T0380908

CHEBOYGAN TWIN LAKES:
COMMUNITY IN THE WOODS

T H O M A S   R .   K N O X

Copyright © 2019 by Thomas R. Knox. 782773
Library of Congress Control Number: 2019900506

ISBN: Softcover   978-1-7960-1061-9
         Hardcover   978-1-7960-1062-6
         EBook   978-1-7960-1063-3

The views expressed in this work are solely those of
the author and do not necessarily reflect the views of
the publisher, and the publisher hereby disclaims any
responsibility for them.

Print information available on the last page

Rev. date: 02/27/2019

To order additional copies of this book, contact:
Xlibris
1-888-795-4274
www.Xlibris.com
Orders@Xlibris.com

(Photograph courtesy of Ken Rocheleau)

Cheboygan Twin Lakes: Community in the Woods

Thomas R. Knox

Cheboygan Twin Lakes: Community in the Woods

Maps: Cheboygan County
Twin Lakes

Contents

Introduction

Of the states in the continental United States, Michigan has, by far, the largest percentage of its total area under water, 41.5 percent. In Southern Michigan, that water is essential to the personal and environmental health of its large urban populations, as shown by crises in Kalamazoo and Flint. In Northern Michigan, much less urban and industrial, the quality of the water is no less essential to the economy and the culture.

There are more than 1,800 lakes in the northern counties of Antrim, Charlevoix, Emmet, and Cheboygan, the western part of Presque Isle County, and the northern portions of Otsego and Montmorency counties. Most of these are kettle lakes, the products of glacial disintegration rather than glacial scouring or manmade impoundment.

Tip of the Mitt Watershed Council (TOMWC), for nearly forty years a protector of these northern waters, designated Twin Lakes in Cheboygan County a "small gem lake," one of fourteen such lakes in the region. The designation is based on water quality measured by several variables over time. "Gem" is significant. But so is "small" as these are the lakes most subject to deterioration as the result of an inability to dilute human presence or accommodate environmental change.

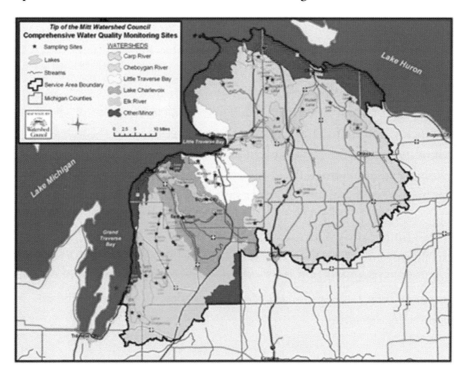

What follows is an investigation of why this small Northeastern Michigan lake acquired such a status and of the role of science professionals and "citizen scientists" in achieving environmentally successful long-term lake management. Part I offers a sketch of Twin Lakes as it now is. Part II concerns itself with the past. The preface to the investigation (chapters 1–4) describes the context—geological, geographical, economic, military, and social—in which Twin Lakes has existed. Chapters 5–10 provide a narrative of the lake's history over the past century or so. And chapter 11 analyzes the crucial element of community in the story. Part III seeks to anticipate the future.

The sources for this study are, by and large, conventional. The local newspapers are useful mostly in the matter of context because, with rare exceptions, Twin Lakes has lain outside their area of coverage. The various property records held in the office of the Register of Deeds in Cheboygan, now accessible electronically, have been invaluable. The office also has originals of the General Land Office survey and of the survey field notes. Similarly, over one hundred years of maps produced by different instrumentalities for different purposes are indispensable. The federal censuses from 1880 through 1940 are essential. State and federal governments in the 1930s contributed the standard bathymetric map of the lake, aerial photographs of the county, and a survey of rural properties. While the tax records of the county go back no further than 1944, the township still has the handwritten tax assessment rolls of the 1930s and earlier. The Millard D. Olds papers, held at the Clarke Historical Library, offer insights into the logging industry of the early twentieth century in Northeastern Michigan. The records of the Cheboygan Twin Lakes Association are not complete, but they are essential. Much hydrological and environmental information is to be found in the reports of the University of Michigan Biological Station (UMBS), TOMWC, the Michigan Department of Natural Resources (MDNR), and the Michigan Department of Environmental Quality (MDEQ).

Thanks are due to the helpful staff of the Archives of Michigan, the Bentley Library of the University of Michigan, the Center for Archival Collections and the Music Library and Bill Schurk Sound Archives of Bowling Green State University, the Cheboygan Area Public Library, the Clark Library of the University of Michigan, the Clarke Historical Library of Central Michigan University, the Library of Michigan, TOMWC, and the UMBS. The staff of various departments of the Cheboygan County government were also very helpful, especially Community Development, the Register of Deeds, and the Treasurer.

Thanks are due as well to Randolph Mateer, who had the prescience and the perseverance to interview "old-timers" on Twin Lakes in 1989 and 1990 and to assemble the document referred to in this book as *Twin Lakes Oral History*. Thanks too to Charles Rodriguez, who conducted and preserved the tape of a long 1991 interview with Lyle and Catherine Page.

And I must not forget local historians and fellow academics, most of them not historians, who have responded quickly and as fully as possible to my queries. Any misstatement, misapplication, or misinterpretation of their responses is my fault, not theirs.

In keeping with the admonitions of the great English local historian W. G. Hoskins, this writer has not been afraid to get his feet wet (often literally and as much as possible for a newcomer to the area). The field work that Hoskins considered so important for the local historian has taken the form of walking, paddling, boating, skiing, trail riding, and asking.

And the last, talking to neighbors who have given freely of their time, knowledge, memories, and photographs has been enormously fruitful.

The photographs of Twin Lakes and Black Mountain, unless otherwise attributed, were taken by Judith Knox or, less expertly, by the author.

I The Present

From the north shore of the Big Bay, the sunset can be seen obliquely. It is rose toned, often golden, light playing off a wall of trees and quiet water, mediated by the juvenile light green of leaves and needles in spring, the mature dark green in summer, and the dying oranges and browns in fall—Golden Pond without the granite.

From the south shore, the blazing, blinding solar light in its many shades and variations dominates, the water turned electric, the trees forming the dark boundary of Earth on which the light burns.

In each of the other bays of Twin Lakes as well, the sunset is unique because each bay has its own orientation, its own outlook, and its own background.

Tip of the Mitt says of Twin Lakes that it "stands apart from other lakes in the region in that it consists of a group of ten interconnected water bodies. The peaceful, mesmerizing waters of these well-preserved lakes are soothing yet vibrant, populated by a diverse array of aquatic plant and animal life." (When the wind is up, which seems to be occurring more often, the Big Bay will show threads of scud, usually moving to the northeast, and, less often, whitecaps and waves. The channel at the southern end of the island may be rough, while the other, smaller, and more sheltered bays show nothing out of the ordinary.)

At the northern foot of Black Mountain, roughly four miles northeast of the top of Black Lake, Twin Lakes lies just beyond the band of agricultural land that more or less parallels the Black River as it works its way northwestward from Black Lake to a junction with the Cheboygan River.

The shoreline is sinuous and, as a result, far longer than a lake of its modest acreage would seem to require. Originally a wetlands, reeds and grasses protect much of the shoreline. Elsewhere, cedars perform the same function. There is no beach. Grass lawns to the shoreline are rare, as is revetted shoreline. (The MDNR has noted that this absence of "shoreline armoring" is "atypical for a Northern Michigan lake."[1])

The waters of the lake are home to a self-sustaining population of fish, predominantly pike, bass, and various panfish. The presence of cisco (lake herring) is notable. A threatened species that is unusual in natural lakes in Northern Michigan, cisco require a lake that stratifies thermally in the summer and contains high amounts of dissolved oxygen in the colder water below the thermocline. Human presence tends to lessen the oxygen level.

The lake has also been home, for longer than living memory, to one or two pairs of breeding loons and, nearly as long, to a pair of sandhill cranes. The cries of the loons—tremolos when there is an eagle in the skies, simple wails and hoots on a soft, lazy afternoon—are a part of lake life. In spring, late summer, and early fall, transient loons drop in to rest and socialize.

(Photograph courtesy of Jerry Beehler)

The other distinctive voices on the lake are frogs—greens, leopards, minks, and spring peepers. Their fellows in other areas of the Northern United States and in other parts of the world are dying out for reasons that are not fully understood. The voiceless, numerous nevertheless, are turtles, including painted, snapping, and the threatened Blanding's.

These waters are also home to single-minded beavers swimming about their business (and the occasional insouciant backstroking beaver who, contrary to stereotype, appears to have nothing in particular on his schedule). Deer will come to the lake to drink and swim to and from the cedar-filled island at its middle. Otters have enjoyed both the waters and sunning themselves on docks. It is best that no one knows where the spawning redds of the bass are to be found, but squads of juveniles of several species are easily seen in shadowed shallows, and at depth, there are small cisco and large pike.

The shoreline and the lake now confront the threat of purple loosestrife displacing native vegetation and choking shallow channels and the presence of zebra mussels, both introduced from outside. The latter, in particular, is a hazard for a lake that is, by its nature, clear because it has relatively low levels of nutrients. This oligotrophism is also the source of a perpetual concern with the number of fish taken from the lake. While self-sustaining, the population is limited and slow growing by virtue of the modest nutrient resources of the lake.

Watch needs to be kept for quagga mussels, recently observed in lakes to the west, and invasive plant species such as Eurasian watermilfoil, curly-leaf pondweed, and European frogbit, the first of which has spread rapidly in Northern Michigan. And beyond these known threats, there is the unknown of the effects of climate change.

Heavily forested at the beginning of the twentieth century, Twin Lakes was one of the last areas in the region to be logged. It is again heavily forested, in part because it is nearly surrounded by state forest. The forest, planted and managed now for nearly ninety years, is predominantly, though by no means exclusively, red pine. Among other creatures, it is home to coyotes, deer, wild turkeys, grouse, foxes, and the occasional black bear.

Professional scientific management of the forest in the abstract is ideal. Professional scientific management of the forest in practice is a highly mixed blessing. The inescapably destructive process of logging, even if "selective," has been on display on the western side of the lake. The all-too-similar consequences of clear-cutting have been readily apparent along Twin Lakes Road to the east and west of the lake, on and near Orchard Beach Road to the west of the lake, in neighboring Presque Isle County to the east, and, most recently and grievously, on Loon Nest Lane, Krouse Road, and Godin Circle on the east side of the lake. In this sort of management, cycles, planning, contracts, and schedules dominate, and property lines are seen as no more than logging limits, not a part of a physical context, much less environment, that involves aesthetics and creates value.

Twin Lakes has become a residential lake and, only secondarily, a recreational lake. Its greatest attractions are natural beauty, fishing, hunting, quiet, and solitude. It has developed rather than been developed.

Residences, for the most part, fit the character of the lake, as do the personalities of many of its residents. Building has progressed at a fairly leisurely pace, easily observable by residents. And generally, what has been built (or expanded) has been modest and discreet, both aesthetically and environmentally. By and large, properties have preserved much of the shoreline, in part because most structures are not, in a literal sense, on the shoreline, often because of the way in which the bays were originally formed. As a result, properties along the lakeshore are home to red and white pine, white birch, maple, cedar, tamarack, beech, hemlock, willow, and aspen as well as bushes, grasses, and reeds. This in itself helps account for the "microclimates" that can be found from bay to bay on the lake and for the condition of the lake as a whole. Nevertheless, substantial further development, especially if concentrated, would seriously threaten the ability of the lake to absorb the human impact.

Many of its residents would accept the words of Henry David Thoreau as expressing their approach to life, at least on the lake. "I wish so to live ever as to derive my satisfactions and inspirations from the commonest events, every-day phenomena, so that what my senses hourly perceive, my daily walk, the conversations of my neighbors, may inspire me, and I may dream of no heaven but that which lies about me."[2]

Small neighborhoods exist, as many as there are bays, most accessed by a single dead-end dirt road through forest. By and large, the neighborhoods have been stable for years. Properties do not easily or frequently change hands, nor has development significantly reshaped neighborhoods. (Very recently, the pace of property ownership changes has increased. Some are transactional, some intrafamilial.) Proximity and ordinary contact over time help explain neighborliness, but in many cases, family relationships are also a factor.

There is a larger lake community built, in part, on personal relationships and ordinary contact (often on the water and/or involving shared interests in fishing and hunting) and, again, in some instances, on family relationships. But at the core of the larger lake community is the Cheboygan Twin Lakes Association.

The CTLA, founded in 1978, was the product of a particular time, a particular set of circumstances, and a particular generation. Its focus from the beginning was not on "improvement" or the protection of property values, but on lake maintenance and environmental preservation. In these, it has been largely successful. Forty years later, it is a living demonstration that scientific knowledge acquired and applied by ordinary citizens, combined with voluntarism, can, without great expense, accomplish much to prevent the deterioration of kettle lakes.

At the same time, it must be said that special circumstances—broadly speaking, nature and the lake's history—conferred a higher degree of protection on Twin Lakes than is true in many other cases. The CTLA was dealt a good hand.

It also needs to be said that the CTLA faces a problem common with citizen organizations: how to preserve its purpose, impetus, and membership when the founders have passed, the second generation is disappearing, and those who are younger have different agendas in their lives and no experience of what gave rise to the CTLA. Continuity is important. Reorganizing and relearning anytime there is a crisis is not an effective approach. Equally, intimate knowledge of the condition of the lake and its surroundings requires continuing engagement. There is also a need, no matter the degree of voluntarism, to find means to generate income to cover ordinary operating costs and the occasional major expenditure.

---

[1] Tim A. Cwalinski, Senior Fisheries Biologist, Gaylord, *Michigan Dept. of Natural Resources Status of the Fishery Resource Report*: Twin Lakes, 2-5 (2014),

https://www.michigan.gov/documents/dnr/2013-1 68_447221_7.pdf.

Hereafter, the MDNR will be identified as the DNR.

[2] *The Writings of Henry David Thoreau, Journal*. VIII November 1, 1855-August 15, 1856. F.B. Sanborn and Bradford Torrey, eds. (Boston and New York: Houghton Mifflin and Company, 1906), p. 204 (March 11, 1856).

II The Past

Chapter 1 Water and Ice

As is true in the relationship of geology and history throughout the world, its geologic past has shaped the history of Twin Lakes. And for much of that past, this area of Northeastern Michigan has lain beneath water or, briefly, in geological terms, beneath ice.

The Precambrian period, covering nearly 90 percent of the earth's existence, extends backward four and a half billion years. Michigan's geologic history begins three and a half billion years ago with igneous rock thrown up by volcanic eruptions and the movement of tectonic plates. This rock can still be seen in the western portions of the Upper Peninsula. In the Eastern Upper Peninsula and in the Lower Peninsula, this formative base lies beneath sedimentary rock, that is, new rock formed from the weathering and eroding of older rock. But in the basement of time, thousands of feet below Cheboygan Twin Lakes, lies Precambrian rock between eight hundred million and one and a half billion years old.[3]

Atop this foundation are layers of sedimentary rock formed in different periods of the Paleozoic era approximately 542 to 251 million years ago. Bedrock beneath Twin Lakes, as in all of the northern tip of the Lower Peninsula, is Devonian, formed roughly 416 to 359 million years ago. Outcrops of this aged bedrock can be found in each of the four northernmost counties of the Lower Peninsula.[4]

In Devonian times, what is now Cheboygan Twin Lakes was part of the Michigan Basin, a shallow granite basin that included all of the Lower Peninsula and the eastern part of what would be Michigan's Upper Peninsula. The center of the basin lay in the middle of the Lower Peninsula. The area that would be Cheboygan and Presque Isle counties resided toward the outer shallower edge of the basin. Even before the formation of the basin, the area had been submerged beneath an inland sea, and it remained submerged by the shallow Ordovician sea, which covered much of North America, leaving behind layers of limestone and shale. Shelled organisms had existed since Precambrian times and trilobites, the most enduring of Paleozoic creatures, since the Cambrian period. But stony corals made their first appearance in Ordovician waters, as did various mollusks and fish (jawless and eel like, to be sure). The corals would be responsible for large barrier reefs on the periphery of the basin and pinnacle reefs nearer its center.[5]

ORDOVICIAN SEA FLOOR

Subsequently, the smaller, shallower, and warmer Silurian sea covered the area. The sea and the climate were tropical because what would be North America lay along the low latitudes near the equator throughout the Paleozoic era. The laying down of lime muds continued, and large quantities of halite (rock salt) were deposited as well. (The Michigan Basin may hold sixty trillion metric tons of Silurian salt deposits.) Reef-building coral thrived by extracting lime from the water and hundreds of feet of lime-infused mud consolidated to become the Niagaran Escarpment, running from Western New York State through the Upper Peninsula to Chicago, "the backbone of the Michigan Basin rock structures."[6]

Along with the formation of bedrock, this period saw specialization in the development of fish (jawed fish had developed earlier in the Silurian period), the appearance of bony fish and of amphibians, and the presence of other forms of sea life, including corals, bryozoans, mollusks, arthropods, and echinoderms. (Mass extinction occurred near the end of the Devonian period, "the second extinction," as it had at the end of the Ordovician period, "the first extinction.")[7] Plants had emerged in the Silurian period, and ferns and trees were abundant in the Devonian world; forests appeared for the first time. Devonian breccia (or collapse breccia), hardened limestone resulting from the dissolution of halite, the collapse of the overlying limestone, and the recementing of the underlying fragments with limestone as the matrix, supports the piers and abutments of the Mackinac Bridge. Brecciated limestone can be seen in the form of the Arch Rock and Sugar Loaf on Mackinac Island, St. Anthony's Rock, Castle Rock, and Gros Cap just beyond the northern end of the Mackinac Bridge, and other "stacks" along the shoreline of the Upper Peninsula. In nearby forest, the water flowing over Ocqueoc Falls in Presque Isle County is moving over Rockport Quarry limestone from the middle Devonian period.[8]

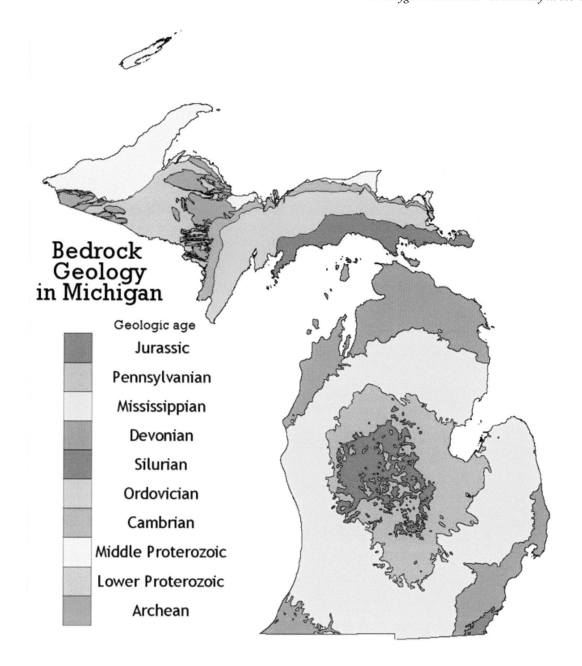

The eras, periods, and epochs shown in this map of bedrock geology are dated as follows (all dates are "millions of years ago"): Archaean, 4,000–2,500; Lower Proterozoic, 2,500–1,600; Middle Proterozoic, 1,600–1,000; Cambrian, 542–488; Ordovician, 488–444; Silurian, 444–416; Devonian, 416–359; Mississippian, 359–318; Pennsylvanian, 318–299; and Jurassic, 200–145.

The subsequent Mississippian and Pennsylvanian epochs—warm, prolific in deposits of sand, anhydrite, and lime muds, marked by coastal swamps and deltas around the center of the Michigan Basin and the first amphibians and reptiles—produced bedrock in the Central and Southern Lower Peninsula. Thereafter, except for late Jurassic rock in the central portion of the state, the geological history of Michigan, like that of other Great Lakes states, is a blank until nearly the end of the Pleistocene epoch, a "lost interval" of well over 250 million years.

Arch Rock, Mackinac Island

Sugar Loaf, Mackinac Island

That blank is a product of the collision of two continents at the end of the Pennsylvanian period to form the "supercontinent" of Pangaea, an event that made Michigan an upland environment inconducive to the sedimentation that had been occurring for millions of years.[9]

Much happened in the "interval." The first seed-bearing plants (gymnosperms) appeared in the Permian period (299–251 million years ago), as did mosses, beetles, and flies. In the Triassic period (251–200 million years ago), archosaurs dominated—dinosaurs on land, ichthyosaurs and nothosaurs in the seas, and pterosaurs in the air. (Twin Lakes was a part of the tropical environment in which the archosaurs flourished; the construction of a new home on the lake in 2004 exposed a dinosaur coprolite.[10]) Small mammals made their appearance, as did the only archosaurs surviving in the modern world, crocodilians. Ancestral sturgeon swam in the seas. At both the beginning and the end of the Triassic period, mass extinctions occurred ("the third and fourth extinctions"), the earlier one by far the largest known in the history of the earth.

The Jurassic era was a world in which ferns, gymnosperms (especially conifers), and small mammals were common, and birds and lizards appeared. It was also one in which the ancestors of the unloved bowfin of Twin Lakes, the only survivors of the order *Amiiformes*, appeared and in which Pangaea broke up. The Cretaceous period (145–66 million years ago) saw the flourishing of flowering plants and the evolution of new types of dinosaurs, including the tyrannosaurs, as well as the breakup of Gondwana, one of the two continents that had made up Pangaea and the parent of most of the land masses of the southern hemisphere. (It would be millions of years yet before the continents would assume their present-day positions.)

Dinosaur coprolite (Courtesy of Bruce and Judy Spiekhout)

In the late Cretaceous period, "true" sturgeon of the sort found in Black Lake and the Black River appeared. In the transition from the Cretaceous to the Paleogene period, dinosaurs disappeared, the "fifth extinction," but mammals diversified. The first large mammals appeared, as did modern plants. The loons of the northern lakes, if they had not originated in the late Cretaceous period seventy to eighty million years ago, existed by the middle of the Paleogene era forty to fifty million years ago; the ancestors of the sandhill cranes that nest on Twin Lakes' island were not far behind, though the sandhills themselves would appear later.

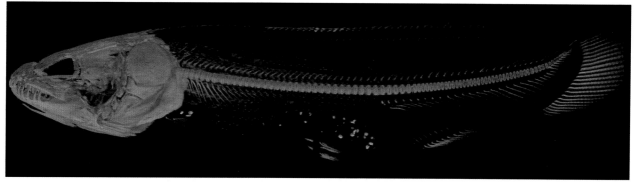

Bowfin

Similarly, not far behind were northern pike and, a bit further on, largemouth and smallmouth bass. These two periods also saw the origins of many of the forest-floor dwellers in Michigan's northern forests. Over the course of sixty million years, the trend of climate change was toward coolness, transforming the hitherto tropical environment into an "icehouse" environment that has lasted for millions of years and has experienced several "ice ages."

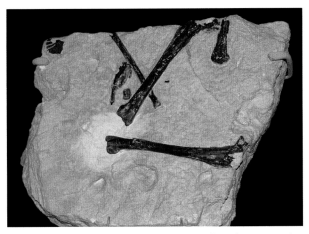

Loon fossils: Naturhistorisches Museum, Vienna

Glaciation

Two million years ago, at the beginning of the Pleistocene epoch, the climate of the northern part of the North American continent cooled. Great masses of ice came together in the Laurentide ice sheet, a continental glacier as much as two miles thick, more than five million square miles in extent, incalculably heavy, occupying virtually all of what is now Canada and most of what is now the North Central United States. Over the better part of these two million years, glaciers advanced and retreated many times.

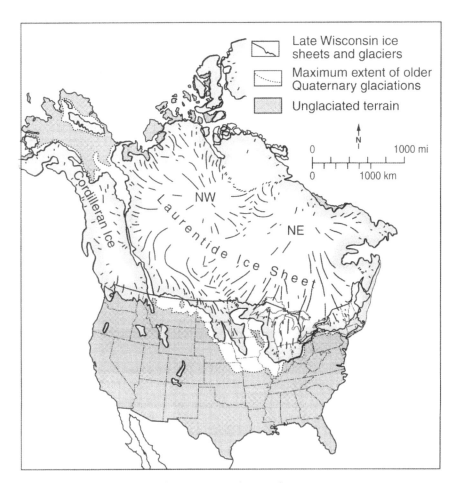

The Laurentide ice sheet

In periods of retreat, climate moderated, and soils formed. It is probable that the first three cycles covered Michigan in ice, but evidence of these glaciations is found only in neighboring states. The fourth cycle, the Wisconsinian, begun more than eighty thousand years ago, wrapped all of Michigan in more than a mile of ice, along with most of Ohio, Indiana, Illinois, Wisconsin, and the northern part of the continent to the immediate east and west. The soil and landforms of Michigan are the evidence of the Wisconsinian cycle.[11]

About fifteen thousand years ago, the northern climate began to warm, and the glacier slowly retreated northward with only occasional and limited readvances thereafter. A thousand years later, much of the southern part of the Lower Peninsula was deglaciated, and the ice that affected the area, previously a single undifferentiated sheet, appeared as three separate fingers or lobes: the Michigan, Saginaw, and Huron-Erie lobes. Soon after, about half of the Lower Peninsula was ice free. The Port Huron readvance covered the coastal and near-coastal northeast of Michigan in ice thirteen thousand years ago. But a thousand years later, the area was ice free. Yet before long, the northern tip was again beneath ice (the Valders or Greatlakean readvance). In a few hundred years, however, the glacier had permanently retreated, and all of the Lower Peninsula was free of ice. Responsible for the glacial sedimentation of the state, this Greatlakean advance of the Wisconsinian glacier is the only one about which much is known in Michigan.[12]

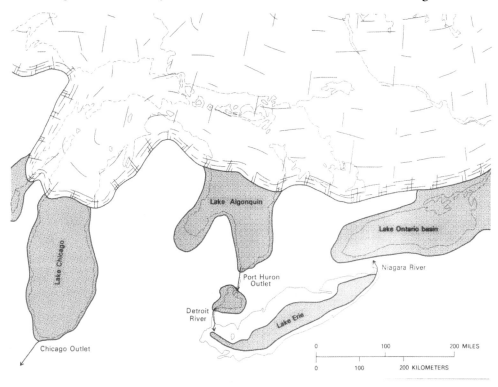

Calumet-level Lake Chicago/Main Algonquin level of Lake Huron, c. 11,600–11,300 years BP (before present)

As they appear in photographs, glaciers may seem to be enormous white stillnesses. But any glacier is a dynamic mass for all its life, accumulating, flowing, retreating, calving, opening and closing subglacial channels, grinding, scouring and shaping whatever is beneath it and, in its retreat, whatever is before it, sometimes softly, more often in overwhelmingly powerful expulsions of meltwater and debris. Glaciation and deglaciation generated a complex set of landforms to the east, west, and south of Twin Lakes and Black Mountain that contrasts with the relatively simple till-floored lake plain that prevails to the north. The two sit near a geomorphic edge, on the border of the complex disintegrations of glacial retreat. Black Mountain, the dominant landform in the area, and Twin Lakes, sitting at its base, resulted from deglaciation, which, in this immediate area, produced what appears to be a kame-and-kettle topography. [13]

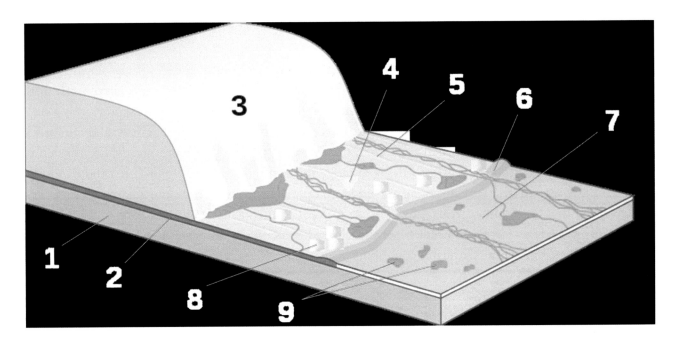

1	Rock bed	6	Terminal moraine
2	Ground moraine	7	Floodplain
3	Receding glacier	8	Kame
4	Esker	9	Kettles
5	Drumlin		

In the absence of detailed research, the exact nature of Black Mountain is open to question, and conclusions are unavoidably speculative. It has been labeled a drumlin, a dune or system of dunes, and a moraine. Of these, it is not a drumlin; its size and composition eliminate that possibility. To describe it as a dune or system of dunes raises difficult questions about the means and timing of its creation. It is a moraine in the generic sense that it is a glacially formed accumulation of unconsolidated soil and rock. But if it is a moraine in the narrower sense of the word, it is only a small remnant of a larger ridge otherwise unidentified.

Most likely, Black Mountain is kamic in origin, a product of glacial movement and decay. A kame is a hill, isolated or one of a cluster, often irregular in form, steep sided or merely mounded, varied in height, formed of sand, gravel, and glacial till deposited by meltwater into depressions or crevasses, usually at the edge of a glacier. Alternatively, Black Mountain may be an esker or serpent kame. (As the last term suggests, the two landforms are closely related, and both are found in association with each other and with kettle lakes. Indeed, one theory of origin sees eskers as a string of kames.) Eskers were formed by streams within and under glaciers or in channels and crevasses atop a glacier. The movement of water deposited silt, especially as the glacier retreated, and what remained was a long winding ridge. At the extreme, eskers may be as much as 275 feet high, a third of a mile wide, and nearly 500 miles long. (The largest identified esker in Michigan is 50 feet high, 400 feet wide, and 22 miles long.) In both cases, when the glacier melted away, what remained was the sediment, in the form of a kame or an esker.[14]

While kames and eskers have been readily identified in Cheboygan County and elsewhere in Michigan, Black Mountain has not been recognized as either (or both). The noticeable flatness of Black Mountain at its summit may be one indicator of a kamic origin. On the other hand, the length and profile of Black Mountain may suggest that it originated as an esker. In Cheboygan County, other much smaller kames can be found to the west and south of Black Mountain, the Silver Lake kames, and the Wolverine kames. Many other kames are found elsewhere in the state. Similarly, eskers are present in Cheboygan County; a three-mile long esker lies north of Douglas Lake and another near Osmun Lake. Other eskers can be found in the Lake Nettie and Hawks complexes in Southeastern Presque Isle County and in Alpena and Otsego counties. Eskers are common in Southeastern Michigan.

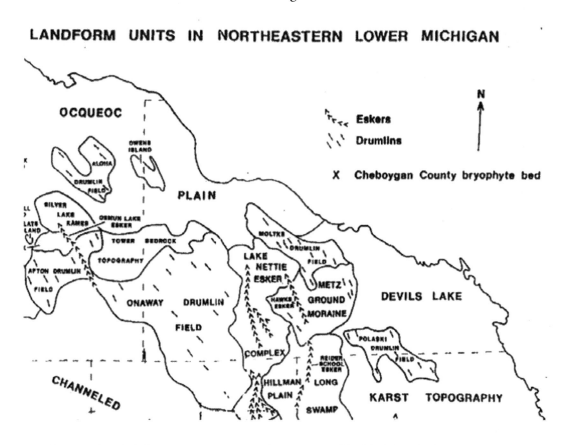

Twin Lakes is a kettle lake or, more accurately, a series of kettle lakes linked by shallow channels. (In a UMBS list of research sites, Twin Lakes is described as "a deep hardwater lake with [seven] different depressions, very distinctly separated." There is an eighth depression at the south end that is not connected to the other seven and has neither inlet nor outlet.[15]) Thousands of such lakes exist in the belt of glacially deposited sand, gravel, and silt lodged between the hard rock of Northern Canada and the clays of the Southern United States. This belt of lakes stretches from Maine to Montana, but it is in Michigan, Wisconsin, and Minnesota that kettle lakes are, in Robert Thorson's phrase, "signature landforms."

Kettles or kettle holes resulted from chunks of ice breaking off from the front of a stagnant or receding glacier and being wholly or partially buried by glacial outwash, meltwater that flowed away from the glacier, bearing sediments with it. Kettle holes vary significantly in size and depth, depending in part on whether they are in a terminal moraine area or an outwash area.[16]

Eventually, most kettle holes filled with water, sediment, and/or vegetation. Depending on its source of water, its vegetation, and the acidity of its water, the hole became a kettle lake (or lakes in the case of Twin

Lakes), a kettle pond, a kettle wetland, a kettle bog (in the case of Hoop Lake, just east of Twin Lakes), or a kettle peatland.

To the west and to the south of Black Mountain and Twin Lakes are drumlins created by the last advance of ice into Northeastern Lower Michigan, notably the Aloha drumlin field and the much larger Onaway drumlin field. Drumlins are elliptically shaped hills as much as one hundred feet high and a mile or more long. Unlike kames, drumlins were shaped by the ice itself, not by meltwater. As a result, their long axis is aligned with the movement of the ice, the material comprising them is clay or shale rather than sand or gravel, and they usually have concentric layers of material, a result of movement of the ice.[17]

Cheboygan Twin Lakes and Black Mountain also reside in terrain characterized by flowing wells and karst. Flowing wells, common throughout Michigan, result from geological or topographical conditions in which pressure in an aquifer forces groundwater to the surface. There is a heavy incidence of such freshwater wells in Cheboygan County, especially along the Lake Huron shore from Mackinaw City eastward and in the west central part of the county; Indian River is well known for such wells, and flowing wells have supplied water to Cheboygan City and Mackinaw City. Michigan Central passenger trains drew their drinking water from artesian wells close by the depot in Topinabee. In 1949, at the summer cottage resort of "Pa and Ma" Collis, just west of Cheboygan city, well-drilling resulted in a "column of water shooting up at an estimated 300,000 to 500,000 gallons a day." A map prepared in 1970 by the U.S. Geological Survey and the Geological Survey Division of the Michigan Department of Natural Resources (DNR) shows a flowing well in glacial drift on the edge of Twin Lakes as well as several flowing wells to the southeast.[18]

Karst refers to shallow soluble bedrock that is subject to dissolution by acidic groundwater, the chemical interaction of precipitation and carbon dioxide in the atmosphere producing a weak carbonic acid. One of the forms of this soluble bedrock is Paleozoic carbonate rock, which exists in two bands extending from Emmet County southeastward through Cheboygan County and across Presque Isle County. Devonian limestone relatively close to the surface is acutely subject to the effects of acidic groundwater. The consequences are abrupt ridges, caverns, earth cracks, disappearing surface streams, underground streams, and, best known, sinkholes. Sinkholes themselves may produce sinkhole lakes, sinkhole-controlled lakes, and solution lakes. Examples of each of these exist in Southern Presque Isle County and along the border between Presque Isle and Alpena Counties. There are also sinkholes just south of the Cheboygan County border in Northeastern Otsego County, two of them, ironically, designated North Twin Lake and South Twin Lake.[19]

Lake Algonquin and Its Successors

Eleven thousand years ago, the Lower Peninsula was free of ice. But glaciation had not yet fully played out its role in the geological history of the northern part of the peninsula. The earliest form of Lake Algonquin (or the Algonquin stages of the Great Lakes) appeared a bit less than twelve thousand years ago, when a local readvance of ice in what is now the Trent Valley of Ontario blocked drainage to the east.[20]

Algonquin, eventually a single lake occupying what is now Lake Michigan and Lake Huron, had its own history of fluctuating water levels, its highest stage lasting roughly eight hundred years (11,200–10,400 BP). Its maximum level was approximately 740 feet. Thus, the contour lines of 750 feet and higher in topographical maps of the Northern Michigan counties mark the outlines of the lake at its highest. (Elevations in Northern Cheboygan County range from 600 to 750 feet above sea level; those in the southern part of the county vary from 800 to over 1,000 feet above sea level.) The clays and sands of Northern Cheboygan County were originally deposits on the Algonquin lake bed. The Twin Lakes area was submerged beneath the lake, except for parts of Black Mountain, one of the "islands" (shown below, with its small "satellites," in brown on the border of Cheboygan and Presque Isle counties) in the lake. Black Lake was also submerged, along with Mullett and Burt Lakes and the smaller lakes that make up the Inland Water Route. (The elevation of Twin Lakes is roughly 680 feet. Black Lake is 610 feet, Mullett and Burt Lakes are 594 feet, and present-day Lakes Huron and Michigan are 577 feet above sea level. At its summit, Black Mountain is over 900 feet above sea level.)[21]

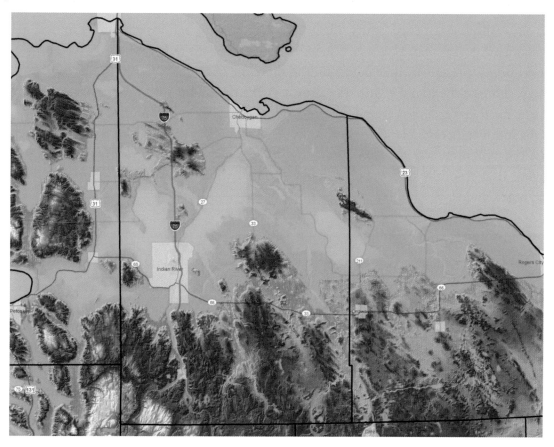

Lake Algonquin (Courtesy of Randall J. Schaetzl)

As the glaciers melted farther to the north, a low outlet valley, North Bay (Ontario) and the Ottawa River, drained the successor lakes, Chippewa and Stanley, and produced a low water period. With the weight of the glacier removed, the earth's crust began to rebound. About five thousand years ago, when the North Bay outlet had risen to 605 feet, the same level as outlets at Port Huron and Chicago that had not functioned since the Algonquin stage, the result was Lake Nipissing, a single stable body of water that covered present-day lakes Superior, Michigan, and Huron for the better part of two thousand years. Nipissing inundated the shoreline of Cheboygan County and flooded Burt and Mullett Lakes and the corridor that would later become the Cheboygan River. The city of Cheboygan and Mackinaw City are built on the floor of Nipissing, and US-23 is built on terraces formed by Nipissing. But neither Twin Lakes nor Black Lake were submerged by Nipissing, as they had been by Algonquin.[22]

Soils

Consistent with its geological history, the soils of Twin Lakes are predominantly sandy, with a single exception. The lakeshore soil group (or soil association) on the west side of Twin Lakes from Page Road north for a short distance is the "Rudyard-Bruce-Ontonagon Association: Deep nearly level to rolling, well drained to poorly drained, loamy, silty, and clayey soils that formed in lacustrine deposits, stratified material, or clayey material; on lake plains." This soil association exists in only 5 percent of Cheboygan County.[23]

The lakeside soil association to the north, east, south, and remainder of the west is "Rubicon-East Lake Association: Deep, nearly level and undulating, excessively drained and somewhat excessively drained, sandy soils that formed in sandy deposits or in sandy material over gravelly deposits; on lake plains, outwash plains, deltas, beach ridges, and eskers." This soil association is found in 17 percent of the county.[24]

Tawas peat is present at three points on the shoreline of the northernmost bay of Twin Lakes. The northwest shore of the island is also Tawas peat.[25] The dominant soils on the northwest side of Twin Lakes, the northeast side, the island, and most of the lake shoreline south of a line drawn east–west across the south end of the island are various kinds of sand. The 1991 soil survey of Cheboygan County indicated that all these were unsuited or poorly suited for septic tank absorption fields. (See Appendix I.) Moving away from the lake, the predominant soils are different sorts of sand to the west, the south, and the north and east.

Vegetation, Animals, and People

Donald I. Dickmann and Larry A. Leefers summarize what followed the retreat of ice and water:

> Although the land left in the wake of the Pleistocene's glacial mauling was raw and coarse, it harbored a remarkable potential to support life.[26] The deposits of glacial till . . . and the lacustrine muck left behind by receding meltwater lakes were in reality crude, undeveloped soils. As such, they only awaited the arrival of something that would grow in them. It did not take long. Windborne seeds and spores quickly began   to fall on the virgin earth. When these pioneering propagules germinated and their fresh sprouts took a tentative hold on the new land, the stage was set for the eventual establishment of a new forest. Plants provided food and cover, so the green immigrants attracted creatures large and small . . . Among these creatures were Michigan's first human settlers.

Over the course of nearly seventeen thousand years, the Northern Lower Peninsula went through a series of vegetation changes that progressed from south to north and that were deeply influenced by climate changes. In all of Michigan, tundra succeeded the ice. As of four thousand years ago, a series of rapid evolutionary changes had produced forests and forest zones that included most of the tree species that now exist in Michigan and that closely resembled what Europeans encountered in the sixteenth and seventeenth centuries.[27] By 1,000 BC, pine-dominated forests existed with oak as a subdominant, and the northern hardwood forests had hemlock as their leading species. (Pine and hemlock were the trees of prime interest to loggers in the Cheboygan area.)

All evidence of vertebrates in Ice Age Michigan has been recovered in the lower half of the Lower Peninsula, south of a line that excludes the four northernmost tiers of counties. Within that southern zone, fauna familiar to modern humans were plentiful: bass, perch, Northern pike, sunfish, bullfrogs, toads, turtles, turkeys, voles, muskrats, rabbits, black bear, and white-tailed deer. Unfamiliar fauna were present as well, notably giant beavers in lakes, ponds and bogs that provided a diet of aquatic plants, mammoths in the spruce-pine forests, and mastodons on grasslands.[28]

The period of prehistoric human habitation of the western hemisphere is divided by anthropologists into the Paleo-Indian period, which concluded about 10,000 years ago; the early Archaic period, which ended about 5,000 BC; the middle Archaic, lasting until 3,000 BC; the late Archaic, which ended around 1,000 BC; and the early, middle, and late Woodland periods, the first two lasting about 500 years each and the third lasting twice that long in Northern Lower Michigan and ending with sustained European contact. The descriptive terms applied to these successive cultures are *early hunter* for the Paleo-Indian, *hunter-forager* for the early Archaic, *forager* for the middle and late Archaic, and *prairie-forest potter* and *village farmer* for the Woodland periods.[29]

Paleo-Indian peoples entered the main body of the Americas about fourteen thousand years ago or perhaps a bit earlier.[30] Within two millennia, some of them were in the Great Lakes basin, living off the plentiful game to be found on the southern edge of the glacier. The best known and most widely spread of the Paleo-Indians in the early Americas were the Clovis people. Meat eaters and nomadic hunters, their defining cultural artifact was the Clovis point, a distinctively shaped, fluted spear point that has been found in most of North America and part of Central America. The Clovis culture was short-lived. From Clovis times, however, there is a continuous line of successor cultures in the Paleo-Indian period (such as Folsom and Plano; a relative of the latter was present in Northern Michigan).

In Michigan, a human presence waited on deglaciation, the emergence of plants, and the subsequent appearance of animals. Paleo-Indians first appeared in Michigan about twelve thousand years ago. The Paleo-Indian population was limited to the tundra plain of the lower half of the Lower Peninsula. It is nearly certain that twelve to eleven thousand years ago, humans butchered, not necessarily hunted or killed, a mastodon at Pleasant Lake in South Central Michigan. (The appearance of Paleo-Indians in the Upper Peninsula came later, ten to nine thousand years ago, and from what is now Northern Wisconsin rather than from the south.) Even before the end of the Paleo-Indian period, populations had begun to limit their nomadism and to create regionalized cultural identities and diversity. In the West, Folsom culture came to depend exclusively on the bison, and Plano culture replaced fluted points with the practice of driving game off cliffs. In the east, Paleo-Indians adapted to individualized hunting of non-herd animals and learned to exploit woodland and water for food.[31]

In Michigan, the five thousand years of the Archaic saw the division of the land into deciduous forests in the south and coniferous forests in the north, significantly varying water levels in the upper Great Lakes that finally settled to roughly modern levels, a warming climate in the mid-period, the first domestic plants (cultigens, specifically squash) in Southern Michigan, and early but extensive regional exchanges of goods. By the late Archaic period, at least three discernible regional linkages or affinities had appeared, one of which tied together people in the Eastern Upper Peninsula, the Straits of Mackinac, the Northern Lower Peninsula, and parts of Ontario. In the Archaic period, changes in Stone Age tool technology were frequent and widespread; familiar northern artifacts such as canoes, fish hooks, sleds, and snowshoes are almost certainly creations of Archaic peoples. Near the end of the period, pottery and crop cultivation appeared. Burt Lake and Douglas Lake were used and possibly occupied by humans in the Archaic period; surface scatters judged to be Archaic have been found along the Cheboygan River.[32]

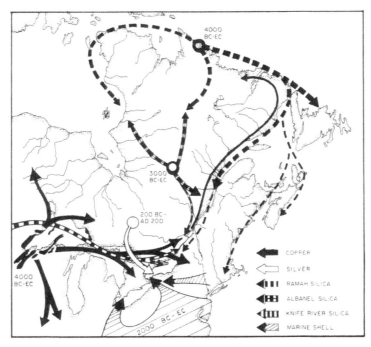

Figure 1. Major trade routes in eastern North America of selected materials. Geologic sources of materials are represented by circles, and arrows point to archaeological sites where the pertinent material has been either instrumentally or judgmentally identified. Arrow thickness reflects the intensity of the trade, and dates at the geologic sources indicate estimated time span of source utilization. EC = European contact. Adapted from Plate 14 (Wright and Carlson 1987) of Volume 1 of the *Historical Atlas of Canada* (R. Cole Harris, ed.), University of Toronto Press, 1987.

The hallmark of the Woodland period was the appearance about 2,600 years ago in Southern Michigan of fired ceramic containers for storage and cooking. (Fired ceramics showed up about five hundred years later in the Northern Lower Peninsula and the Upper Peninsula.) Neither ceramics nor the introduction of domesticated plants changed the hunting-gathering core of early Woodland culture. What appears to have been an early Woodland fishing camp has been found on the southeastern shore of Black Lake, and a middle Woodland site has been identified on the Cheboygan River. Sites on the south end of Black Lake and the southwestern shore of Lake Sixteen (Presque Isle), represented by fire-cracked rock and a single projectile point or fire-cracked rock only, offer too little evidence to date. Late Woodland peoples in the Saginaw Valley and Southeastern Michigan, however, were exploiting the vast wetlands (e.g., wild rice) and raising and storing crops (e.g., sunflower seeds and squash), even choosing to locate to lands better suited to horticulture.

North of the line marking the limit of the 120-day growing season, a line that approximates the forest division, hunting, gathering, and shallow-water fishing remained the norm. But about 1,200 years ago, a technological leap, deep-water nets, made whitefish and lake trout the basic, plentiful, reliable, and preservable food of these northerly peoples, much as beans, maize, and corn were for others. The late Woodland period in the Northern Lower Peninsula and the Eastern Upper Peninsula is subdivided into the relatively short Mackinac and Bois Blanc phases and the longer Juntunen phase, which prevailed in Northeastern Michigan on the eve of European intrusion.[33] Each phase is characterized by numerous fishing sites or villages, intensively occupied, if only seasonally. The Juntunen site on Bois Blanc was occupied over the course of more than five hundred years between the ninth and fourteenth centuries.

The Woodland period also saw the building of circular earthworks and burial mounds. Most earthworks in Michigan were built between 1,000 AD and 1,300 AD, most mounds between 500 BC and 1,200 AD.

Both served several purposes and reflected greater complexity in social relations between members of the group and among groups.[34] The largest known mound in Michigan was the "Great Mound," at the junction of the Rouge and Detroit Rivers in the southeast corner of the state; the largest surviving mound is the Norton Mound site, near Grand Rapids in the southwest corner. As of the publication of W. B. Hinsdale's *Primitive Man in Michigan* in 1925, three mounds had been identified in Cheboygan County, ten in Emmet, and one in Presque Isle. By contrast, the numbers of authenticated mounds in the more southerly counties of Lenawee, Kent, and Saginaw were fifty-one, forty-six, and thirty-three, respectively.[35]

These were the societies Europeans encountered. Perhaps "savage" by their standards, although Europeans had little room to condemn "savagery," the indigenous cultures were complex and, in some respects, admirable even by European measures.

---

[3] See the extraordinarily comprehensive view of Michigan's geological and geographical history, to which chapters 1 and 2 of this book are much indebted and which contributed usefully at other points as well, in: Randall Schaetzl, editor in chief, *Michigan Geography and Geology* (New York: Pearson Custom Publishing, 2009). The following chapters of *MGG* contributed to the first portion of "Water and Ice": Danita Brandt, "Geology: Introduction and overview," pp. 11–23; Theodore J. Bornhorst and Danita Brandt, "Michigan's earliest geology," pp. 24–39; Steve LoDuca, "Paleozoic environments and life," pp. 40–59; and Michael A. Velbel, "The 'lost interval': Geology from the Permian to the Pilocene," pp. 60–68.

The references for this paragraph are Brandt, in *MGG*, pp.12–22.

The specific phrase "in the basement of time" is Norman Macleod's in *A River Runs Through It*. Geologists commonly use *basement* to designate rock beneath a cover of sedimentary rock.

[4] John Adam Dorr and Donald F. Eschman. *Geology of Michigan* (Ann Arbor: University of Michigan Press, 1970), pp. 87–89; *Geology in Michigan — DEQ*, http://www.michigan.gov/documents/deq/ogs-gimdl-GTLH_geo_307674_7.pdf.

[5] *MGG*, pp. 40–50; Dorr and Eschman, p. 87; R. W. Kelley, comp. Geology Notes for Upper Peninsula Traveling Workshop (Lansing: Geological Survey Division, Michigan Department of Conservation, 1957), p. 2, http://www.michigan.gov/documents/deq/GIMDL-GGGNUP_302335_7.pdf; Allan M. Johnson, Robert V. Kesling, Richard T. Lilienthal, and Harry O. Sorensen, "The Maple Block Knoll Reef in the Bush Bay Dolostone (Silurian, Engadine Group), Northern Peninsula of Michigan" (Ann Arbor: University of Michigan, Museum of Paleontology, Papers on Paleontology No. 20, 1979), p. 3; Kenneth K. Landes, George M. Ehlers, and George M. Stanley, "Geology of the Mackinac Straits Region and Sub-surface Geology of Northern Southern Peninsula" (Lansing: Department of Conservation, Geological Survey Division: Publication 44, Geological Series 37, 1945), pp. 9–18. For descriptions, depictions, and photographs of fossil invertebrates, see *MGG*, p. 46, and Dorr and Eschman, ch. XIII.

[6] *MGG*, pp. 42, 45–52; Kelley, p. 2.

[7] See Elizabeth Kolbert, *The Sixth Extinction* (New York: Henry Holt & Co., 2014) for an accessible history of extinctions.

[8] Geology in Michigan — DEQ; Dorr, pp. 113, 116, 123, 178; Landes; *MGG*, pp. 52–54.

[9] The Mississippian and Pennsylvanian periods are also labeled the Carboniferous period. The phrase "lost interval" is that of Dorr and Eschman in their standard text *Geology of Michigan*;_Geology in Michigan — DEQ at http://www.michigan.gov/documents/deq/ogs-gimdl-GTLH_geo_307674_7.pdf. See also *MGG*, pp. 57–60, 66.

[10] The coprolite was examined and confirmed as such by Prof. Grahame J. Larson of the Department of Geological Studies, Michigan State University.

[11] William R. Farrand, "The Glacial Lakes around Michigan" (Bulletin 4, revised. Lansing: DEQ, Geological Survey Division, 1998), pp. 5–6.

[12] "Glacial Lakes," http://www.geo.msu.edu/geogmich/glacial.html.

[13] This type of topography is known by other names as well. Ice-contact topography is a "steep and irregular topography formed when a continental glacier (ice sheet) stagnates and retreats. Typical features of ice-contact topography include eskers, kames, and kettle lakes. Ice-contact topography is sometimes called kettle-kame or ice-disintegration topography." Dennis A. Albert and Patrick J. Comer, *Atlas of Early Michigan's Forests, Grasslands, and Wetlands* (East Lansing: Michigan State University Press, 2008), 105.

The diagram of deglaciation in the text is a slightly modified version of one widely available in many languages on the internet.

[14] What follows is a more sophisticated description of kames.

KAMES are rudely stratified deposits of cobble, gravel, sand, and silt which were sorted out of the ice by rapidly swirling waters whose activity was concentrated largely in depressions or plunge basins where melt waters flowing over the surface of the glacier plunged over the ice front on to the accumulating moraine. They are recognized by their "knob-like" structure and by their common occurrence in areas of interlobate moraines. It is not surprising that kames should abound in regions where several ice fronts were retreating simultaneously because it was here that pockets were most readily formed to supply the environment in which an excessive supply of melt waters had an opportunity to churn up and deposit the material.

Kames are scattered in various type of moraines and occur frequently in areas of till plains as well. In certain regions of till plains developed under conditions of ice stagnation, series of kames were tied into extended chains to form eskers. (S. G. Berquist, "The Glacial History and Development of Michigan" (no date), http://www. michigan.gov/documents/deq/Glacial_History_Bergquist_306034_7.pdf[, p. 7)

For the various descriptions of Black Mountain, see DNR, Black Mountain Plan: Development and Management Guidelines, Draft, September 1988, p. 9; Lawrence M. Sommers, ed., *The Atlas of Michigan* (East Lansing: Michigan State University Press, 1977), p. 33; interpretive posting on the all-access trail at N 45°29′196″/W 84°12′252″ in the Black Mountain Forest Recreation Area; Cheboygan County Planning Commission, Cheboygan County Comprehensive Plan, adopted February 20, 2002, map 4.1; Sommers, p. 32.

Otherwise, see Albert and Comer, p. 105; Myrna M. Killey, *Illinois's Ice Age Legacy* (2nd ed., Champaign: Illinois State Geological Survey, 2007), pp. 18–19, 72; Robert M. Thorson, *Beyond Walden: The Hidden History of America's Kettle Lakes and Ponds* (New York: Walker & Co., 2009), p. 32; and W. A. Burgis and D. F. Eschman, "Late-Wisconsinan History of Northeastern Lower Michigan," Midwest Friends of the Pleistocene Thirtieth Annual Field Conference, May 29–31, 1981 (sponsored by the Department of Geological Sciences, University of Michigan), Landform Units in Northeastern Michigan. On glacial movement and landforms and soils in Northeastern Michigan, see Randall J. Schaetzl, "Late Pleistocene Ice-flow Directions and the Age of Glacial Landscapes in Northern Lower Michigan," *Physical Geography*, 22 (2001), 28–41 and Randall J. Schaetzl, Frank J. Krist, Paul R. Rindfleisch, Johan Liebens, and Thomas E. Williams, "Postglacial Landscape Evolution of Northeastern Lower Michigan Interpreted from Soils and Sediments," *Annals of the Association of American Geographers*, 90:3 (2000), 443–466. I also thank Randall Schaetzl for his electronic communication on February 15, 2011.

[15] http://umbs.lsa.umich.edu/research/researchsite/twin-lakes.htm?order=field_project_years_active_value2&sort=asc. This isolated lake has been known variously as South Twin Lake, East Twin Lake, Twin Lake 1, and other less formal names, such as Bullhead Lake.

[16] Albert and Comer, p. 105; Killey, pp. 18–20, 72; Thorson, pp. 6–8, 31–36.

[17] William L. Blewett, David P. Lusch, and Randall J. Schaetzl, "The physical landscape: A glacial legacy," in *MGG*, pp. 264–266.

[18] David P. Lusch, "Groundwater and karst," in *MGG*, pp. 235–241; Schaetzl, "Karst Country of the NE Lower Peninsula," http://web2.geo.msu.edu/geogmich/NE-MIkarst.html; Frank Leverett et al., Flowing Wells and Municipal Water Supplies in the Southern Portion of the Southern Peninsula of Michigan (Washington, DC: GPO, 1906); *Cheboygan Daily Tribune* (hereafter referenced as *CDT*), August 23, 1949, August 2, 2000; W. B. Allen, Flowing Wells in Michigan 1974 (Water Information Series Report 2, prepared by the United States Geological Survey in cooperation with the Michigan Department of Natural Resources, Lansing: State of Michigan, Dept. of Natural Resources, Geological Survey Division, 1977), p. 6 and plates 1 (map showing flowing wells in glacial drift in Michigan) and 2 (map showing flowing and nonflowing artesian wells in bedrock in Michigan).

West of Cheboygan County, in Emmet County, the Oden State Fish Hatchery, established in 1921, was unique among state fish hatcheries in that its water supply came entirely from artesian wells and springs (Department of Conservation Biennial Report, 1933–1934, p. 126, 1935–1936, p. 129).

[19] Lusch, pp. 235-241; "Karst Country of the NE Lower Peninsula," http://web2.geo.msu.edu/geogmich/NE-MIkarst.html; NEMCOG Presque Isle. The Michigan Nature Association and the Michigan Karst Conservancy (MKC) have worked collaboratively to preserve and manage the seventy-six-acre Mystery Valley Karst Preserve and Nature Sanctuary in Posen Township, Presque Isle County. It contains what is "regarded as the finest known example of a karst valley with a swallow hole in Michigan."

[20] "Glacial Lakes," http://www.geo.msu.edu/geogmich/glacial.html.

[21] Randall J. Schaetzl, Scott A. Drzyzga, Beth N. Weisenborn, Kevin A. Kincare, Xiomara C. Lepczyk, Karsten Shein, Cathryn M. Dowd, and John Linker, "Measurement, correlation, and mapping of glacial Lake Algonquin shorelines in Northern

Michigan," *Annals of the Association of American Geographers*, 92:3. Based on the presence of deep sands on the Riggsville island southwest of Cheboygan, the argument has been made that Algonquin, at some stage, had to have submerged at least some of these "islands."

[22] Cheboygan County Planning Commission, "Cheboygan County Comprehensive Plan" (2002), p. 4-2. The phenomenon of rebound is called isostasy.

[23] United States Department of Agriculture, Soil Conservation Service, in cooperation with Michigan Department of Agriculture, Michigan Agricultural Experiment Station, and Michigan Technological University, Soil Survey of Cheboygan County, Michigan, 1991, p. 8. See the General Soil Map for the spatial distribution of the soil associations.

[24] Soil Survey, p. 10.

[25] This and subsequent soil information is taken from Soil Survey, Map Sheets. For specific details of each type of soil, see Appendix I.

[26] Donald I. Dickmann and Larry A. Leefers, *The Forests of Michigan* (Ann Arbor: University of Michigan Press, 2003), pp. 53–54.

[27] Dickmann and Leefers, pp. 59–66; Christina M. Hupy and Catherine H. Yansa, "The last 17,000 years of vegetation history," in *MGG*, p. 95–101. Leaves of the first postglacial, cold-tolerant species, nearly fourteen thousand years old, have been recovered from a moss (bryophyte) bed just west of Cheboygan City.

[28] J. Alan Holman and Danita Brandt, "Pleistocene fauna," in *MGG*, pp. 106–114. See also the chapter on fossil vertebrates in Holman's *Ancient Life of the Great Lakes Basin* (Ann Arbor: University of Michigan Press, 1995).

[29] Despite the differences in description, all these cultures hunted in some way and to some degree. William A. Lovis, "Between the glaciers and Europeans: People from 12,000 to 400 years ago," in *MGG*, pp. 390.

[30] A convenient summary of current knowledge and hypothesis can be found in Guy Gugliotta, "When Did Humans Come to the Americas?", *Smithsonian*, February 2013 (and http://www.smithsonianmag.com/science-nature/When-Did-Humans-Come-to-the-Americas-187951111.html?c=y&page=5). See also Glenn Hodges, "Tracking the first Americans," *National Geographic*, January 2015 (and http://ngm.nationalgeographic.com/2015/01/first-americans/hodges-text). A recent study of ancient genomes of people who lived in Alaska, California, and Ontario as much as 4,800 years ago suggests a more complicated picture of human migration in the Americas than has existed up to now (C. L. Scheib et al., *Science*, 360:6392, pp. 1024–1027). The easternmost of these people would have been ancestral Algonquinian speakers.

[31] Lovis, pp. 389–391

[32] Lovis, pp. 391–393; Scott Herron, "Human history," in Knute J. Nadelhoffer, Alan J. Hogg Jr., and Brian A. Hazlett, eds., *The Changing Environment of Northern Michigan* (Ann Arbor: University of Michigan Press, 2010), p. 15; electronic communication with the state archaeologist on August 1, 2014. The linkage of the inhabitants of the Southern Lower Peninsula was with cultures in Ohio, Indiana, and Illinois. The other major affinity involved the Western Upper Peninsula and inhabitants of what is now Wisconsin.

[33] Helen Hornbeck Tanner, ed., *Atlas of Great Lakes Indian History* (Norman: University of Oklahoma Press, 1987), pp. 24–28, map 5; Lovis, pp. 393–99.

[34] Lovis, pp.393–399.

[35] W. B. Hinsdale, *Primitive Man in Michigan* (Ann Arbor: University of Michigan, 1925), pp. 116–117, Plate II.

Chapter 2 Anishnaabeg, Wemitigoji, Jagonash, and Chemokmon

We have no spirit to celebrate with you, the great Columbia Fair . . . The cyclone of civilization rolled westward; the forests of untold centuries were swept away; streams dried up; lakes fell back from their ancient bounds; and all our fathers once loved to gaze upon was destroyed, defaced, or marred; except the sun, moon, and starry skies above, which the Great Spirit in his wisdom hung beyond their reach.
— Potawatomi chief Simon Pokagon, speaking at the World's Columbian Exposition in Chicago in 1893[36]

Visitors to the Northern Lower Peninsula of Michigan may be excused if they are unaware that its land and lakes were the land and lakes of the Odawa (Ottawa) and the Ojibwa (Chippewa) for centuries. Few place-names preserve their memory. Of the nine northernmost counties in the Lower Peninsula, for example, three have French-origin names, two relate to Ireland, two are "Indian-sounding" names created by a white man, and one, also "Indian-sounding," was imported from New York. Only Cheboygan originates in the languages of the Odawa and Ojibwa. Virtually no city, village, township, river, or lake bears a name referencing the nonwhite history of the region. Even places that have relatively well-established or recognizable Native American names, such as *Waganakising*, are shown on maps with an English name. Other than casinos, their traces are invisible as far as most visitors are concerned.

But in the seventeenth and eighteenth centuries, what is now Michigan was the core of *Anishinaabewaki*, a part of what the French called the "high country" (*pays d'en haut*), stretching from Montreal to the Mississippi and farther, a land in which a European presence was slight and conditional, the center of which was not Montreal but Michilimackinac. The high country in these centuries was neither conquered nor settled by Europeans, and its inhabitants were not submissive to French or British authority.

The people who encountered the first Frenchmen (*Wemitigoji*) on the Upper Great Lakes in 1634 were divided into the northern *Anishnaabeg* ("human beings," "original people") and the southern *Anishnaabeg*, a division corresponding to the distinction between the fishing/hunting people of the Northern Lower Peninsula, Upper Peninsula, and Canadian shore of the Great Lakes and the farming people to the south. Beyond this broadest identity, the native peoples thought of themselves in terms of kin (members of a family by birth), clan (defined by the father's kin identity), and band ("a small local economic and sociopolitical group" with a territorial association that might take its name from a leader, a village, a geographical feature, or an animal). What did not feature in the layers of identity was tribe; that would be a seventeenth- and eighteenth-century development growing out of defeat and displacement by the Iroquois and out of relations with Europeans and Americans.[37]

The scholar Charles Cleland breaks down the century and a half of relations between the French and the native peoples of the Great Lakes into three periods: from 1603 (French settlement on the St. Lawrence) to 1649 (beginning of the Iroquois Wars); from 1649 to 1700 (the Iroquois Wars); and from 1700 (end of the Iroquois Wars) to 1763 (expulsion of the French from Canada by the British).[38]

Jacques Cartier had explored the St. Lawrence Valley in 1535; Samuel de Champlain established Quebec in 1606. Within a few years of the second event, the French had formed positive relationships with Algonquian-speaking peoples in St. Lawrence Valley and to the west and north, notably with the Nipissing and the *Cheveaux Releves* ("High Hairs"). The French also allied with the Iroquoian-speaking Huron of the Ottawa River and Georgian Bay. In the process, the French became enemies of the "League of the Iroquois," the Five Nations (Cayuga, Mohawk, Oneida, Onondaga, and Seneca), who were linked in trading relations to the Dutch. Like the French, the Dutch found themselves drawn into already existing conflicts between the Five Nations and the allies of the French.[39]

In the early seventeenth century, the Huron Confederacy, composed of at least four different groups numbering just over twenty thousand persons, lived in an area between Lake Huron and Lake Simco in Southern Ontario. A much smaller but closely related band, known to the Hurons as the *Tionnontatehronnon* but called the *Petun* or tobacco Hurons by the French, occupied the base of the Bruce Peninsula. Manitoulin Island was the habitation of those several groups the French called the *Cheveaux Releves*; they called themselves the *O-dah-wah* or *Adawa* ("trader" or "traders" is the common translation).

Algonquinian-speaking bands, fishermen and hunters, were to be found along the entire eastern shore of Georgian Bay. The *Nipissings* lived along the Ottawa River and Lake Nipissing. To the west, near the mouth of the French River, were several bands known as the *Atchiligouan*. Farther to the west lived the "beaver people" (*Amikouai*) and then the "eagle people" (*Mississauga*) and then, at the falls of St. Mary's River, the "people of the falls" (*Pahouitingwach Irini*, called by the French the *Saulteaur*). The south shore of Lake Superior and the Eastern Upper Peninsula, including the Lake Michigan shore, was home to the *Mikinac* ("turtle people") and the *Nouquet* ("bear people"). These peoples living on the shores of Lakes Superior and Michigan were the ancestors of the Ojibwa.[40]

Two other groups need to be noted. In Southwestern Ontario, to the south of the Hurons, lived the *Attiwandaron*, called by the French the Neutral, an Iroquoian-speaking people who did not ally themselves with the Huron or with the Iroquois and who usually managed to remain at peace with both. But the

Neutral, in conjunction with the Odawa, did war with the "Fire Nations" (*Atsistaehronons*), a large number of small independent Algonquinian-speaking agriculturist bands occupying the southern third of the Lower Peninsula. These were the ancestors of the Potawatomi and the Mascouten.[41]

Disease, Christian evangelism, and war would radically alter this distribution of native peoples over the next two centuries. Diseases endemic among Europeans—influenza, measles, smallpox, and whooping cough—decimated Native Americans. In less than twenty-five years, these reduced the Huron population by more than half. The Winnebago around Green Bay, a place of refuge for eastern Indians in the 1650s, had suffered the same or even greater losses by the end of the 1640s. The Iroquois also lost perhaps as much as half of their population; replacement provided one of the motives for the league's aggressiveness. Jesuit missionaries succeeded in converting perhaps 15 percent of the reduced number of Hurons. These supported the French and, in turn, were favored by the French with, for example, firearms that were denied to the unconverted traditionalists. (By contrast, the Iroquois were supplied firearms by the Dutch and then by the English as a part of the fur trade without regard to conversion.) Thus, it was a demographically weakened and politically fragmented Huron Confederacy that, at mid-century, entered on intensified warfare with the Five Nations of the Iroquois Confederacy.

The Iroquois Wars and Diaspora

The year 1649 is a nominal date for the beginning of the Iroquois Wars; 1641 or 1642 would do as well. Earlier, war had rarely been absent for long in the relations among the various bands in the region, and these merged into the greater conflict. At mid-century, the Five Nations assembled the largest and best armed war party yet seen and raided northward and westward with unprecedented success. In 1649, that war party attacked the Hurons and, in a matter of a few months, turned them into refugees who fled first to Christian Island in the Georgian Bay and then to Manitoulin Island, where they joined with *Petun* and Odawa refugees, and then to Mackinac Island.[42]

In 1650, it was the turn of the Neutral, who were destroyed. Soon after, the Fire Nations had to abandon the Lower Peninsula. Typically, those who were attacked by the Iroquois suffered one of three fates. They were killed or captured and later killed, a death often preceded by torture. They escaped and sought a place of security, often quite distant. Or they were adopted into the Iroquois. Adoption was a means by which the Iroquois compensated for their numerical inferiority to the Hurons and the Algonquinian-speaking peoples and replaced at least some of their battle casualties.

In 1654, the Iroquois attacked the Erie peoples living along the south coasts of Lake Ontario and Lake Erie, ending a war begun a few years earlier. Erie survivors either escaped or, more commonly, were absorbed into the Seneca Nation. By then, the Iroquois had also cleared much of the Ohio country and the Illinois country.

In the face of Iroquois raids, the southern *Anishnaabeg* fled Michigan, moving by land to Green Bay, where refugee *Petun* and Odawa also gathered. Driven by rumors of Iroquois raids, these *Petun* and Odawa moved farther west to Lake Pepin on the Mississippi, where they encountered and traded with indigenous Siouan peoples. A few years later, conflict with the Sioux caused the *Petun* to move northward up the Black River in Wisconsin and the Odawa to settle briefly on Lac Courtes Orielles, near Hayward, Wisconsin. Soon after, both groups fled to Chequamegon Bay on Lake Superior near Ashland, Wisconsin.[43] From this diaspora emerged the tribes known as Ottawa, Ojibwa, and Potawatomi.

The success of the Five Nations was not unbroken, nor did it come cheaply. In 1653, the Iroquois sent a war party even larger than that of 1649 against the many different bands gathered around Green Bay. Threatened with starvation and unable to gain succor from those they had planned to attack, the Iroquois broke into two groups. One group headed toward the falls of St. Mary's River, the land of the *Saulteaur* and another refuge for displaced Algonquinians. These Iroquois never returned, simply disappearing from all records.[44] (By this point, the *Anishnaabeg* at Michilmackinac were already preparing a large counterattack with Hurons, Nipissing, *Petun*, Ojibwa, and *Susquahannock*.) A year later, a large Iroquois force tried to cross the straits at Michilmackinac, only to be driven back by Odawa and Ojibwa. In 1658, yet another large Iroquois war party, seeking revenge for the deaths of their kin, was defeated. Four years later, a band of Mohawk and Oneida came again into the *Saulteaur* lands and was destroyed by a force of *Saulteaur*, Odawa, and *Amikwa* at or near what is known as Iroquois Point. *Anishnaabeg* were never driven from Manitoulin, Michilimackinac, or the St. Mary's.

Diminished by disease and exhausted by war in all quarters—by now, the Iroquois were at war with the *Susquahannocks* to their south—the Five Nations secured a peace with the French in 1667. That release from the terrifying pressure of the Iroquois, even if partial and temporary, ended the western diaspora and allowed the displaced to move eastward to Green Bay and southward along the Lake Michigan shore, to the Straits of Mackinac, and to Manitoulin Island.

The last quarter of the seventeenth century saw renewed warfare over an even larger area between the Iroquois, on the one hand, and the French and several Indian nations, primarily the Huron, Odawa, and Potawatomi, on the other. The latter part of the Iroquois Wars intersected the European conflict known as the War of the League of Augsburg (1688–1697), generally referred to in North American history as King William's War. In Cleland's words, the entire period is one of "plot and counterplot, alliance and betrayal, war and peace."

What is hidden in Cleland's words is *Anishnaabeg* functioning as autonomous, even dominant, actors, pursuing their own interests, not those of the French or English, and focusing on the politics and wars of the Indian lands, not those of Europe and its colonial possessions. It is in this period that the Odawa made Michilimackinac the crucial conduit of the fur trade and of European trade with the *Anishnaabeg* and others to the west, conditioned the terms of a European presence in *Anishinaabewaki*, and, using their role as trade intermediator, made themselves the leading political player in relationships with the French and the other Indian nations. Their focus was the Iroquois and, to a lesser degree, the Dakota Sioux. (The word *sioux* derives from the Ojibwa-French *nadowessioux*, "little snakes"; the Iroquois were the "big snakes.")[47] It was the *Anishnaabeg*, far more than the French, who were responsible for an end to more than a half century of intermittent war in the form of the Great Peace of Montreal in 1701, signed by the French, the British, and chiefs from fourteen nations.[48]

French Policy and the Seven Years' War

Within weeks of the treaty's signing, Antoine Laumet de La Mothe, *sieur de Cadillac*, commander of the now-abandoned *Fort de Buade* at St. Ignace, established *Fort Pontchartrain du Détroit*. One of its purposes was to block tribes of the Upper Great Lakes from pursuing relations and trade with the Iroquois and the English, especially in the Ohio country. Another was to break the control of trade with the western nations exercised by the Odawa at Michilmackinac. Cadillac invited Huron and Odawa from Michilimackinac to settle in the Detroit River valley. Those who did were joined by Sauk, Masquakie (Fox), and Mascouten from the Green Bay area, Potawatomi and Miami from Southwestern Michigan, and Mississauga Ojibwa from Northern Lake Huron.[49]

In the half century before the onset of the French and Indian War in 1754 (the first act in the worldwide Seven Years' War of 1756–1763), the French, haunted by fear that their "allies" would link up with the English and the Iroquois, built forts to protect a revived fur trade in the north and west, embarrassed themselves in a conflict with the Cherokee, and, as they saw it, employed Indians to keep the Ohio country clear of English traders and tribes willing to trade with the English. Over the course of time, the repeated conflicts produced changes in native conduct of warfare. Beginning with the bow and arrow, axe, and club as weapons and the ambush of the unsuspecting or lightening raids on lightly protected villages as tactics, Indians acquired firepower in the form of guns, developed a capacity to attack and even besiege heavily protected forts, and ultimately became heavily armed irregular military units, often mercenary, under the (often nominal) command of French officers or the leadership of a *métis* (Euro-Indian) or an admired *ogimaa* ("chief").

For example, at mid-century, the French failed to convince a Miami chief in the trading town of *Pickawellany* (near modern-day Piqua, Ohio) to resume trade and alliance with the French, mounted an unsuccessful raid in 1751, and then were unable to recruit a war party to attack the town. In 1752, however, a band of 240 Ojibwa and Odawa from Michilimackinac, assembled by an Odawa-French *ogamaa*, also an officer in the French militia, descended on *Pickawellany*, drove out the British traders, and, in a pungent phrase, "made a broth" of the Miami chief. The Miamis abandoned the town, moved back to the Wabash River, and resumed an alliance with the French. Within two years, all British traders were gone from the Ohio Valley.[52]

What is notable about this episode is that the motive of the Indians was to preserve peace among themselves as a precondition to continuing to play off the French and the English against each other, that *Anishnaabeg* diplomacy independent of the French assured nonintervention by the English or the Iroquois, and that the attack was a tightly controlled piece of political theater. Michilimackinac had a better understanding of Montreal than Montreal of Michilimackinac.[53]

Similarly, in 1757, the Indian force with the French army operating south of Lake Champlain in New York exceeded 850. Of these, nearly 340 were Odawa from Michilimackinac, Saginaw Bay, and Detroit, and 160 were Ojibwa (*Sauteurs*); almost 90 were Potawatomi from Detroit and Southwestern Michigan. (The commander at *Pickawellany* distinguished himself again in 1757 in the successful siege of Fort William Henry, the British fort on Lake George, as he had in the defense of Fort Duquesne against the Braddock expedition in 1755.)[54]

Most of the fighting in the North American theater of the war had ended in 1760 with the British taking possession of Quebec, Montreal, and all French fortifications west of the Alleghenies. Clumsy at best in their relations to native populations, contemptuous of the northern tribes, and committed to policies that ran up against the interests of those who had been allies of the French, the British (*Jagonash*) unknowingly—but deservedly, perhaps—prepared their own retribution. (Like the French, the British looked for centralization and authority in *Anishnaabeg* society. What they found was intricate, decentralized kinship relations, which they never fully understood, and leaders who could persuade but not command.)

In May and June 1763, all British forts west of the Alleghenies were attacked in Pontiac's War. Of fourteen fortifications, eight were taken by Indians and one abandoned by the British. Of the eight, one was Fort Michilimackinac. Seventy British were killed and the rest taken prisoner; the French Canadians living in the fort were not disturbed. The attack, including the subterfuge that gave the war party armed entry to the fort, was the work of the Ojibwa chief *Minavavana* (*le Grand Saulteaur*), who lived near Michilimackinac, and the war party was led by the Ojibwa war chief *Matchekewis*, who lived at Cheboygan in the summer and Saginaw Bay in the winter. (In his classic *History of the Ojibway People* (1885), the Ojibwa-French interpreter William Warren devoted many pages to the attack on Fort Michilimackinac, as the episode survived in mid-nineteenth-century Ojibwa tribal memory. The first pages of Andrew J. Blackbird's *History of the Ottawa and Chippewa Indians of Michigan* (1887) concern the role of the Odawa, his people, in the aftermath of the attack.) It was late 1764 before military operations ceased in the large area that is Trans-Appalachia.[55]

British Policy and the Struggle for the Ohio Country

British policy was to close off the Ohio Valley and Great Lakes region to settlement, recognizing the area as Indian property by right of immemorial occupancy and leaving it as an Indian hunting and trading preserve (to the benefit of the imperial budget). This was the policy enunciated in the Royal Proclamation of 1763 and the policy to be accomplished in another way by the Quebec Act of 1774. But it ran directly contrary to the interests of colonial land speculators and squatters. The Indian response to their incursions was to raid American settlements. Even before the outbreak of the American Revolution, the struggle for the Ohio country and the Great Lakes had begun. It would last another forty years. In that struggle, Great Lakes Indians would consistently ally themselves with the British, who presented no immediate threat to their interests, and against the Americans (*Chemokmon*), who did.[56]

In the last decades of the French colonial presence in the Great Lakes, there were three major Indian settlements in the Northern Lower Peninsula: a mixed Ojibwa and Ottawa village at the mouth of the Au Sable; the Odawa village of *Waganawkezee* (*L'Arbre Croche*) on the Lake Michigan shore, established in 1742; and the Odawa settlement at Michilimackinac, occupied before 1720 but abandoned in 1742 with the move to *Waganawkezee*. After 1763, when what had been New France became British (or Spanish) territory by the Treaty of Paris, the Northeastern Lower Peninsula slowly became the land of the Ojibwa, the Northwestern Lower Peninsula the land of the Odawa, at least according to maps. In fact, kin relationships were so close and intricate that many settlements were mixed. As at the Au Sable, both Ojibwa and Odawa lived at Saginaw. But in 1768, only two major Indian villages appear in the northeast, both identified as Ojibwa, one at the mouth of the Au Sable, the other near Cheboygan. Similarly, there were only two major Indian villages in the northwest, both identified as Odawa: *Waganawkezee* and *La Croix*, a newer village to its north.[57] In fact, villages were most often clusters of villages, in the case of Michilimackinac dozens of them and more than six thousand inhabitants within a few miles.

After the Treaty of Paris ended the Revolutionary War, the British remained at Detroit and Michilimackinac (they had built a stonewalled fortress on Mackinac Island in 1780–1781 to replace the old French fort on the mainland). From both but especially the former, the British followed a policy of supporting the Miami, Shawnee, Delaware, Wyandot, Potawatomi, Odawa, and Ojibwa, who resisted American land claims and intrusions into the Ohio country and who defeated most of the American military expeditions sent against them. But the British were careful to avoid overt acts of war or acts that might easily be interpreted as acts of war.[58]

In 1794, the British built Fort Miamis on the Maumee River in Northwest Ohio, a primary line of Indian defense. The fort was to support the Indians and to block the approach to Detroit. A punitive American military expedition under the command of Gen. Anthony Wayne had begun marching north from Cincinnati the previous year, building forts along its way. One of these was Fort Recovery in West Central Ohio, very near what would be the Indiana–Ohio border.

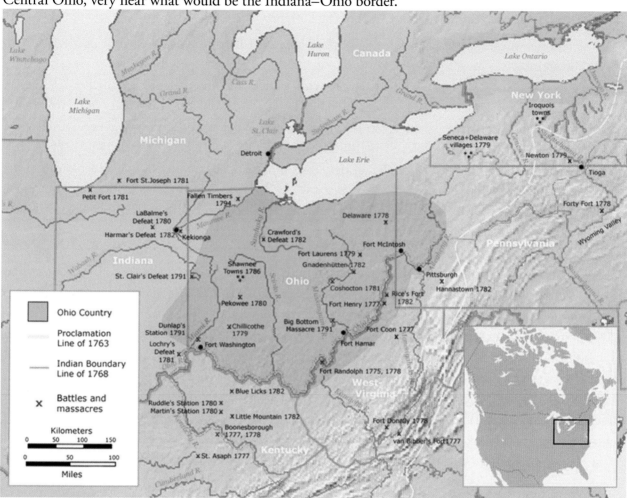

The Ohio Country

In the summer, an Indian force of as many as 1,600 warriors moved south and attacked a supply column and, on its retreat, the fort itself. Of the warriors, at least half were Ojibwa and Odawa from Northern Michigan; others were Potawatomi from the Huron River in Southern Michigan. Angered by the lack of support from local Delaware and Shawnee in what proved a bloody action for the Indians, many of the Ojibwa, Odawa, and Potawatomi returned to their villages, reducing the number of Indians that faced Wayne on the Maumee in the decisive Battle of Fallen Timbers in 1795.

The defeat of the Indians at Fallen Timbers (and the refusal of the British at Fort Miamis to protect or aid fleeing Indians) led to a year of negotiation between Wayne and the Indians. The result was the treaty of Greeneville, signed in August 1795, "a treaty of peace between the United States of America and the tribes of Indians called the Wyandots, Delawares, Shawanees, Ottawas, Chippewas, Pattawatimas, Miamis, Eel Rivers, Weas, Kickapoos, Piankeshaws, and Kaskaskias." Its primary effect was to grant virtually all of Ohio to the United States. But among its articles was a provision to cede to the United States:

the post of Michilimackinac and all the land on the island on which that post stands and the main land adjacent, of which the Indian title has been extinguished by gifts or grants to the Frewnch [sic] or English governments; and a piece of land on the main to the north of the island, to measure six miles, on lake Huron or the strait between lakes Huron and Michigan and to extend three miles back from the water of the lake or strait; and also the Island De Bois Blane [sic], being an extra and voluntary gift of the Chippewa nation.

The signatories included the Ojibwa chiefs *Mashipinashiwish* from *Waganawkezee* and *Masass* from Michilimackinac.

The land ceded by Greeneville filled rapidly with whites, and the pressure for further land cessions intensified. Northern Indians could see what had happened (especially after the Treaty of Detroit in 1807 ceded much of Southeastern Michigan to the Americans and the treaty of Fort Wayne in 1809 yielded another three million acres to whites in Illinois and Indiana) and what threatened to happen in the Upper Great Lakes. It was these Indians on the edges of American expansion who became the primary supporters of the Shawnee brothers, *Tenskwatawa* and *Tecumseh*, the one known as the prophet preaching cultural rejection of the whites and the other organizing a political and military resistance that resulted in Tecumseh's War (1811) and merged into the War of 1812.

At this time, seven major Ojibwa villages existed in the northern part of the Lower Peninsula: four along Saginaw Bay, one on the Au Sable, one on Thunder Bay, and one at Cheboygan. The Odawa villages of *Waganawkezee* and *La Croix* remained on the Lake Michigan coast, along with a third Odawa village on Walloon Lake and two Ojibwa villages and a mixed Odawa-Ojibwa village in the area of Grand Traverse Bay and the Leelanau peninsula.[59]

In July 1812, Fort Mackinac was taken by British forces, three-quarters of whom were Indians, including local Ojibwa and Odawa. With the defeat of the British and the death of *Tecumseh* in the Battle of the Thames in October 1813, many Indians withdrew from formal military operations, returning to their villages in the Upper Great Lakes, content to do no more than raid American farmsteads and settlements. Nevertheless, the American effort to retake Fort Mackinac in July 1814 was thwarted by a combination of British guns and Indian allies. (The Americans occupied the fort a year later by virtue of the Treaty of Ghent.)

American Policy and Expropriation

The years after the war saw the peak of the fur trade. Mackinac was its hub, the headquarters of the northern department of John Jacob Astor's American Fur Company, the dominant player in the American fur trade. Furs and trade goods, of course, had long been essential elements in the economies of the northern Indians and important contributors to the violent history of the region. Since the 1790s, the policy of the federal government was to prevent exploitation of Indians by traders, to ensure Indian access to trade goods, to prevent Indian acquisition of alcohol, and, in time, to regulate the fur trade. Federal policies were a failure. The fur trade eventually died, its animal base exhausted, its products no longer fashionable, and the national economy in depression.

The legalistic expropriation of Indian lands in Michigan continued throughout the first half of the nineteenth century. Two treaties, that of Saginaw in 1819, pressed by territorial governor Lewis Cass as the commissioner of the federal government and that of Washington, brokered between the federal government and Native Americans by Henry Schoolcraft, conveyed first Northeastern and then Northwestern Michigan to white hands.

The Treaty of Saginaw referenced the boundaries established by the Treaty of Detroit and defined the northern border of the new cession as running from the western boundary "to the head of Thunder Bay River; thence, down the same, following the courses thereof, to the mouth" at Thunder Bay. Among other land reservations, the treaty provided that there should be "one tract, of eight thousand acres, on the east side of the river Au Sable, near where the Indians now live."

As of 1830, there were eleven major Ojibwa villages in the Northern Lower Peninsula, including *Mishcotawagamish* at the base of Black Lake and six villages on Thunder Bay and two Odawa villages: *Cheboygan* on the west shore of Burt Lake and *Chingassamp* on the Cheboygan River just north of Mullett Lake. (In 1830, the Indian population of the Lower Peninsula was roughly 14,000 persons living in 131 villages, the vast majority of which were located south of a line drawn from Muskegon to the Saginaw Bay. In the same year, the white population was slightly less than 32,000, most also living in the southern half of the Lower Peninsula. In only a few years, the number of whites was nearly 175,000.)[60]

Much more extensive in the land ceded and in its other provisions, the Treaty of Washington referenced the Thunder Bay River line and reflected a need (or desire) to deal with many more Native American leaders than seventeen years earlier. While he did not sign the thirteen clauses that make up the core of the treaty, "Chingassanoo— or the Big Sail, on the Cheboigan"—did add his mark to the supplemental article. He and "Mujeekewis, on Thunder-bay river," were each to locate one thousand acres to be held in common by their bands for five years. Both appeared in the first class of the list of chiefs entitled to share in a fund of $30,000, in their cases to receive $500. Two chiefs in the second class, receiving $200 each, were "on the Cheboigan, Chonees, or Little John, Shaweenossegay; on Thunder bay, Suganikwato". "Poiees or Dwarf and Pamossay of Cheboigan[, and] Gitchy Ganocquot and Pamossegay of Thunder Bay" fell into the third class and were to receive $100.

In 1830, Pres. Andrew Jackson, known not only for his defense of New Orleans in 1815 but also for his campaigns against the Creeks (1813–1814) and the Seminoles (1817–1818), eagerly signed the Indian Removal Act. Federal policy became to purchase Indian lands in areas of white settlement and to compel tribes to move west beyond the pale of settlement. (This policy of separating Indians and whites ultimately failed in large part because white settlement moved westward, uncontrolled, at a rapid rate.) By the end of 1840, with some exceptions, the Potawatomis in Michigan had been removed to Kansas.

The fate of the Odawa and the Ojibwa was different. The Treaty of Washington had provided that they would receive fourteen substantial reservations within the ceded lands to be used as permanent homes. (They might also hunt and fish within the ceded lands until the lands were needed for settlement.) In addition, for twenty years, the Indian would receive subsidies to address matters such as agriculture, health, and education on these reservations. The U.S. Senate unilaterally altered the agreed terms to limit occupancy of the reservations to a period of five years. This period might be extended at the will of the United States.

But if the tribes wished to move west, the government would provide them land. The chiefs subsequently and reluctantly accepted the changes under pressure of the government withholding all promised payments until they gave their assent and with the promise that the reserved lands would not be needed for many years.

For several reasons, many Odawa and Ojibwa were able to remain in Michigan until federal policy abandoned removal and substituted a policy of reservations and individual allotments. Contrary to all their history and tradition, Indians were to be civilized into Jeffersonian "cultivators" or "husbandmen." Treaties signed in Detroit in 1855 created three reservations in the upper half of the Lower Peninsula, the Little Traverse reservation of the Odawa, the Grand Traverse reservation of the Odawa and Chippewa, and the Isabella reservation of the Saginaw Chippewa. Even these, however, failed to provide secure land tenure for the Indian signatories; that struggle would continue for decades into the future.[61] (Hostile to Indians and an advocate of the policy of reservations, William Tecumseh Sherman knew the whites even better; in 1865, at the very beginning of the campaigns against the Plains Indians over which he presided, he defined a reservation as "a parcel of land set aside for Indians, surrounded by thieves.")[62]

But as late as 1870, the eve of the logging boom in the northernmost Lower Peninsula, eight substantial Ojibwa villages remained in the northeast, including one at Ocqueoc in Presque Isle County, and five in the northwest. There were a dozen Odawa villages and a mixed Odawa-Ojibwa village in the northwest. But a census in 1907 "of persons of Indian descent" in Cheboygan County, taken "to determine [their] eligibility . . . to receive payment of monies as the result of Congressional legislation," totaled only 114 persons, nearly 40 percent of whom were partners in mixed marriages and most of whom lived in Cheboygan City or Mackinaw City. (As of 2000, the Native American population of the county was slightly less than 700.)[63]

Cheboygan

Like the rest of Northern Michigan, Cheboygan County has failed to preserve in its place-names a substantial memory of an Indian presence. Of the thirteen cities, villages, and unincorporated places in the county, only two have names linked to the Indians of Northern Michigan. Of nineteen townships, none has a name so linked. The name of the county and city, Cheboygan, is Ojibwa in origin. Its specific meaning or meanings may never be known with certainty. Mackinac ("turtle") and its variants are also Ojibwa. On the eastern shore of Burt Lake, Waubun (or Wauban) Beach derives from the Ojibwa for "east." On that same shore, Chippewa Beach recalls Ojibwa, who probably never lived there. Point Nipigon on Lake Huron has roots in the Ojibwa (or, more generally perhaps, in Algonquian) language. East of Indian River, Gokee Creek, the largest tributary of Milligan Creek, is a trout-fishing stream.[64]

Other names are either generic or misplaced. The river and the community at the southern ends of lakes Burt and Mullett are two of over seventy places in Michigan that have "Indian" as a part of a name. Indian Point (a county map of 1902 identified the peninsula as Colonial Point, then a newly minted name) on the western shore of Burt Lake was a site occupied by Native Americans for centuries (in the eighteenth and nineteenth centuries largely by Odawa) until their village was burned and they were driven out in 1900 by a Cheboygan timber speculator and the sheriff of Cheboygan County. Miami Beach, on the south shore of Mullett Lake, refers to a tribe that never lived in Northeastern Michigan.[65] Nunda Township uses a shortened form of the name by which the Seneca referred to themselves. But the Seneca likely never set foot in Northeastern Michigan; the name is a transfer from a township in New York State. Tuscarora Township refers to the last tribe to join the Iroquois Confederacy; expelled from North Carolina in the early eighteenth century, the tribe moved to New York State. The Tuscarora had no connection to Michigan; the name is probably a settler import from New York.[66] The settlement of Topinabee, on the western shore of

Mullett Lake, commemorates a Potawatomi chief whose band lived on the St. Joseph River in Southwest Michigan; the town was named in 1881 by the hotelier and resort developer from Niles, Michigan, who had platted the village.[67]

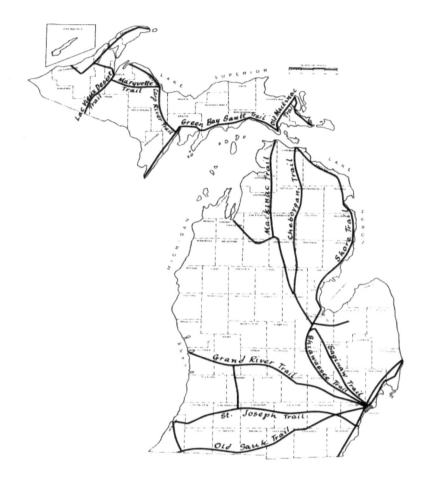

However, despite a paucity of archaeological evidence, there is reason to believe that Native Americans were aware of and probably hunted, fished, and gathered in the area of Twin Lakes and Black Mountain, possibly as early as the Woodland period. Several long-occupied Indian villages lay within a relatively few miles of the lake. The two major trails in the northeast passed nearby. Twin Lakes sits at the northern base of Black Mountain and near Black Lake and the Black River, each of which is an important geographic feature in the much-traveled landscape slanting southeastward from Mackinac and Cheboygan to Thunder Bay and Saginaw. The area provided an abundance of sugar maples, blueberries, cranberries, huckleberries, fish, and game. The annual movement of families or small groups between Saginaw Bay and the northern tip of the peninsula was habitual in the Ojibwa culture of the northeast, as was the phenomenon of retreat into winter hunting camps (or into small summer camps). Similarly, temporary encampment for specific purposes in the business of survival (e.g., fishing, maple sugaring, berry picking) was common. More generally, Northern Michigan was their land; they knew it intimately and moved through it continually for centuries. Even if the physical evidence is scant, there is every reason to believe that Twin Lakes and its environs were a part of their universe and their economy of survival.[68]

Two longtime residents of Twin Lakes, interviewed in 1990, reported the discovery of arrowheads by other persons at one of the old campgrounds on the lake and on surrounding farmland. Each of the interviewees possessed stone artifacts that they described as grinding tools, but there is not agreement among experts about the true nature of these objects.[69]

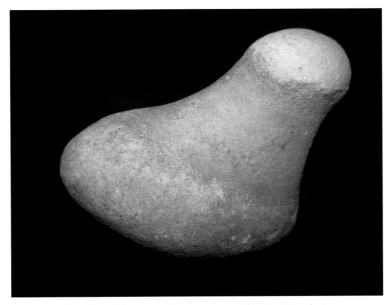

Pestle? (Photograph courtesy of John Ressler)

For its part, the state archaeologist's office has only a few records of archaeological activity or recovery of Indian artifacts in the corridor in question, Grant and Benton Townships in Cheboygan County and Bearinger Township in Presque Isle County.[70] There is a site on the southwestern shore of Lake Sixteen in Bearinger Township at the foot of Black Mountain that is represented only by fire-cracked rock. Similarly, there is a site on the southeastern shore of Black Lake that is represented by fire-cracked rock and a single projectile point. These remains are too scant to permit any sort of conclusions about the sites. Along the same shore, there are remains of a fishing camp probably dating to 700–900 AD, the Juntunen phase of the late Woodland period. A handful of sites or scatters exists near and along the Cheboygan River, all of them dating to the middle Woodland period or earlier. On the other hand, the much later villages of *Chingassamo, Mishcotawagamish, Shavinaws, Mujekewis, Sagonakato, Shoshekonawbegoking, Shingabawassinekegobawat, and Ocqueoc*, ranging along the Huron shore and sitting at the base of Black Lake and the head of Mullett Lake, are facts.

---

[36] Quoted in Edmund J. Danziger, *Great Lakes Indian Accommodation and Resistance during the Early Reservation Years, 1850–1900* (Ann Arbor: University of Michigan Press, 2009), p. 220. Like Henry David Thoreau, Pokagon underestimated the reach of white men; see part III, note 1.

[37] Charles E. Cleland, *Rites of Conquest: The History and Culture of Michigan's Native Americans* (Ann Arbor: University of Michigan Press, 1992), ch. 2. Alvin M. Josephy Jr.'s *The Indian Heritage of America* (Boston: Houghton Mifflin, 1991) is an accessible survey of Indians throughout the Americas.

[38] Cleland, p. 79. As the reader will see, this chapter is heavily indebted to two classic pieces of research, Cleland's Rites of Conquest and Helen Hornbeck Tanner's Atlas of Great Lakes Indian History. Its other major debt is to the much more recent Masters of Empire: Great Lakes Indians and the Making of America by Michael A. McDonnell.

[39] Cleland, pp. 79–88.

[40] Cleland, p. 86. Eventually, the Huron—or some of the Huron—became known as the Wyandot and settled around Detroit and on Sandusky Bay in Ohio; see Virgil J. Vogel, *Indian Names in Michigan* (Ann Arbor: The University of Michigan Press, 1986), pp. 15–16. From 1840 to 1853, the southern part of what is now Cheboygan County, including Burt, Mullett, and Black Lakes, was Wyandot County.

[41] Cleland, pp. 86–87.

[42] Christian Island is now an Ojibwa reserve.

[43] Cleland, pp. 88–94.

[44] The other group of Iroquois moved south along Lake Michigan and was wiped out by the Illinois.

[45] Cleland, p. 96.

[46] Cleland, pp. 94–96; Tanner, pp. 29–35.

[47] Josephy, p. 116.

[48] Cleland, pp. 111–116; McDonnell, pp. 34–67.

[49] Helen Hornbeck Tanner, ed., *Atlas of Great Lakes Indian History* (Norman: published for the Newberry Library by the University of Oklahoma Press, 1987), p. 39.

[50] Cleland, pp. 114–115; Tanner, map 9.

[51] Cleland, pp. 118–123.

[52] Cleland, pp. 122–123; Tanner, pp. 44–45. The attackers also ritually ate the heart of an English blacksmith in full view of the defenders.

[53] See McDonnell's analysis of this episode, pp. 142–159 (Michael A. McDonnell, *Masters of Empire: Great Lakes Indians and the Making of America*, New York: Hill & Wang, 2015).

[54] Tanner, p. 46. "Map: North America, 1763," from America: A Narrative History (5th ed.) by George Brown Tindall and David E. Shi. © 1999, 1996, 1992, 1988, 1984 by W. W. Norton & Company Inc. Used by permission of W. W. Norton & Company Inc.

[55] John A. lko, comp., *An Annotated Listing of Ojibwa Chiefs 1690–1890* (Troy, NY: Whitston Publishing Co., 1995), pp. 35–36.

[56] In a statement of work done "for the King by order of Major [Arent Schuyler] DePeyster Governor at Michelmackinac," P. Durand included the following.

March 5 [1780] For having pulled down a house of twenty four feet long by twenty deep and having transported it six leagues on rollers of white wood, having furnished the necessary wood for repairs and having put the key of the said house into the hands; the said house for the great Chief of the Sauteaux named Macquiquiovis [Matchekewis] for the price and sum of 4500 livres 4500

For having been down the river besides the house of the Chief Macquiquiovis to examine & find the pineries of red and white pine to make a saw mill & to examine the different sorts of wood and land for the good of the King 250

This house, moved to the Ojibwa village on the Cheboygan River, was a tangible part of the British policy of cultivating and using Indians as a counter to the Americans and their Spanish allies.

In 1780, Patrick Sinclair, lieutenant-governor and superintendent of Michilimackinac, while carrying out the transfer of the fort to Mackinac Island, organized an expedition against the village of St. Louis on the Mississippi. The force included perhaps two dozen white fur traders and 750 to 1,000 Indians—Ojibwa, Menominee, Winnebago, Sioux, Sac, and Fox, the Indians under the overall command of the Ojibwa chief Matchekewis, the successful attacker of Michilimackinac in 1763 and a signatory of the Treaty of Greeneville in 1795. While the attack was less than an unalloyed success, the British policy of employing Indians would endure into the nineteenth century.

For the statement of work, see Historical Society of Michigan, *Michigan Pioneer and Historical Collections* (Lansing, 1888), vol. 10, pp. 365–366. For letters concerned with the expedition, all from Sinclair to Frederick Haldimand, "Captain General and Governor in Chief in and over the Province of Quebec and the territories depending thereon in America, Vice Admiral of the same, General and Commander in Chief of His Majesty's forces in the said Province and the Frontiers thereof, &c., &c," see vol. 9, pp. 546, 548, 549, 558–560.

[57] See Tanner, maps 13, 20, 24, 25, 33, and associated text.

The area of Michilimackinac had a nearly continuous Native American presence for 2,500 years—semi-nomadic peoples from roughly 1,000 BC until the seventeenth century AD, by which point *Anishnaabeg* people were present. Over the next two hundred years, the Odawa were the most prominent tribe at the Straits of Mackinac, followed by the Ojibwa. Odawa and Ojibwa tradition identified the site of the earth's creation with Mackinac Island, *Mishee Mackinakong*, the place of the Great Turtle's back. See Cleland, p. 35, n. 4; Basil Johnston, *Ojibway Heritage* (Lincoln: University of Nebraska Press, 1976), pp. 13–14. See also Johnston, *The Manitous: The Spiritual World of the Ojibway* (New York: Harper Collins, 1995).

Michilimackinac was an economic, military, and transportation center where all those in the region met for a variety of reasons. In his narrative journal of travels, Henry R. Schoolcraft commented that "the old peninsular fort . . . continued to be the seat of the fur trade and the undisturbed rendezvous of the Indian tribes during the whole period that the crown of France exercised jurisdiction over the Canadas" (*Narrative Journal of Travels through the Northwestern Regions of the United States Extending from Detroit through the Great Chain of American Lakes to the Sources of the Mississippi River in the Year 1820*, (East Lansing: The Michigan State College Press, 1953), p.84).

The summer population of Michilmackinac itself might increase substantially as Indians from the south and west visited or passed through. (Tanner, p.130).

[58] For post-Revolutionary relations between Native Americans and the British and Americans, see Cleland, pp. 150-160, and McDonnell, pp. 311-329.

[59] Tanner, map 20. Henry Schoolcraft provided this account of a stopover at the Au Sable village in 1820:

On reaching the river aux Sablés, we found a number of Chippeway Indians upon the shore and a permanent village at the distance of two miles above its discharge. They appeared friendly and, as soon as our tents were pitched, came formally to the Governor's [Lewis Cass] marquee. A chief of the Chippeways [Black Eagle] then addressed the Governor in a speech in which he told him that he was glad to see him there—that he had heard of his coming—and hoped he would see and relieve their wants &c. The pipe of peace was then smoked in the usual style of Indian ceremony by handing it to all present, each one taking a whiff, which is all that is required: when this ceremony was ended, they commenced that of shaking hands, beginning with the Governor, and passing round in a circle to each individual composing his suite. They afterwards presented some fresh sturgeon (*accipenser*), which are caught in abundance in that river, and received in return some tobacco and whiskey and then departed to their villages.

Lewis Cass had negotiated the Treaty of Saginaw the previous year, by which the "Thumb" had been ceded to the United States as far north as Thunder Bay. (As Secretary of War in the Jackson administration, Cass would play a major role in the removal of Indians from the Eastern United States to lands beyond the Mississippi.) A companion, David Bates Douglass, a Yale graduate, veteran of the War of 1812, West Point instructor, professional engineer, and eventually the president of Kenyon College, noted in his journal, "June 2nd . . . There is an Ottowa Camp about a mile up this river [the Au Sable] & we found near our own a small camp of Chippewas from some of whom we attained some fine fresh sturgeon for supper . . ." (Schoolcraft, pp. 74, 367).

[60] Tanner, map 25.

[61] For a broad regional view of American and Canadian government policy and of the variety of Native American responses, see Danziger, *Accommodation and Resistance*. His summary of the experience of Native Americans in Michigan's Lower Peninsula follows.

[O]n Michigan's Lower Peninsula, moderately acculturated Indians were distinguished by extensive land loss [as of c. 1900]. In the rush to integrate them into the state's mainstream, the federal government's allotment scheme lacked adequate safeguards—in effect, throwing them "to the wolves." Lands were lost and federal services abruptly withdrawn. Scattered native families, many of them landless, survived through their inherent pluck and adaptability. Living along the banks of rivers and on the shores of Lake Michigan, they played service roles or supplied labor for minimal pay instead of living as the coequal, self-sufficient farmers envisioned in 1855. For them, life on the new reservations did not last long, unlike the experiences of Lake Superior Ojibwa and the natives of Canada and New York, whose land bases were more secure. (pp. 230–231)

[62] The statement and attribution can be found in Robert Burnette, *The Tortured Americans* (Englewood Cliffs, NJ: Prentice-Hall, 1971), p. 12; Peter Matthiessen, *In the Spirit of Crazy Horse: The Story of Leonard Peltier and the FBI's War on the American Indian Movement* (New York: Penguin Books, 1992), p. 17; Joe Starita, *I Am a Man: Chief Standing Bear's Journey for Justice* (New York: St. Martin's Press, 2008), p. 85; and elsewhere.

[63] Tanner, map 33.

[64] In the TOMWC watershed area, Antrim, Cheboygan, and Emmet Counties account for almost all of fewer than two dozen Indian-language–based place-names. Gogebic County in the Western Upper Peninsula, also a part of Ojibwa territory, contains more such names by itself.

[65] In all of Michigan, this is one of only two uses of "Miami" to name a place. A third use is an arm of Maumee Bay that is (barely) within the southeastern border of Michigan; "Maumee" is a variant of "Miami." In the late seventeenth and early eighteenth centuries, the Miami briefly had villages in Southwest and Southeast Michigan, but their homeland in the eighteenth century was the Wabash, St. Joseph, and Maumee River watersheds of Western Ohio and Eastern Indiana (Vogel, p. 12).

[66] Vogel, pp. 20–21.

[67] See the appropriate entries in Walter Romig, *Michigan Place Names: The History of the Founding and the Naming of More Than Five Thousand Past and Present Michigan Communities* (contributor Larry B. Massie, Detroit: Wayne State University Press, 1986).

[68] The trails map, taken from Philip P. Mason, *Michigan Highways from Indian Trails to Expressways*, shows only major trails. It omits several significant east–west trails in Central and Southern Michigan, an important trail on the western edge of the state that ran, roughly, from the Pere Marquette River southward to the Old Saux Trail, trails on the Leelanau peninsula, and, especially important, in Northern Michigan, a complex of trails between Michilmackinac and the northern shore of Little Traverse Bay. It also fails to show short trails linking major routes near their convergence, as in Cheboygan.

[69] Lawrence M. Sommers, ed., *Atlas of Michigan* (East Lansing: Michigan State University Press, 1977), p. 108; *Oral History*, "Indians." See also Wilbert B. Hinsdale, *Archaeological Atlas of Michigan* (Ann Arbor: University of Michigan Press, 1931). There is disagreement among students of Native American culture in Michigan as to whether the one artifact now available is even a human artifact. The balance of opinion is that the object is a pestle. A pestle clearly has different implications for an Indian presence on the lake than do arrowheads alone found on a slope up from the lake or scattered in area fields. Perhaps coincidentally, the name of Ernie Hover's resort on the south end of the lake was "Camp Arrowhead."

[70] Electronic communication from the state archaeologist, August 1, 2014.

Chapter 3 Stump Farms and Fire Storms

Logging

Michigan's lumber industry had its origins in the 1840s and 1850s as New Englanders and New Yorkers working the rapidly depleting northeastern forests looked for new sources of timber. Of 131 "leading lumbermen" in the Great Lakes states of Michigan, Wisconsin, and Minnesota, nearly two-thirds came from New England or New York. Of the owners of the largest lumber companies in Cheboygan in 1884, the vast majority originated in New York. Between 1840 and 1870, most loggers in Michigan came from New England, New York, Pennsylvania, or Ohio.[71]

The industry's heyday lay in the years after the Civil War and before World War I. Production in the Great Lakes states rose from 3.6 billion board feet in 1869 to almost ten billion board feet in 1889. The peak production of Cheboygan's sawmills came nine years later.[72]

The opening of the forests of Northern Lower Michigan resulted from infrastructure development, federal government policy, and an insatiable demand for lumber. The Erie Canal, finished in 1825, had made possible the movement of bulk cargoes from the Great Lakes to eastern markets. The locks on the American side at Sault Ste. Marie opened traffic from Lake Superior to the lower lakes. The lakes themselves made transport to growing lakeshore cities inexpensive, if not always safe. And it was the federal government that dredged the harbor at Cheboygan to a depth that made it a significant Great Lakes port.

The Land Ordinance of 1785, which established the Public Land Survey System, committed the federal government to survey the frontier lands it had acquired as a preliminary to their sale. The first area to be surveyed under terms of the ordinance was the northwest territory, beginning with the lands that would be admitted to the United States as the state of Ohio in 1803. The General Land Office carried out this arduous task over the course of decades, first in the southern portion

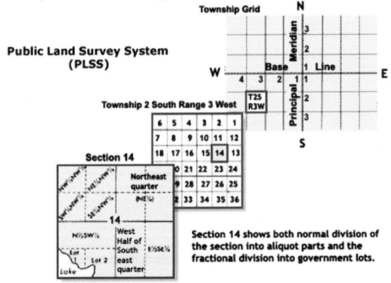

Section 14 shows both normal division of the section into aliquot parts and the fractional division into government lots.

of the territory and much later in its northern sections. Its surveyors (William Austin Burt and John Mullett were two of them) laid down survey lines, measured out townships, and established section corners. But they also made notes on the nature and resources of the land they surveyed. The surveys of the northern Lower Peninsula were carried out mostly in the 1840s and 1850s. The surveyors' notes indicated the presence of an unbelievable quantity and quality of timber (so unbelievable that they greatly underestimated its volume).

The federal government also wanted to divest itself of the surveyed land. Directly or indirectly, it was extraordinarily generous with those who built infrastructure in the wilderness as a preliminary to settlement. So were state governments once they had received public lands.

Land in large quantities was granted to the builders of canals, railroads, and roads. St. Mary's Falls Canal Co., the company that had built the first locks on the American side of the border at Sault Ste. Marie in 1853, received a land grant of 750,000 acres. In 1869, the Jackson, Lansing, and Saginaw Railroad Company received nearly 75,000 acres in Cheboygan County alone. In 1871, the Michigan Central Railroad acquired 750,000 acres as an incentive to its northward expansion. Twenty thousand acres in Cheboygan County went to the contractors who improved the Inland Water Route. Merritt Chandler of Cheboygan and Onaway, an important timber owner in the later nineteenth and early twentieth centuries, received 40,000 acres for building roughly ninety miles of road from Presque Isle to Petoskey and from Black Lake to the southeast corner of Allis Township in Presque Isle County.

Ordinary citizens could buy public lands at a standard price of $1.25 per acre; the minimum purchase was eighty acres. With passage of the Homestead Act in 1862, acquisition became even cheaper and easier; a settler could claim 160 acres in exchange for a small fee, building a house with two windows and remaining on the land for five years. No cheaper way of buying timber has ever been invented.[73]

The almost exclusive focus of logging was the white pine—cream colored, often knot free for much of its height, easily floated, light, strong, durable, and easy to work. Red (Norway) pine, often found with its relative but also existing in pure stands, frequently smaller but more fire-resistant and reproductively more vigorous in fire-scarred land, was a distinct second best. In time, however, it became an inescapable choice. And as it too disappeared in a holocaust of harvesting, hardwoods, by default, became what was left.[74]

Rivers were the primary conduit by which logs reached sawmills. In the Northeastern Lower Peninsula, the important logging rivers, in addition to those feeding into the Saginaw River, were the Au Sable, the Thunder Bay, and the Black. The equivalent rivers in the northwest were the Muskegon and the Manistee, along with the White, the Pere Marquette, the Little Manistee, the Betsie, and the Boardman. At the mouths of these rivers lay some of the preeminent lumber towns: Saginaw, Bay City, Oscoda, Alpena, Cheboygan, Muskegon, Manistee, and Traverse City.[75]

The industrialization of the logging industry came in the 1870s with the introduction of "big wheels" (or "Michigan logging wheels") and logging railroads. What had been relatively selective cutting near rivers in winter became unselective cutting year-round in the deepest parts of the forest; the transportation problem—of timber out but also of labor and supplies in—had been solved.[76]

The Black River

The lone sawmill in Cheboygan in 1874 produced seven million board feet of lumber. Four years later, six mills produced over fifty million board feet. In 1883, the major sawmills in Cheboygan, ranked by sawed lumber, were Thompson Smith, the masters of Duncan City on the east side of the Cheboygan River, Nelson & Bullen, W. & A. McArthur, owners of the primary "pier" in Cheboygan whose "sawdust mountain" would become a landmark, J. B. McArthur, William Smith, Southern Michigan Cedar & Lumber Company, Mattoon, Ogden & Company, Young & Company, and Quay & Son.[77] The number of sawmills in Cheboygan peaked in 1888 and again in 1891 at twelve (a few years earlier, there had been 112 mills on Saginaw Bay). The following year, production exceeded one hundred million board feet for the first time. The highest total of nearly 124 million board feet occurred in 1898.

Big wheels

Logging train

But Cheboygan sawmills had become increasingly dependent on imported Canadian logs, and the end was near. In response to the Dingley Tariff of 1897, Canada embargoed the exportation of logs. The rafting of logs from the Upper Peninsula to Cheboygan was not enough to support the industry for very long. In 1900, nine mills produced over sixty million board feet of lumber. In the next seven years, the number of mills was cut by more than half. Production exceeded fifty million board feet in only one year and forty million board feet in only one other. Otherwise, production ranged downward from just under forty million board feet to less than thirty million board feet.[78]

At the beginning of the nineteenth century, Twin Lakes lay in an area of conifer swamp and northern hardwood-conifer forest, with pine/oak forest to the south along the eastern shore of Black Lake. Just north of Twin Lakes, sprawled across secs. 34, 35, 28, and 27 of T37N R1E on the General Land Office dependent survey of 1854 is this description: "Surface moderately rolling soil loamy timber Sugar Beech Hemlock Maple W Pine." In sections of the township farther north are the phrases "Land mostly swamp and generally wet Timber Cedar Tamarac B. Ash Balsam Maple W Pine and Spruce" and "Sandy soil — Timber Y. and W. Pine Beech Hemlock &c." Even in late 1904, just past the peak of logging in the northeast, Frank Leverett described Cheboygan County in this way: "The eastern half of the county is largely unsettled except in a strip running southeastward from Cheboygan past Black Lake to Onaway, and much of the southeast quarter is still covered by hard-wood forests. The western half is largely cleared and much of it is settled."[79]

Two years earlier, the land touching Twin Lakes was held by six individuals, one corporation, and the federal and state governments.[80] Only one property was less than thirty-one acres, and most were significantly larger. One couple (William and Catherine Gainor) and two individuals (E. Hall and George D. Richards) owned two parcels each, totaling in the last two cases at least eighty acres.

New York–born William Gainor was a "farmer and dairyman [and] Lumber Manufacturer and timber jobber" with a "sawmill & creamery at Black Lake." (Years before, Gainor had sued the Cheboygan River Boom Company, organized by William Chandler, the brother of Merritt Chandler and the editor and publisher of the *Northern Tribune* in Cheboygan. The company operated a "sorting gap" at the fork of the Black and Cheboygan Rivers. The Michigan Supreme Court reviewed the case in Gainor's favor in 1891.)[81] The Canadian-born George D. Richards was a "Real Estate Dealer, Land Looker and Estimator," "a strong temperance man," and the founder of the village of Wolverine.[82] Most likely, another landowner, "E. Baker," was Emeline Baker, the widow and heir of Sanford Baker, an important lumberman in the years immediately following the end of the Civil War.[83] The corporate owner was Pfister & Vogel Leather Company, headquartered in Milwaukee and then the largest tannery in the world. Its interest was in hemlock bark for its tanning processes. Between them, the federal and state governments possessed nearly two hundred acres.

The privately-owned properties appear to have been held solely for the timber that stood on them. The large acreages of state tax land in the township, the identity of the largest landowners in the township, and the fact that the owners of Twin Lakes properties were either in the timber trade or lived elsewhere than the township reinforces that impression.

In this respect, Twin Lakes did not differ from Grant Township generally. Merritt Chandler, Pfister & Vogel, Merchants Bank of Canada, and four Cheboygan lumber companies owned 20 percent of the properties in Grant Township that did not belong to the state of Michigan or the federal government. Chandler, Pfister & Vogel, and Merchants Bank of Canada held 25 percent of the roughly 32,000 total acres in the township and a much higher percentage of the acres in private hands.[84] The Report of Commission of Inquiry, Tax Lands and Forestry to the Governor and Legislature of the State in 1908 identified C. H.

Fultz and his wife, Catherine, the L. Haak Lumber Company, William C. Laird of Bay City and Indian River, and Silas McTiver of Onaway, along with Merritt Chandler, as large purchasers of "tax homestead" lands, usually sold at lower than bargain basement prices. Between them, they had bought almost 7,500 acres of such lands in Cheboygan County. All of them owned properties in Grant Township, in the case of C. H. Fultz over 1,000 acres of such lands.[85]

As of November 1907, state tax lands and undisposed-of homestead lands in Cheboygan County amounted to 42,214 acres out of the county total of 507,492 acres, placing it in the mid- to upper range of the counties listed by the Commission of Inquiry. Commission data show sale of 5,407 acres of tax lands in Cheboygan County (a quarter of the total acreage sold in the eleven counties surveyed by the commission's special examiners) for $10,499 (a third of the sale income from the eleven counties). The commission valued the timber sold in Cheboygan County at $61,590 (39 percent of the estimated total value of timber in the eleven counties) and the land at $13,117 for a total of $74,707. Thus, the state lost $64,208 on the sales in Cheboygan County (29 percent of the total loss calculated by the commission in the eleven counties). "Most of the land examined was not sold to actual settlers, but to people who are either in the timber business or to persons regularly engaged in land traffic and who evidently purchased them for speculative purposes."[86]

Fire

What came in the wake of logging were farming and fire. As elsewhere in Michigan, timbered properties near Twin Lakes became farms, most notably the Page and Reynolds farms. Logging had been wasteful, leaving huge quantities of slash, the discarded and flammable residue of a careless and irresponsible harvesting of the first-growth forest. But fire was also a common tool of farming. Setting slash ablaze cleared land for the plow. The remains of one harvest were burned to prepare for the next. Fires were set to encourage the growth of blueberries and to push the growth of pasture. What was missing were reliable means of controlling and suppressing fire.

Where lumbering involved spark-spewing timber locomotives, the process itself incinerated untold acres, as did locomotives on the freight and passenger lines built to the tip of the Lower Peninsula. Most of the towns in the northeast threatened or destroyed by fire in 1908 and 1911 were on the Detroit and Mackinac rail line from Alpena to Cheboygan, a track that had been bought in 1895 (Alpena to LaRoque) or built soon after (LaRoque to Onaway in 1898 and then Onaway to Cheboygan).

"The greatest handicap to effective forest fire protection at this time was public indifference and, on the part of many, active antagonism to forest fire control, since it was widely held that forest fires stimulated agricultural development."[87] Lumbermen encouraged the idea that all the timbered land, once cut, would become farmland, not illogically since often their intention was to sell the denuded land to whatever innocents wandered into range. (The *History of Northern Michigan and Its People* said admiringly of Merritt Chandler that "he has sold about ten thousand acres of [the forty thousand acres he received from government for road-building], and is gradually disposing of more. It is covered with fine hardwood timber, and as fast as this is cleared off he offers the land for sale for farming purposes, giving new settlers every possible inducement to locate on it.")[88] Thus, both lumbermen and fire were to be regarded as agents of progress.

But fire was also a product of the late nineteenth- and early twentieth-century environment in Michigan. Enormous quantities of slash were joined with very hot and dry summers and autumns, plentiful oxygen in the atmosphere (at least 17 percent), and strong winds typically generated by cool fronts moving northeastward. It needed only a trivial ignition source to produce large uncontrollable fires and, in several instances, virtual firestorms.[89]

At the Forestry Convention in Grand Rapids in 1888, Arthur Hill, addressing the subject of legislation to prevent forest fires, cited statistics from the U.S. Census Report of 1880 for Michigan regarding the origination of forest fires. Clearing land was purportedly the source of 60 percent of reported forest fires. Twenty-two percent were started by hunters and 16 percent by locomotives.[90]

Fire was an inescapable feature of two seasons of the year in late nineteenth- and early twentieth-century Michigan. "Summer and smoke" was not simply a poetic phrase. Haze, most often from small but numerous fires, often land-clearing fires, was a constant presence in these seasons in Michigan: "dangerously the summer burned."[91] The following article, taken from the *Cheboygan News* of July 28, 1909, but originating in the *Alpena Pioneer*, may reflect the norm for summers in Northeast Lower Michigan. The year 1909, sandwiched between catastrophic fires in 1908 and 1911, is never mentioned in accounts of Michigan forest fires.

> Deputy Game, Fish and Fire Warden R. E. Ellsworth came down from the north and left again for Alcona county.
>
> Mr. Ellsworth has, for several days, been giving his attention to forest fires, which are quite prevalent in the counties north of [Alpena]. Mr. Ellsworth says that with the exception of Metz and Posen townships, fire is quite general in Presque Isle county and a large section of Cheboygan. In Metz and Posen, the supervisors, who are fire wardens, have performed splendid service in suppressing fires, and both townships are practically free from danger.
>
> In Presque Isle county, Mr. Ellsworth made complaints against two men employed by Merritt Chandler who persisted in setting fires after they had been warned not to do so.
>
> In Cheboygan county, Mr. Ellsworth caused James Bader to settle a loss of $15, sustained by a neighbor through fires started by Bader.
>
> Mr. Ellsworth drove through a considerable part of Presque Isle and Cheboygan counties, warning the people that under no circumstances shall fire be started contrary to the provisions of the law and that complaints would be made against every person who violated the law.
>
> Mr. Ellsworth went to Alcona county to look into the fire situation.

Perhaps a response to the fire of 1908 or possibly standard procedure before that, the papers of the M. D. Olds Lumber Company of Cheboygan contain forms that provide a detailed accounting of fire damage on Olds timber properties by township and section for 1910, also a "quiet" year.[92]

Some of these fires became catastrophes, most often in the fall, but partly at least as a consequence of conditions in the spring and summer. The first of these was in early October 1871. Its best known manifestation was the Great Chicago Fire. But the same conditions also produced the Peshtigo Fire in Northeastern Wisconsin that burned almost 1.3 million acres, killed nearly 1,500 people, and spread into the Upper Peninsula. And the same set of conditions was responsible for the simultaneous Great Michigan Fire in the Lower Peninsula, a series of fires that began with the destruction of Glen Haven, Holland, and Manistee but that also devastated the Saginaw Valley, the Thumb (four towns were destroyed), an area north of Lansing, the Au Sable River valley, and the area around Thunder Bay near Alpena. (Alpena had been wholly or partially destroyed by fire in 1862, 1863, 1867, and 1869.)[93] In Michigan, two and a half million acres (including fifty thousand acres in the Upper Peninsula) burned, and two hundred people died.[94]

Almost exactly a decade later, fire swept the Thumb again, officially killing 282 people but possibly more and burning over a million acres. Ironically, this fire completed the process of deforesting the Thumb that lumbermen and farmers had pursued and opened it up fully to agriculture.

For nearly three decades, the Lower Peninsula was spared a genuinely catastrophic fire, although summer and smoke remained the norm. In the Upper Peninsula, however, the same logging and farming protocols and the same environmental conditions produced significant but generally unreported fires. In terms of news coverage, the exception was the fire of August 1896 that destroyed the lumber town of Ontonagon and over two hundred thousand acres of forest.

But October was a fatal month in the Lower Peninsula. In mid-October 1908, a fire started west of Millersburg in Presque Isle County, one of several fires burning in the county. High winds drove it eastward from late morning until, by evening, it had reached the shore of Lake Huron, whereupon it turned back to the west. It destroyed the villages of South Rogers and Metz (with forty-three deaths) in Presque Isle County and Bolton and Cathro in Alpena County while threatening Millersburg, La Roque near Hawks, Belknap, Hagensville, Nagel's Corner, Posen, and Rogers City in Presque Isle County as well as Long Rapids and Alpena in Alpena County.[95] In fact, much of Northeastern Michigan was burning. "Presque Isle and Cheboygan counties are all aflame and the 75 miles between this city [Alpena] and the city of Cheboygan is reported to be almost a solid mass of fire. Alpena county is ablaze in every direction."[96]

> From Cheboygan comes a report that the huge accumulation of sawdust there, known as the "Sawdust mountain," is on fire and that several hundred people on the east side of the city have been smoked out of their homes. A high south wind is fanning the fire into a spectacular blaze, against which the city firemen can do little. Morris Fitzgerald, a farmer near Cheboygan, lost his farm buildings, worth $4,000 [well over $100,000 in current terms].

For a time, Cheboygan was surrounded by fire on all its land sides. In a 1990 interview, a resident of Twin Lakes since the 1930s recalled that in 1908, a fire started "near Donovan's farm [immediately south and west of Twin Lakes] and burned as far as Saginaw." He also mentioned a steam boiler burned in the fire somewhere between Twin Lakes and Black Lake. M. D. Olds's 1909 and 1910 contracts with Alva Page to strip and cut trees on the Page property and that of Pfister & Vogel and deliver everything by March 1910 implies that fire burned close to Twin Lakes. (There are blackened stumps still to be found around Twin Lakes. They may be remnants of the 1908 or 1911 fires or the result of a later and more local fire or a residue of logging.)

The sixty passengers aboard a Detroit and Mackinac Railroad train bound for Alpena from Cheboygan spent the night at La Roque, surrounded by flames, unable to go forward or back, saved only by "hard work." Subsequently, a train with relief supplies left Cheboygan for southern Presque Isle County but retreated in the face of the egregious danger. Another train passenger, Bishop Charles D. Williams, later wrote, "At Posen, I got an upbound train to Cheboygan. We passed through fifty or sixty miles of country with a forest fire every mile or two." Pfister & Vogel lost a large tract of virgin hemlock at High Banks, less than a dozen miles east of Cheboygan in Benton Township. As the fire that hit the hemlock was a crown fire, M. D. Olds, then one of only two large mill owners in the area, bought the land, sold salvaged bark to Pfister & Vogel, and cut and sold the lumber as quickly as possible. But Olds himself lost standing timber farther south of Cheboygan, his crew abandoning the new camps and escaping with only their clothes and one horse along the Lake Huron shore. Another logger, surrounded by flames, made his way to the beach, spent the night in a flat-bottomed boat driven out onto the lake by the winds, was picked up by a freighter, and dropped off at Mackinaw City. "Lakeside resort [on the Lake Huron shore on the northwest edge of Cheboygan] has been burned, the groves and cottages. County farmers are saving their homes, but all the stuff in the woods has burned. The Indian Reservation south of Mullett Lake has burned over and the Indians are homeless."[97]

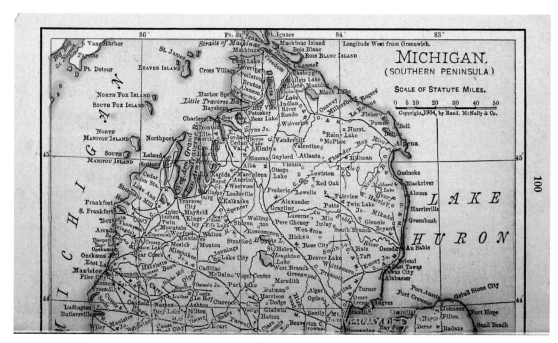

1904 map

Though concentrated in the upper portion of the northeast, fire was not limited to that area in this October. "A report brought in tonight from Alcona county says a strip 20 miles wide from Hubbard lake to [the] Au Sable river is burning." "Bad forest fires" were reported as well "in the neighborhood of Elmira, Gaylord, and Johannesburg, in Otsego County; Cadillac, in Wexford County; Grayling in Crawford County, where 4,000,000 trees planted by the State Forestry Commission were destroyed; Grawn, in Grand Traverse County, and Caseville and Bad Axe, in Huron County, in the 'Thumb' district." In the Upper Peninsula, fires were burning around Sault Ste. Marie, Menominee, Escanaba, Houghton, and Calumet. Incomplete reports placed the area burned at 2.4 million acres and the damage costs at almost $2.6 million.[98]

A fire story with a Detroit byline offered an explanation of the inferno and a solution to the fire danger in Michigan.[99]

> The Cheboygan woods are full of dry fallen timber left by the woodsmen, and it is this condition which keeps the fires ablaze. Everything has been parched with the drouth for weeks back, and yet people have been clearing and with fire. It is simply miraculous that scores of towns have not been burned before this. The situation demands reforestation. Strong statutes must be secured, requiring timbermen to clear forests of debris of the cuttings which are now left in the woods. Mills and towns must be required to provide fire protection. We must also have officials who will vigorously enforce such laws. Unless we quit our greedy and careless ways, we shall have many, many horrors.

Catastrophic fire would strike once more in Michigan before the "greedy and careless ways" began to give way. On July 11, 1911, in an extremely dry and hot summer, fires burning near Au Sable came together into a large conflagration driven by strong west winds. The towns of Au Sable and Oscoda stood in its path to Lake Huron and were destroyed. Five persons, perhaps as many as twelve, died. But as in 1908, this fire was only one element in a situation that generated companion blazes in Alpena, Cheboygan, Iosco, Oscoda, and Presque Isle Counties. The cities of Alpena and Cheboygan were again threatened; the towns of Metz and Posen were again destroyed. W. & A. McArthur Company's mountain of sawdust in Cheboygan, already burning for weeks, got beyond control. Merritt Chandler lost nine of his registered

Hereford cattle and more than one hundred tons of timothy hay to fire; subsequently, he had to euthanize the most severely burned of the surviving cattle. The towns of Tower in Cheboygan County, Millersburg and Onaway in Presque Isle County, and Waters in Otsego County barely escaped the fire or survived with great damage; La Roque did not. (Ironically, the downtown of Indian River was destroyed a week earlier not by a forest fire but by a fire started in the back of a local hotel). After a few days, "the district from Alpena to Cheboygan ha[d] plenty of smouldering [sic] forest fires, but no further losses [had] been reported." The official state records show nearly two hundred reported fires in 1911 and 156,000 acres burned. Monetary losses, according to unofficial sources, exceeded $1.5 million.[100]

A small portion of Cheboygan's sawdust pile

In the forty years after 1911, Michigan did not suffer another catastrophic forest fire. But there were bad fires and bad fire years; 1915, 1919, 1921, 1923, 1925, 1930, 1931, 1933, 1936, 1946, and 1947 were the years with the largest number and the most severe forest fires. (In 1925, in Cheboygan County, two fires burned more than eleven thousand acres, and in 1930, fire charred six thousand acres. In 1938, a quiet year, the Department of Conservation reported twenty-three fires in the county burning 75 acres. More than two-thirds of the acreage was forest land of some kind.)[101] Between 1911 and 1920, nearly two million acres in Michigan were destroyed by wildfires; in the 1920s, the figure reached almost two and a half million acres. In general, however, the extent of forestland burned diminished radically in the 1930s, again in the 1940s, and has remained relatively low and constant for more than a half century. The area destroyed in the 1990s was less than one hundred thousand acres. Nevertheless, as recently as 1999, firemen spent twenty-four hours suppressing a fire in the Alverno swamp, just northwest of Twin Lakes.[102]

The reduction was, in part, the product of lessening two activities closely associated with forest fires, logging, and clearing farm land. (Indeed, as if in synchrony with the "opening of the north," the causes of fires acquired a modern look. Smokers accounted for well over a third, according to the Department of Conservation's figures for 1925–1934. Brush burning was responsible for 14 percent, railroads for just under 9 percent, and lumbering for less than 1 percent. The other causes were "unknown" (12 percent), "incendiary" (10 percent), "campfires" (7 percent), "miscellaneous" (6 percent), and "lightning" (2 percent).)[103]

But it was also the result of the emergence of forestry as a science and of a conservation ethos and conservation legislation (at both the federal and the state level). It was not coincidental or incidental to this change that the "big burn" in Washington, Idaho, and Montana, which garnered national attention and became the founding myth of the Forest Service, occurred in August 1910, between the last two great fires in Michigan, both of which also drew national attention.

The prevention and suppression of forest fires were central elements of both forestry and conservation. That the first fire tower was built in 1912 (in Montmorency County) is symbolic of the change.[104] Two towers were built in the Twin Lakes area, both in Presque Isle County: the Black Lake tower east of Black Mountain near Lake Sixteen and the Owens tower on Black Mountain (N 45°31′32″/W 084°16′23″). Alva Page appears as the Grant Township fire warden in 1915–1916, and Sidney Godin was fire warden at the Black Lake tower for three years in the early to mid-1920s before moving into Cheboygan. By 1929, there were three fire towers in Cheboygan County: at Hebron; south of Indian River and east of the old US-27; and between Afton and Tower on the old US-23.[105]

A few of the fire and game protection signs issued by this department.

Twin Lakes

The Twin Lakes area was extensively logged in the early years of the twentieth century. (The 1937 bathymetric map of Twin Lakes labels all the adjacent land "second growth," and aerial photographs of 1938 show large swaths of land in a fairly early stage of reforestation.) As noted before, in 1902, the properties touching the lakeshore were not in residential, recreational, or agricultural use; they were likely held for their timber. (A significant share of shoreline property on the northwest and northeast sides of the lake was in state hands.) On the Grant Township plat map of that year, most of the properties to the east and north of the lake were owned by names prominent in logging. Properties sandwiched between the shoreline and the deeper forest were generally in the hands of residents (Henry and Mary Leonard, Kenneth McLeod, John LaFleur, Isaac Mauk, Joseph Robideau) who were listed in the 1900 and/or 1910 census as "farmer."

The largest landowners in the immediate vicinity of the lake were Pfister & Vogel Lumber Company (Government Lot 4 in T37N R1E sec. 34), Edmund Hall[106] (Lots 4 and 5 along the southwest shore), the State of Michigan (in all four sections), and George D. Richards (over 600 acres in T37N R1E, secs. 34 and 35, and T36N R1E sec. 2).

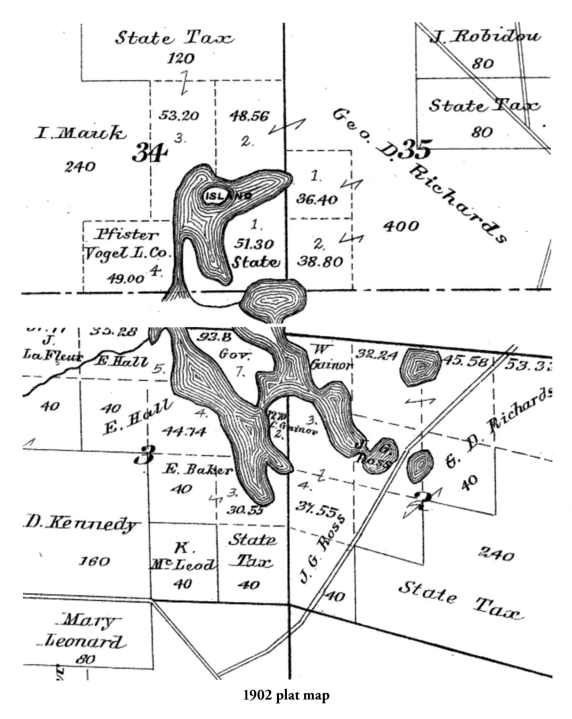

1902 plat map

In early December 1902, M. D. Olds had approached Richards regarding these lands, producing a reply that has the directness characteristic of much correspondence in the lumber business.[107]

> Yours of the 5th inst. at hand. No, there is no use of spending any time to look [survey the timber on] those Twin Lake lands of mine, unless you are willing to pay the prices I have asked you.

> I may change my mind sometime about their value; but think when I do, it will be to raise the price.

The land remained in Richardson's hands until his death in 1937.

The two highest valuations listed in the 1910 Polk City directory for property owners in Grant Township were M. D. Olds (nearly 4,100 acres valued at more than $20,000) and Embury-Martin Lumber Company (almost 800 acres valued at nearly $7,500). Both held land in sections touching

Twin Lakes. Three others in the timber industry—Merritt Chandler, S. Harris Embury, and McTiver & Hughes—owned properties totaling over 1,700 acres valued at $11,150. Excluding these, the average property holding was slightly below 100 acres and valued at $620. Alva Page's 80 acres were rated at $200 and Herbert Reynolds's 160 acres at $350. Black Mountain was a mix of state tax land, state homestead land, and lumber company property. (The number and identity of patrons of the 1903 Presque Isle plat book from Bearinger Township, which includes the eastern side of Black Mountain, reflects the nature of the township. The number of patrons is only five, a small figure compared to other townships, and those patrons were a single clergyman and four lumber companies. Only fourteen farmers are listed for the entire township.)

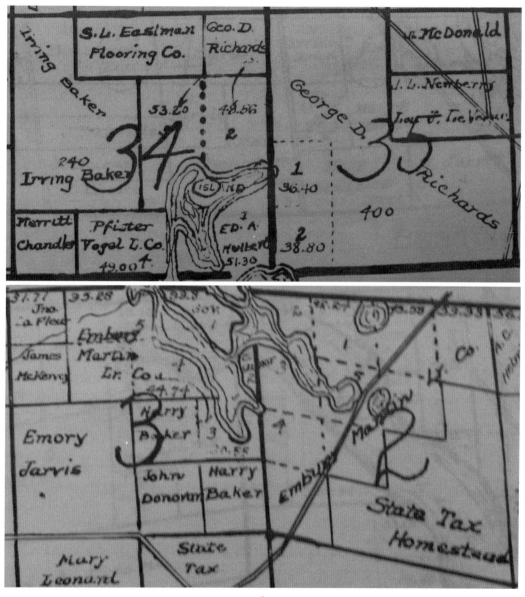

1913 plat map

By 1913, ownership of land contiguous to Twin Lakes had changed significantly, according to the plat book. In essence, the north side of the lake was (still) owned by George D. Richards, the west side (from north to south) by Pfister & Vogel, Embury-Martin Lumber Company, and Henry Baker, the south side by Embury-Martin, and the east side (from south to north) by Embury-Martin and Edward

A. Hulbert.[108] Land on the west and north sides of the lake adjacent to the properties of Pfister & Vogel and George Richards was owned by Merritt Chandler, Irving Baker, and the S. L. Eastman Flooring Company of Saginaw. (In the years after 1902, Richards, Hulbert, and Eastman Flooring Company had acquired state lands, and the Merchant Bank of Canada appears to have divested itself of all holdings in Grant Township. By 1916, average timber properties in Grant Township had dropped 50 percent in size and 75 percent in valuation, while other properties had, on average, increased slightly in size and roughly 70 percent in valuation.)

Tracking land ownership in the area in the late nineteenth and early twentieth centuries is shooting at a moving target with a slightly misaligned sight. Turnover of farmland may not have been great, but turnover of timberland was. Most of the people involved dealt repeatedly with others in their relatively small circle. Deeds were often registered long after the conveyance had taken place. Some, undoubtedly, were never registered at all and thus never public record. Deeds of the era are inconsistent in the details entered in the document. Plat books are not completely reliable; they often lag actual ownership and, in two instances on Twin Lakes, government resurvey of a section. Often it is difficult to provide a certain narrative of property ownership.

For example, Edward A. Hulbert unquestionably owned substantial acreage in T37 R1E sec. 34, as of 1905, specifically Government Lot 1, what is now Godin Circle. It is shown in the 1902 plat book as 51.30 acres of state land and in the 1913 plat book (and that of 1930) as 51.30 acres owned by Hulbert. Hulbert's actual patent of 1905 (certificate 20526) shows 38.38 acres and identifies the property as government lot 5. The difference was a resurvey of the section in 1904.

The original survey of 1841 laid out six lots in a not wholly logical sequence around a woefully inaccurate drawing of the northern lake. It included a 30-acre Lot 1 on the west side and tiny Lots 5 and 6 on the east side. The dependent resurvey of 1854 substituted a more logical order of lot numbers, beginning with a 51.30-acre Lot 1 on the east side and swinging around the north end of the lake and down the west side to what would be Page Road. In 1904, a supplemental plat substituted a 38.38-acre Lot 5 for the 1854 resurvey's 51.30-acre Lot 1.

A deed of April 27, 1907, shows that Edward A. Hulbert sold Lot 5, T37N R1E sec. 34, in Benton Township to Charles M. Horton, a land agent who dealt with most of the logging companies in the area at one time or another. (In the years under discussion, he was engaged with Merritt Chandler, individual copartners in the Embury-Martin Lumber Company, and repeatedly with the Embury-Martin Lumber Company.) The identification of the political township is written in the deed, but there is no statement of acreage.

But a year and a half earlier, on October 9, 1905, Horton had executed a timber deed by which Embury-Martin acquired the right to all timber on various properties, including Lot 5, T37 R1E sec. 34. On what basis Horton did so is unknown; there is no record that Hulbert had transferred timber rights to Horton.

Less than six months after acquiring Lot 5 from Hulbert, Horton, on October 8, 1907, conveyed a property with the same locational references to Embury-Martin Lumber Company. There is no identification of the political township in the deed and no statement of acreage. A clerk in the register's office, however, entered the deed as Benton Township.

At least two problems arise. First, no part of Benton Township was in T37N R1E sec. 34. The principal meridian was surveyed in 1815 and did not change thereafter, in part because it was an essential reference in treaties by which Indians ceded lands to whites. (Specifically, the meridian was chosen because, from the mouth of the Auglaize River (Fort Defiance) in Ohio northward, it was the western boundary of the land ceded by Indians in the Treaty of Detroit. It is also referenced in the Treaty of Saginaw.) In its march to Sault Ste. Marie, the meridian forms the eastern border of T37N R1W and the western border of T37N R1E. It runs through Grant Township to the west of Twin Lakes. So T37N R1W sec. 34, is about two miles into Benton Township, but its eastern cousin is over three miles into Grant Township. And as of the dependent resurvey, the only other Lot 1 or 5 in T37N R1E was on Lake Sixteen, and there is no record that Hulbert or Horton owned either lot, nor is it likely that either man did.

One solution is to assume that it is all a matter of error, misstatement, and omission. After all, August 1938 aerial photographs show that most of the section had been logged. Seven years earlier, on August 11, 1931, a quit claim deed conveyed from Embury-Martin Lumber Company to Herbert Bockes, Trustee, properties that were specifically described in the usual manner as well as "all the other real estate and property in which the said first party [Embury-Martin] has any interest whatsoever, of every kind and description and wheresoever situated," presumably including Lot 5. Finally, it was the same Herbert Bockes, Trustee, who had sold Lot 5 to Edsel Page in May 1942. (In the previous seven years, he had sold lots owned by Embury-Martin on the other side of the lake to Clyde Page and Bert Reynolds.)

But the second problem: a deed of July 21, 1920, shows that Edward A. and Caroline Hulbert sold Lot 5, T37N R1E sec. 34, containing 38.38 acres, to Kenneth McLeod. (McLeod appears in "Cheboygan Up-to-Date" (1898) as the Grant Township supervisor, in the 1902 and 1913 plat books as the owner of Highland Farm and other properties in Grant Township, in the 1920 census as a farmer, and in many property records of the late nineteenth and early twentieth century.) The records of McLeod and his heirs are a dead end with respect to the property.

Some of the early residents around Twin Lakes came out of logging backgrounds. Alva Page[109] was originally a logger who, according to oral testimony, bought land from the M. D. Olds Lumber Company to run sheep. Perhaps he did, but there is no record of the purchase. He did contract with Olds in 1909, in the wake of fire in 1908, to peel bark, skid, and bank it "where it is practically safe from fire," to make ties, and to cut, skid, and deck all logs from trees on his property and lot 4 in T37N R1E sec. 34. In January 1910, he agreed, before the end of winter, "to deliver to M. D. Olds' railroad track on the marsh on Section 11, T37N of R1E [in Benton Township, northeast of Twin Lakes], alongside Branch 2, all the logs and Cedar which he lumbered for [Olds] during 1909."[110] The 1913 plat map shows a block of land owned by Merritt Chandler between the Page farm and Lot 4, then owned by Pfister & Vogel. Eventually, Alva Page acquired both.

The two properties that made up the Page farm west of the lake were bought in early 1907 from John and Gina Lafleur for $150 and in late 1908 from Isaac and Almira Mauk for $50. On his hand-seeded land, it is said, he lost nearly half of the first forty sheep to bears. But a justice of the peace would view the carcass, if it could be found, and the county would pay for the loss of the sheep. (It was also said that his neighbor, Herbert Reynolds, raised sheep to shoot bears.)

William Godin appears in the 1910 census as a laborer in a lumber works. Sidney Godin logged in the area, probably after his marriage in 1906 and the birth of a daughter, Gladys, in Ocqueoc in 1910. His father-in-law, Wesley Bedgero, had his own saw mill, which he moved to wherever logging was going on.[111]

The 1910 census listed nearly a quarter of Grant Township heads of household as employed in the logging industry. One of the many Owenses in the township cut timber at Twin Lakes. Other surnames that would be common in the region—Baker, Crawford, Elliott, and Gannon among them—appeared as laborers in the lumber industry. There was a lumber camp on Krouse Road with a stable, blacksmith shop, and store. This camp probably accounts for the "open links used by blacksmiths," the "forged weldings," and the "parts of horses bits" found on two properties at the southern end of Krouse Road. The resident of one of these also found "chunks of wood" on his land and wood laid into the lake, perhaps for water wagons. (It is likely that at least some, perhaps a large number, of the logs lying on the lake bottom served a function in the logging operations and were then abandoned.) The same camp may have been responsible for a fifteen-foot-wide bridge at or near a narrow crossing of the lake. It was built for logging but was also used for picnics. It too was abandoned around 1915 and deteriorated. Lyle Page camped on the lake in 1909 (at age six) and remembered about six logging camps in the area (perhaps on Black Mountain and the Alpena State Road in addition to Twin Lakes), a camp that included a barber shop and "hand cars on small railroad."[112]

Logging Trains

Cheboygan had two logging trains in operation in the years immediately before World War I and during the first years of the war. And thereby hangs a confused and confusing tale.

McArthur, Smith & Co. laid track and was building its own cars as early as 1878 to remove logs left in the woods for lack of snow. In the same year, Thompson Smith had "a tramway runs camps to the river." The *American Lumberman*'s industrial statistics showed that in 1906, the Haack Lumber Co. ran a logging railroad with one steam log loader and an electric light plant. (It was not listed in directories of 1910 and 1912.)[113]

The grandly named Cheboygan & Presque Isle Railroad was owned and operated by M. D. Olds. Created as a part of his response to the fire of 1908, its purpose was to remove bark and lumber in the year or so before the trees died. In 1910, it consisted of eighteen miles of track running east from his mill in Cheboygan, with five miles more under construction, a single locomotive, thirty cars, a log loader, and an electrical generator.

However, the trains involved in this story did not run on rails. They were tractor-sleigh trains, a steam locomotive with skis in place of the front wheels and caterpillar treads to provide traction and a line of sleighs on skis to haul logs. In winter, they could pull logs from the deep forest to a railhead or, indeed, all the way to the mill in Cheboygan.[114]

The tractor-sleigh train owned by M. D. Olds, the "hemlock special," could move twenty-five sleds at a time. A team of horses could haul one sled with a load of 5,000 to 10,000 board feet; the steam log hauler could pull 125,000 board feet. One of its drivers was Charles Martineau. (The 1910 and 1920 censuses list Charles Martino as living in Cheboygan's Second Ward and show his occupation in 1910 as railroad brakeman and in 1920 as boiler maker. Polk's 1910 directory lists his occupation as laborer and the 1916 directory as boiler maker at Schwartz Bros. & Co. He was born in Michigan, but both his parents were born in French Canada.)[115]

The other tractor-sleigh train was Cheboygan's "pulpwood special," owned by Embury-Martin.[116] It was operated by George Michelin, who had a contract with Embury-Martin to cut and deliver logs from lumber camps to the vicinity of Twin Lakes. The crew was Joseph Eno and John McLaughlin.[117] (George Michelin appears in the 1920 census as a lumberman and employer working in a lumber camp; his residence was in Benton Township. Polk's 1916 directory lists him as a lumberman. The 1920 census lists a Joseph Eno whose occupation was "engineer" and who worked a steam hoist and lived in the Third Ward of Cheboygan City. Polk's 1916 directory lists a Joseph Eno as a "life guard." The only John McLaughlin listed appears in the 1900 and 1910 censuses as a marine engineer or engineer on a lightship living in the First Ward of the city and in the 1910 Polk's as a laborer. Two were born in Canada; all three had ties to Canada.)

"Hemlock Special" (above), "Pulpwood Special" (below)

Two trains, two stories. What they share is the destruction of capital equipment by the driver out of anger with bosses. In one version, M. D. Olds was notorious for "firing workers to maintain discipline," though often hiring them back the next day. He fired Martino once too often. Told to take the log hauler back to the mill before he left, Martino drove off the grade at full speed into a swamp where the hauler was permanently entombed. In the other version, George Michelin became angered by some element of his relationship with the company and drove the engine into an all-embracing swamp somewhere in the area.

Could such events have occurred? The area in question, Northern Grant Township and especially Benton Township, is low-lying and lacustrine, at one time the bed of Lake Algonquin, later the site of a peat moss farm, and now home to the largest cranberry bog in Michigan as well as millions of trees that flourish in or tolerate wet soils. A road passes through this area, whose history reflects the nature of the terrain; twelve years after the first contracts were let, the Alpena–Duncan City road had not been completed, and "it [was] not passable for teams, the whole length, in summer."[118] Logging, road-building, and railroading history abound in tales of equipment and track sunk in such terrain, as in this account of logging railroads in Minnesota.

> In many places, spurs had to cross swampy areas, and there were but few pieces of track that did not have one or two "sink holes," where the track settled in the soft ground. Both locomotives and railroad cars were lost when they sank into swamps, and many spurs had to be abandoned because it was impossible to keep the track from sinking.[119]

Abandoned and rusting equipment, frequently sunken or overgrown, is to be found in the forests of Cheboygan County. ("Ernie Hover mentioned a steam boiler that was somewhere between Twin & Black Lakes burned in the 1908 fire."[120]) Roughly three hundred miles to the south, the Black Swamp of Northwest Ohio provides tales of entire stretches of corduroy road and railway line disappearing. The striking height of the Detroit and Mackinac roadbed in many of its sections as it runs from Onaway to Aloha bespeaks efforts to address the same sort of problem. It did not even require a logging railroad, as witness this report from Eaton Rapids, Michigan, published in the *Cheboygan Democrat* in 1913: "ROAD OVER SWAMP DROPS FROM SIGHT," "Highway Finished Week Ago Entirely Disappears."[121]

Did such an event occur? By itself, failure to find rusted remnants, despite many searches, is not conclusive, though it suggests the likelihood that it did not happen. But there are other grounds for skepticism.

One is the incidence of tales of buried, hidden, or lost locomotives; the disappeared locomotive is an archetypal story. Aside from logging areas, such as the Great Smoky Mountains and Ontario, hidden locomotives are said to be or to have been found beneath the streets of Brooklyn and under a mountain of tires in California, in states as distant from each other as Virginia and Alaska, and in areas remote from the United States such as New Zealand. (Not all the tales are untrue.)

The tale shows another characteristic common to such stories, knowing the location or actual sighting, followed by failure to find the object or to find the spot again. Gordon Turner cites well over a dozen such instances. "Bill Rapson relates that in 1982 . . . he chanced upon it, and was right up to it, and banged on it with his gun. He went home, but tried to go back later. He wandered around futilely, because, he said, his marker tree for a turn off had been cut down."[122] Affirmation of the locomotive's existence and explanation of the failure to be able to find it.

> The engine seems to be on the property of the Abitibi Company of Alpena, which cuts the trees for their wood value and leases a lot of the land to hunting clubs. The Abitibi Company has conducted a couple futile searches. By 1983, Abitibi had cut off 14,000 acres, or 45 percent, and an official said the engine . . . might be in the uncut area, representing more than half its property which had not yet been thoroughly worked.[123]

The uncertainty of location counts against it. ("Railroad grade from Black Mtn. the whole way across. — Claude Ressler." "That's that ones [sic] supposed to have that locomotive buried in it. — Elnora [Godfrey]." "Jim Leister thinks the sand cut mentioned in my [Randolph Mateer's] reading may have been back [on] the road off Alpena State. He refers to it as a sand cliff. He claims the road goes back to the ridge." (The sand cut, accessed off Krouse Road according to Gordon Turner, is near Twin Lakes.) "Claude Ressler thinks it might be in the area of the old Badger Truck Trail (Orchard Beach [Road])."[124]

So does the absence of a date. Not a single one of the accounts assigns a specific date to the event or even an approximate date ("during the War" or "after the big fire," for example). By inference, it must have occurred between 1898 and 1928; closer specification requires focusing on the timing of the introduction of logging trains by Olds and Embury-Martin.

So does the uncertainty about the employer. There were only two possibilities in Cheboygan at this time. (The original source of the story was allegedly Joseph Viau, a local merchant and the mayor of Cheboygan, who had worked for M. D. Olds as a youth.) So does the absence of any source independent of the story that refers to the loss of a locomotive. There is no mention in the local newspaper or in surviving records of either company. (The records of the Olds Lumber Company are especially detailed, inventorying supplies in individual logging camps down to salves and ointments, providing a daily count of camp meals served by type of employee ("monthly," "skidder," "piece makers," "extras") and including the nationality of workers in injury reports ("English," "French," "Swede," "Polish," "German"). A missing locomotive would have been noted.) Interesting but not especially helpful are the facts that Martino a few years later was a boiler maker and Michelin was in a lumber camp as an employer.

What might have happened, if anything? One possibility is the embroidery of a not-uncommon accident in logging, fitting it out with an explanatory motivation, perhaps in the context of labor discontent and the death throes of the local industry.

In the case of Olds, that discontent may have resulted from an idiosyncrasy of the owner and thus have been a one-off. On the other hand, the Olds papers often refer, explicitly or implicitly, to labor tensions. They were virtually unavoidable, given the nature of the turn-of-the-century lumber industry; low production costs were its lifeblood. It must also have been apparent to some that after the fire of 1908, Olds was preparing, in a short term, to end lumber operations in the area, with the inevitable loss of jobs.

In the case of Embury-Martin, discontent may have been even more substantial. In the years between 1909 and 1915 (specific records disappear from the annual report of the Michigan Department of Labor as of 1916), Embury-Martin Lumber Company accounted for half (50.7 percent) of all industrial injuries in Cheboygan County. These injuries (37 in all, more than a third categorized as "severe") were concentrated in 1913 and 1914. By contrast, the other three large employers in the area—Cheboygan Paper Company (17 injuries), M. D. Olds (6 injuries), and Pfister & Vogel (3 injuries)—accounted, respectively, for 23, 8, and 4 percent of industrial injuries.

Another accident in January 1915 resulted in the death of Ephraim Tuttle, a farmer in Munro Township, who was hauling logs for Embury-Martin from a skidway to the mill over a private road built and maintained by the company. Before the Industrial Accident Board, his widow, Sarah, sought compensation for his death from Embury-Martin under the Workmen's Compensation Act. Embury-Martin and its insurance company appealed the board's ruling in favor of the widow. The crucial issue before the Supreme Court of Michigan, as before the Industrial Accident Board, was whether Tuttle was an employee (or "servant" in the language of common law) or an independent contractor. The Supreme Court upheld the board's judgment that Tuttle was an employee, not an independent contractor, and therefore, the provisions of the Workmen's Compensation Act applied. The case, *Tuttle v. Embury-Martin Lumber Co*, 192 Mich. 385, 400; 158 NW 875 (1916), was frequently cited in state courts across the country during the twentieth century and appeared in a brief before the Michigan Supreme Court as recently as 2012.[125]

The story of the locomotive focuses on a dispute and anger with the employer as the motivation for the (alleged) action. The number of injuries associated with Embury-Martin was high and concentrated, even allowing for the hazards of logging and milling. As testimony in the Tuttle case made clear, the terms of employment for the company's workers were various and complicated and open to different interpretations. (Similarly, a letter of December 1908 from M. D. Olds to Thomas McCarty at camp 2, Mullett Lake, reveals the complexities of worker pay and the power of the camp foreman to make decisions about pay.)[126] The vice president of the company—effectively, it seems, the operating officer—was George Patterson, a hard-headed veteran timber man who provided the lead testimony for the company in the court case. The company, if only for financial reasons, did not want to accept responsibility in a case of worker fatality. By this point, Embury-Martin was the only local sawmill left standing. All this may suggest labor friction, which could serve as fuel to a story about an accident in the field that affirmed the hostile attitudes of workers at the time. Or it may have been a workingman's fantasy. Even a storyteller's invention.

---

[71] Michael Williams, *Americans and Their Forests: A Historical Geography* (Cambridge: Cambridge University Press, 1989), p. 201; Maria Quinlan, "Lumbering in Michigan," http://seekingmichigan.org/wp-content/uploads/2013/09/Lumbering-in-Michigan.pdf.

[72] Williams, p. 224, table 7.2.

[73] Dickmann and Leefers, pp. 119–121; Ellis Olson, *Wood Butchers of the North, with Cheboygan Logmarks*, 2nd ed. (Cheboygan: Cheboygan Daily Tribune, printer, 1989), p. 6; Lloyd M. Atwood, *Cheboygan as a Nineteenth Century Lumber Area*. Wayne State University MA Thesis, 1947; Forrest B. Meek and Carl J. Bajema, *Railways and Tramways: A Chronicle of Michigan's Logging Railroads* (Clare, MI: White Pine Historical Society, 1989), p. 138.

[74] Dickmann and Leefers, pp. 125–126. In his annual report of 1896, the president and general manager of the Detroit and Mackinac Railroad addressed the implications of disappearing pine forests.

> The main business of [the] road continues to be in the haudling [sic] of logs and lumber, but the decrease in the pine which is now practically exhausted is more than made good by the increase in the shipments of hardwood logs, lumber and manufactured products. This seems to answer the question so often asked "What will become of the road when the Pine is gone?"
>
> It will take many years to work up the hardwood and unlike much of the land on which pine grew, the hardwood land is all good farming land.

The obituary of M. D. Olds in the *Cheboygan Daily Tribune* of September 9, 1935, praised him as "a shrewd, clear visioned [sic] businessman," precisely because he anticipated and adjusted to the depletion of the different species.

> When Michigan was being denuded of its pines, he bought up hardwood options, and when the pines were gone, he had large holdings of beech and maple to convert into board feet at his mill. When this gave out, he was ready for a new lumbering enterprise, and bought a tract of timber and railroad in Oregon.

[75] Dickmann and Leefers, pp. 123–124.

[76] Dickmann and Leefers, pp. 142–143.

[77] *The Traverse Region, Historical and Descriptive, with Illustrations of Scenery and Portraits and Biographical Sketches of Some of Its Prominent Men and Pioneers* (Chicago: HR Page & Co., 1884), p. 104.

[78] James B. Smith. *Lumbertowns in the Cutover: A Comparative Study of the Stage Hypothesis of Urban Growth* (Dissertation, University of Wisconsin, 1973), pp. 43–46, Table III.

[79] Dickmann and Leefers, p. 102; Frank Leverett et al., *Flowing Wells and Municipal Water Supplies in the Southern Portion of the Southern Peninsula of Michigan* (Washington: GPO, 1906), p. 353.

[80] *Plat Book of Cheboygan County, Michigan*, drawn from actual surveys and the county records, P. A. & J. W. Myers, Surveyors and Draughtsmen (Minneapolis: The Consolidated Publishing Co., 1902), http://cheboygancountymi.org/maps/1902plat/1902grant2.html, http://cheboygancountymi.org/maps/1902plat/1902grant3.html (a part of the MIGenWeb Project). The plat book is readily available electronically at other locations.

[81] http://cheboygancountymi.org/news/trib1906.html; *Plat Book*, 1902 Cheboygan County Land Owners, http://cheboygancountymi.org/history/1902plat.html; *Plat Book*, Patrons, Grant Township; http://cheboygancountymi.org/maps/1902plat/patrons.html; Olson, p. 6; *Michigan Reports: Cases Decided in the Supreme Court of Michigan*, vol. 86, pp. 112–121;

Northwestern Reporter, vol. 48, pp. 787–789; Polk's County Directory 1916, http://cheboygancountymi.org/dir/1916cc7.html. The present-day spelling of the surname is "Gaynor." Gainor was probably also a young contractor on a section of the Alpena State Road more than thirty years earlier.

[82] Polk's County Directory 1916, http://cheboygancountymi.org/dir/1916cc7.html; *Biographical History of Northern Michigan Containing Biographies of Prominent Citizens* (B. F. Bowen and Company, 1905), pp. 794–797. As a young man, Richards (1855–1937) "worked on farms, in the lumber woods, [and] drove the Flint and Thunder Bay rivers." In 1880–1881, he settled "at the junction of the Sturgeon rivers, Cheboygan county," established the post office at Wolverine and became postmaster, took up "a government homestead," and married. "For an income, he has built new roads, bridges, looked lands, scaled logs, lumbered for self and others, was trespass agent of the J. L. & S. R. R. Co. several years; at the same time, and since, doing a general real estate, land-looking and timber estimating business." He was twice elected "county road commissioner," served on the Wolverine school board, and, in 1902, was sent to the Michigan Legislature. (*Michigan Official Directory and Legislative Manual for the Years 1903–1904* (Lansing: R. Smith Print. Co., State Printers and Binders, 1903) p. 813. He owned shoreline on Twin Lakes until his death in 1937.

[83] *Plat Book*, Patrons, Grant Township, http://cheboygancountymi.org/maps/1902plat/ patrons.html.

[84] See the Grant Township maps and the list of property owners in the *Plat Book*. On Chandler, see http://www.everingham.com/family/data2/article011.html and *Plat Book*, Patrons, Miscellaneous, http://cheboygancountymi.org/maps/1902plat/patrons.html.

[85] *Report of the Commission of Inquiry, Tax Lands and Forestry, to the Governor and Legislature of the State* (Lansing: Wynkoop, Hallenbeck, Crawford, 1908), pp. 53–69. Fultz was a "Real Estate Dealer," "lumberman," and a director of the Cheboygan State Bank. The L. Haak Lumber Company were "Manufacturers of and Dealers in Lumber and Lands." McTiver is listed as a "Manufacturer of and Dealer in Lumber, Ties and Telegroph [sic] Poles. Cedar pavement a specialty," Laird as a "Dealer in Lands and Timber," and Chandler as a "Dealer in Cedar, Hardwood and Farming Lands." See Polk's Cheboygan City Directory 1916, http://cheboygancountymi.org/dir/1916cc2.html; *1907 Dun & Bradstreet Rating Book*, http://cheboygancountymi.org/dir/1907db.html; http://cheboygancountymi.org/ news/trib1906.html; *Plat Book*, Patrons, Cheboygan, http://cheboygancountymi.org/maps/ 1902plat/patrons.html; *Plat Book*, Patrons, Mentor, http://cheboygancountymi.org/ maps/ 1902plat/patrons.html. See also the Grant Township maps and the list of property owners in the *Plat Book*.

[86] *Tax Lands*, pp. 8, 12, 101–103, 124–125, 128. The commission or the printer of its report was mathematically challenged at several points, notably in listing 22,130 acres of state tax land and 20,084 acres of tax homestead land in Cheboygan County for a total acreage of 22,214 acres. The cheap sale of tax-reverted lands also appeared to involve corruption among state employees (see Dempsey, pp. 60–61).

[87] J. A. Mitchell and D. Robson, *Forest Fires and Fire Control in Michigan* (Lansing: Michigan Dept. of Conservation in cooperation with U.S. Dept. of Agriculture, Forest Service, 1950), p. 27. Native Americans had used fire "to maintain trails and forest openings, clear fields for domesticated crops, herd animals toward a harvesting zone, and fertilize cropped land and encourage wild food plants" (Dave Dempsey, *Ruin and Recovery: Michigan's Rise as a Conservation Leader* (Ann Arbor: University of Michigan Press, 2001), p. 14).

[88] Perry F. Powers, *A History of Northern Michigan and Its People* (Chicago: Lewis Publishing Co., 1912), p. 575.

[89] Dickmann and Leefers, p. 152.

[90] *Proceedings of the Forestry Convention Held in Grand Rapids, Michigan, January 26 and 27, 1888, under the auspices of the Independent Forestry Commission*, Bulletin 32, Department of Botany and Forestry, Agricultural College, Michigan (Lansing: Thorp & Godfrey, 1888), pp. 22–23.

[91] The two quoted phrases in this paragraph come from poems of Hart Crane, "summer and smoke" from "Emblems of Conduct" and "dangerously the summer burned" from "Passage." Leigh J. Young recalled (a half century later) that as late as 1907, "whenever the wind got in the north in the fall the smoke was so thick in Ann Arbor that you could see it blowing by the street lights at night, you could smell it first thing in the morning. You couldn't travel from Ann Arbor to the Straits of Mackinac at any time during the summer without seeing the smoke of several fires along the way" (quoted in Dempsey, p. 53). Young was a graduate of the University of Michigan, later a professor of silviculture at the university, and the mayor of Ann Arbor during World War II.

The fate of Michigan's original forests was summarized in a USDA technical bulletin:

> Of Michigan's original stand of 280 billion board feet of saw timber, approximately 35 billion feet was cut and burned in clearing land, 73 billion feet was burned and wasted during or after lumbering or destroyed by forest fires independent of lumbering operations; 204 billion feet was cut for lumber; and 40 billion feet was cut for other products, such as railroad ties, shingles, staves, ship timbers, poles, pulpwood, veneer logs, furniture and vehicle dimension stock, and the like. In many parts of the State the amount of timber destroyed by fire exceeded

the amount cut. In the region tributary to the Au Sable River, for instance, it has been estimated that 20 billion feet of pine was burned, and only 14 billion feet was cut by loggers. (W. N. Sparhawk, *The Economic Aspects of Forest Destruction in Northern Michigan*, U.S. Dept. of Agriculture Technical Bulletin No. 92 (1929), in Mitchell and Robson, p. 6, n. 2.)

[92] Olds Papers, Box 11, Fire Damage (Inventory of Timber, 1910).

[93] Mitchell and Robson, p. 7.

[94] For the fires of 1871, 1881, 1896, 1908, and 1911, see the appropriate sections of Dickmann and Leefers, Mitchell and Robson, and Betty Sodders, *Michigan on Fire* (Thunder Bay Press, 1997).

[95] The *Eleventh Biennial Report of the State Game, Fish and Forestry Booklet* (1909) explained the cause of the fire in terms remarkably free of any human agency.

> The cause of the Metz fire and other related forest fires in this area of the state in 1908 was traceable directly to climatic conditions. The deficiency in rain fall for the months of July, August, September and October in that year was shown to be greater, in the records of the Michigan Agricultural College, than for the same months of any year since 1864, when the meteorological station at the college was established Weather conditions covering the period from April to November were most unusual and favorable for destructive forest fires. The warm humid weather with frequent warm rains, covering a long period during the early season, produced a heavy growth of brakes, ferns, fireweed and other forest ground vegetation. This condition was followed by continued dry hot weather, beginning in the month of June and ending the last part of the month of October.
>
> In the Upper Peninsula and northern part of the Lower Peninsula, the frosts during the months of August and September killed much of the forest ground vegetation, which the hot and dry weather soon converted into tinder of the most inflammable nature. Severe killing frosts occurred in the Upper Peninsula on October 2 and in the northern counties of the Lower Peninsula on October 3. These frosts added dead hardwood leaves to the dry ground growth, and the hot dry weather following, with hot southerly winds, produced a condition for fires not before occurring in Michigan. On October 14, 1908 the very air seemed to be charged with inflammable gases, and fire would travel at great speed. (in Sodders, pp. 259–260)

[96] *Evening Telegraph* [Elyria, OH], October 17, 1908, datelined Alpena, Michigan, October 17; *Evening Mirror* Warren [PA], October 16, datelined Detroit, October 16.

[97] *News Tribune* Duluth [MN], October 17, datelined Alpena, Michigan, October 16, 1908; Williams, quoted in Herbert Nagel, *The Metz Fire of 1908* (Presque Isle Historical Society, 1979); *Evening Mirror* Warren [PA], October 17, datelined Detroit, October 16; *Detroit News*, October 17, 1908, in Sodder, p. 286; *Detroit News*, October 19, 1908, in Sodder, pp. 280–281; *Oral History*, "Fires," "Logging Tractor."

In an article datelined October 17, 1908, from Detroit, Michigan, the *New York Times* reported that the Reverend Williams had driven "overland to Cheboygan last night after being fire-bound for two days at Hagensville, back of the burned village of Metz," and quoted him as saying, "The whole country is a firetrap. The woods are full of dry fallen timber, left by the old lumber men; slashings and old mills with seasoned lumber are everywhere. There are not sufficient clearings about the towns and no fire protection. Everything is parched with drought, yet the people carelessly clear the lands with fires. It is simply miraculous that more towns do not go like Metz" (Oct 18, 1908).

M. D. Olds is listed in the 1910 Polk Directory for Cheboygan City under "Lumber-Wholesale" and "Shingle Manufacturers" at "ft of B North"; valuations in 1910 show him to have been a large landowner in Aloha, Grant, and Koehler Townships in Cheboygan County (http://cheboygancountymi.org/dir/1910value3.html). Earlier, Olds had operated a stave mill in Cheboygan; it burned in 1897. Aside from timberland in Michigan and Oregon, Olds came to own or co-own a California orange and poultry farm, an Ohio sugar company, property and a company in Cleveland, apartments in Detroit, and a coal and wood delivery business.

Olds's assessment of the fire's damage to his property in a letter to a friend dated October 27, 1908, may have more accurately reflected his state of mind than the facts on the ground; he had "forty to fifty million hemlock and I think about forty million of it burned." (Olds Papers, Box 30, Correspondence 1908 C). He added, "this is only the Hemlock alone. There is all the pulp wood, and the cedar and the other timber that has been damaged, some of it burned up. The muck in the swamp has burned so that a good deal of this timber has fallen down and by the time the winter winds get through with it, it will practically be in a brush heap."

Olds's energetic and imaginative response to the fire was the making of his later career as a businessman.

[98] *NYT*, October 18, 1908, datelined Detroit, Michigan, October 17; Mitchell and Robson, p. 11.

[99] *Times Leader* Wilkes-Barre [PA], October 17, 1908, datelined Detroit, Michigan, October 17.

[100] Sodder, p. 319; *Detroit News*, July 13, 1911, in Sodder, p. 327; http://www.ferris.edu/faculty/hillm/MYWEB7/Personal/TOPINABEE/Topinabee%20Pics.htm#Indian River; *Dallas Morning News*, Dallas [TX], July 14, 1911, datelined Detroit, Michigan, July 13, http://www3.gendisasters.com/michigan/9784/oscoda-mi-area-fire-jul-1911.

The "mountain of sawdust" in Cheboygan lasted more than a half century longer than the company that created it, a thirty-foot high, thirteen-acre, eighty-thousand-ton waste wood pile. Efforts in the 1970s to contour the site were defeated by the physical dangers posed by large voids within the pile. "Testing in the 1990s showed that groundwater near the enormous pile contained mercury, copper, nickel, lead, and zinc discharging to the Cheboygan River at unsafe levels. In 1999, the state put a first installment of $1.5 million of public funds into the partial removal of the sawdust, also sinking monitoring wells to determine the exact level of contamination entering the river" (Dempsey, p. 238).

Removal of the pile was not universally welcomed. "What is wrong with our town. It's suppose [sic] to be an historical town, but by the looks of everything, they've either torn it down and now they want to get rid of the sawdust pile, which in my way of thinking is very historical, our forefathers would turn over in their graves if they seen [sic] all the hard works just pushed aside . . . Historical town is not going to be for long. Our sawdust pile is the world's largest, but again not for long. Too bad" (*CDT*, June 28, 1999).

[101] Mitchell and Robson, p. 12. The *CDT* of May 20, 1925, reported, "In the Black River district between Cheboygan and Onaway, miles and miles of plains and cutover lands were burned over during the night."

[102] Dickmann and Leefers, p. 181, figure 8.2; *CDT*, May 14, 1999.

[103] Michigan Department of Conservation, Forest Fire Report Calendar Year 1938.

[104] For the details of this change, see Dickmann and Leefers, ch. 8, and Dempsey, chs. 1–4. On the "big burn," see Timothy Egan, *The Big Burn: Teddy Roosevelt and the Fire That Saved America* (Boston: Houghton Mifflin Harcourt, 2009). The Montmorency Tower was built of wood. The first cross-braced steel tower was erected in the Houghton Lake State Forest in 1913 (Dickmann and Leefers, p. 181).

[105] Official map showing state parks, fish hatcheries, game reserves, fire towers, and national forests purchases units in Michigan (Lansing: Department of Conservation, 1929); *Proceedings of the Public Domain Commission* (Lansing: Wynkoop Hallenbeck Crawford, 1916), vol. 7, p. 237; *Oral History*, "Fire Towers."

It was only in 1928 that the Department of Conservation added fire towers to its "Official Map showing state parks, fish hatcheries . . ." Two children were born to Sidney and Sadie Godin while living on Lake Sixteen, Forest Lincoln Godin in 1923 and Mary Genevieve Godin in 1926.

[106] New York–born, Detroit-based Edmund Hall (1819–1903) was a wealthy lumberman, lawyer, and contractor, the largest part of whose timberlands were in Clare and Isabella Counties.

[107] Olds Papers, Box 27, Correspondence, Q-Z, 1902, letter, Richardson to Olds, December 9, 1902.

[108] W. R. Middleton, Cheboygan County Atlas (Cheboygan: W. R. Middleton, 1913), pp. 14, 18. Hulbert, then twenty-two, was a member of the Thirty-Third Michigan Volunteers, Company H, in 1898 (http://www.mifamilyhistory.org/spanam vetscountyasp?s_County=Cheboygan&SpanishAmericanCompany_SpOrder_Sorter_Given&SpanishAmericanCompany_SpDir=ASC), the chief clerk of the Michigan Central Railroad (1916 Polk's City Directory) and the county treasurer (CDT, September 20, 1906). He bought 38.38 acres of what had been state land for $2.50 an acre in December 1904 and in June 1905 received a federal patent signed by Theodore Roosevelt (Oral History, "Land Purchases"; U.S. Archives: Michigan Land Patents Database).

[109] Alva (or, rarely, Alvah) Russell Page (1876–1952) was born in Michigan, married Nettie Isabell Jewell (1884–1976), fathered seven children, and farmed in Grant Township for four decades before retiring and moving into the city of Cheboygan. He was township supervisor during much of the Great Depression (1930–1936), township treasurer in seven years between 1911 and 1928, and five times a justice of the peace between 1911 and 1944. Alva Page's parents both came from Canada, and Nettie Jewell was born in Canada.

[110] Olds Papers, Box 6, Agreements — Timber, 1903–1917.

[111] *Oral History*, "Logging Camps," "Krouse Road." Godin was a common name in Case Township, Presque Isle County, around the turn of the twentieth century. The 1910 census of the township included adult male Godins with given names of Fred, Joseph, Lewis, Louis, Oscar, Sidney, and William. The William Godin in the 1910 census of Grant Township, Cheboygan County, was the son of William Godin of Case Township and had grown up there. The son appears in the 1900 census of Case Township as a "woods laborer" with a wife, a son, and three daughters. There also lived in Case Township William Godin, the father of Sidney Godin, who grew up there as well. The first of the fathers was listed as a "mill laborer," the second as a farmer.

[112] *Oral History*, "Krouse Road."

[113] Meek and Bajema, pp. 15, 31.

[114] The locomotives in question were Phoenix log haulers, a small number of which (175) were built in Eau Claire, Wisconsin, in the early twentieth century.

[115] Meek and Bajema, p. 31; Gordon Turner, *Pioneering North*, p. 13; William C. Fitt, "Locomotives Without Tracks: Michigan's Phoenix Log Haulers," *Michigan History* (September/
October 1982), pp. 46–48; "Our Story," Celebrating 150 Years of Cheboygan Business History, Special Supplement to the *Cheboygan Daily Tribune*, August 2010.

[116] In 1907, Embury-Martin Lumber Company was a partnership of S. Harris Embury, William L. Martin, Hugh L. Cox, George E. Patterson, James Stokan, Kate K. Boggs, and Lorne M. Meyer.

[117] Turner, p. 13.

[118] *Alpena*, p. 149.

[119] J. C. Ryan, "Minnesota logging railroads," http://collections.mnhs.org/MNHistoryMagazine/ articles/27/v27i04p300-308.pdf.

[120] *Oral History*, "Logging Tractor."

[121] *Cheboygan Democrat*, September 12, 1913.

[122] "In search of the hidden locomotive," *Pioneering North*, p. 46.

[123] "In search of the hidden locomotive," *Pioneering North*, p. 45.

[124] *Oral History*, "Logging Tractor."

[125] See the plaintiffs-appellees' supplemental brief in *Marcy Hill, Christopher Hill, and Patricia Hill v. Mark Pritchard and Timothy Dameron, Sears, Roebuck and Co.*, filed April 10, 2012, in the Michigan Supreme Court.
The 1920 census showed the widowed Sarah Tuttle, then thirty-nine years old, with her two children, living in the household of her brother in Munro Township, Cheboygan County. Her parents were members of the same household.
Olds Lumber Company also had its share of injuries, rigorously detailed in company accident reports describing a splinter in the elbow, a loss of fingers or a leg, or a fatality. Similarly, Olds, in one or two instances, encountered a widow seeking compensation for the loss of a husband. See Olds Papers, Box 5, Accident Reports, 1905–1927.

[126] Olds Papers, Box 6, Camp Reports, 1908–1913.

Chapter 4 The Opening of the North

The years between World War I and the U.S. entry into World War II saw developments that shaped post–World War II Northern Michigan. Specifically, these were the success of the conservation movement and the emergence of forestry, changes in state policies toward tax lands and forestation, and the development of highways. The first two of these had a significant impact on Twin Lakes and Black Mountain. The effect of the third was just beginning to appear as the United States entered the war.

Conservation

Conservation in Michigan had roots after the Civil War in the interests of well-off fishermen and hunters—"the fish and game boys," as Genevieve Gillette would famously call their descendants—and in the appearance of forestry as a science and academic discipline at the turn of the twentieth century. Both were informed by an awareness of the massive destruction of the state's natural resources by industrial-scale fishing, hunting, and logging.

The first legislative steps toward conservation in Michigan were laws passed in 1859 that prohibited netting fish on inland lakes in Southern Michigan and established closed seasons for certain game. These laws were stimulated by economic concerns, not a conservationist ideology. But they showed features that would be characteristic of conservation efforts (and the response to conservation efforts) in the next half century and beyond.

The initiative came from citizens, not from state government or the legislature. The legislature was not enthusiastic about any kind of regulation. The laws actually passed, usually after many failed efforts, fell short of what had been originally proposed. The mechanisms for implementation were awkward at best, and the laws went largely unenforced.[127]

A state board of fish commissioners was created in 1873. Its primary goal was still economic—large-scale reproduction in a state fish hatchery of the commercially valuable whitefish. Its secondary goals were more nearly those of conservationists—supervision of fishery management and enforcement of fishing laws.[128]

More important to conservation than these early legislative enactments was the appearance of sportsmen's clubs, such as the Lake St. Clair Fishing and Shooting Club, incorporated in 1872, and the coming together in 1875 of many of these clubs in the Michigan Sportsmen's Association. The purpose of the association was political, and its underlying rationale, despite the obvious self-interest, was conservationist. The Association sought the enactment of judicious and effective laws for the protection of

> . . . wild game of fur, fin and feather, whose flesh affords nutritious food, and the pursuit of which furnishes a healthful recreation, and also all birds that assist the agriculturist and horticulturist in the production of their crops, by the destruction of noxious animals and insects, and the enforcement of all laws for such purposes.[i]

Conservation was not a matter of absolute protection, nor was it a concern for the environment as a whole. It was a matter of using—but using wisely—available natural resources for the benefit of humans, especially well-off professionals and businessmen. From this point on, there would be a conservation interest in Michigan seeking to counter the market hunting, commercial fishing, and logging interests.

An 1877 bill prohibiting transport of Michigan game across state lines, aimed at commercial hunters who killed huge numbers of deer and whose markets were mostly in the large cities of the east, reflected the difficulties of achieving any movement. The original bill was defeated in the Michigan Senate. Brought back two years later and passed, it was vetoed by the governor. Another two years later, it became law. But local officials and local juries (if matters got that far) refused to enforce the law.[130]

The Association's ultimate answer to the problem of enforcement was the creation of the office of state game warden, appointed by the governor, paid, and empowered to appoint deputy wardens (who were to be paid by county boards of supervisors). The first bill was defeated in 1883; the fourth bill passed in 1886 and took effect in 1887. Resistance to the wardens and regulation continued, but for the first time, there was at least modestly successful enforcement of fish and game laws in Michigan.[131]

With the creation of the state game warden, the Association ceased to play an important role in the history of conservation. Instead, the leading role shifted to William B. Mershon, scion of a wealthy Saginaw lumbering family and an active member of the Sportsmen's Association, and to the Michigan Association for the Protection and Propagation of Fish and Game that he organized. Other parties also joined the play. For example, Mershon's proposed fish and game commission, with powers to manage wildlife and fish, not merely enforce game laws, passed the Michigan Senate in 1911 with the support of the Michigan Audubon Society, formed in 1904, and the Conservation Committee of the Michigan State Federation of Women's Clubs. (The bill did not make its way out of the Michigan House of Representatives.)[132]

Forestry

The first formal course in forestry in the United State was taught in 1882 by Volney M. Spalding at the University of Michigan. The first course in forestry at Michigan Agricultural College (MAC, now Michigan State University) was taught by William J. Beal in 1883. Forestry-related courses proliferated at the Agricultural College in the 1890s, and in 1902, the Department of Forestry was created. In the next year, the University of Michigan instituted the School of Forestry, which offered graduate education in the discipline.[133]

In 1887, the State Board of Agriculture, which would eventually create the Department of Forestry at MAC, established the Independent Forestry Commission, with Beal and Charles Garfield, a horticulturist and an active and influential conservationist, as its directors. The next year, the commission sponsored a forestry convention in Grand Rapids, the first of its kind in Michigan. It was lightly attended by lumbermen. Topics of discussion included forest fires and forest preserves (advocated by Garfield and proposed by the Michigan Sportsmen's Association). The commission made a few recommendations, including one to establish a forest preserve, and then sank from sight.[134]

The Forestry Act of 1899 reestablished the Forestry Commission (the "permanent" commission), with Garfield as president and authority to withdraw two hundred thousand acres of abandoned tax-reverted lands for forest preserves. Within a few years, these preserves amounted to forty thousand acres in Roscommon and Crawford Counties, and in 1903, the legislature officially recognized Michigan Forest Reserve Districts 1 and 2. These were northwest of Higgins Lake and south of Houghton Lake. The chairman of the University of Michigan's new School of Forestry, Filibert Roth, was appointed as forest warden.[135]

What still had not been addressed were the questions of what to do with the cut-over and burned-over lands of Northern Michigan, how to deal with the threat of forest fire, and how to begin reforestation.

Ironically, the answers involved the dissolution of the Forestry Commission to consolidate power and jurisdiction in the Public Domain Commission. (The Public Domain Commission took over jurisdiction in matters that previously had been handled by a clutch of independent officials—the commissioner of the land office, the auditor general, and the game, fish, and forestry wardens.)

The most powerful stimulus to legislative action was the fires of 1908, strong enough even to overcome the logging interest's lobbying against measures to prevent forest fires. Important also was the *Report of Commission of Inquiry, Tax Lands and Forestry* (1908), which showed the incompetence, corruption, and cost involved in the State Land Office's administration of reverted lands. The Commission of Inquiry recommended expanding the state's forest preserves, paying local governments compensation for lost tax revenue, changing the tax code in ways to encourage the growth of forests, relying on natural rather than artificial reforestation, and, above all, establishing effective fire protection. (Regarding the tax code, the commission said, "forest raising is impossible as a commercial venture, because, if the assessing officers do their duty and tax annually what the law directs them to tax, the result must be the confiscation of all the profit within the period of years necessary to grow a tree from the seed to maturity.") Less important was an awareness among some that, barely past the peak of logging, population in Northern Michigan was declining and poverty was rising.

But conservationists at the time were not at all certain that the commission represented a victory for those who advocated on behalf of the forests. By and large, it proved to be.[136]

State Forests and State Parks

The Public Domain Commission, created in 1909, represented an abandonment of the policy of selling off tax-reverted lands cheaply without realistic regard to their potential use. Its goals were to build forest reserves and, after legislative amendment in 1911, to facilitate settlement of the cutover lands. (In a few years, the commission largely gave up on the second goal and concentrated on the first. As the Commission of Inquiry had pointed out, pine lands rarely made good farmlands.) The Commission was authorized to withdraw a minimum of two hundred thousand acres of tax-reverted lands for reserves. The creation of state forests and tree planting would be its primary activities, the latter drawing on a science-based tree nursery that had existed at Higgins Lake since 1904.[137]

In the 1911–1913 biennial report of the Commission, Marcus Schaaf, the State Forester, recommended that at least two of the new state forests be brought under management in the next year. The state forests in question were Ogemaw, Kalkaska in Grand Traverse and Kalkaska Counties, and Black Lake, which then consisted of 4,200 acres in Cheboygan and Presque Isle Counties. Black Lake State Forest was not mentioned in later biennial reports.

But by 1922, work had begun on a new state game refuge unit north of Black Lake in Cheboygan and Presque Isle Counties that was called the Black Lake State Game Refuge. The 1925–1926 Department of Conservation biennial report showed the refuge as 5,067 acres with a fire-line system 25 percent complete, headquarters buildings 90 percent complete, permanent improvements, lookout control and equipment 75 percent complete, telephones complete, and additional acreage to block up the hunting grounds properly "not yet determined."

The next biennial report bespoke poor planning and failure.[138]

> *The Black Lake [State Game] Refuge*, when surveyed, was found to be so poor in cover, so broken in acreage, and so poorly stocked with game that for the present, it could best be handled as a State Forest. Since this refuge had never been given definite boundaries and so had never been

posted, it had never actually functioned, and its transfer to become a State Forest, under active administration, therefore put it to work for the first time and in the most effective way. Later on, when blocking operations have given control of the essential lands and when cover and game have become fairly well established, a refuge will no doubt be practicable in connection with the State Forest.

The transfer to the Forestry Division took place in 1927. At this point, the forest consisted of two districts, "one immediately south of Black Lake in Cheboygan County and the other north of the Lake and extending eastward some twelve miles into Presque Isle County." The forest contained fifty-six thousand acres, nearly half of which were owned by the state. Tree plantations existed to the extent of 1,899 acres, and the "skeleton" of a fire-line system extended for thirty-four miles. The forest was dedicated in 1928.

By the middle of 1930, Black Lake Forest had expanded to 80,678 acres, 46 percent of them state-owned. Plantations, predominantly though not exclusively red pine, had been established on nearly 6,000 acres, and fire lines totaled seventy-two miles. Two years later, the forest covered 93,959 acres, 52 percent of them state owned. Tree plantations totaled 9,800 acres and fire lines 101 miles. The overall size of the forest would remain very nearly the same for the next few years but with expanded plantations and more fire lines.[139]

The increase in the number of campers, fishermen, and hunters in state forests by the end of the 1920s caused the Forestry Division to adopt a policy of establishing camping sites that would bring campers together in areas relatively well protected from the spread of fire. (These campgrounds would also help protect the forest from the campers.) The first of these camps was built in Fife State Forest in 1929. A camping site was built in Black Lake State Forest the next year; it appears as Camp Agaming State Tourist Camp on the shore of Black Lake in the 1933 Cheboygan County map.[140]

A state park commission was created in 1919. The Public Domain Commission had been authorized to accept gifts of property as parks, and in 1917, the legislature appropriated funds to buy two hundred acres of virgin white pine at Interlochen as the state's first independently established park. (Two state parks preceded Interlochen. In 1895, Mackinac Island State Park became the first state park; founded in 1875, it had been the second national park, behind Yellowstone, until deeded to the state. In 1909, Michilimackinac State Park was created in Mackinaw City under the auspices of the Mackinac Island State Park Commission.) In 1921, the Public Domain Commission was replaced by the Department of Conservation, headed by a director and, as of 1927, administered by a seven-person conservation committee with the power to appoint the director. The Park Commission and several other previously separate boards and commissions were folded into the department at or soon after its creation.[141]

In 1921, the Park Commission presided over twenty-two state parks totaling approximately 1,500 acres. One of these was Cheboygan State Park, formerly O'Brien's Grove, just east of the city of Cheboygan. A second was Onaway State Park, on the south shore of Black Lake, a part of which was previously a Presque Isle County park known as Indian Orchard and the rest of which was privately donated. The commission acquired the land in 1920 and dedicated the park in 1921. (Aloha State Park on Mullett Lake opened as a thirty-four-acre park in 1923.) "Cheboygan on the Straits of Mackinac," a map and textual celebration of the county published by the Cheboygan Chamber of Commerce in the mid-1920s, referred to the Onaway Park as "another one of the state's most popular summer tourist stopping places." (With its faint aroma of boosterism, this statement requires some perspective. Only 220,000 people visited state parks in 1922. By the later 1920s, that figure had more than doubled, and in the 1930s, visitors to state parks numbered eight to nine million annually. Given its location, attendance at Onaway State Park was perhaps surprisingly high in the 1920s, but the number of its visitors was far less than at parks such as Tawas Point on Lake Huron or Grand Haven on Lake Michigan or Burt Lake State Park a relatively few miles away.)[142]

Highways

The 1920s saw the creation of a road system that ultimately opened Northern Michigan in a way lake steamers and railroads had not. (That said, it should be noted that all eight state parks in Northeastern Michigan as of 1925 could be reached by rail as well as road.) In 1905, fewer than three thousand automobiles were in use in Michigan. At the beginning of 1913, nearly forty thousand automobiles were registered in the state (registration had begun in 1906).

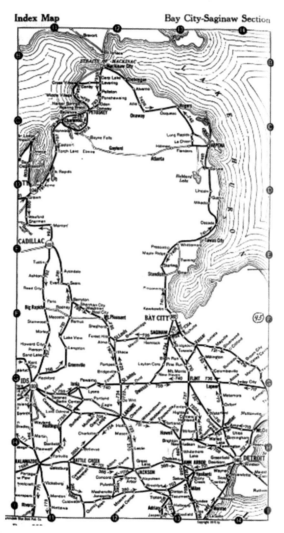

Official Automobile Blue Book, 1915. Vol. 4: Middle West . . .
(New York: Automobile Blue Book Pub. Co., 1915)

In 1903, maps of the resort area of Northern Michigan showed "State and County Wagon Roads"; in 1913, they showed these and "Automobile Roads." B. F. Bowen Co.'s 1916 Michigan atlas carried the title *Michigan State Atlas 1916 Automobile and Sportsmens Guide*. A 1915 road map of the state, however, presents a Northern Michigan that is virtually without roads except for one up the East Coast and one up the West Coast. A map of the trunk-line system prepared by the State Highway Department in 1919 shows a more extensive network of roads in Northern Michigan, almost all of them unimproved, even to the extent of being graveled.[143]

The state created the Highway Department in 1905, though the building and maintenance of roads remained at the local level. In 1913, the legislature passed the State Trunkline Act, which called for a three-thousand-mile system of roads to be built by townships and counties, with the state paying twice the "reward" it had previously conveyed to localities building roads. Two years later, the Covert Road Law encouraged road building by allowing the organization of districts to finance and construct roads. At the same time, it increased the financial share of counties in building trunk lines. In 1919, legislation reversed the relationship that had prevailed up to that point; the state highway commissioner would initiate trunkline highways and oversee their construction, while local government provided financial aid to the state.[144]

In November 1926, the U.S. Highway System was introduced, a matter much more of numbering and rerouting state roads to create interstate routes than of physical construction or expansion. In that year, US-23, running from the Ohio state line at Toledo through Ann Arbor, Flint, Saginaw, Standish, Tawas City, Alpena, Posen, Rogers City, Onaway, Aloha, and Cheboygan to Mackinaw City, replaced all or most of M-65 and M-10. (North of Alpena, the road was gravel.)

---

[i]*Transactions of the Michigan Sportsmen's Association for the Protection of Fish, Game, and Birds*, 4th Annual Session, January 21-23, 1879, quoted in Dempsey, p.40.

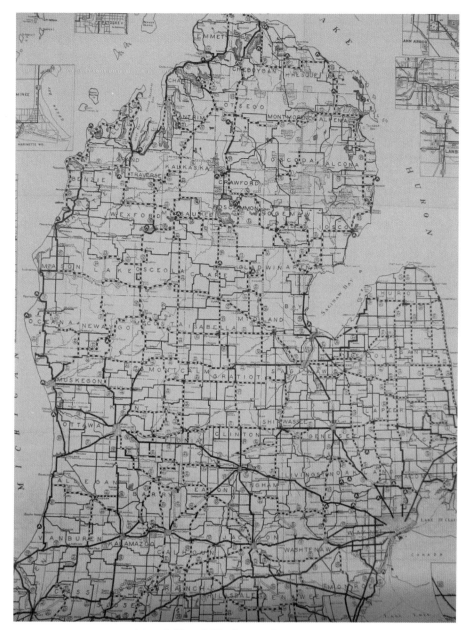

1927 Official Highway Service Map

In 1927, what had been M-14 and M-29 became US-27, extending from the Indiana border through Lansing, Mt. Pleasant, and Clare to Cheboygan. (In 1923, M-14 had been realigned to run along the south and east sides of Houghton Lake and through Grayling and Indian Rivers to Cheboygan.)

For much of the 1920s, the only north–south road in Northeastern Michigan between the coastal M-10 and the central M-14 was M-33. In 1928, it was extended from Atlanta and Mio as far south as the edge of West Branch. (Previously, it had run from Mio to Roscommon.)

M-58 and M-11, running from the Indiana border through St. Joseph and then up the entire West Coast to Mackinaw City, were redesignated as US-31. What had been M-13, adjusted often in the early 1920s and running from the Indiana state line through Kalamazoo, Grand Rapids, Cadillac, and Petoskey to Harbor Springs, became US-131.

A series of Michigan routes became US-10, the northernmost major east–west road in the Lower Peninsula. (M-32 occupied much of its current route but ended at Elmira in the west and Lachine in the east. What is now known as M-68 did not exist until the 1940s.)

As of late 1926 then, four major north–south roads led into Northern Michigan, including the central part. East–west travel, however, depended largely on local roads.[145]

One correlation to the expanding road system and the explosion in the number of vehicles (by the end of 1928, there were more than a million automobiles in Michigan) was the growth of hunting in Northern Michigan. The sale of small-game licenses in Michigan increased almost 40 percent during the 1920s (from just over 245,000 in 1920–21 to nearly 341,000 in 1929–30), and the sale of deer licenses soared almost 275 percent (from just under 28,000 in 1921 to over 76,000 in 1930).

These new faces in the woods (what was left of them) were urban-dwelling recreational hunters for whom travel north was now more convenient and far less daunting. As early as 1924, the director of the Department of Conservation lamented, "Man, the gun and automobile in ever increasing number combine in an agency of destruction that exceeds today natural reproduction of game, even when augmented by the productive efforts of man, on a basis of existing seasons and bag limits." (In 1940. H. D. Ruhl, then "In Charge" of the Game Division, would reflect, "The unprecedented development of travel facilities in Michigan during the past twenty years has brought hitherto remote game areas within easy reach of sportsmen and sightseers from distant populous centers until there are now few extensive wild land areas inaccessible to motorists in search of recreation or sport.")[146]

Maps of Cheboygan and Presque Isle Counties in the 1930s, however, reveal how few roads existed in Eastern Cheboygan and Western Presque Isle Counties, none of them paved. A 1939 soil survey of Cheboygan County noted of the county as a whole, "the roads in the settled communities are surfaced with gravel or are graded dirt roads; but in the less settled parts, the roads are not improved, and automobile travel over them is slow."[147]

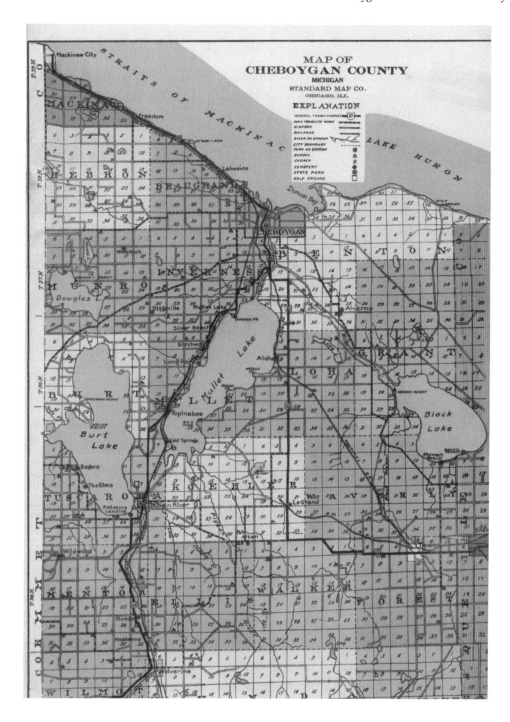

US-23 ran west from Rodgers City to the Ocqueoc River and turned south toward Millersburg and then west again through Onaway to a point east of Afton where it turned north to Cheboygan. (The route is essentially that of present-day M-68/M-33 to the point east of Afton where M-33 peels off to the north; the northern route had once been M-10.)

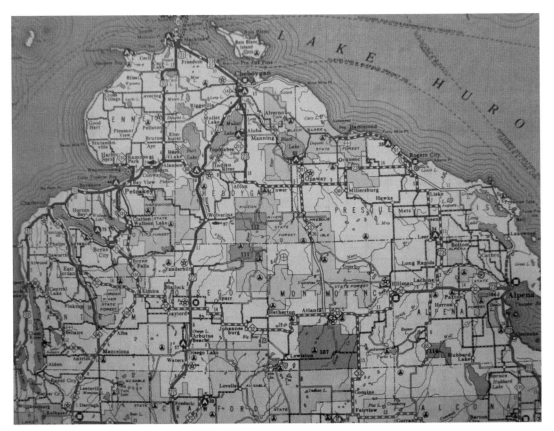

1938 official highway map

An "improved" road (in the finely tuned language of the era) ran north out of Rogers City along the coast to Hammond Bay. A "connecting" road continued northward along the coast as far as Grace; no coastal road existed in Presque Isle County beyond that point. Farther along the Lake Huron shore, a road ran along the north coast eastward from Cheboygan to a point just short of the Cheboygan County line. (Re-routing of US-23 to the coast from Rogers City to Cheboygan occurred in 1941, once construction of an "improved" but not hard surfaced coastal roadway had been completed.)

Two dirt roads twisted westward off the improved coastal road north of the new P. H. Hoeft State park, both joining the present-day Ocqueoc Lake Road east of Ocqueoc Lake. A road, the present-day North Ocqueoc Road, ran from Ocqueoc to meet the southernmost of these dirt roads.

An "improved" road, the present-day North Allis Highway, ran west out of Ocqueoc, becoming dirt to the west of M-211 and then running northwest on the farther side of Black Lake to Manning (the present-day Mograin Road) and, after crossing the Black River, north through Alverno to Cheboygan. SR-211, an "improved" road, ran north out of Onaway to the state park and then cut northeast to meet present-day Presque Isle County Road 646 (Town Hall Road).

A connecting road slanted northwestward off SR-211 parallel to the east shore of Black Lake and then west (the present-day Ross Road) before meeting the road to Cheboygan south of Alverno. North of Black Lake, just before it headed due west, this road intersected a "connecting" road that ran west from Grace and then southwest, crossing the Alpena State Road on its way.

The Alpena State Road ran southeast out of Cheboygan, and a road ran south from High Landing on the coast, the two joining just northeast of Twin Lakes (T37 R1E sec. 35); the Alpena Road then continued to meet the present-day Presque Isle County Road 646 (Town Hall Road).

Official map of Cheboygan County, 1933

The Civilian Conservation Corps

In 1920, P. S. Lovejoy wrote,

> A third of Michigan virtually is bankrupt, unable to pay its way with schools and roads, getting poorer instead of richer from year to year, producing less and less of value. This third of Michigan takes ten million acres or so, the most of it being in the northern part of the Lower Peninsula, the rest in the Upper Peninsula . . . Whenever we get ready, we can grow all the timber we want. Growing timber is a simple affair. All you have to do is stick a little tree right into the right sort of ground and wait.[148]

Many of those little trees were stuck into the ground by members of the Civilian Conservation Corps between 1933 and 1942. The CCC was a public-works relief program for unemployed, unmarried men, aged eighteen to twenty-five, from families on relief. (Later, other groups of men were allowed to enroll.) It operated as Franklin D. Roosevelt indicated in his address to Congress on relief in 1933:

> I propose to create a civilian conservation corps to be used in simple work, not interfering with normal employment and confining itself to forestry, the prevention of soil erosion, flood control, and similar projects. I call your attention to the fact that this type of work is of definite, practical value, not only through the prevention of great present financial loss but also as a means of creating future national wealth.

Northern Michigan—rural, poor, cut over, and burned over—was exactly the kind of area at which the program was aimed. As of December 1933, 63 percent of the population of Cheboygan County depended in whole or in part on some form of public relief. In 1940, a study of local government in the county commented that while the relief burden had lessened, "it appears that a large part of the population of

Cheboygan as well as the other cut-over counties will continue to be dependent upon public relief of some sort unless employment is provided through the development of new economic activities."[149]

Between 1933 and 1942, the CCC, operating an annual average of fifty-seven camps in Michigan, enrolled over 102,000 men from the state. These men planted nearly 500,000 trees and improved over 200,000 acres of forest stand, stocked over 150,000 fish, improved 1,200 miles of stream, spent 140,000 man-days fighting forest fires, built 500 bridges and almost 7,000 miles of truck trails and minor roads, installed over 2,000 miles of telephone line, erected 95 lookout houses and towers and 222 buildings, and built state parks or provided amenities at existing parks. Fire prevention, detection, and suppression on forest lands were the primary goals, thus the building of lookout houses and towers, the improvement of forest stands, and the construction of trails and roads as well as actual firefighting. The second goal was reforestation, to which Michigan added an emphasis on improving habitat for fish and game and stocking fish.[150]

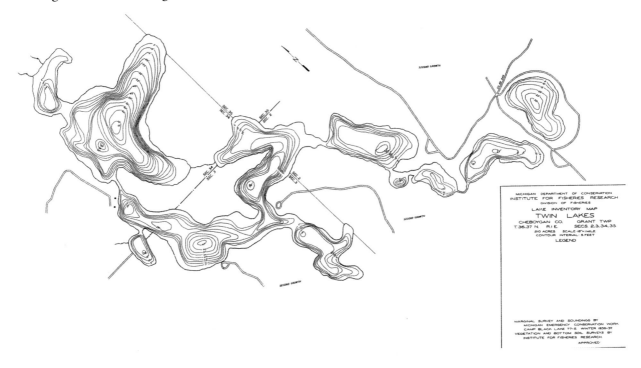

The nearest CCC camp to Twin Lakes was the Black Lake camp at Ocqueoc Lake in Presque Isle County, designated 77-S. (The buildings still stand as the Ocqueoc Outdoor Center, a county facility acquired from the federal government in 2004.) In 1933, under the Michigan Emergency Conservation Work program and as a part of the Forestry Division's policy of building campsites in state forests, the CCC built the first campground on Twin Lakes, ten camping sites on ten acres, on the steep slope down to East Twin Lake. (The campground was well sited in terms of a view but poorly sited in terms of erosion stimulated by the human presence. Much later, in the Black Mountain Forest Recreation Area Development Plan of 1989, the DNR thought it necessary to say regarding development criteria for horseback riding, "Use of East Twin Lake for watering only to the extent erosion not detrimental to fish populations."[151]) In the winter of 1936–1937, the CCC did the marginal survey and soundings for the Michigan Institute of Fisheries bathymetric map of Twin Lakes. Just what its role in tree planting in the Black Lake Forest around Twin Lakes may have been is unknown. (Alva Page "ran the tree planting crew" under the direction of Dave Green, the first superintendent of the Black Lake Forest. But this was a program of the Michigan Department of Conservation that did not involve the CCC unit at Ocqueoc. Tree planting in the forest predated creation of the CCC by several years. Green died in 1942 and is buried on Black Mountain.) Throughout the 1930s, details of fifteen to twenty CCC men from the Black Lake camp worked in the Onaway State Park, carrying out "forest improvement," mapping boundaries and topography, installing fencing, and building parking surfaces, foot trails, water storage and supply systems, and sanitary facilities.

Electrification

In 1935, the federal government created the Rural Electrification Administration (REA) to bring electricity to rural areas (90 percent of urban residents had electricity; 90 percent of rural residents and farms did not). Private companies, aware of the costs and skeptical of the rural market, were not interested. As of 1935, Consumers Power Co. and Detroit Edison Co. did provide power to some farms, mostly in Southern Michigan, but in Michigan as a whole, less than 25 percent of farms had electricity. So the mechanism to achieve this became locally created electricity cooperative companies, which received federal funding in the form of low-interest loans to finance the construction of generation and distribution facilities and power lines. By the outbreak of World War II, the REA had helped establish well over four hundred cooperatives, and by the end of the war, 90 percent of farms were electrified.

In Michigan, the Republican administration of Gov. Frank Fitzgerald stalled rural electrification by refusing to recognize cooperatives as legal entities. The election of the Democrat Frank Murphy in November 1936 provided the opening for electricity coops; as of early 1937, they were recognized as legal bodies by the state. One of these coops was the Presque Isle Electric Cooperative (PIEC), which originated with a meeting in Metz of a county extension agent and a small group of farmers in the fall of 1936. It was incorporated in March 1937, set its first pole in Posen on September 22, and, three months later, on Christmas Eve, activated seventy miles of line from Norway Dam in Alpena County to Moltke Township in Presque Isle County, bringing electricity to eighty-two farm families, the first REA-financed line to be put into use in Michigan. By 1943, the PIEC had bought Onaway Light & Power Co., acquiring the Tower dam/hydroelectric plant and adding a diesel plant at Tower, extended lines into Cheboygan and Montmorency counties, and was providing electricity to 2,900 farms and rural residences. Twin Lakes, however, lacked utilities of any kind.[152]

The plant in Tower responsible for generating more than half the power produced by the PIEC in the early 1940s (Courtesy of *Michigan County Lines*)

[127] Dempsey, pp. 38–39. Gillette (1898–1986), "the lady of the parks," graduated from Michigan Agricultural College with a degree in landscape architecture, worked professionally as a designer and landscaper, developed a lifelong friendship in the 1920s with P. J. Hoffmaster (1892–1950), the first superintendent of state parks and subsequently director of the Department of Conservation, and worked for sixty years to create and fund the state's system of parks.

[128] Dempsey, p. 39.

[129] *Transactions of the Michigan Sportsmen's Association for the Protection of Fish, Game, and Birds*, Fourth Annual Session, January 21–23, 1879, quoted in Dempsey, p. 40.

[130] Dempsey, pp. 41–42. As logging and farming increased forest openings and edge habitat, the deer population of Northern Lower Michigan should have increased. Instead, it peaked between 1875 and 1886 and then collapsed. The cause was unrestricted market hunting. "Populations throughout the state were depleted, and white-tails were completely extirpated from many areas in the south." Hunting licenses were first required in 1895, and market hunting was closed down by legislation in 1900. Still, in 1914, the state game commissioner estimated the deer population of Michigan as only 45,000; by 1937, it was 1.1 million (Phil Myers and Barb Lundrigan, "Mammals," in *Changing Environment*, p. 124).

[131] Dempsey, pp. 41–43.

[132] Dempsey, pp. 46–48. The Michigan State Federation of Women's Clubs had been founded in 1895 and had created a Forestry and Town Improvement Committee in 1902, the precursor of the Conservation Committee.

[133] Dickmann and Leefers, pp. 176–177. It should be noted that these courses preceded the early work of Gifford Pinchot as chief forester at George Vanderbilt's Biltmore estate in North Carolina and that of his successor in the position, Carl Schenck. Both were educated in forestry in Europe and are often seen as the fathers of forestry in the United States. Pinchot endowed the Yale School of Forestry in 1900, created the Society of American Foresters in the same year, and founded the U.S. Forest Service in 1905. Schenck originated the Biltmore Forest School in 1898, referred to as the first forestry school in the United States and "the cradle of forestry," and, in 1908, held the Biltmore Forest Fair to demonstrate the effectiveness of forest management.

[134] Dickmann and Leefers, pp. 177–178; Forestry Convention. In his opening remarks, Professor Beal noted that the commission sent out over three thousand circulars and one hundred and fifty personal letters. The letters were mostly requests to prominent men to be present . . . and talk upon some topic or send a short communication to be read at some of the meetings. A large part of the letters went to lumbermen, a class of men we thought were directly interested in the subject. From these men, we received only a few favorable replies, and I see only two or three of them with us now. (p. 3)

Arthur Hill set the purposes of the commission and the convention in a broad framework: "It was said by the philosopher Humboldt that men in all climates bring upon future generations two great calamities at once, a want of wood and a scarcity of water" (p. 22). (The "philosopher" in question was the explorer, geographer, and naturalist Alexander von Humboldt, not his elder brother, the linguist and philosopher Wilhelm von Humboldt.)

[135] Dickmann and Leefers, p. 178; Dempsey, p. 55.

Fifteen years earlier, at the Forestry Convention in 1888, Garfield had advocated one or more forest reserves and had targeted the Houghton/Higgins area as a site. Regretting an earlier generation's failure to reserve forest at the headwaters of the Grand, Raisin, Kalamazoo, and Huron Rivers in Southern Michigan, he went on to say,

> It can still be done at the head waters of the Muskegon and Au Sable rivers. Take six townships, including Houghton and Higgins lakes, that are almost worthless for agriculture, and they will make under State control the best kind of a forestry reserve. There were a few pines, but most of them have been removed. There is a wide range of herbaceous plants, for the character of the soil varies widely. It is a charming wild tract. There are a few settlers, but they would be glad to leave if paid a nominal price for their claims. The land is mostly in the hands of large owners, who hold it cheap . . .
>
> The advantage to science of such a reserve is no small item. There, the native flora and fauna would be preserved for future study.
>
> * * *
>
> Such a reservation would give us data as to facts of tree culture and forest influence that we could not otherwise get. It would enable the State to test these questions on a scale of such magnitude as to be of great value. (pp. 50–51)

Asked if he would limit the reserve to six townships, he replied, "Not if we could get more."

The rationale of the Michigan Sportmen's Association's resolution for a "State Park" intersected but did not entirely match Garfield's justification of a forest reserve. A "State Park" would serve "as a protection to fin, fur, and feather; as a sanitary influence for the whole State; as a preserver of the Manistee, Muskegon, and Au Sable. As a preserve for game, it would serve as a breeding and development grounds for animals and fishes to go out into the rest of the State" (p. 51).

[136] Dickmann and Leefers, pp. 178–179; Dempsey, pp. 60–64; *Report of Commission of Inquiry, Tax Lands and Forestry*, pp. 22–40 (the quoted statement may be found on p. 31; on the centrality of fire control, see pp. 27, 29, 39)

[137] Dempsey, pp. 108–109; Dickmann and Leefers, p. 179.

[138] Department of Conservation, *Biennial Report 1927–1928*, p. 222.

[139] *Biennial Report 1929–1930; 1931–1932; 1939–1940*.

[140] *Biennial Report 1933–1934*, p. 209.

[141] Dempsey, p. 93; for an overview, see Claire V. Korn, "Yesterday through Tomorrow: Michigan State Parks" (East Lansing: Michigan State University Press, 1989).

[142] *Presque Isle County Advance*, August 18, 2011; Korn, pp. 152, 155–156. "Cheboygan on the Straits of Mackinac" appears to have been published in 1925 or 1926. It refers to the "New Rustic Hotel on the Cheboygan River" in its entry on Hackmatack. The "big Log Inn" at Hackmatack had burned to the ground and, "after long planning and careful preparation, the new log hotel" was completed for the 1925 season. It opened with a dinner dance on July 6, 1925 (*CDT*, July 3, 1925, July 6, 1925). "Cheboygan" refers to all roads as trunk-line highways or by their state designation, not by a U.S. number. The U.S. road system came into effect in November 1926 with approval by the American Association of State Highways Officials.

[143] *World Almanac and Encyclopedia 1905*; *Automotive Industries*, vol. 28.

[144] See p. 3 of the article written by Dorothy G. Pohl and Norman E. Brown, "The history of roads in Michigan," and posted at the Michigan Highways site, http://www.michiganhighways.org/history4.html.

[145] See the history of the individual highways at Michigan Highways.

[146] Dempsey, p. 117; *Biennial Report 1927–1928*, p. 8; *Biennial Report 1931–1932*, p. 34. The sale of hunting licenses dropped sharply in 1931 and 1932, began to recover in 1933, and in 1939 reached nearly 538,000 (small game) and over 169,000 (deer) (*Biennial Report 1939–1940*, p. 55). Ruhl's observation appears in the same biennial report (p. 219).

[147] United States Department of Agriculture, Soil Conservation Service, in cooperation with the Michigan Agricultural Experiment Station, and the Michigan Department of Conservation, *Soil Survey of Cheboygan County, Michigan*, 1939, p. 3.

[148] Dempsey, p. 108. P. S. Lovejoy was the author of an important tax reform in 1925—the Commercial Forest Reserve Act, which capped taxes on lands with productive timbering potential. Fire *and* tax rates both discouraged forest management for the long term (the Commission of Inquiry had seen that in 1908, "forest raising is impossible as a commercial venture because if the assessing officers do their duty and tax annually what the law directs them to tax, the result must be the confiscation of all the profit within the period of years necessary to grow a tree from the seed to maturity"). Lovejoy's reform substituted a stumpage tax when the land was logged and the owner had his profit. "The act proved a decisive factor in reforestation of the millions of acres of cutover northern Michigan lands still in private ownership" (Dempsey, pp. 110–111).

[149] Robert S. Ford and Frank M. Landers, *Local Government in Cheboygan County* (Ann Arbor: University of Michigan Press, 1940), p. 6.

[150] Perry H. Merrill, *Roosevelt's Forest Army: A History of the Civilian Conservation Corps 1933–1942* (Montpelier, Vermont: Perry H. Merrill, 1981), pp. 138, 140; Dempsey, p. 114; Dickmann and Leefers, pp. 185–191.

[151] Appendix E, pp. 41–42.

[152] See Raymond G. Kuhl, *On Their Own Power: A History of Michigan's Electric Cooperatives* (Okemos, MI: Michigan Electric Cooperative Association, 1998), especially pp. 146–149. PIEC began to provide electricity to Twin Lakes in the 1970s. Only in 1998 did Aurora Gas Company install lines on the roads into the lake (with the exception of Truscott Drive).

Chapter 5 Local Change

"Twin Lakes"

The first map to label Twin Lakes "Twin Lakes" appeared in 1920, printed by the Standard Map Company of Chicago. *Bowen's Atlas* of 1916 and the Michigan State Highway Department road map of Cheboygan County of 1917 both show Twin Lakes accurately but do not name it. Neither did a map of lakes and rivers in Cheboygan and Presque Isle Counties drawn circa 1910 and a detailed 1914 map of state forests in Cheboygan drawn by R. R. Havens for the Public Domain Commission.[153] Earlier maps, back into the mid-nineteenth century, never named the lake; most did not show it. (The original GLO survey of 1841 and the dependent resurveys of 1854 and 1856, of course, did show the lake. The depiction of the lake in the original survey is inaccurate.) Before 1920 and long after that in the mind of the Department of Conservation, the only "Twin Lakes" in Cheboygan County was in Koehler Township, the two lakes now known as Cochrane and Roberts.[154] But on the other hand, George Richards, in his letter of December 1902 to M. D. Olds, referred to "those Twin Lakes lands" in Grant Township, and presumably Olds had used the same reference in his earlier letter to Richards. In 1909, Olds company records used the phrase "Twin Lakes Timber" to refer to hemlock in T37 sec. 34.[155]

"Twin Lakes" is one of the most common lake names in Michigan. (Even the Ojibwa-language name of the Nijode Lakes in Mecosta County in Central Michigan is rendered "Twin Lakes.") Why this lake acquired the name has to be conjectural. In an interview, Elnora Godfrey said that the name comes from the two lakes at the south end of the system near the Black Mountain Lodge, those being the twins.[156] If one stands on Twin Lakes Road as it runs between the southernmost bay and the isolated lake, it is difficult to see northward beyond that bay, especially when there is any foliage. It seems there are two lakes of similar size, if not of quite similar shape. The two also have similarly steep slopes and the same forestation. (On the other hand, her explanation leaves open the question of why a map publisher in Chicago in 1920 chose to label these uninhabited and little visited bodies of water "Twin Lakes" and what caused Richards and Olds to use that name almost twenty years earlier.)

There is oral evidence that the lake may also have been called "Chain of Lakes" by local residents and nonresident fishermen. The secretaries of the Twin Lakes Association used that term in correspondence as late as 1980 and 1981.[157] The "Cheboygan on the Straits of Mackinac" map of the mid-1920s also used the phrase "a chain of lakes" to describe what it referred to as Twin Lakes. Why it might do so is evident today and would have been equally obvious in the 1920s. (However, "Cheboygan" does say that the channels are large enough to get rowboats through. It did not specify whether that passage could be made by rowing or required a portage.)

In the 1920s, Cheboygan County (and much of the rest of the Northern Lower Peninsula) began to make a transition from an overwhelmingly extractive economy to an economy that relied heavily on recreation and tourism. A succession of articles with the theme "RECREATIONAL DEVELOPMENT TURNING TIDE" and a close reportorial watch on the "resort industry" and related topics distinguished the *Cheboygan Daily Tribune* (*CDT*) in 1925 and subsequent years from the newspaper in its previous forty years.[158] (A year earlier, a headline had advised, "Cheboygan Should Bend Every Effort to Get Resorters.")

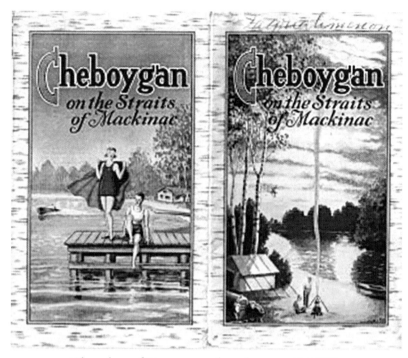

Chamber of Commerce brochure, mid-1920s

Among the pleasures on offer in the county, "Cheboygan on the Straits" listed "three splendid nine-hole golf courses"; Mullett, Burt, Black, Douglas, Long, Silver, and Twin Lakes; and a half dozen resorts on Black Lake as well as similar facilities on Mullett and Burt.

Thus, it contained among its many listing and descriptions of lakes, resorts, and activities the following: "**Twin Lakes** — A chain of lakes connected by channels large enough to get rowboats through, nestling among some great hills and in an undeveloped and away-from-civilization country, offering delightful campsites and where the fishing is splendid, the water cold and crystal. Twelve miles from Cheboygan on good roads." ("Good roads" was not defined.) This transition would affect the few residents near Twin Lakes and those who owned property in the surrounding area.

Grant Township

Twins Lakes lies close to the center of Grant Township, a lightly populated, largely agricultural township in the first half of the twentieth century. The township was imperfectly formed in 1870 and then reorganized in 1879 by the legislature. Censuses between 1880 and 1940 reflect its settlement, the peak of lumbering, a significantly diminished number of households following that peak, and renewed (but unsustained) settlement on the eve of World War II.

As the table below shows, in only a few decades did the population pattern of Grant Township mimic that of the county. Except for the years in the immediate aftermath of the end of large-scale logging, the county population rose from decade to decade. Grant Township shows an almost unbroken line of declining population for roughly seventy years. Until 2000, the township had its highest population in 1880.

Population

	Cheboygan County	% Change	Grant Township	% Change
1880	6,524		773	
1890	11,986	83.7%	459	-40.7%
1900	15,516	29.5%	542	18.0%
1910	17,872	15.2%	462	-14.8%
1920	13,991	-21.7%	312	-32.5%
1930	11,502	-17.8%	245	-21.5%
1940	13,644	18.6%	377	53.8%
1960	14,550	6.6%	296	-8.5%
1980	20,649	41.9%	579	95.6%
2000	26,448	28.1%	947	63.6%

The reconstituted census of 1890 shows 63 households in the township. Of the 43 heads of household for whom occupation is indicated, 42 were farmers and one a laborer. Of the 51 heads of household for whom birth place is recorded, 49 percent were born in Canada, 27 percent in Michigan, 12 percent in Great Britain, 8 percent in the state of New York, and 3 percent in Germany. William Gainor appears as a farmer; the entries for Gilbert O'Connor and James O'Neill do not indicate occupation.[159]

The 1900 census listed 99 heads of household. Of the 88 legible entries, 56 (64 percent) were farmers and 24 (27 percent) laborers, possibly farm laborers, though this enumeration lists "day laborers," "farm laborers," and "laborers," leaving posterity to guess at what they were laboring. One each of the following occupations was listed: carpenter, health resort operator, postmaster, land looker, blacksmith, and housekeeper. Two heads of household had no occupation entered. The names Boyea and Owens appear.[160]

Places of birth and the unusually high percentage of laborers suggest that the population was the product of recent immigration to Michigan. Of heads of household whose place of birth is indicated and legible, 51 percent came from Canada; 10 percent from each of Michigan, New York, Northern Europe (Germany, Norway, Prussia, Sweden), and other U.S. states; and 8% from Ireland. The occupations of the township population were weighted very heavily toward labor; while 38 percent of all occupations listed was "farmer," 43 percent was "laborer" of one kind or another. Adding the 8 percent of occupations entered as "housekeeper" brings the total of these three to nearly 90 percent of occupations in the township. Singular occupations other than those mentioned above were engineer, stage driver, hotel waiter, store clerk, insurance agent, journalist, dressmaker, and boiler maker. Two individuals were entered as "at School."

The 1910 census reflected the logging of Grant Township. Ninety heads of household are listed; the occupations of 88 are legible. Of the legible entries, 70 percent are farmers and only 3 percent farm laborers. But 23 percent are laborers, teamsters, packers, or sawyers in the logging industry. (It is very likely that some "farmers" also worked as loggers.) The rest are a house servant, a stone mason, and a charity case. The lumber workers included William Godin. Two of the farm laborers were William Boyea and John Owens. The farmers included Adeline Boyea, William Gainor, four Owenses, Alva Page, and Herbert Reynolds. Of all occupations reported, two-thirds were in agriculture (farmers and farm laborers). The lumber industry accounted for 18 percent. Surprisingly, the next largest occupational category was servants (7.5 percent). Single entries for occupation included nurse, blacksmith, machinist, bookkeeper, and telegraph operator.[161]

Overwhelmingly, heads of households were born in Canada or Michigan, 42 percent in each case. New York accounted for 9 percent and Ireland, Iowa, Maine, and Ohio for the remainder.

The 1920 census listed only 57 households. Two are illegible. Seventy-five percent of heads of household listed their occupation as farmer and 13 percent as farm laborer. In contrast to the previous census, only 4 percent were engaged in the lumber industry, specifically a lumber camp laborer and a lumber camp foreman. The remaining heads of household were a farm manager, a grocer, a trapper, a general laborer, and a female for whom "None" was entered under occupation. Of all occupations listed, 74 percent were in agriculture (farmers, farm manager, farm laborers). The next largest occupational groups were servants (7 percent) and lumber camp laborers (6 percent). Single listings of occupation appearing for the first time included dressmaker, sailor, and steam fitter and drill press operator (both in the automotive industry).[162] For the first time, Michigan dominated as the birthplace of heads of household (56 percent). Canada still was the birthplace of 28 percent, and Ohio, Ireland, Germany, England, and New York accounted for the rest.

The 1930 census showed even fewer households, only 46. Of the 41 male heads of household listed in the township, nearly 90 percent were farmers. These included George Gaynor, Herbert W. Gaynor, Alva R. Page, and Herbert Reynolds. Of the remaining male heads of household, one was a carpenter, one was a trapper, and three were farm laborers. There were five female heads of household, all listed as having no occupation. Of all occupations reported, 85 percent were in agriculture. "Laborer, woods" accounted for 5 percent of occupations and "Teacher" for 3 percent. One individual was "Laborer, forest reserve" and another "Laborer, dredge."[163] Sixty-three percent of heads of household had been born in Michigan, 27 percent in Canada, and the remainder in England, Germany, Iowa, and Ohio.

The 1940 census showed a significantly larger number of households, 83, than the preceding two censuses. It also showed a wider range of occupations, some of them distinctly modern. Still, 61 percent of the heads of household were farmers. These included Willard Boyea, Henry L. Chamberlain, Raymond P. Cronan, Herbert W. Gainor, Daniel O'Neill, William E. A. Owens, Alva Page, and Herbert E. Reynolds. No other occupation accounted for more than 5 percent. (Eight percent of heads of household had no occupation stated.) The seven listed as laborers included two construction laborers and four Works Progress Administration (WPA) laborers but only a single farm laborer. ("Bert A. O'Connors" and Bert Reynolds were WPA laborers.) The more traditional occupations included three carpenters, two proprietors of retail grocery stores, a caretaker, a lumberman, and a water driller. Newer occupations included two truck drivers, a garage mechanic, an automobile metal finisher, a steel-pipe fitter, a private administrator, and a salesman for a scales manufacturer (Jefferson A. Crawford for Toledo Scale Co.).[164]

Of the total of 132 individuals in the township whose occupations are specified, 69 percent were engaged in farming (farmers or farm laborers). Seven percent were in the construction industry (four carpenters, three truck drivers, two laborers). Nearly as many were employed in the CCC and WPA (a surveyor, a truck driver, six laborers). In addition to those instances already mentioned, occupations followed by only a single individual included a dredge operator, a grade-school teacher, a stenographer, and a sewer in a garment factory.

Of the heads of households, more than three-quarters had been born in Michigan and 6 percent in each of Canada and the state of Ohio. The remainder came from Kansas, Kentucky, Indiana, Iowa, Minnesota, and Missouri.

Land Ownership

Industrial decline came early to Cheboygan County. M. D. Olds ended his lumber operations in 1916. The Pfister & Vogel tannery in Cheboygan City closed in 1926 with the loss of hundreds of jobs and the rapid disappearance of the tannery itself, most of the houses Pfister & Vogel had built for workers, and the other physical structures associated with the tannery. The Embury-Martin sawmill burned down in 1928, and the company did not rebuild, as it had after a 1919 fire. Another major employer, the paper mill on the Cheboygan River, closed in 1929. Subsequently, the Great Depression brought widespread abandonment of land by nonpayment of taxes and consequent forfeiture to the state. With regard to Twin Lakes, the result was a significant exchange of land ownership that continued through the 1940s and set the framework of the lake's future development.[165]

The shoreline of Twin Lakes was surveyed as a series of government lots.[166] T36N R1E sec. 2, contained five lots, with Lots 2, 3, and 4 arrayed north to south on the west side of the section along Smith Road, Lot 5 on both sides of the southern bay, and Lot 1 to its north.

T36N R1E sec. 3, also contained five lots. Lot 1 was the island that had been in continuous federal ownership until 1922, when the State of Michigan received a patent on its northern half. Lot 2 was a sliver of less than 13 acres on the western tip of the Smith Road peninsula. Lots 3, 4, and 5 ran south to north on the west side of the lake from the Crawford Road area to Page Road (the line between the township and T37N R1E sec. 34).

T37N R1E sec. 34 held four lots and a bit of confusion. Lots 4 and 3 were on the northwest shore of the lake and lot 2 on the northeast shore. The original survey of 1841 shows a Lot 2 that is considerably larger than ultimately it would be and no Lot 1 or lot 5. The Dependent Resurvey of 1854 produced an accurate depiction of the lake and introduced a Lot 1 of 51.30 acres that included land that became Godin Circle. A supplemental plat of 1904 showed instead a Lot 5 of 38.38 acres, as did a supplemental plat of 1922. In 1952, the Department of Conservation presumed the 1922 plat to be the authority for the designation of lots.[167]

T37N R1E sec. 35 required only two lots. Lot 1 just barely touched the eastern end of the Big Bay, and the southwestern corner of Lot 2 brushed the lake south of Godin Circle.[168]

In 1902, in T36 sec. 2, Lot 1 was owned by George D. Richards, Lot 2 by William Gainor, and Lots 3, 4, and 5 by James G. Ross. (In 1899, it appears that all the lots in the section had been transferred to Anselm McIntosh by the estate of William Ross. McIntosh does not appear often in the property records but was a partner in the timber firm of McIntosh & Small in 1898 and appears in Polk's Cheboygan directory of 1910 and of 1916 as a dealer in timberlands.)

To the west in T36 sec. 3, Lot 2 was owned by Catherine Gainor, Lot 3 by Emeline Baker, and Lots 4 and 5 by "Edmund Hall of Detroit" (as he is listed on a deed). In T37 sec. 34, Lot 1 was state land, Lot 2 was owned by George D. Richards, Lot 3 was state tax land, and Lot 4 was owned by Pfister & Vogel Lumber Co. George D. Richards owned both lots in T37 sec. 35.

According to a plat map of 1913, ownership in T36 sec. 2 had changed only in that Embury-Martin Lumber Company owned the Ross properties (Lots 3, 4, 5). Similarly, in T36 sec. 3, Lots 3, 4, and 5 had passed to Embury-Martin Lumber Company (Hugh Cox, a partner in Embury Martin, conveyed Lots 4 and 5 to the company in May 1904.) In T37 sec. 34, Lot 1 (or 5) was shown as owned by Edward A. Hulbert, and George D. Richards had added Lot 3 to Lot 2. (In all likelihood, the Hulbert property had actually been conveyed through Charles Horton to Embury-Martin Lumber Company.) No change had occurred in T37 sec. 35.

A plat map of 1930 showed that Anselm McIntosh had taken over the Embury-Martin property in T36 sec. 2 and no change of ownership in T36 sec. 3. The same map showed that ownership in T37 sec. 34 was unchanged. In fact, however, Alva Page had bought Lot 4 from Pfister & Vogel in 1919 and conveyed it to his son, Lyle Page, in 1927, and Lot 1 (or 5) might have been sold to Kenneth McLeod in 1920. (See chapter 3, "Twin Lakes," for the uncertainties of ownership of this lot.) Richards's ownership of Lots 1 and 2 in T37 sec. 35 continued. His properties in secs. 34 and 35 exceeded 800 acres.

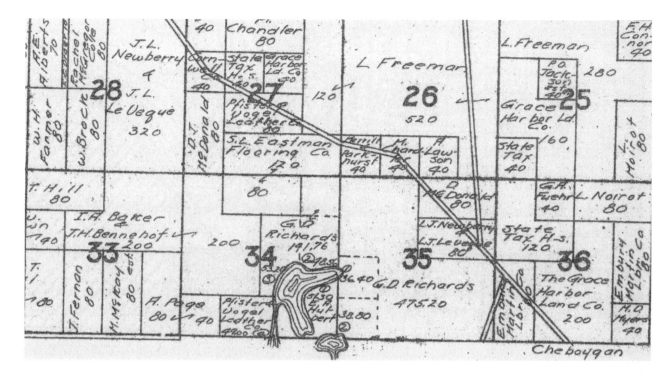

A little farther afield, Irving Baker and John H. Bennehoff, both of Tiffin, Ohio, held 400 acres, bought in 1912, in secs. 33 and 34 that included land west and north of the top of the lake. North of Twin Lakes, much of sec. 27, traversed by the Alpena State Road, was owned by S. L. Eastman Flooring Co., Pfister & Vogel, Merritt Chandler, the Grace Harbor Land Co. and Leonard Freeman of Fenton, Michigan, who also owned the greater part of sec. 26 to the east; in 1911, M. D. Olds had assigned ten thousand acres of land in Cheboygan and Presque Isle Counties to Freeman in exchange for all the stock of Prospect Holding Company of Cleveland.[169] Property to the west of the lake was owned by Alva Page, John LaFleur, James McKervey, Harry Baker, John Donovan, and Herbert Reynolds.

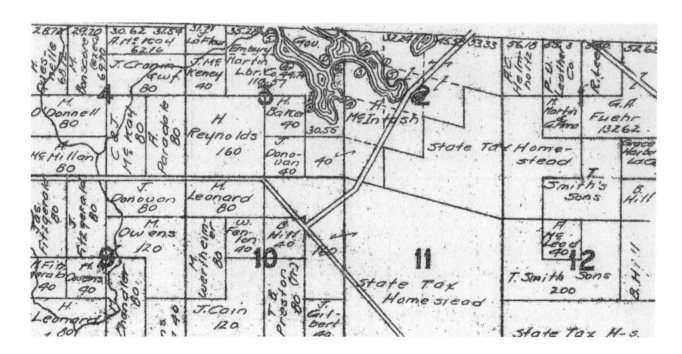

A rural property inventory for Cheboygan County, carried out between 1936 and 1939, draws a somewhat different picture of property holding on the shoreline of the lake.[170] The five government lots in T36 sec. 2, the southeastern quadrant of the lake, were all owned by George D. Richards. None had dwellings or buildings. He also owned, as he had since at least 1902, the two government lots in T37 sec. 35, which included the northeast shore of the lake. They also lacked dwellings or buildings.

In T36 sec. 3, the southwestern side of the lake, Government Lot 2 (present-day Smith Road Circle and Westervelt Road) was owned by Herbert Gainor. The property, just under 13 acres, had been in the Gainor family since at least 1902 but had no dwellings or buildings. Government Lot 3 had been acquired by Richards from Anselm McIntosh (or Embury-Martin Lumber Co). Government Lot 4, nearly 45 acres, was owned by Bert Reynolds, contained 6.5 acres of untillable pasture and 38 acres of mixed hardwoods, and held a one-and-a-half-story, one-room house and a cabin. Government Lot 5, just over 35 acres, was still shown as assessed to Embury-Martin Lumber Company In fact, Lot 5 had been bought in 1936 by Clyde Page from Herbert D. Bockes, Trustee, for $150. (Bockes appeared in Polk's directory of Cheboygan City for 1910 as a lumber scaler for Embury-Martin Lumber Company, in the 1916 directory as a lumber inspector with no affiliation, and in many property transactions over the course of nearly a half century. He functioned as a trustee for Embury-Martin properties throughout the 1930s and into the early 1940s.)

In T37 sec. 34, the northwestern quarter of the lake, Lots 2 and 3 were owned by Richards, as they had been since at least 1913. Government Lot 4, 49 acres, all classified as mixed hardwoods, was owned by Lyle Page. It contained two "tourist" cabins, both built in 1937. Government Lot 5 (or 1), over 50 acres, was administered by Herbert D. Bockes as trustee for Embury-Martin.

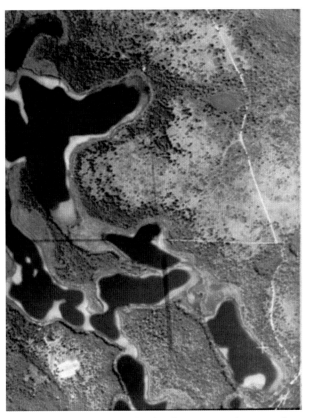

East Side, Twin Lakes, 1938 (island, the future Godin Circle, Krouse Road, Smith Road peninsula); the vertical and horizontal lines are section lines

George D. Richards died in 1937. In 1939, Jefferson A. Crawford and William A. Quesnell, as tenants in common, bought from the Richards family all the lots in T36 sec. 2, along with Richards's other holdings in sec. 2, and Lot 3 in T36 sec. 3. In addition, they bought Lots 2 and 3 and other Richards property in T37 sec. 34 and Lots 1 and 2 and other property in T37 sec. 35. Two lots in T36 sec. 2, one in T36 sec. 3, and one in T37 sec. 35, totaling 125 acres, had passed to the State of Michigan for delinquent taxes and had to be redeemed in 1941.

Crawford did not redeem all the properties. In particular, the state appears to have already transferred Lot 3 to the Department of Conservation. Lot 3, which years later would become the site of the Twin Lakes campground on Smith Road, included a substantial stretch of shoreline and many uncut trees, and it connected to land that the state already owned. Dave Green, superintendent of the Black Lake Forest, reported planting red and white pine nearby as early as March 1932. The *Michigan County Atlas of General Highway Maps for 1940* shows the Smith Road peninsula as state forest.[171]

By the late 1930s, the Department of Conservation was committed to state acquisition of water frontage to provide public access to lakes and streams. The public fishing site program was officially established by Act 337, PA 1939, which became effective January 1, 1940. This act set aside forty cents from each dollar of fishing license fees for acquisition of land to insure public access, for lake and stream improvement, and for fisheries research. By the end of World War II, the department had acquired considerable water frontage but had put off development.[172]

The years 1937–1946 were also a time of enormous expansion of the Black Lake Forest. The overall acreage of the forest increased 65 percent, from just over 92,000 acres to nearly 153,000 acres. State holdings within the boundaries of the forest increased even more impressively, doubling from slightly less than 52,000 acres to over 102,000 acres. The largest biennial increase occurred in 1941–42, an overall expansion of 41,500 acres, 38,500 (93 percent) of which were state holdings. Reversion for nonpayment of taxes appears to have been the primary reason for the acquisitions. The 1943 tax rolls of Grant Township suddenly abound in entries reading "State" and "State Conservation," all written in vibrant red pencil that contrasted with the stolid graphite gray of all other entries.[173]

Quesnell acquired more land in T36 sec. 2 in 1942 and 1944. With those acquisitions, Crawford and his wife, Alberta, and Quesnell and his wife owned much of the lakeshore on the east side as well as extensive land on the north side. In 1944, Crawford and Quesnell paid taxes on over 835 acres in the four sections that include Twin Lakes. Crawford alone paid taxes on an additional 142 acres. In that year, Crawford, Quesnell, and the State of Michigan owned over 80 percent of the four sections. In T36 sec. 2, all the land was owned by Crawford, Quesnell, or the state or was property bought from Crawford and/or Quesnell in the four years preceding 1944. Crawford and Quesnell owned all of T37 sec. 35. However, they ended their common tenancy the following year, with the properties passing to Crawford.

Beginning in 1940 and 1941 with the granting of warranty deeds by Alberta Crawford and William Quesnell to Catherine Elizabeth Cody and to Charles Krauhs, the land in T36 sec. 2 was sold off in small parcels. (In June 1941, the Crawfords also sold a property in the same section to Clifford Canfield, who promptly sold it to a pair of buyers from Wayne and Oakland Counties. The deeds expressly prohibited the property being used for "a gas station, beer or liquor tavern, restaurant, lunches or grocery business." They also provided that "at no time shall this property be sold or transferred, rented or leased to persons other than members of the Caucasian race.") The largest number of sales was in the years 1945–1953, but the process continued at a slower pace until the death of Alberta Crawford in 1990 (her husband died in 1961). Most of the current properties on Krouse Road from its intersection with Twin Lakes Road to Godin

Road (but not including Godin Road and Godin Circle) track back to the ownership of Jefferson and/or Alberta Crawford in the early 1940s.[174]

In the late '30s and early '40s in T36 sec. 3, Lot 1 remained federal property, and Lot 2 was owned by Herbert Gainor. (Gainor sold this lot to Leonard Smith in 1946.) Lot 3 had been acquired by Crawford, Lot 4 became the property of Bert Reynolds in 1938 with the fulfillment of a land contract entered into in 1935, and Lot 5 was owned by Clyde Page.

In T37 sec. 34, Lots 2 and 3 had been acquired by Crawford. Lot 4 was returned by Lyle Page to Alva Page in 1941 and sold by Alva Page to Lewis and Junellda Cross in 1944.[175] Lot 5 (or 1) was sold by Herbert D. Bockes, Trustee, to Edsel Page in 1942 and then conveyed by Edsel Page to Sidney Godin in 1945. (Godin had sold his meat market in Cheboygan in 1944 and owned a farm and other properties on Black River Road near Alverno.) Over the course of many years thereafter, shoreline parcels were transferred to family members and relatives and to others.

The Truscott family—Thomas J. Truscott and his wife, Marion, and their son, Gerald, and his wife, Doris—were also large-scale buyers (and eventually sellers) of land.[176] Lyle Page recalled selling land to Truscott in 1939. But the land records show only a transfer of land from Lyle Page to Alva Page in 1941, none by Lyle Page to Truscott at any time. The largest amount of the land Truscott owned appears to have been acquired from Lewis and Junellda Cross in 1946, 1947, and 1953. The land in question lay in T37 secs. 33 and 34 and had been acquired by the Crosses from Alva Page and Jefferson Crawford. From 1962 onward, the Truscott family sold parcels along the northwestern shore of the lake.

The last of these buyers and sellers of Twin Lakes lands was Herbert Killian.[177] In 1952, Killian acquired Lot 4 and the southeast quarter of the northwest quarter in sec. 3, nearly 85 acres. These two had been jointly held since at least the beginning of the century—by Embury-Martin Lumber Company and then by Bert Reynolds, who bought them in the midst of the Depression, and then by Roy Huff in the five years before Killian's purchase. Throughout the 1950s and into the early 1970s, Killian sold parcels accessed by Reynolds Road.

Virtually all the current properties on Twin Lakes can be traced to the acquisition and ownership of land by the Crawfords, Sidney Godin, Thomas Truscott, and Herbert Killian between 1939 and the early 1950s. Their decisions to parcel out the land (over the course of decades in some cases) changed the nature and created the present appearance of Twin Lakes. What had been an almost entirely unoccupied lake, except for a brief period of logging, would become a largely residential and recreational lake.

This pattern of distribution is one reason why the lake is in its present condition. Building on the lake has been individualized and staggered over time. There has not been the building of a development nor has there been successful large-scale land acquisition and building by a developer or contractor. Similarly, there are no properties with a cluster of cabins or layered residences. Thus, there is not the residential crowding that exists on many lakes in Northern Michigan and elsewhere throughout the state.

Depression and War

The economic shift from extractive to recreational, in combination with the greater ease of travel, gave residents of Twin Lakes an opportunity to augment their livings and brought in new residents who similarly tried to benefit from hunting and fishing.

As of 1930, the major properties on the periphery of Twin Lakes not assessed to Embury-Martin, Pfister & Vogel, or George Richards were the 120 acres of Alva Page west of the lake and the 160 acres of Herbert Reynolds south and west of the lake, both listed as farmers in the census and both longtime residents by 1930.

Of the 120 acres homesteaded by Alva Page in T37 secs. 33 and 34, 45 were classified as "cropland and farmstead" in the Rural Property Inventory, one was classified "road," and the remaining seventy-four were classified "farm woodlot" and described as mixed hardwoods. His eighty-acre property was approached on a gravel road, had rural free delivery, was two miles from the nearest school, four miles from an electric line, and one mile from a telephone, and, according to the Rural Inventory, had no adequate water supply. His forty-acre property differed little, but there was no road, no water supply, and no rural free delivery. (Oddly enough, there is no mention or drawing of a farmhouse on the "cropland and farmstead.")

In contrast, Herbert Reynolds's 160-acre farm, also on a gravel road, was slightly over half cropland and farmstead. It contained a one-and-a-half-story wood-frame house, thirty-six by twenty-two by eighteen feet, including a twelve-by-fourteen-foot covered porch, built in 1898. The foundation was concrete, the roofing wood shingle, the walls rolled, the interior finished board, and the floors hardwood and pine. Heat was provided by a stove and light by oil lamps. Like all the structures on or near the lake, it lacked plumbing. Its overall condition was "fair." The property also contained a barn ninety-six by forty-eight by sixteen feet, built in 1932. Its foundation was posts, its exterior rough lumber, and its gambrel roof covered with rolled mineral membrane. Its overall condition was "poor."

Bert Reynolds's shoreline property, Lot 4, contained a one-and-a-half-story wood-frame house, built in 1938, and a cabin. The house was twenty by twenty-four by twelve feet, with a wood post foundation, rolled roofing, finished lumber walls, pine floors, and an unfinished interior; as in the Reynolds farmhouse, heat came from a stove and light from oil lamps. Its overall condition was "fair." The cabin was twenty by eighteen by eight feet of log construction with rolled roofing and hardwood floors. Its overall condition was "good." A well provided adequate water.

Alva Page and Herbert Reynolds supplemented farming as best they could and as opportunity arose. In 1919, Page bought Government Lot 4 in T37N sec. 34, nearly fifty acres, including shoreline, from Pfister & Vogel Leather Company. He had logged on this lot under contract to M. D. Olds; eventually, he began to build boats—thirteen-foot flat-bottomed three-seaters that required soaking and tar in the spring—and rent them. Some of these are probably to be found in the population of boats residing in the mucky lake bottom. At some point, he began to build cabins, eventually four at least, sell the lumber to build cabins, and operate the White Birch Cabins Resort along the shoreline in Lot 4.[178] He was also in charge of the tree-planting crew in the Black Mountain Forest. Reynolds hunted bear and trapped. Fishing and rabbit and grouse hunting were good.

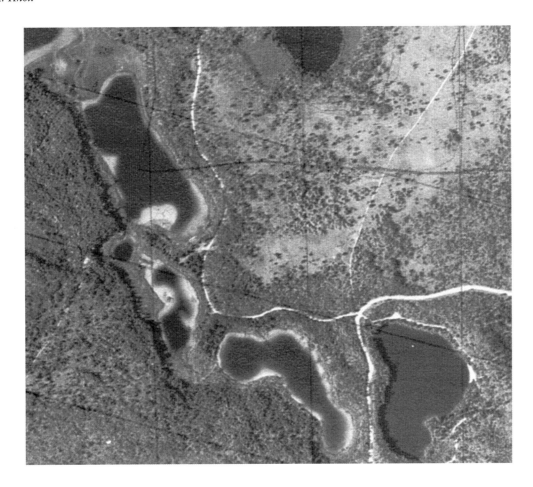

Southeastern quarter of Twin Lakes, 1938. Lower right: Twin Lakes Road and the isolated lake. Bottom: the southernmost bay. Shoreline on the left is the Smith Road peninsula and adjacent state land. The isolation of the bays is repeated elsewhere on the lake.

In 1927, Lyle Page bought Lot 4 from Alva and Nettie Page for "one dollar and other considerations" and in 1941 sold it back to them for $1,000. In 1938, the Rural Property Inventory classified the entire property as "forest and timber area" and showed two cabins, one twenty-two by sixteen by ten feet, the other sixteen by fourteen by ten feet, and the Twin Lakes outlet. (Unlike his immediately older and younger brothers, Alton and Clyde, Lyle seems to have spent the Depression at home. He appears in the 1930 census as a twenty-three-year-old farm laborer in the household of Alva Page, as does his eighteen-year-old brother, Clyde. Twenty-six-year-old Alton Page was living in Wayne County, Michigan. In 1940, both Alton and Clyde lived in Wayne County. The 1940 census lists Lyle (and his wife) in his father's household, indicates that he lived there in 1935, and shows his occupation as "Operator Dredge." In 1941, Lyle appears to have been living in Bay City.)

In the thirties, a dam was built in Lot 4 at the western end of the bog at the lowest point of the lake. The dam consisted of a low earthen levee and a wooden gate; it may have included some form of drainage channel. (See the photographs of the dam outlet in 1984 in chapter 8.)

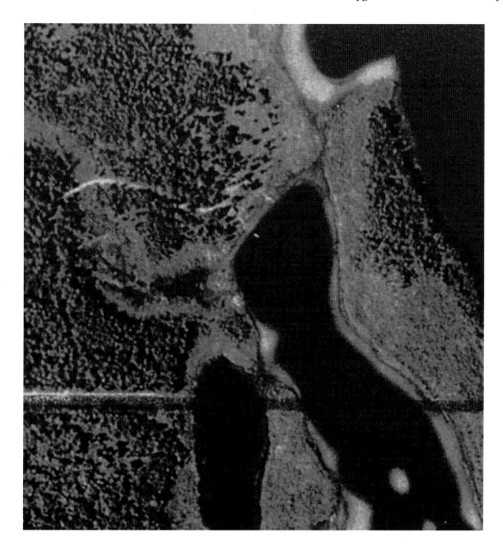

Page Road access bay, dam-and-outlet bay, resort, island, 1938

While Lot 4 had been the property of Lyle Page since 1927 and he would make a career as a marine dredger on the Great Lakes, it is nearly certain that Alva Page built the dam, possibly as late as 1936, certainly not much earlier. He had bought the nearby Page home properties in 1907 and 1908. He had clear-cut Lot 4 in 1909 and 1910 under contract to M. D. Olds. He had acquired the property between the Page farm and Lot 4, probably from Merritt Chandler and probably between 1913 and 1916. In 1919, he bought lot 4 from Pfister & Vogel. He built a log cabin at what is now the intersection of Page Road and Truscott Lane as early as 1926, and as mentioned, he built boats (the bog may have provided some of the materials with which they were built). He probably built the two new cabins that appear on the 1937 bathymetric map and in the 1938 aerial photograph and are described in the Rural Property Inventory. The directional sign to "Twin Lakes Cottages" bears the name "Alva Page," and Alva Page operated the resort.

That does not preclude collaboration between father and son in building the dam or, more likely, the cabins. But tradition, the preponderance of what evidence exists, and the 1991 interview of Lyle Page point to Alva Page as the builder. Indeed, it appears that the return of Lot 4 to his parents in 1941 marked the end of any direct link between Lyle Page and Twin Lakes. [179]

Building a dam may have been an effort to make Twin Lakes more attractive to visitors; the lakes were shallow, and boats had to be portaged or poled from one to the other, hence the flat bottoms. An entry in the GLO survey for T36 sec. 3 reads, "Land all Swamp and Swampy"; an entry for T37 secs. 34 and 35 reads, "Land most all swamp." "Swamp," "swampy," or some variant appear to be the most common words or phrases describing the land in these sections. (But in fairness, the surveyors did discover "2ⁿᵈ rate" and "1ˢᵗ rate" soils and land and "land good for agricultural purposes.") A map of lakes and rivers in Cheboygan and Presque Isle Counties, dated uncertainly as 1910, shows Twin Lakes fairly accurately, small creeks flowing into Owens Creek, and Owens Creek emptying into the Black River, very much the drainage system that still exists. But it does not name Twin Lakes and does not show an outlet, much less one joining Owens Creek. However, it does sprinkle symbols indicating marsh or swamp all over Twin Lakes. In Lyle Page's interview of 1991, recalling Twin Lakes in the 1930s, the words "swamp" and "marshy" or variants are repeatedly used to describe the small bay in which the dam is located and the land to its west.

A map of 1914, excellently drawn for the Public Domain Commission, shows T37 sec. 34, which includes the northwest shore of Twin Lakes, notably Government Lot 4, and nine sections to the immediate west of Twin Lakes as largely marsh or swamp. (The sections are 33, 32, 31, 30, 19, 16, 15, 10, and 9.) It also shows an outlet from Twin Lakes that peters out in T37 sec. 4 rather than joining Owens Creek.

The official Cheboygan County map of 1933, drawn by Royal Fultz, a man who knew the features of its terrain by virtue of his business, showed no drainage from Twin Lakes, though he did show feeders and drainage elsewhere on his map.[180]

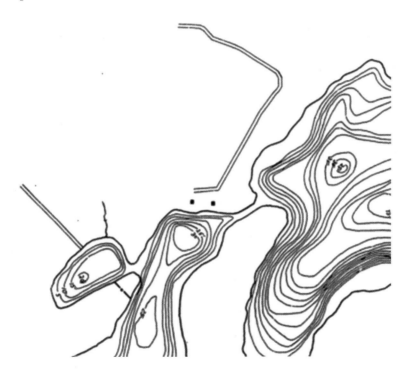

Same area, 1937 bathymetric map

More specifically, the dam may have been a response to the drought of 1932–1937 and the generally low water levels on the lake, levels that needed to be raised as a precondition of a successful resort. Aerial photography in 1938 makes it clear that most of the bays were isolated or land-locked, notably the southernmost bay and what is now the Page Road access bay, but also what is now the dam-and-outlet bay, the northwest side of the island and the shore of the island across to the Godin peninsula. (Much of the island also appears to be deforested.) Shallows are very pronounced in all parts of the lake. The drought of the 1930s would seem an obvious explanation. But Twin Lakes is a spring-fed lake, and the extent of drought diminishment of groundwater in Northeast Michigan is not precisely known (drought is measured by surface stream flow). Nevertheless, rainfall may have been a necessary supplement to groundwater and its lack enough to account for the appearance of the lake despite the newly built dam.

Fish and Game

The animal presence around the lake may have been greater than now despite deforestation, the farms nearby, and the discouraging description of the Black Lake Game Reserve in the late 1920s. (Aerial photography shows early-stage second growth to the east and north and farms to the west. There is a thin belt of forest along most but not all of the lakeshore; the Smith Road peninsula and state land to its southeast do not appear to have been cut as of 1938.) As early as 1922, the Black Lake Game Reserve covered nearly five thousand acres of Grant Township and Bearinger Township. (The Cheboygan Game Reserve, bordering on Black Lake, occupied four thousand acres of Waverly Township to the immediate south of Grant Township.) "Cheboygan on the Straits of Mackinac" said that the county had "deer, bear, partridge, pheasants, squirrels, and rabbits."

> There are perhaps more bear in the county than in any other county in the state, more partridge as there have been no ice storms in recent years to kill them off as it has elsewhere, and deer are coming back in goodly numbers. There are lots of rabbits everywhere and many fur-bearing animals.

Bears were indeed plentiful. Ernie Hover[181] recalled going to Bert Reynolds's farm and seeing many bear hides drying on a fence. He also recalled one morning seeing a dozen sets of bear tracks coming off Black Mountain in the light snow cover and at other times tracking bear in the area north of the lodge and west of the Alpena State Road. The back of his Camp Arrowhead trifold brochure showed only the small silhouette of a bear. Sidney Godin, as a part of his duties on Lake Sixteen in the mid-'20s, hunted bear. An article with a photograph of a hunting cabin off the Alpena State Road indicated that Godin never lacked for friends while hunting. (There was no regulation of sport bear hunting until 1925, when the state legislature declared bears to be "game animals." Before then, bears could be killed at any time in any circumstances by any means. Bert Reynolds at some point had a special permit to shoot bears to protect his livestock; protection of livestock was also the rationale for Godin's bear-hunting responsibility. State-wide regulation was abandoned in 1939, but counties could request bear protection.)

Deer were plentiful. (A favorite lake story from a slightly later time is of a doe called Babe that drank from a washtub, invited herself into cabins on South Krouse Road, and moved from diner to diner at the table looking for gifts of food.)[182] There were reported sightings of lynx, a "predator" in the eyes of the Department of Conservation, bobcats, and what may have been a cougar. Present-day fauna would almost all have been present, perhaps in larger numbers in some cases: coyotes, foxes, beavers, river otters, martens, rabbits, squirrels, chipmunks, a variety of frogs, several species of turtles, other amphibians, bald eagles, ospreys, hawks, common terns, belted kingfishers, blue herons, swans, common loons, mergansers, owls, pheasant, grouse, and many smaller woodland birds.[183]

Fish, it seems, were bigger and more plentiful. (This testimony is from fishermen and from individuals looking back to a past thirty to fifty years earlier than when they spoke.) Pike worth talking about were in the thirty- to forty-inch range. In 1957, Leonard Smith received newspaper coverage for catching a forty-inch pike while ice fishing on Twin Lakes. (The minimum legal "keeper" size for pike in most of Michigan is now twenty-four inches; the most common pike catches in Wisconsin are on the order of eighteen to twenty inches; the largest northern pike catch on record is fifty-nine inches in New York.) Bass were at the upper end of the weight range for their species and significantly heavier than the three-pound fish the DNR thinks are the bass most commonly seen by Michigan fishermen now. "You could slip out and get a few bass most anytime you took a notion."

Similarly, bluegill were reported at the upper end of the size scale. "It was nothing to catch a 10″ bluegill way back in the [1960s]. Big fat ones. You didn't have to go out there and use any special thing either.

(Photographs courtesy of Dolores Madden)

You'd see [them] jumpin' all over the lake, breakin' water, feeding, just throw your line out, 2 or 3 feet deep, and catch 'em." (Occasional creel surveys in the 1930s, 1940s, and 1950s offer support for the memories of plentiful bluegill.)[184]

> I can tell you back in 1960 how long it took to catch a mess of fish. About an hour, you could get all you needed . . . bass or bluegills. An hour of an evening, you could get all the fish you want.

(At least some present-day fishermen assert that as far as pike and bass are concerned, nothing has changed in fifty years or more.)

The lake provided ice in winter ("Built an ice house around 1920. Herb Gaynor . . . also had an ice house. Miles from Black Lake came to Gaynor for ice. Cut the blocks 18″ wide, and sometimes it would be 24″ thick.") Winter cedar cutting continued even after larger-scale logging had ceased. "One winter two men cutting cedar had a cabin where the entire front was just a canvas cover." They may have been on the small northern bay near the Page property on which the dam is located. This was nearly a northern bog in earlier days. Still extremely shallow, it has by far the greatest density of cedar stumps of any place on the lake and also has tamaracks, both trees suited to that sort of wet environment. [185]

Tamaracks are plentiful to the west and north of this bay, wherever the shore is low. They are also present on the northwestern shore of the island, which is opposite the bay, and in a few other places on the northern and western shore of the lake. (The GLO field notes so often reported tamaracks that their author resorted to abbreviation, "Tamk.") Pine and hardwood dominate to the east. (The only other abbreviation of the names of trees in the notes was "W. & Y. Pine.")

Certain sections of the present-day shoreline probably resemble the shoreline as it was before lumbering, farming, and residential building altered it. In general, these are areas where the tree line stands back from the shore. Most notably, these areas are along the northernmost edge of the lake and along much of the island littoral. A few other small areas preserve remnants of the original shore. In its earlier form, the Twin Lakes shoreline was much more obviously a wetland than in the last century.

On the other hand, the nature of this shoreline made it the primary area to be filled in, probably beginning with the dam and cabins of the 1930s, continuing at least into the 1950s, and affecting especially Lot 5 in T36 sec. 3 and T37 sec. 34.

---

[153] Archives of Michigan, MS 2011-34, Map of Rivers and Lakes, Cheboygan and Presque Isle Counties; RG 58-017, Public Domain Commission, State Forests — Cheboygan.

154 The presence of "Twin Lakes" and "Twin Lake" just in Cheboygan County can be misleading. A 1902 plat map of Koehler Township shows two lakes east of Indian River that are labeled "Twin Lakes," whereas the plat map of Grant Township for the same year assigns no name to the body of water apparently known even then as Twin Lakes. In its biennial report, 1921–1922, p. 118, in a table of perch fingerlings planted by the Cheboygan Field Station, the Department of Conservation lists "Twin Lakes" five times. Four of these are located "in the vicinity of Cheboygan," and the fifth is in Koehler Township. Given the locational reference and knowing that Twin Lakes, Grant Township, is much larger and much deeper than Twin Lakes, Koehler Township, it would be reasonable to believe that at least one of these plants, perhaps the largest, was in Twin Lakes, Grant Township.

Not so. Although county maps did not list the two Koehler Township lakes separately, the Department of Conservation's stocking records for 1938 listed them as North and South Twin, and residents contacted in a 1945 fishery survey apparently referred to them as North and South Twin. (G. P. Cooper, "A fisheries survey of Twin lakes, near Indian River, Cheboygan County," Fisheries research report 1044; 1946, p. 1). And a letter of February 9, 1945, quoted in the survey, confirms that the thirty thousand perch planted in 1921 were planted in these lakes (pp. 8, 12). Why the Department of Conservation chose "Cheboygan" as a geographical reference point rather than Indian River or Wolverine is a mystery.

The confusion is the greater because there are superficial similarities in the history of the two sets of lakes, the important ones involving land acquisition by the Department of Conservation and dams.

In its 1945–1946 biennial report, the Department of Conservation congratulated itself on the acquisition of lake shoreline (pp. 243–244), specifically the "Twin Lakes property in Cheboygan County." At a glance, the acres and feet of frontage cited could fit Twin Lakes, Grant Township, and the timing approximates the department's acquisition of the east side of the Smith Road peninsula and other shoreline on the east side of the lake. However, the purchase referred to is of the last major pieces of shoreline on Roberts Lake and Cochrane Lake. (The Cheboygan County supervisors requested the change in names in 1950 to honor two Cheboygan County soldiers killed in World War II; *CDT*, July 11, 1950.)

The 1948–1949 biennial report, p. 79, referred to a dam and bridge built at the outlet of Twin Lakes in 1948. Twin Lakes, Grant Township, of course, has a dam of less than certain history and a roadway over the dam at the outlet of the lake. Fortunately, coordinates were provided, which showed conclusively that the Twin Lakes in question was not in Grant Township. (Unfortunately, the coordinates, as stated, showed that the dam had been built in the middle of Mullett Lake.)

Similarly, there exists a "Twin Lake" or "East Twin Lake" north of Carp Lake in Hebron Township that shares a name with the isolated basin of Twin Lakes, Grant Township. This "Twin Lake" has been designated Reswell on recent Cheboygan County maps; its "twin," in Emmet County, is now labeled Dow Lake. (*Changing Environment*, p. 80; http://umbs.lsa.umich.edu/ research/research_sites). As noted in chapter 1, there are twin lakes—North Twin Lake and South Twin Lake—in Northeastern Otsego County just south of the Cheboygan–Otsego county line.

155 Olds Papers, Box 31, Correspondence, Land Descriptions, 1909. While never occupied, Richards's properties included both the isolated lake and the southernmost bay of Twin Lakes, and a trail, now Twin Lakes Road, ran between them.

156 Vogel, p. 147; *Twin Lakes Oral History*, "Chain of Lakes."

157 *Twin Lakes Oral History*, "Chain of Lakes"; letter, Elnora Godfrey to Steve Swan, October 15, 1980; letter, Bonnie George to Steve Swan, September 8, 1981. In 1956, the Department of Conservation, with its propensity to assign directional names to lakes, referred to North Twin Lake and South Twin Lake, names that were never used by local residents. (*CDT*, February 17, 1956.)

158 See the *CDT* passim for examples of the concern with recreational development; Ford and Landers, pp. 4–5. This concern was not entirely new, though the emphasis was *Cheboygan Up-to-Date* (1898) had touted the healthy air and water of the county. One article in the *CDT*, however, was entitled, "CHEBOYGAN COUNTY PROMISES GREATEST FARMING SUCCESS." And "Cheboygan on the Straits" contained text praising the agricultural prospects of the county: its soil was "exceedingly fertile," and the county contained "soil adapted to every purpose." But by then, it was becoming known that a large portion of the local market for farm products had disappeared with the lumber industry and that only a small fragment of land in the county was prime agricultural soil. A later study classified only 5 percent of the land as first grade—"well suited to farming." The remaining lands were divided fairly evenly between second grade ("less well suited to farming") and third grade ("generally not suited for farming," "recommended for forestry not because they will produce better trees—in fact, they will not—but because [they are] unsuitable for agriculture"). (Z. C. Foster et.al., *Soil Survey of Cheboygan County* (Washington, DC: U.S. GPO, 1939), pp. 9–10, 46.)

159 The population schedules of the 1890 census were mostly damaged or destroyed in a fire at the Department of Commerce building in Washington in 1921 and the remainder destroyed in the earlier 1930s.

160 United States Census Bureau, Twelfth Census, 1900. Michigan. The population of Cheboygan County as a whole reported in the 1910 census a decade later was nearly eighteen thousand. That number would not be reached again or exceeded until the 1980 census.

[161] United States Bureau of the Census, Thirteenth Census, 1910. Michigan.

[162] United States Bureau of the Census, Fourteenth Census, 1920. Michigan.

[163] United States Bureau of the Census, Fifteenth Census, 1930. Michigan.

[164] United States Bureau of the Census, Sixteenth Census, 1940. Michigan.

[165] The Pfister-Vogel tannery occupied twenty-five acres and the adjoining grass lands on the edge of Cheboygan, consisted of thirty buildings, employed roughly 150 men, and bought fourteen to fifteen thousand cords of hemlock bark yearly.

State forest acreage increased greatly at two points in the twentieth century: during and immediately after the Depression (reversion for nonpayment of taxes) and 1946 (transfer of state game lands in the northern two-thirds of Michigan to the administrative control of the Forestry Division). William B. Botti and Michael D. Moore, *Michigan's State Forests: A Century of Stewardship* (East Lansing: Michigan State University Press, 2006), p. 75.

[166] Frequently located along meandering bodies of water, the "government lot" or "fractional lot" is often irregular in shape, and its acreage varies from that of regular subdivisions of sections (such as a quarter or quarter-quarter). For its terms, see a glossary of the Public Land Survey.

[167] The confusion was actually greater than indicated in the text. See Appendix 3.

[168] In the interests of simplicity, all future references to township, range, and section will be more economical. Unless otherwise indicated, all references are to T36N, T37N, and R1E. References will drop the "N" and the "R1E." References will be to T36 sec. no. or T37 sec. no.

[169] Olds Papers, Box 5, Agreements — Leonard Freeman 1911.

[170] Rural Property Inventory, Cheboygan County, 1936–1939, Archives of Michigan, RG 94-380. The Rural Property Inventory was established in 1935 by the State Tax Commission in cooperation with the Works Progress Administration. It was intended to employ unskilled, unemployed workers and to produce detailed descriptions of 1.5 million parcels of land in Michigan outside Wayne County.

[171] Library of Michigan, Folio MDoc G1411 P2 M53 1940. It also shows the present-day drainage from Twin Lakes to Owens Creek to the Black River.

[172] See the Department of Conservation's *Biennial Report 1945–1946*, pp. 243–244, celebrating the acquisition of the final acres on "Twin Lakes."

[173] Archives of Michigan, RG 91-37, State Forest Plantation Record, 1910–1941, 1949–1959; Ninth to Thirteenth Biennial Reports, Department of Conservation, 1937–1946.

[174] Jefferson Crawford (1899–1961) was born in Missouri and worked for the Toledo Scale Company in the Flint, Michigan, area. Alberta Crawford was born in Chesaning, Michigan, in 1904. The two married in 1934 and lived in Flint as of 1935. They, with a daughter, are listed as residents in Grant Township in the 1940 census. His occupation is given as salesman. Jointly or severally, they owned and operated the Black River Lunch restaurant on Black River Road and the All Sports Bar at the intersection of Black River Road and Twin Lakes Road.

William Anthony Quesnell, born in Michigan in 1890, is listed in the 1920 census as a farm laborer and in the 1930 and 1940 censuses as a farmer in Grant Township. According to Catherine Ross Page, he was the first of many owners of a grocery at the intersection of Twin Lakes Road and Black River Road (T36N R1E sec. 5), a site that he and Jefferson Crawford appear to have reserved for their own commercial activity (hence the provisions in early deeds on the south end of Twin Lakes that disallowed "a gas station, beer or liquor tavern, restaurant, lunches or grocery business"). Quesnell died in 1972.

Charles Krauhs owned the property he had acquired in 1941 until his death in 1965. The road running by his property is the eponymous but misspelled Krouse Road. The alternative spelling on maps is Krause, a name that appears on many property documents in Cheboygan County but on none in Grant Township.

[175] Lewis C. Cross was a realtor from the Detroit area with family ties to Northeastern Michigan. The couple divorced in 1954. In addition to child support and alimony, Junellda Cross got the family home in Wayne County, property with 1,320 feet of lake frontage on Black Lake, along with the lake home, cottages, and farm buildings, and a 1946 Plymouth four-door sedan. Lewis Cross retained property on Black Lake and received Lot 4 and thirteen acres of Lot 3 on or adjacent to Twin Lakes.

[176] Thomas J. Truscott (1891–1973), born in Canada, as was his wife, Marion V. Truscott (1896–1967), was a railroad supervisor living in Detroit when he had first bought property on Twin Lakes. Gerald N. Truscott (1917–1994) was born in Detroit where he married Doris I. Truscott (d. 2000) and made his living as a painter.

[177] Herbert D. Killian (1893–1982), born in Union County, Pennsylvania, was a farmer and then a Highway Department worker in St. Joseph County, Indiana (South Bend is the major city in the county). He was a summer resident of Cheboygan beginning in 1952 and a permanent resident after 1967. He and his wife, Laura L. Killian (1905–1987), owned and operated

the Silver Birch Resort on Twin Lakes and resided on North Black River Road just west of its intersection with Butler Road. Laura Killian was born in South Bend, Indiana, married Herbert Killian in 1944, and taught for more than forty years in Indiana and in Cheboygan.

[178] Post WWII, Ernie Hover would build cabins near the southernmost of the connected bays, and Herbert Killian would operate the Silver Birch Resort.

[179] *Twin Lakes Oral History,* "Krouse Road." Lyle Page's comments as reported in *Oral History,* made when he was nearing age ninety and had not lived on Twin Lakes for a half century, need to be used with caution. There are errors and statements that cannot be substantiated by documents that should exist. For example, there is no record of a land transaction between Alva Page and M. D. Olds or between Lyle Page and Thomas Truscott. Other comments are vague or ambiguous, such as the date when Alva Page built the dam ("around 1930") and who built the cabins ("Started building cabins around 1935. Had four at one time").

[180] Archives of Michigan, MS 2011-34, Map of Rivers and Lakes, Cheboygan and Presque Isle Counties; 58-017, Public Domain Commission, State Forests — Cheboygan. On the other hand, a county map in the 1902 plat book shows the modern drainage system, as does the map of the county in "Cheboygan on the Straits."

[181] Ernest O. Hover (1908–1997), a carpenter (and fisherman), was born in Missouri. His family roots, however, were in West Central Ohio, as were those of his wife, Helen Daisy Hover (1907–2003). They were married in 1930. Ernie Hover first came to Twin Lakes in 1934 and subsequently purchased land on the southerly bay in 1945 and 1946. He was a discerning collector and a talented woodworker and jewelry maker. Members of his family remain property owners on the lake. See *Oral History,* "Bears", "Wildcats."

[182] *Twin Lakes Oral History,* "Babe."

[183] The first three were prominent on the state's list of predators to be destroyed—"all practical means must be used in order to rapidly eliminate predatory animals in Michigan" (Department of Conservation, *Biennial Report 1921–1922,* p. 327). As of 1935, wolves, subject to bounties for more than a century, were considered extinct in the Northern Lower Peninsula. Beavers and otters were grudgingly excluded from the list as, on balance, more valuable than destructive (and, like fishers, martens, and mink, much diminished in population). "Wildcats" (or "wild cats"), owls, and certain hawks could be killed at any time. Crows and woodchucks carried bounties (*Report,* p. 85). On bears, see *A Review of Bear Management in Michigan* (Lansing: DNR, 2008). Bear population estimates for the Northern Lower Peninsula in 2008 were around two thousand (p. 10, figure 1). In 2014, there were sightings of a young cougar and a bobcat at or near the lake and a raft of river otters in the lake near the island. (In the past, otters have been known to sun themselves on unoccupied docks.) In 2015, tracks seen near a residence were identified as a hybrid wolf-coyote, and in 2015 and subsequent years, there have been several cougar sightings.

[184] *Oral History,* "Fish." The comments are from Herbert "Red" Zattau and Claude Ressler. The largest specific size given for a pike that was caught was thirty-nine inches (Ernie Hover). There is mention of a forty-two-inch pike that was not taken (Red Zattau) and of a pike "almost as long as the boat" that was caught (Gladys Spiekhout).

[185] The quoted statements are those of Lyle Page in *Oral History,* "Krouse Road."

Chapter 6 After the Good War

The United States Air Force and the Air National Guard

Postwar military policy and the early years of the Cold War transformed Michigan into a forward air defense sector, a home base for strategic bombers, and a major military training arena. Beginning in the late 1940s, these changes affected many Northern Michigan communities in the 1950s and thereafter. Already in the 1960s, the island in the middle of Twin Lakes was used as a dry-run gunnery range by tree-top–flying fighter aircraft. In the 1980s, a perfectly reasonable plan—from the viewpoint of the Air National Guard (ANG)—would have created an even more disturbing and dangerous situation (see chapter 7).

On September 18, 1947, the United States Air Force (USAF) appeared as an independent military service. On the same day, the ANG came into existence. Both were products of the National Defense Act of 1947. The ANG units were largely fighter-interceptor squadrons; their primary mission was air defense of the continental United States. USAF leaders were convinced that these reserve units, which had been the aviation component of the prewar National Guard, could not perform adequately in combat without extensive training after they were mobilized; "flying storage" and "state-sponsored flying clubs" were two phrases used to refer to the ANG. Mobilization for the Korean War proved the Air Force right. But the National Guard had had and still had the political clout to protect its stake in aviation, a stake which in Michigan went back to 1917. Reforms of training followed, and the ANG did manage to make some contribution in Korea and to preserve itself as an air reserve distinct from the Air Force Reserve.[186]

From the perspective of the USAF and the ANG, Northern Michigan was both a borderland requiring air defense and a forward area from which to launch strategic bombing sorties. It was also a remote area with large apparently uninhabited swaths of land and open water and therefore suited for air gunnery and bombing training. (In 1955, for example, the USAF, with little notice, designated a "danger area," the eastern end of which lay between Bois Blanc Island and Cheboygan on the mainland and which extended northwestward up the Straits. It was used by F-80 fighters from Kinross AFB as a rocketry range.[187]) In addition, it was a poor region whose towns could be expected to welcome the economic boost of military facilities and an area in which political resistance to USAF or ANG plans was unlikely.

The oldest continuously operating air base in Michigan in 1950 was Selfridge Air Force Base (AFB), near Mt. Clemons. Under different designations and with different missions and diverse tenants, it had functioned since 1917. Briefly in 1919 and then from 1922 until late 1941, Selfridge was the home station of the First Pursuit Group, the first air combat group formed by the Air Service of the American Expeditionary Force in 1918. (The unit was again stationed at Selfridge from 1955 to 1961.) In 1971, the facility would become Selfridge Air National Guard Base (ANGB).[188]

What in 1953 was named Wurtsmith AFB, near the community of Oscoda in Iosco County, began as Loud-Reames Aviation Field in 1923, became Camp Skeel the next year, and was used for winter flying and aerial gunnery for the next twenty years, mostly by planes flying out of Selfridge. With the addition of three concrete runways in 1942, it became Oscoda Army Air Field (AAF), a remote training facility for the unwanted: the pilots of the 332nd Fighter Group—the Tuskegee airmen—and the FAFL, the Free French Air Force. It became a permanent installation in 1951 as an air defense command (ADC) alert-status and training base, was subsequently a strategic air command (SAC) and then an air combat command (ACC) base before closing in 1993.[189]

Wurtsmith is the source of perfluorinated chemicals (PFCs) that, twenty years after its closure, caused authorities to advise a number of people living in Oscoda to stop drinking and cooking with water from their wells and to advise everyone to avoid eating any fish from nearby Clark's Marsh and to consume only migratory fish caught in the lower Au Sable River. The PFCs were elements in foams used in fire-fighting training. In addition, trichloroethylene (TCE), used to clean jet engine parts, was found in the base's water system and in the surrounding community at levels astronomically higher than prescribed in the federal Safe Drinking Water Act.

The Alpena County Regional Airport, which contains the Alpena ANGB (or Phelps Collins ANGB) and the Alpena Combat Readiness Training Center (CRTC), originated as Phelps Collins Field, a strip built on privately donated land in a flat open area that had been used by early aircraft as a dirt field. The site, given to Michigan in 1931 to be a state-owned field, was surveyed by the Army Corps of Engineers and subsequently cleared and prepared by the WPA. The first military use of the field was by the First Pursuit Group from Selfridge in the late 1930s as a supplement to air gunnery at Oscoda. In 1940 and 1941, the group used Phelps Collins to train pilots in the new all-metal fighter aircraft built by Seversky, Curtiss, and Lockheed. In 1942 and 1943, three concrete runways were added, as at Oscoda, along with greatly expanded personnel facilities, and the field became the Alpena AAF. Redesignated the Alpena Army Air Base (AAB), in 1944, its missions were training, air defense of the locks at Sault Ste. Marie, and maintenance, modification, and overhaul of B-24 Liberators built by Ford at Willow Run before their overseas deployment. Military surplus at the end of the war, the base became the Alpena County Regional Airport. By 1954, however, the regional airport was a joint-use facility housing both ANG facilities and an ADC radar station detached from Wurtsmith.

Alpena AAF

The present-day Alpena CRTC ("your destination of choice for full-spectrum operations and four-season joint training") boasts the largest airspace east of the Mississippi River, 147,000 acres for ground maneuver units, and the Grayling Air-to-Ground Range.

Kellogg AAB, now W. R. Kellogg Regional Airport and the Battle Creek ANGB, was a troop carrier command base in World War II. Adjoining Fort Custer trained over three hundred thousand infantrymen during the war and another seventeen thousand in the Korean War and has remained a heavily used training center.

The facility best known as Kincheloe AFB, twenty miles south of Sault Ste. Marie, originated as Kinross Auxiliary Field in 1941–1942, a subordinate base of the Army Air Transport Command at the Alpena AAF. Its missions were to defend the locks at Sault Ste. Marie and to refuel aircraft flying to Alaska. It was quickly deactivated in 1945 and the airfield leased to the city of Sault Ste. Marie to be used as a civilian airport.

Army troops returned in 1950, and in 1952, Kinross was transferred to the control of the USAF as Kinross AFB. It was to be used as a fighter-interceptor base for the ADC to defend the Sault locks and the Upper Great Lakes. In 1958, the main runway was greatly extended to accommodate SAC bombers and tankers. After two more years of construction, SAC aircraft deployed to what, in 1959, had been renamed Kincheloe AFB. In 1960, a long-range anti-aircraft missile squadron was installed northwest of the base, under the command of the ADC at Kincheloe. Threatened with closure as early as 1971, the base was deactivated in 1977.

Almost twenty years later, the Army Corps of Engineers had to construct a new well house and two new wells in 1999 after TCEs were discovered in nearby municipal wells. Long-term monitoring of groundwater wells has followed. It also removed 150 tons of soil and tar material from the tar spill area at one end of the main runway, searched for possibly buried rocket propellant sticks, and attempted to remove volatile compounds from the soil of a firefighting training area.

K. I. Sawyer AFB, near Marquette in the Upper Peninsula, originated in the early 1940s as a civilian field, becoming a joint civilian and military installation only in 1956 and an exclusively military installation in 1959. Initially an ADC installation, it became, more famously, a SAC base before being decommissioned in 1995.

What eventually was named the Kalkaska AFB was planned by the USAF in 1954 as an ADC fighter-interceptor base to be built in Benzie County, near Traverse City. The two sites favored by the USAF were each within less than ten miles of the Interlochen Music Camp, which would be ill served by the deafening scream of fighter-interceptors scrambling at full throttle. The proposal was fought by Third District Congressman Paul W. Shafer, a longtime member of the House Military Affairs Committee. Subsequently, the location was changed to land near Cadillac in Wexford County and then to a site near Kalkaska, where construction actually began and the base received its name in December 1955. Soon after, the site was again moved, to Manistee County this time, and then the entire project was abandoned.[190]

The one other military base to play a role in the postwar history of Northern Michigan was Camp Grayling, the largest National Guard training facility in the United States. Sprawling over 147,000 acres in Crawford, Kalkaska, and Otsego Counties, Camp Grayling began in 1913 with a land grant of 13,000 acres for a permanent military training site (and game refuge and forest reserve) from a local lumber baron. (The grant carefully preserved his logging rights for five years. The next year, he founded the Grayling Fish Hatchery in a vain effort to restore Michigan grayling, decimated by the habitat destruction of logging, to the Au Sable River.) The camp, then called Camp Ferris, first trained troops in 1914.

In 1927, what is now McNamara Field, a joint-use military and civil aviation airfield northwest of Grayling itself, began as a field just barely cleared of the residue of logging. In World War II, it was expanded to become the Grayling AAF. Artillery began "long range shooting in the area east of Frederic," north of the camp, in or after 1935. (The small community of Frederic is ten miles northwest of Grayling.) In 1949, Camp Grayling began to expand significantly with the transfer of over fifty thousand acres from the Department of Conservation. Much of the expansion was buildings and infrastructure. But in the summer of 1950, artillery practice was to be conducted north of the road connecting Frederic and Lovells. (The very small community of Lovells is roughly twenty miles northeast of Grayling.) "At the same time, there will be tank firing south of the area," and "the Air Forces will use the area as an air-to-ground target range at varying times during the encampment." The last of these became the issue that affected Twin Lakes.[191]

In early 1953, the air force announced that it might shift the ANG center at Grayling to Alpena. A week earlier, the state representative for Alpena, Gerald W. Graves, had introduced a resolution in the state House of Representatives that a jet training base be established at Alpena. While Maj. Gen. Earl Ricks, the deputy chief for the National Guard Bureau, spoke of the transfer as tentative, Graves said that guard officials had told him that the center for jet aircraft would have to be located at Alpena "and no place else." The issue appears to have been the costs of expanding WWII airfields to accommodate jet aircraft. Grayling would require the purchase of land and construction of a new runway. The runways at Alpena could be extended without the purchase of land, and the construction of a new runway would not be required. Ricks also noted that Alpena was nearer than Grayling to the gunnery ranges over the Great Lakes and had more hangar and aircraft parking facilities. The move to Alpena and the attitude of the ANG toward the land and its residents eventually spelled trouble for Twin Lakes.

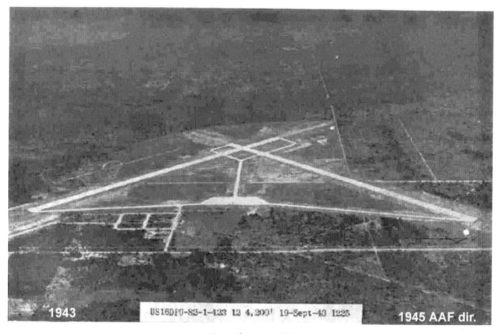

Grayling AAF

The Department of Conservation

The Department of Conservation seems to have paid little attention to Cheboygan Twin Lakes in the decades after World War I and, beneficially or not, continued to ignore the lake after World War II. The exceptions to this statement are the campgrounds, some creel surveys, and one episode of fish planting.

At the state level, it pursued policies of acquiring water frontage to increase public access to lakes and streams ("one of the most popular programs of the Department of Conservation"), building dams, and propagating "preferred" fish. The last was described in the 1959–1960 biennial report as "chemical treatment of lakes to remove all fish, corrective stocking, and improvement of northern pike spawning habitat became major tools for improvement." All three policies were tied to serving the perceived growth of interest in fishing. Eventually, Twin Lakes would be caught up in at least some of the department's commitments.

The department did stock the isolated lake with bass and bluegill in 1956 after a major fish kill resulting from deep snow coverage of the lake. The first record of "fish management" activity on Twin Lakes by the DNR, however, is a fish survey in 1968, the first of what would be decennial surveys.

The Black Mountain Ski Area — 1956–1988

There were few ski areas in Northern Michigan before World War II. Only three (near Alpena, Cadillac, and Petoskey) had a tow. Boyne Mountain opened in 1947. A cluster of ski areas near Gaylord also appeared at about the same time. Griswold Mountain, just north of Indian River off US-27, opened at the beginning of the 1950s. But the mid- and late 1950s saw a wave of openings in Northeast Michigan, of which the Black Mountain Ski Area was one.[192]

In July 1956, the Department of Conservation approved plans to establish the Black Mountain Ski Area "to serve the winter sports interests of Rogers City, Onaway, and Cheboygan." The newly formed Bi-County Winter Sports Association (BCWSA) was authorized to use a 360-acre tract in T36 secs. 1 and 12, just east and south of Twin Lakes. Dr. Carl F. Rauch of Cheboygan, physician and surgeon and president of the association, announced on August 1 that three ski runs and a tow had been staked out a few days earlier and that the next day, the group would begin to raise $25,000 by selling non-interest-bearing bonds priced at $100.[193]

Enthusiasm about the prospects of Black Mountain ran high. Rauch, president of the Caberfae Ski Club in 1945–1946, suggested that in a few years, it might become another Caberfae, which, the *Tribune* noted, had three to four thousand skiers a weekend. The manager of Caberfae, looking at Black Mountain, said it might become the fifth best ski area in Michigan.

Three brushing bees in September, volunteer labor in what was understood to be a community project, cleared a road into the ski area, the ski tow, the parking lot, and the site for a shelter house. The Grant Township board, recognizing "what a fine community endeavor this ski project is," allocated $500 (an extraordinary amount for the township) to brushing the area to speed the effort. The *Tribune* managed to dress up the brushing bees in the rhetoric and themes of turn-of-the-century histories of settlement: "men, women, and children" came to the bees "to attack the wilderness which is Black Mountain, to wrest from it an additional source of economic security for the entire area upon completion."[194]

While the BCWSA was a nonprofit entity, there was a strong economic motivation in building the ski area. A subheadline in the *Tribune* read, "EXPECTED TO BE FINE ECONOMIC BOOST." The paper reported that the Caberfae ski facility the previous winter took in $172,000 in tow fees and that skiers who came to Cadillac spent $500,000. Similarly, the Gaylord ski area reported $156,000 in tow fees and that skiers spent on average $41 each in Gaylord. It was speculated that the area would lose some summer tourists as a result of the rerouting of US-27 and that the Black Mountain project would more than make up that loss.[195]

In a remarkable demonstration of planning, organization, and volunteerism, the BCWSA, in a bit over four months, created a ski area where before there had been only forest. By mid-October, four runs were nearing completion, and two tows and the "lodge" (a warming house with certain facilities) were under construction. Union carpenters donated their labor to build the lodge, and a construction company provided the necessary power tools. Just before Thanksgiving, water was hit at 330 feet to supply the warming house; the following week, one tow was tested, and a week later, a second was installed. The opening and dedication were set for the weekend of December 21–22, 1956, coincident with "the REA" (a local nickname of the Presque Isle Electric Cooperative) beginning to set poles to bring in power.

Ironically, there was no skiing at the opening for lack of adequate snow. The New Year's weekend of 1957 was the first weekend of actual skiing on Black Mountain. Several weeks earlier, the dedication had been postponed until January 26 in order that members of Nick's Crusaders, contributors to BCWSA, could come north from Detroit. (They made an additional contribution at the dedication.) The dedication, complete with a Black Mountain Snow Queen, was covered extensively by the *Tribune*, which several weeks earlier had devoted a front page to the ski area, with large photographs running from top to bottom down the middle of the paper.[196]

The numbers at the Black Mountain Ski Area were not as impressive in its first year as those at Caberfae and Gaylord. The board of directors reported $4614.00 in receipts, while operational costs were $1,876.46. Bond sales slightly exceeded the target. Nevertheless, by early September 1957, clearing had begun for three new runs, four new tow paths, and an enlarged beginners' area. These were part of a $21,000 expansion, to be financed by further sale of bonds, to make the area competitive with other major ski areas.

The largest expenditures for the upcoming season were to be six permanent electric tow units, four new runs, and a threefold increase in the size of the beginners' area. Marketing was not ignored. Edward J. Slezak, a professor of physical education at the University of Michigan and the owner of the Michakewa Lodge on Long Lake, took on responsibility as the downstate promotional director of Cheboygan-area resort interests and promised to open the lodge each weekend of the ski season for university groups of thirty to fifty people.[197]

By mid-1959, there were clear signs of trouble. A year earlier, Rauch had appealed for men to work at the ski area "because of an emergency condition." Grass had been planted on the runs, but erosion was beginning before the seed could grow. Hay, of which the BCWSA had twenty tons, needed to be spread to protect the ground. Arguably, it should have been known that steep runs, dropping an advertised two hundred feet and stripped of their vegetation, on a mound of sand and gravel would erode and could not be held together by grass, even if it could be successfully planted. If nothing else, the first camp ground on Twin Lakes should have been an object lesson. The DNR posts signs in the old ski area, now a scramble area, limiting the size of vehicles allowed because of "steep slopes and loose soil."[198]

In June 1959, bondholders agreed to extend the due date of their bonds five years in order that the board of directors could buy a mechanical lift to replace the rope tows. Total income for 1959 was $5,295, whereas in 1958, it had been $6,024. Tow fees from nonmembers had decreased, as had overall patronage.

These figures provided the rationale for the new lift. In July, the board of directors voted to raise $20,000 at 6 percent interest to construct the mechanical lift. It also voted to negotiate a land transfer with the Department of Conservation that would be needed for the lift and new ski runs. In February 1960, the board of directors voted to install a T-bar lift (and buy land to swap) at a cost of $25,000: "[W]e have found this season that we cannot be very successful in attracting groups so long as we have only rope tows." Additionally, the board planned to cut and clear to reorganize the layout of the ski area and provide an 1,800-foot run with 200 feet of vertical drop. The land transfer took place in 1961, when the state received the Fisher property in Duncan Bay, recently bought by the BCWSA and needed by the state for a new Cheboygan state park, in exchange for 125 acres of land on Black Mountain on which the ski area was located. Nevertheless, the BCWSA was losing the competition.[199]

In the seasons of 1960 and 1961, the *Tribune* continued its heavy coverage of the ski area and its sponsorship for the fifth year of a "free ski school" on Wednesday evenings, even printing the names of the eighty enrollees in 1960. The new Detroit-based owners of Camp Walden (formerly Camp Michakewa for

Girls) on Long Lake brought skiers from the Ann Arbor–Detroit area north to ski at Black Mountain and Boyne Mountain. Several Central United States Ski Association–sanctioned meets were held, the number of skiers modest and the winners mostly local skiers.[200]

The official county map issued by the Cheboygan County Commissioners in 1967 described the ski area as "400-acre areas [sic] with diversified ski runs. 8 slopes, 6 tows, and a T-bar lift. Certified instructors — individuals — groups. Ski lodge — food — rest room facilities." But by this date, the run had almost certainly ceased to operate. Despite early heavy snow and the usual coverage anticipating the winter season, there was no mention of Black Mountain in the December 1964 editions of the *CDT*. (But there was coverage of a meeting of the Cheboygan Winter Sports Club in which there was discussion of developing a hill near Cheboygan, already used by the high-school ski team as a ski slope.) In 1966, the BCWSA conveyed the property to the Black Mountain Recreation Corporation, and at the end of 1988, the corporation conveyed it to the State of Michigan. A 1994 plat shows the land as owned by the Real Estate Division of the DNR.

The Flood from the South: Parcelization and Seasonal Homes

The process of parceling out the shoreline areas of Twin Lakes had begun as early as 1940. But at the beginning of the 1950s, Twin Lakes remained sparsely populated and intensely quiet. So much so that on two occasions in mid-May 1951, Company C, 125th Infantry, National Guard from Cheboygan held nighttime maneuvers near Twin Lakes and Black Mountain.[201]

Krouse Road near Twin Lakes Road, November 1947
(Photograph courtesy of Dolores Madden)

But the region of which it was part was being transformed. As of 1961, only one in six of new "REA Customers" was a farmer. The explanation was an explosive growth of vacation homes and cabins. PIEC had the highest percentage of seasonal consumers in Michigan, about 60 percent. The highest peak demand for electricity in the Presque Isle system "is the night before deer hunting season opens" (The first easements granted PIEC on Twin Lakes came on the south side in 1972 and 1973).[202]

By 1976, 49 percent of households in Cheboygan and Emmet Counties were second-home owners, 31 percent year-round residents, and 20 percent vacationers. The years 1965–1974 was a period of concentrated second-home purchases (52 percent of such properties) and also of movement into year-round residences (76 percent of such properties). (The population of Cheboygan County increased 13.9 percent and of Emmet County 15.3 percent between 1960 and 1970.) Of the second homes, only 22 percent of the properties had been bought in or before 1954.[203]

By 1990, over half of the homes in Cheboygan County (and Presque Isle County as well) were seasonal. Typically, these homes were used approximately eighty-five days a year, with summer use accounting for roughly 60 percent of the total annual usage. Of the seasonal home owners, just over a third had incomes of $30,000–$60,000, and a quarter each had incomes of $60,000–$100,000 and $100,000 or more. (Median household income in the United States was $8,486 in 1970, $16,841 in 1980, and $30,056 in 1990. Except for Ohio in 1990, median household incomes in these years in Michigan and Ohio were 3 to 18 percent higher than the figures for the nation.) Forty-one percent were retired, 40 percent were not retired and did not plan to retire, and the rest planned to retire in a near future. Twenty-nine percent thought it likely or very likely they would convert their seasonal home into a permanent home, 18 percent thought there was a small chance they would convert their seasonal home into a permanent home, and 53 percent thought it unlikely.[204]

What brought people to the area? As part of its study of the attitudes and values of lakeshore property owners, the Gannon-Paddock report of 1972–1974 asked full-time and seasonal residents in Cheboygan, Presque Isle, Emmet, and Charlevoix Counties several questions bearing on that subject. Of those responding to the study's questionnaire in Cheboygan County, 31 percent were year-round residents, 51 percent were second-home owners, and 18 percent were vacationers (N=501). In Presque Isle County, the number of respondents was far smaller, the first and second percentages were significantly lower, and the percentage of vacationers was substantially higher (N=39). Of the second-home owners and vacationers in Cheboygan County, nearly three-quarters had their primary residence in Michigan, and of these far and away, the largest percentages came from Wayne, Oakland, or Macomb Counties in the southeast. Outside Michigan, Ohio accounted for the largest percentage (12 percent). The percentages were much the same in Presque Isle County, though Michigan and Wayne County were even more heavily represented.[205]

Seven percent or less of second-home owners, year-round residents, or vacationers in the overall study area wanted to see a great deal of development in the future; the vast majority (roughly 70 percent in each case) desired only some or a little development. Of over two thousand opinions given in response to the question "[W]hat do you like about your being here in this part of northern Michigan?" nearly a quarter, by far the largest percentage, involved peace, quiet, and solitude. The water and lakes, the natural setting, and the recreational opportunities each accounted for roughly 12 percent, the climate/weather and the clean air/water for smaller percentages. Familiarity with the area and the people/friends and family brought up the rear.[206]

By and large, Twin Lakes conformed to these patterns. Between 1960 and 1975, there were roughly sixty new property owners on the lake. Unlike earlier land transfers, these properties were mostly parcels. (Studies of Twin Lakes in the early to mid-1970s variously estimated that there were fifty "widely scattered cottages," sixty-eight "dwelling units," eighty-four "dwelling units," and ninety-eight "households" on the lake.) A departure of degree from the norms was that, beginning with Ernie Hover in the 1930s, Ohio has accounted for an unusual number of seasonal and year-round residents of the lake. For example, of the first nine officers of the CTLA (1978–1980), four came from Ohio. As well, the southernmost portion of Krouse Road acquired nicknames that recognized the high incidence of Ohioans settled there. While no nicknames have survived, there was a similar grouping of new residents on Reynolds Road, in this case from Northwest Indiana, not Ohio. The first president of the CTLA came from this group.

In 1960, the major landowners on Twin Lakes were Clyde H. Page, H. D. Killian, Jefferson and Alberta Crawford, Leonard Smith, the State of Michigan, Jerome B. Galloway, Harry G. Spiekhout, and Thomas J. Truscott. Seven years later, the only changes were the addition of Richard M. Curtis and Francis J. Sawyer.[207]

The acreages of Page and Killian had been owned previously by Embury-Martin Lumber Company. The Page property has remained intact, but Killian had already begun to parcel out shoreline. Crawford owned three unconnected allotments of land—between Reynolds Road and Smith Road (both roads existed long before 1960), where Crawford Lane is now found; at the southwestern end of the lake, entirely surrounded on the land side by state forest; and along Krouse Road, northward from the Galloway property and including the still undeveloped northern shore of the Big Bay and the small Northern Bay.

The Curtis property on the east side of the lake had been acquired from George Nimmo in 1954; Nimmo had bought the property from Jefferson Crawford in 1949. Jerome Galloway owned a strip of land along the shoreline on the southeast side of the lake, properties bought from Sophia Curtis Blair and Jefferson Crawford between 1948 and 1953. (Blair had acquired her property from Crawford in 1945.)

Harry Spiekhout owned the land that makes up Godin Circle, essentially the old Hulbert patent. F. J. Sawyer bought property in T37 sec. 35 in 1959, 1960, and 1966 from Jefferson Crawford and then Alberta Crawford. (He completed three other purchases in the same section with Alberta Crawford in the next ten years. Most of these transactions are mislabeled "36.35" in the records.)

Much of the state land lay to the north, east, and south of the lake. But it also included the land still owned and logged by the state along Twin Lakes Road from Reynolds Road to and around the south end of the lake as well as the land that would be the Smith Road campground.

The Gannon-Paddock study estimated there to be sixty-eight "dwelling units" on Twin Lakes. (At another point, its estimate is eighty-four.) By contrast, the larger lakes had as many as fifteen times that number: Mullett, 1,043; Burt, 715; and Black, 609. Paradise (Carp) Lake, Crooked Lake, and Douglas Lake, while not approaching the numbers of the large lakes, nevertheless had many more housing units than Twin Lakes. Nearby Long Lake, with ninety-one units but nearly twice the size of Twin Lakes, and more distant Pickerel Lake, with nearly twice the housing but five times the surface area, arguably had comparable densities.[208]

(Some of these "dwelling units" would have been rental cabins. Truscott seems to have rented the cabins built by the Pages; eventually, these became residential properties. Ernie Hover built Camp Arrowhead, a small number of cabins on both sides of Krouse Road, two of which still stand as parts of larger properties. Like Alva Page, he also built and rented boats; his daughter painted the boats. Herbert Killian had six rental cabins spaced along the western shore of the lake on what had been the Reynolds property; all have been removed and replaced by homes.)

Ernie Hover (Photograph courtesy of Jerry Beehler)

A study done in 1974–1975 and published in 1978 calculated the density of shoreline development and "motorboat" ownership. Twin Lakes is shown with 14.1 kilometers of shoreline and an estimated 98 households and therefore a density of 6.9 households per kilometer, far and away the lowest of the lakes listed. The only other lakes with densities below 10 households per kilometer (between 8.4 and 9.9) were Long, Munro, and Douglas. The densities on Black and Mullett were four times that on Twin Lakes, and Paradise (Carp) Lake, a lake with a shoreline length nearly identical (14.3 kilometers) to that of Twin Lakes, had five and a half times the density. Ironically, Twin Lakes had the highest number of motorboats per hectare of surface water area, barring only Lance Lake. The authors concluded therefore that Lance and Twin Lakes were the "most heavily used," Burt, Black, and Mullett the least used. In fact, this conclusion confuses ownership per hectare and use and fails to distinguish between different kinds and uses of "motorboats."[209]

In these years, especially from the early 1960s through the early 1970s, people arrived who would soon play important roles in the future of the lake, among them Killian, Newland, Godfrey, Seconsky, Kraatz, Ressler, Westervelt, Grim, Boyea, Griewahn, and King. A lesser sign of change in the nature of the lake was the arrival of its first pontoon boat in the late 1960s. (The most common watercraft on the lake today are pontoon boats, small aluminum fishing boats, kayaks, and canoes.)

That change was also signaled by purchases of relatively large properties, apparently for purposes of investment or, in some cases, protection, and by the first efforts at development oddly delayed, as if developers did not have their ears to the ground. Much of both stemmed from the disgorgement of land held by Alberta Crawford in T36 sec. 2 and T37 sec. 34.

In April 1973, John Stuart of Bridgeport bought from Crawford over six hundred feet of shoreline property in T37 sec. 34 for just over $15,000. In 2000, he would sell it for more than ten times that figure. From 1959 through 1977, Francis J. Sawyer brought a total of roughly thirty acres in T37 sec. 35 from the Crawfords. Louis and Paul Spens, in the form of Spens Realty & Construction Co. of Ocqueoc, were very active. In 1976 and 1977, they had over twenty-five acres of shoreline property surveyed in T36 sec. 2. In 1976, they bought substantial property in Government Lot 2, T36 sec. 2, from Richard Curtis for $19,000. The next year, they entered a land contract with Alberta Crawford to buy two parcels, totaling nearly twenty-five acres for $21,800. And in 1978, they bought another substantial chunk of shoreline property from Crawford. In the same years, they sold two properties, totaling over twenty-five acres, to Frederick Janz and Raymond Carlson. (Janz sold the property to its current owners in 1989, Carlson in 1995.) Spens remained a property owner in T37 sec. 34 into the mid-1980s and, in a minor way, even into the mid-1990s.

In 2000, Secluded Land Company of De Soto, Wisconsin, planned development on both Twin Lakes and the Black River (Black River Shores, off Twin Lakes Road). In April of that year, the company bought the Stuart property (Government Lot 2, T37 sec. 34) with its 660 feet of shoreline. It then discovered that Twin Lakes was not a no-wake lake and, within a matter of months, sold off the property in parcels. (Much of the Black River is a no-wake zone.)

One of the buyers was Melvin O'Connor Jr. O'Connor had acquired land in T37 sec. 34 from three sellers between 1992 and 1994, two of the properties linked to the Crawfords and the third to the Truscotts. He acquired more in 2001 from two sellers; both these properties had been owned previously by Spens. Operating since 2005 as OC Land Development LLC, he has laid out and provided infrastructure for Loon Nest Estates Condominium.

This condominium, occupying parts of Government Lots 2 and 3 and currently marketing four shoreline and five "lake view" (back lot) properties averaging just over 0.65 acres, is a departure from previous building on Twin Lakes. The overall area of this phase is over seven acres, and the "proposed future development area" is nearly twenty-nine acres.

The Lodge

One of the stories of the lake, its source long unknown, was that "at one time in the 1940[s] to mid-'50s at the present site of Chateau Lodge [now the Black Mountain Lodge] was a very private lodge and even a private airstrip for its owners. The airstrip is now grown over, adjacent to the back entrance to the Chateau Lodge's parking area." The tale sometimes involves hints of a retreat for Detroit hoodlums of the era, as if it were a latter-day version of Al Capone's hideout. Little of this can be documented or seems likely.

The land had been in several hands, including Embury-Martin Lumber Company and George D. Richards, before it was acquired by Jefferson Crawford in 1939. Aerial photographs in 1938 show no clearing and no structure on or near what became the Chateau property. The area where the runway was supposed to exist is fairly heavily treed, more so than adjoining land, and would not have served well as even an emergency landing spot. What does show is a trail that runs off Twin Lakes Road, where it curves near the Chateau down along the shore of the isolated lake and two cleared areas on the shore, both probably associated with the first campground.

The Crawfords transferred the property by warranty deed to Ednor Corporation in early 1952. Ednor Corporation was incorporated in July 1951 with a Southfield, Michigan, business address. Its principals appear to have been Edward J. Dunn and Norbert J. Stockton. A 1960 plat book shows the property as owned by E. J. Dunn. (Dunn owned Steel Erection Fabricators Inc. and Congress Steel Products Inc. in the Detroit area. The "resident agent" for the latter was Richard W. Look, also the agent for Ednor Corporation. The steel products corporation was dissolved in 1978.) Subsequent plat books of the 1960s and 1970s list the ownership as Ednor Corporation. In these decades, the property appears to have functioned as a private lodge, but for exactly what purposes is unknown. (The lodge, Michakewa, which was to have served skiers on Black Mountain in the 1950s and 1960s, was on Long Lake.) A longtime resident of the lake indicated that attendance at the lodge was by invitation only; he was surprised to have been once invited.

The land adjacent to the Lodge property and on the eastern slope of the isolated lake was acquired by Mark F. Thompson of Cheboygan and his wife, Grace, from Jefferson Crawford in 1946 and sold by his wife's estate to Arlo Smith in 1964 and 1965. Smith and Ednor Corporation exchanged bits of land in 1968, Ednor receiving the west one hundred feet of the southeast quarter of the northeast quarter of sec. 2 and Smith securing "water's edge" property for $500.

In 1976, Dunn granted an easement to PIEC, and later, Ednor Corporation, which dissolved in mid-1979, sold the property to D & P Co., Stockton signing for Ednor and Dunn appearing as a copartner in D & P. In plat books issued in the 1980s; however, N. J. Stockton is shown as owner.

In the 1950s or very early 1960s, a structure looking much like a modernist design of the era was built. It still stands as the dining room of the lodge, though integration into the larger structure has erased some of its modernist edges. An aerial photograph from 1963 shows clearing on the site of the lodge and, not altogether clearly, a fairly large structure. It also shows clearing across Twin Lakes Road down the slope to the isolated lake. It does not show a landing field. Much of the trail along the shore of the lake and the clearings on the shore had been erased in the course of twenty-five years.

At some point in the mid- to later 1960s, an explosion occurred on the property, killing an adult female, injuring at least three children, and doing significant structural damage to "the first dwelling." The apparent cause was an accumulation of gas in a basement used as a kitchen, combined with cigarette smoking. Ernie Hover and Red Zattau heard the explosion and rushed to the scene. Subsequently, state police arrived. The episode is obscure because the only evidence is the brief statements of Hover and Zattau made more than twenty years after the event, along with the testimony of two other persons who heard the explosion but were not otherwise witnesses. The state police do not have or cannot find an incident report in its records, and no newspaper appears to have reported the event.[210]

In the early to mid-1980s, Dunn, then owner of Chateau Inc., had repeated tax liens laid on by the state treasurer. In 1986, Donald L. Miles is listed as president of Chateau Lodge Inc., a corporation formed in late 1983. At this point, the property is described as a "motel, lodge, restaurant, and lounge." (Miles also owned a property on the northern end of Black Lake.) A few years later, the *Detroit News* devoted an article to the lodge.

> Chateau Lodge is owned by Donald Miles of Farmington Hills, who is in the automotive paint business. The lodge is small. There are seven double rooms with two large beds, several overlooking the lake, and there is a suite with three bedrooms and two bathrooms plus a large common room with fireplace. There is also a dormitory room that sleeps nine persons.

In 1995, the property was bought and the lodge-restaurant run by Michael and Rose Telgheder as Chateau North. In 2008, the property was again bought, this time by Ross and Paula Bates, and operated as Black Mountain Lodge.[211] They significantly expanded and renovated the structure. At the same time, the Telgheders developed Chateau Woods, a condominium behind the lodge.[212] The lodge property is once again listed for sale (2016).

---

[186] The official historical statement of the ANG regarding the Korean War is the following.

The Korean War was a turning point for the Air Guard. Some 45,000 Air Guardsmen, 80 percent of the force, were mobilized. That call-up exposed the weaknesses of all U.S. military reserve programs, including the ANG. Sixty-six of the Air Guard's ninety-two flying squadrons, along with numerous support units, were mobilized. Once in federal service, they proved to be unprepared for combat. Many key Air Guardsmen were used as fillers elsewhere in the Air Force. It took three to six months for some ANG units to become combat ready. Some never did. Eventually, they made substantial contributions to the war effort and the Air Force's global buildup. Largely as a result of the Korean War experience, senior ANG and Air Force leaders became seriously committed to building the Air Guard as an effective reserve component. (http://www.ang.af.mil/history/heritage.asp)

[187] *CDT*, March 21, 1955.

[188] Information about military bases in Michigan is scattered in bits and pieces on the internet (as is information concerning units and aircraft). But there is no single source, electronic or print, that is comprehensive.

Selfridge and Alpena, like Wurtsmith and Kinchloe, have contaminated water supplies. In the first two cases, the contamination is PFAS (per and poly fluorinated alkyl substances) in drinking water at five to eight times the safe level.

[189] Capt. Burt E. Skeel commanded the Twenty-Seventh Pursuit Squadron of the First Pursuit Group at Selfridge. A winner of the Mitchell Trophy air race in 1923, he died as he prepared for the Pulitzer Trophy race of 1924 when the wings of his Curtiss CR racing aircraft fell away from the fuselage.

His death was cited by the lead defense attorney in the Billy Mitchell court martial in 1925 as an example of the truth of Colonel Mitchell's assertion that "the lives of the airmen are being used merely as pawns" by the War Department and Navy Department leaderships. "Both of those officers [Skeel and Alexander Pearson, holder of the world speed record in 1923] were killed in dilapidated racing airplanes which were not constructed for the race for which they were entered but were constructed for a race two years previous. These ships broke in the air because they were not strong enough to stand the strain" (*NYT*, November 10, 1925).

In the same trial, then major Carl Spaatz testified that "the one pursuit squadron on the Government's service [the First Pursuit Group]" had difficulties "in finding a suitable spot for gunnery practice." In time, a place was found in Michigan that the Air Service could lease for one dollar—"the War Department was loath to let go the dollar." Eventually, it did (*NYT*, November 10, 1925).

Spaatz was subsequently the commander of the Eighth Air Force (1942–1944), commander of Strategic Air Forces in Europe (1944–1945), and the first chief of staff of the new USAF (1947–1948).

[190] *CDT*, June 22, 1954, August 7, 1954, August 12, 1954, March 14, 1955, July 29, 1955.

[191] For Camp Grayling, see Jean Gothro, "The Story of Camp Grayling," typescript, 1949.

[192] In October 1956, the East Michigan Sports Council announced that with the opening of three new winter sports ski parks in the coming winter, the area now had seventeen winter sports parks. That winter Michigan as a whole had fifty-nine major winter sports areas. *CDT*, October 1, 1956, January 8,1957.

[193] *CDT*, August 1, 1956.

[194] *CDT*, September 21,1956, September 1, 1956.

[195] *CDT*, September 17, 1956.

[196] *CDT*, October 12, 1956, November 24, 1956, December 4, 1956, December 13, 1956, December 15, 1956, December 20, 1956, December 21, 1956, December 24, 1956, December 31, 1956, January 2, 1957, January 7, 1957, January 26, 1957.

[197] *CDT*, September 5,1957, September 6, 1957.

[198] *CDT*, May 16, 1958.

[199] *CDT*, June 13,1959, July 16, 1959, February 20, 1960, January 27, 1961.

[200] *CDT*, January 4, 1960, January 5, 1960, January 6, 1960, January 7, 1960, January 21, 1960, January 25, 1960, January 28, 1960, February 4, 1960, February 8, 1960, February 15, 1960, January 27, 1961, February 11, 1961, February 15, 1961.

[201] *CDT*, May 14, 1951, May 28, 1951.

[202] Kluge, p. 148.

[203] Robert W. Marrans et al. *Waterfront living: A report on permanent and seasonal residents in northern Michigan* (Urban environmental research program, Survey Research Center, Institute for Social Research, the University of Michigan, Ann Arbor: The Institute, 1976).

[204] Daniel J. Stynes, JiaJia Zheng, and Susan I. Stewart, *Seasonal Homes and Natural Resources: Patterns of Use and Impact in Michigan*, General Technical Report NC-194 (St. Paul, MN: U.S. Dept. of Agriculture, Forest Service, North Central Forest Experiment Station, 1997), pp. 2, 10, 12; http://www.census.gov/hhes/www/income/data/historical/state/state1.html.

[205] John E. Gannon and Mark W. Paddock in cooperation with project staff of the Northern
Michigan Environmental Research Program, *Investigations into Ecological and Sociological Determinants of Land-use Decisions — A Study of Inland Lake Watersheds in Northern Michigan* (Pellston, MI: University of Michigan Biological Station, 1974), tables 1, 2, pp. 272–273.

[206] Gannon and Paddock, tables 4, 5, pp. 275–276.
Ironically, quiet is now "the latest trend in luxury resorts." See http://fortune.com/2014/09/17/silent-luxury-resorts or *Fortune*, October 6, 2014, 41–44. The World Health Organization has described noise pollution as "an environmental health burden 'second only to air pollution.'" *Sierra* (May/June 2017), 10.

[207] Clyde Page (1911–1970) was a younger son of Alva and Nettie Page and a younger brother of Alton and Lyle Page. In the 1940 census, he appears in Taylor Township, Wayne County, Michigan, and worked at the Fleetwood Fisher Body plant. The eldest brother, Alton, also resided in the township and was a foreman at the body company.
George (d. 1959) and Grace Spiekhout, both born in the Netherlands, appeared in the Thirty-Third Ward of Cook County, Illinois, in the 1910 census, together with young sons John and Harry. George Spiekhout was a baker. Ten years later, George, having taken advantage of Michigan's homestead law and listed as a farmer, resided in Bearinger Township, Presque Isle County, Michigan, with his two sons and a daughter, Annie. (Grace Speikhout died on the eve of WWI.) In 1930, he appears with only his daughter, then seventeen, at home. At age sixty, in 1940, George appears alone but for a housekeeper. John Spiekhout, with his wife and two children, also resided in Bearinger Township in 1940. (In the 1930 census, John appeared as a coastguardsman at the Hammond Coast Guard Station.) Harry G. Spiekhout (1908–1969) married Gladys Godin (1910–1991) and, together with four sons (Sidney G., H. Dale, Bruce N., and Morris L.), resided in New Baltimore, Macomb County, Michigan, in 1940. (Soon after, the family added a daughter, Gayle Susan.)

[208] Gannon-Paddock, p. 12. Crooked Lake was identified as the lake most seriously affected by human impact (p. 71). Comparison of the lakes is complicated because Twin Lakes had a greater total shore length than either Long or Pickerel and a considerably higher shoreline development factor (see p. 72, table 5).

[209] Robert W. Marans and John D. Wellman, *The Quality of Nonmetropolitan Livings: Evaluations, Behaviors, and Expectations of Northern Michigan Residents* (Ann Arbor: Survey, Institute for Social Research, 1978), pp. 65–66

[210] *Oral History*, "Chateau Lodge."

[211] Ross Bates Jr., a businessman in the Detroit area, is the son and grandson of property owners in Benton Township. "My dad had that bell for more than 40 years," he said of a bell that has been hung at the peak of the new northern extension of the Lodge. "Every time he moved, the bell moved too. We don't even know where he got it, but he kept it all that time even though he never hung it up. It was like he was waiting for just the right place for it. Finally, last summer, we mounted it there at the peak, and Dad got to be the first one to ring it. It hadn't been rung in all those years" (http://cheboygantoday.com/wp-content/uploads/2012/07/CT-2010.pdf).

[212] The development consists of a private road and nine properties in woods off Lodge Road behind the lodge. The average property appears to be roughly three-quarter acres, and lake access and lake view are not involved.

Chapter 7 The World Is Too Much with Us

In the early 1970s, recognizing the onset of rapid growth in the area, the University of Michigan Biological Station, located at the southern end of Douglas Lake since 1909, reached out to residents of Northern Michigan. The National Science Foundation's RANN program (Research Applied to National Needs) provided support for the first year-round research project in the history of the station. The goal was to evaluate the water quality of thirty-eight lakes in Charlevoix, Cheboygan, and Emmet Counties and to gather social data regarding their residents and visitors. Limnologists and others dealt with the physical science; social scientists dealt with the attitudes and expectations of the human residents.

Project CLEAR (Community Lakes Environmental Awareness Research), funded by the National Science Foundation and the Kennedy Foundation and led by students, was a closely related effort to promote public awareness of inland lake protection. Among other things, it produced and distributed to lake residents general information packages dealing with the elements of lake health (e.g., greenbelts, septic systems, water quality monitoring, and wetlands) as well as materials focused on particular lakes in the region. One result of this work was the Tip of the Mitt Watershed Council, founded in 1979, based in Petoskey, and still fulfilling its mission to preserve and protect water quality in Northern Michigan.[213]

Cheboygan Twin Lakes was one of the thirty-eight lakes to be assessed by the RANN project. The lead investigators of the project were John E. Gannon and Mark W. Paddock. Their report bore the distinctly unlyrical title "Investigations into Ecological and Sociological Determinants of Land-use Decisions — A Study of Inland Lake Watersheds in Northern Michigan." The language used in the report to describe Twin Lakes had only a bit more lilt.[214]

> The name "Twin Lakes" implies two lakes of similar dimensions lying in close proximity to one another. For Twin Lakes, Cheboygan County, this is certainly a misnomer. Twin Lakes is actually a chain of seven small interconnecting basins separated by narrow channels. An eighth isolated basin lies east of the interconnected depressions. Although it has no surface connection to the chain of lakes, it nevertheless is considered part of the Twin Lakes group. The Twin Lakes basins have a total surface area of 84 [hectares, or approximately 207 acres]. Most depressions are from 10 to 12 [meters, or 33 to 39 feet,] deep, and the deepest basin has a maximum depth of 22.3 [meters, or 73 feet]. The shoreline is extremely irregular, and therefore, the Twin Lakes chain has the highest shoreline development factor . . . of any lake in the study area . . . Twin Lakes is sparsely dotted with 84 dwelling units. Its watershed is relatively small, encompassing an area of 459 [hectares, or 1,135 acres]. Twin Lakes is drained by Owens Creek, which empties into the Lower Black River just north of Black Lake.

The investigations and Project CLEAR were the first linkages of Twin Lakes to formal science and environmental research and concerns. These links would build slowly and quietly over the next decades. The initiative in these two instances came from beyond the lake community, and the communication appears to have been one-way. In later years, the initiative would come from the lake community, and the communication would involve dialogue.

The Campground and Boat Ramp — 1972–1979 (Part 1)

On November 1, 1974, John Gannon sent another document, "Report on the Water Quality Status of Twin Lakes (Grant Twp., Cheboygan Co., Mich.) with Special Reference to the Impact of Campgrounds," to Mr. and Mrs. Brooks Godfrey of Route 2, Cheboygan. This report was a somewhat expanded restatement of observations in the Gannon-Paddock study.[215]

Gannon noted that the staff of the Biological Station had studied Twin Lakes over the course of two years. "Awed by the beauty of this region," he commented that "the series of interconnecting basins, tranquil embayments, and essentially wild shoreland make Twin Lakes a uniquely beautiful region in Northern Lower Michigan." Gannon also expressed concern about human-induced, environmentally adverse change on Twin Lakes, specifically the "three (3) State forest campgrounds presently existing on the shores of Twin Lakes." ("Figure 1" below is his handwritten identification of the basins, locating of the two older campgrounds, and mislocating of the new campground.) He identified five elements as potentially undoing the local ecological balance: the small size of the lake; the total length of the shoreline, with its high shoreline development factor, the highest in Cheboygan County despite the greater size of other lakes; water levels (no legal lake level had been established); sandy soils; and phosphorus loading.[216]

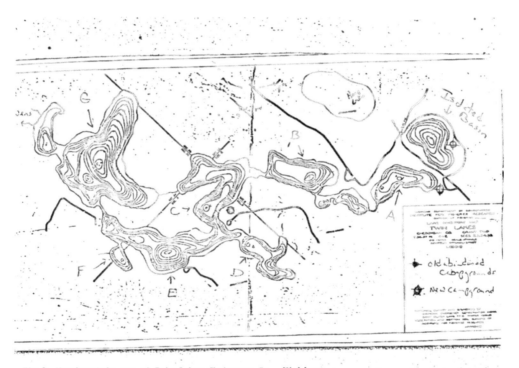

Fig.1. Morphometric map of Twin Lakes, Cheboygan Co., Michigan.

Quite apart from their contribution to human use (or overuse) of the lake, the campsites presented a problem of erosion. The two campgrounds—one on East Twin Lake, the other on the southernmost of the connected bays—were located on steep slopes and had eroded badly. The first had long been abandoned but was still used by campers, and the second was abandoned in late May 1974. Gannon was critical of the decision by the DNR to build yet a third campground on Twin Lakes, the Smith Road campground. (By the time of his letter, as he ruefully acknowledged, this campground had already been built. The only positive he could see was the small amount of money allocated to repair environmental damage at the second campground.)

The better alternative, he suggested, would have been to close the campgrounds for the short time needed to carry out remedial erosion control and abatement measures, as at the Weber Lake campground northwest of Wolverine. On the contrary, he said, the DNR appeared to be following an unsound policy of building for public use without proper safeguards, which produced erosion, and then moving farther along the shore to repeat the process. "Where will camp-ground number 4 be built on Twin Lakes after the new one on basin 'C' becomes badly eroded?"[217]

In all likelihood, the Smith Road campground *was* the fourth Twin Lakes campground. Department of Conservation maps from 1940 through 1957 show "Twin Lakes Campground" on or near Hoop Lake, just east of Krouse Road near its southern end. (The Gannon-Paddock study described Hoop Lake as a bog lake, seven acres in size with a maximum depth of thirty-one feet, and "entirely state-owned with no development anywhere" in its 130-acre watershed. Hoop Lake remains a small, lovely, quiet forest lake.[218]) The maps are almost the only evidence of the campground's existence. Other evidence is the location listed in a pamphlet of Michigan State Forest Campgrounds from the 1950s: "NE 1/4 of the NW 1/4 & NW 1/4 of NE 1/4 sec. 2 T36 N R 1 E Cheboygan County" corresponds to the Hoop Lake area, not to the isolated lake.

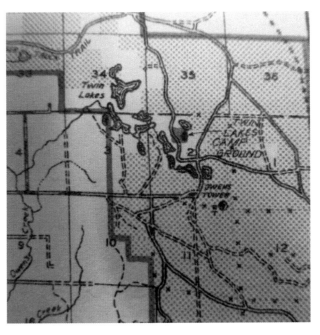

But the likelihood of a campground on Hoop Lake is heightened by the timing of its appearance in the department's maps. George Richards's properties included all the lots in T36 sec. 2. Richards died in 1937, taxes were not paid, and in November 1939, the treasurer of Michigan conveyed many of his properties to the State of Michigan. Jefferson Crawford reached an agreement with the heirs to purchase (and redeem) most of Richards's properties, including Lot 1 in T36 sec. 2, which contained the land to the west of Hoop Lake. (The legal process continued into 1944.) What Crawford did not acquire and may not have been given a chance to acquire was the land to the lake's east. That became part of the Black Lake Forest.

As noted before, this was a time in which the Black Lake Forest expanded enormously, primarily in the form of newly state-owned land. Similarly, the Department of Conservation had, for a decade, followed a policy of creating campgrounds in state forests. It is likely that these factors produced a small campground at Hoop Lake. What needs to be ignored is the red location square on the department's map that would put the campground on the southwestern shore of Hoop Lake and in Lot 1, which was and remained unquestionably a private property. Moreover, that location would not match the references in the 1950s pamphlet.

The land on the eastern shore of Hoop Lake, however, does match the references and looks as if it might have been a site for a small campground. Access would have been easy as much of the surrounding forest land had been scalped. (There is a now well-established trail to the site and plentiful evidence that the field a few hundred yards to the south was later used for large family gatherings.) The position and relationship of the more mature trees on the site makes it easy to imagine camping sites.

However, no one recalls the campground or being told of it, much less using it. On the other hand, none of the department's maps shows a state campground on the isolated lake, and only in 1961 did they cease to show the Hoop Lake campground and begin to show the campground on the southernmost of the connected lakes.

There are several possible explanations. The most likely is that there actually was a campground on or near Hoop Lake that no one remembers or has heard of or that left any discernible traces. The Department of Conservation may not have opened the campground on the southernmost lake until after 1957, even though building it was a part of planning and budgeting at the end of WWII. (A map of Black Lake and Twin Lakes foot trails showing this campground was printed by the Forestry Division in 1959.) The two may also have coexisted for a time.

A second possibility, much less likely, is that the map maker incorrectly interpreted "isolated lake," if that term or a similar one was used, to mean Hoop Lake rather than "East Twin Lake." It may also be that, for some reason, the Department of Conservation did not consider the CCC-built campground in the state forest to be a state campground or closed it before 1940; none of the department maps show the site.

The Smith Road campground issue first arose in 1972, when the Godfreys and other residents heard rumors of a planned campground. DNR offices in Onaway, Indian River, and Gaylord denied that such plans were in the works. (There appears to have been a history of difficulties with nonresidents on Smith Road that can no longer be documented but that helps to explain the sensitivity of the road's residents and the preponderance of Smith Road or nearby residents in the Cheboygan Twin Lakes Association and its leadership.)

A year later, red strings appeared on trees in the area in question. DNR offices again denied that plans were being developed. Days later, a DNR employee appeared with plans, saying they were the first he had known of the project. (The billboard erected by the DNR on site characterized the campground as "a recreational bond project," valued at $2,600,000, in cooperation with the U.S. Department of Interior, Bureau of Outdoors Recreation. It is unlikely that a project like this burst into being on the spur of the moment.) Twenty families then pooled resources to hire a local attorney to try to make their case regarding the adverse effects or dangers presented by multiple privies and many open fires. Legal action failed, and the campground opened the following year.[219]

Cheboygan Twin Lakes Association

One product of the first campground episode, coming to fruition almost simultaneously with the second, was formation of the Cheboygan Twin Lakes Association. As explained by Elnora Godfrey in a 1988 newsletter summarizing its first ten years, the association "was formed primarily because we could see the changes coming and, through the advice of others, thought it best if we could get ours going and could continue what we deemed so precious to us. The quiet beauty of our lakes and watershed and to maintain the high quality of our waters."[220]

Its articles of incorporation were filed with the Michigan Department of Commerce on December 11, 1978.[221] These defined five purposes of the association.

1. — To preserve and attempt to improve the awe-inspiring beauty of Twin Lakes and surrounding area.

2. — To maintain the high quality of Twin Lakes waters by close survelience [sic] of septic systems and water levels. Both old and new. Plus watercraft.

3. — To maintain a watchful eye on any further developments [sic] on Twin Lakes, be it Campgrounds, Cabins, Mobile Homes, Motor Homes, or Homes, whatever.

4. — To ask each member before he or she attempts a project to ask themselves . . . is this the right way? In other words, think first. Our Twin Lakes consist of only 207 acres of interconnecting basins, and overuse can destroy them in a matter of a few years.

5. — To exercise all powers within the law to protect the health, rights, welfare, and ecology of the area.

Its source of income was the $10 annual dues paid by its members. (Annual dues have remained the same to this day.) Its officers were Stephen J. Seconsky (president), Elnora M. Godfrey (secretary), and Jane Smallwood (treasurer). The trustees were Edmond B. Godfrey, Arnold Griewahn, and Glenn Grim. Its constitution and bylaws were drafted in March 1979.[222] These provided that officers—president, vice president, second vice president, secretary, corresponding secretary, treasurer, and seven trustees—should be elected by ballot for one-year terms at the annual spring meeting of the association. The president or the vice president, the secretary, treasurer, and three board members were to be year-round residents. The association would hold two meetings a year, in the spring and the fall; other meetings would be called as necessary. Membership was open to those owning or in the process of buying "waterfront or watershed property on or around Twin Lakes" (the draft carried the handwritten comment "better described as waterfront or with designated private owned easement to Twin Lakes"). A voting member was a husband and wife; each member had one vote. (There was a generational assumption in this provision. See chapter 11.) The original membership was twelve couples. Ten years later, it was sixty.

Elnora Godfrey

(Photograph courtesy of Bob and Margaret Wiest)

Elnora Godfrey (right) and Jane Smallwood examining the dam, 1984

Elnora Godfrey (1917–1996) emerges from the surviving documents as the driving force and public voice of the CTLA. She and her husband, Brooks (1905–1979), originally from the Lima, Ohio, area, settled on Twin Lakes in 1965. An employee of the Internal Revenue Service, he had been assigned to Hawaii and to Mackinac during his career. As a public person, Elnora Godfrey knew clearly what she wanted, was organized, forceful, and indefatigable, could not be intimidated, and would write—as petitioner, critic, or congratulator—to anyone on the planet. It is said that she could always be relied on.

The early activities of the CTLA not related to the immediate issue of the Smith Road campground or to improving fishing on the lake were to secure a special local watercraft control regulation prohibiting high-speed boating and recreational towing by boats (water skiers, water sleds, and such) on Twin Lakes and to take over maintenance of the dam at the lake outlet (see chapter 8), to seek nonprofit tax-exempt status, and to sponsor events that became part of the lake's annual calendar—Memorial and Labor Day picnics, a Fourth of July boat parade, and a Christmas party. The reasons for the regulation, effective in mid-February 1980, were to prevent further damage and erosion of the shoreline, the washing out of bass and bluegill spawning beds, and friction between fishermen and boaters.[223] Taking over maintenance of the dam was taking over control of lake level. Securing tax-exempt status would prevent any of the association's scant funds from going to taxation (though an annual payment to the state was needed to renew the status) and might facilitate donations to the association. The picnics, parade, and party were means of promoting community and increasing membership.

The Campground and Boat Ramp — 1972–1979 (Part 2)

The DNR and the campground continued to present problems. In June 1979, Jim Leister, a summer resident of Twin Lakes who lived in Southern Michigan, received a copy of a public notice issued by the

Army Corps of Engineers, the only copy received by a property owner on Twin Lakes.[224] The notice bore the signatures of Melvyn D. Remus, District Engineer of the Corps, and Howard A. Tanner, Director of the DNR. In conjunction with the construction of "a boat launching facility" at the campground, the corps would dump two hundred cubic yards of sand and twenty cubic yards of 4A stone into the lake. The boat ramp itself was to be a forty-by-twenty-four-foot concrete plank structure.

Interested parties were given twenty days from issuance of the notice to file comments in writing. A lack of response would be interpreted to mean that there was no objection to the permit application. The State of Michigan Water Quality Division had already certified the project without issuing public notice. The preliminary determination of the Corps was that the project would not affect endangered species or their critical habitat, and therefore, no consultation with the U.S. Fish and Wildlife Service and National Marine Fisheries Service was necessary. Despite the discharge of dredged or fill material into a waterway, the Corps also determined that no environmental impact statement was needed.[225]

On behalf of the CTLA, Stephen Seconsky and Elnora Godfrey wrote Remus on June 30, with copies sent to Rep. Steven Andrews, Congressman Robert Davis, Tanner, the UMBS, the Grant Township Board of Trustees, and Thomas Martin of the Cheboygan County Commission.[226] The letter was critical of the notification process and of the lack of local knowledge.

> In response to the letter received by James Leister of Erie, Michigan, from the Army Corps of Engineers, in reference to a public hearing notice to be displayed at the Post Office in regards to a proposed boat ramp to be built at Twin Lakes near Manning, Michigan[, h]ad you not stated Grant Township, no one would have guessed this was our Twin Lakes[.] Manning, Michigan, Grant Township has not been in existence for many, many years, which would leave us to believe your department is not too familiar with Twin Lakes or the surrounding area.[227]

The letter went on to build a case against the Corps project in particular and the public access in general. Why, it asked, was the Corps (and the DNR) to be allowed to do what individual property owners were not permitted to do?[228] Why was there no need for an environmental impact statement when the 1974 UMBS report made clear the environmental consequences of yet another campground, much less a large-scale boat dock? What the DNR and the Corps perhaps saw as a very limited project, the CTLA saw as something quite different.

> We also feel to attempt to make a public beach is not wise. First, you would destroy the natural shoreline, and second, the bottom, being marrow, will not hold sand. The shoreline water is not a gradual drop off. It is a sudden one from one foot to twenty within the distance of twenty-five foot [sic] from shore.

The letter ended with a request for a public hearing.

On July 11, a distinctly secondary administrator in the Corps responded that before any decision was made on a public hearing, regulations required that "the applicant be afforded the opportunity to contact the objectors and attempt to resolve the objections." But a day earlier, the DNR had advised the Grant Township clerk that a public hearing would be held.[229]

By letter of August 16, a site planner from the Waterways Division of the DNR advised the same corps administrator that "the scope of this project has been reduced to a carry-down site which is now existing. Please remove our application to construct a boat launch ramp at this facility."[230] As of August 22, the Corps considered the project denied or withdrawn.[231]

Clear-Cutting — 1984–1985

Clear-cutting near Twin Lakes appeared as an issue in July 1984. Harry Moran, a logger from Onaway, had clear-cut 67 acres of state-owned forest land near Doriva Beach Road and was contracted to clear-cut and selectively cut another 180 acres along the same road. At a meeting with property owners from Black Lake, Twin Lakes, and Black Mountain on the cut site on July 20, Moran, invoking scientific forestry, offered the standard rationale for clear-cutting. He also went out of his way to make it clear that anything other than clear-cutting was unprofitable. And he added that in present-day society, "pressure from special interest groups is hindering forestry management."[232]

An article on the meeting (with a photograph) appeared in the *CDT* on July 23. The next day, Elnora Godfrey, writing as an individual to State Representative John Pridnia, enclosed a copy and offered some vigorous observations. She was a year-round resident of Twin Lakes, which were small and fragile, spring fed, and beautifully clear.

> Why here? So close to lakes and residents. If the DNR call this cutting reforestation at it's [sic] best, I'd sure hate to see at it's [sic] worst. Why not plant as they cut? If they depend on the squirrels to replant, it'll be some time. The acreage they wiped out was planted by the Detroit News thirty years ago.

Dismissal as a "special interest" group hurt.

> We are only trying to retain the beauty of this region, and apparently, they are trying just as hard to wipe it out. At this point, our local flyers are telling us that the Twin Lakes area looks from the air like a bunch of bombs have been dropped, and this, we do not appreciate. When you drive past the mess we have here twice a day, 365 days a year, it is a little hard to put it out of your mind.

Pridnia responded that in a meeting a few days later, County Commissioner Clayton Cannis had said he was pleased with his meeting with the DNR and believed that negotiations between himself, the DNR, and Mr. Moran would resolve the issue satisfactorily.

In February 1985, the decision of the DNR to clear-cut thirty-five acres and to selectively cut one hundred acres between Krouse Road and the Alpena State Road appeared in the *Tribune*. (In Cheboygan County as a whole, between 1,100 and 1,400 acres of state-owned forestland were scheduled for cutting, much of it in Grant and Waverly Townships.) The CTLA, with a hundred members present, had discussed the DNR's forestry policies and decisions in the association's September 1984 meeting. Its response in February was a letter of protest, copies of which were sent to the Director of the DNR, the area forest manager, State Senator Mitch Irwin, State Representative Pridnia, County Commissioner Cannis, and Township Supervisor Clarence Archambo.[233]

The letter mentioned tourism—the draw of the area's "unique beauty" and its "spectacular burst of color in the Fall"—and the danger and damage of logging trucks: "[T]heir lumber truck drivers certainly don't qualify for merit badges in safe driving . . . They have the mistaken idea that they own these roads, and on [sic] one lives up here . . . Our township is constantly paying for the damage they have created to our roads, and that money is coming out of our pockets, not the State's."

But its core was to challenge clear-cutting itself. The Cheboygan Twin Lakes Association wants "to go on record to strongly protest this method of destroying our forests." Thinning was necessary, but "how many acres have already been cut in the Black Mountain–Twin Lakes area, not to mention Grant Township[?]" The DNR was "more interested in selling wood than trying to preserve it."

Why not replant as they cut, as they do in other states? And why not a buffer zone? Our waterfront owners pay a very high price to be able to see the water, yet we are required to leave a ten-foot buffer zone back from the water's edge.

The CTLA had tried to preserve the beauty of Twin Lakes and "would like to see the same respect shown the surrounding area."

If the DNR continues the same rate of cutting, there will be no longer be anything beautiful to see in the Black Mountain–Twin Lakes area. Unless, of course, you consider the scrub Aspen inviting to the eye. We will no doubt be called bleeding hearts or Special Interest Groups (as before); call us whatever suits their fancy, but the hard fact remains. We would like our kids and Grandkids to be able to see the beauty our eyes have seen.

If previous clear-cutting in the area was a good example of reforestation, "there is a lot to be desired with our DNR's methods, and [these methods] should be revamped."

The response of the DNR came in the form of a four-page letter from Henry H. Webster, State Forester, in which he explained patiently, as to a child, the forest management policies of the State of Michigan.[234] A comparison was made between these policies and investing money and using the interest. While there was enthusiastic mention of new or expanded mills of Champion, Meade, Louisiana-Pacific, and Weyerhauser and their need for wood, it was asserted that "much of the harvesting that is done on state land is primarily for the provision of wildlife food or the improvement of wildlife habitat." Two paragraphs were devoted to a primer on aspen. "Many of our clear-cutting harvests are in aspen forest."(That was not the case in the Black Mountain–Twin Lakes area.) There followed a simile of harvesting forests and harvesting corn. Webster also asserted that there was "a deep concern for aesthetics."

We have had training programs for our forestry people on forest aesthetics, provided them with literature on the subject, and have policies designed to reduce the visual impact of timber harvesting. Our field people are conscious of the visual impact and, within the limits of topography, forest type, and several other factors, try to vary the edge boundaries, size, and impact of harvesting. On occasion, buffer strips are left until the cut area regenerates.

However, the only aesthetic issue he seemed to recognize was slash, which was now being cleared away for use as firewood. (There was no mention of environmental issues at all.) The inadequate buffer left on Doriva Beach Road the previous year, he said, was a result of particular circumstances, not policy. The area forest manager had reassured Webster that a buffer would be left between Krouse and the Alpena State Road. The comment on the dangers of logging trucks "has prompted us to prepare an article on driving courtesy and sharing the road," which would appear in the next state forest timber news and be sent to 1,200 timber producers in the state.

Writing to Irwin at the end of March, Webster specified the then current plans for clear-cutting in Grant Township. In T37 sec. 35, along Krouse Road on the west side of Twin Lakes, forty-six acres would be cut, leaving a two-hundred-foot buffer (with aspen and birch cut out so the buffer could be managed for hardwoods). In sec. 36, bordering the Alpena State Road, twenty-four acres would be cut with the same two-hundred-foot buffer. In sec. 37, along Krouse Road and the Alpena State Road, a two-hundred-foot buffer of all trees would be left along Krouse and a two-hundred-foot buffer minus aspen and birch along the Alpena State Road.[235] Robert Van Stee, the DNR's area forest manager, responded to Godfrey in a letter informing her that he would appear at the Grant Township board meeting in mid-March to discuss the DNR's plans for cutting and other issues.

Most important among those other issues was damage to roads. An article in the *Tribune* observed that much of the timber equipment moved on rural roads that could not withstand the weight and speed of the equipment; repair was the responsibility of local government, not the DNR or timber contractors. "The road system damage is not resolved," said Van Stee. "It's a real problem. Every township complains. They feel the DNR should do something, but we don't feel we have the jurisdiction." Bizarrely, the DNR turned the issue into one of local autonomy, an avoidance of heavy-handed state administration. "The roads are not built for the heavy equipment. We [DNR] feel it's not our prerogative to tell people how to use their roads. The regulations should come out of the county road commission."[236]

The policies of the Forest Management Division of the DNR, clear-cutting, and even what the division describes as selective harvesting have continued to raise concern. In 1996, the focus was on Black Mountain, opened for only two years as a recreational area, where the Division authorized clear-cutting of aspen, maple, and birch along the novice ski/hiking trails. "Wide expanses of trail . . . have been laid bare"; "recreational users . . . expressed concern about erosion." They also believed that "the devastating effects can destroy an environment that has provided shelter for wildlife and glimpses of the forest world in its most pristine setting." And they were apprehensive that "the open areas will attract snowmobilers to the ski trail, creating a nuisance problem." Mackinaw Forest District Manager Robert Slater said, "It's good for wildlife." He added that people would now be able to see Black Lake—"the vista will be beautiful"—and that "the rich black soil" would begin to regenerate immediately. "I will not let erosion take place." (A vista of Black Lake did not appear in the original rationale for converting Black Mountain into a recreation area, and rich black soil is difficult to find on Black Mountain. The planning documents for the recreation area expressly precluded this kind of cut along the trails.)[237]

For thirty years, until late 2018, cuts along Krouse Road were carefully conducted and did not raise issues. But in the years after 2007, five cuts occurred on Twin Lakes Road in a distance of less than five miles, several in close proximity to the lake, all on the edge of the road. Arguably, two of these left a screen. (What constitutes a "screen" or "buffer" may never be agreed upon.)

Godin Circle

Loon Nest Lane

The Forest Management Division explained, regarding the most recent of these cuts, that it was for the good of the wildlife. (The good of the wildlife does not appear to have been an urgent issue since cutting was postponed for several years after issuance of the contract for the convenience of the contractor.) Its response to concerns about the slash left by the contractor was that "this course [sic] woody debris can be an eyesore for a year or two until the new undergrowth gets established, but it does provide some important benefits as well. Including small animal habitat, and many nutrients will be released back into the soil as it decomposes." As for fire danger, while there is likely to be an "increase of fire intensity when there is pine slash on the ground, the number of fires does not normally increase." This condition "normally only lasts 2–3 years as pine slash deteriorates rapidly, and the new regrowth provides shade." By way of reassurance, it was said that "the DNR responds to all wild-land fires with large equipment designed for putting out fires in the woods," utilizing "a combination of a bulldozer with a plow on the back and large water units." (If fire and fire suppression were to follow close on logging, a genuine wasteland would be created. Moreover, fire on and around Twin Lakes is highly dangerous and likely to spread more rapidly than the DNR can respond. Two recent residential fires on Twin Lakes shared two characteristics: delayed response and complete destruction).[238]

The Bombing Range — 1986–1988

Insisting that its gunnery and bombing range at Camp Grayling was inadequate and that it must have a new one in Northeastern Michigan, the Michigan Air National Guard asked the DNR to trade state-owned timberland near Alpena for a thirty-one-thousand-acre forest property owned by Abitibi Price Corp., a Canadian wood products company with a mill in Alpena. Nearly eight thousand acres of the property lay in Benton Township and just under four thousand acres in adjoining Grant Township. The remainder was in Presque Isle County. The southwestern edge of Abitibi timberlands lay near Twin Lakes, to the northeast of the lake and north of the Alpena State Road. The range was to begin approximately six miles east of Cheboygan, extend southward from the Lake Huron shore for seven miles, and then slant southeastward toward Rogers City. The *Detroit News* described the proposed range as "a roughly 50-square-mile area running from Lake Huron, north of Huron Beach, west to the shores of Black Lake." Residents in the region were assured that 90 percent of the bombs dropped in the target area would be "inert" and that all bombs would be picked up "regularly."[239]

Once it was publicly known, the guard's plan was opposed by letter writing and petition campaigns led by citizens of Huron Beach and Rogers City but involving residents of Twin Lakes as well. The letters went to every level and sort of political official, the petitions to Governor James Blanchard. In early September 1986, the Cheboygan County Resolution Committee, following in the footsteps of the Presque Isle County Commission, agreed unanimously to recommend to the full county commission that it oppose the transfer, a recommendation that was acted on by the commission. While economic, recreational, and environmental reasons were alluded to by the *Tribune* in its coverage of the recommendation, loss of tax revenue was perhaps more prominent; the two townships and the county would see reduced income, and the Cheboygan area schools would lose very substantial revenue.[240]

U.S. Representative Robert Davis (Gaylord) and State Representative John Pridnia (Harrisville) were especially impressed by the reaction of their constituents. Pridnia commented, "In my meetings with the governor's staff, I made it clear he should take very fast action in opposing this gunnery range. There was not one communication of support to me from one entity. It offered no positives whatever to my district but many negatives."[241]

Davis and Pridnia appear to have been instrumental in convincing Governor Blanchard on September 24 to block the plan, at least temporarily, by ordering the Michigan National Guard to wait on a study by the Pentagon of training sites and facilities nationally. Blanchard added that if the Pentagon recommended a new gunnery range in Michigan, he would direct Maj. Gen. Vernon J. Andrews Jr., the state's Adjutant General, to carry out a comprehensive study of all possible sites in the state. For his part, Andrews said a new range was needed to assure the long-term future of Phelps-Collins Air Base in Alpena. "Phelps-Collins Air National Guard Base is a major asset to the state and helps bring in over $85 million for the Michigan Air National Guard . . . We must assure its future in Michigan." With the naive optimism or perhaps the wishfulness of authorities pushing a project, Andrews had also said, "opposition to the proposal would disappear 'if (critics) will simply allow us to tell them the facts.'"[242]

"The facts" would make no difference to the residents of Huron Beach or Rogers City or to Elnora Godfrey of Twin Lakes, who, in early September, drafted a letter on behalf of the CTLA containing the following comments.

> Twin Lakes lies at the foot of Black Mountain and curves northeasterly, almost to the Peat Moss Company, which, if we understand correctly, is pretty close to where the bombing area will start. The actual bombing, even though smoke bombs that weigh twenty-five pounds, [sic] could prove dangerous if they do miss their target. We have retired elderly people living in the area, and it could prove dangerous to their health.

> We do have many expensive homes located on Twin Lakes, and there is no question in our minds that living near a bombing area will decrease the property value of all parcels of ground. Please give this some consideration also.

> We have not, in the past, complained of the noise created by the low flying bombers or their keeping the tops of our trees pruned, but when you mention bombing, it is a horse of a different color! We have reasons of our own to object to this. First, we live within a mile of the area. We have tried to keep our waters and watershed as quiet and clean as possible. We have nesting Common Loon and Osprey (which are pretty much in danger of becoming extinct) and which don't much care to be disturbed. We have also sighted Bald Eagles once again. I think, in essence, what we are trying to say is, we would like our quiet pristine country to stay that way, if possible.

In addition to Davis and Pridnia, her cc list included Cannis, now a Grant Township supervisor, MacGregor, Col. Paul Pochmara, base commander of Phelps Collins, Rod Brown, manager of the Atibibi plant in Alpena, Janice Baers, the secretary of the Doriva Beach Association, the governor, and Senator Carl Levin.[243]

By the spring of 1987, the issue was alive again. In the CTLA newsletter of March 23, 1987, Godfrey tried to rouse the troops.

> They are really after it in earnest this time, and letters will help. Most of us are afflicted with a disease called apathy. I had a call from Don Riegles [sic] [Donald Riegle, U.S. senator] office saying they had only sixty letters from this whole area, and that is not a very good showing. They are talking 4,000 flights per year and will "on rare occasions" drop live bombs. [The majority of the four thousand sorties would be flown in the summer.] The bombing area is within two miles back of us, and I would think this is a serious situation and should not be taken lightly or [that we should] wait around for someone else to do the letter writing. Do we or do we not care? Maybe we'll win, or maybe we'll lose. You'll never know unless you try. At least we can't be blamed for lack of caring. Do hope you'll cooperate. Individual letters count so much more than one from an Association.

Earlier in March, a Godin Circle resident had written Pridnia, receiving in reply a reaffirmation of his opposition. Godfrey had signed a petition sent to Davis and had written to Gordon Guyer, Director of the DNR. Davis commended her for her involvement in "the grassroots effort to bring your concerns to my attention," and the deputy director of the DNR responded for Guyer that "there are no negotiations occurring." She later wrote to Sen. Carl Levin.[244]

Yet as of June 1987, a spokesman for the National Guard said that the guard "had not abandoned the possibility of acquiring the land from the Abitibi Corporation for use as an air-to-ground range," although further negotiations waited on the results of a needs assessment. Weeks earlier, Rep. Bob Davis had made his position clear.[245]

> I think we have made some progress on the National Guard's Plan to locate a bombing range in Cheboygan and Presque Isle counties. This controversy is far from over, and the Guard is now in the process of studying possible locations throughout the state.
>
> Several weeks ago, however, I made my position known: I will oppose any efforts to locate that range in northeastern Michigan.
>
> I have always been a strong supporter of Phelps Collins Air National Guard base, the Alpena home of aircraft that would use a bombing range. But my own analysis of the situation, based on the military situation and the views of the residents of the proposed tract, made it clear to me that looking elsewhere was the best strategy for everyone.
>
> I continue to pledge to use my position on the House Armed Services Committee to keep the Air National Guard's bombing range out of Cheboygan and Presque Isle counties.

At a meeting with Representative Davis on January 3, 1988, Clayton Cannis asked Davis if "there was anything new" on the bombing range. Davis replied that federal money was needed to establish and run the range, and as far as he was concerned, "the money was not available." However, David Sherman concluded this portion of the newsletter with the comment "Until the Abitibi Range issue has no chance of resurfacing, The [sic] Association must remain vigilant and ready to oppose any moves toward its establishment."[246]

The need for vigilance was also implicit in Elnora Godfrey's comments in the summer newsletter.

> We have . . . been involved in a ground to air battle with the ANG and the Bombing Range.[247] Many, many letters and meetings. At this point, thing [sic] have quieted down somewhat. Probably due to election year. The only thing we can report is heresay [sic]. We probably won't here [sic] much until they drop the first bomb!

The Black Mountain Forest Recreational Area — 1988

The district office of the Mackinaw State Forest produced a draft of development and management guidelines for Black Mountain in September 1988. Planning had begun as soon as the DNR was able to acquire the 125-acre ski area in January 1988. In all, over nine thousand acres of Black Mountain were now state lands. There were several reasons offered in the draft to plan and develop the area. It was unique in Northeastern Michigan, "having more relief and numerous scenic vistas than any other parcel in that region of the state"; it was an area of "exceptional scenic beauty." It was also an area of increasing recreational use. But that recreational use was unplanned and uncontrolled, producing environmental damage and user conflict. In particular, "the Black Mountain area and . . . the old ski area [have] a considerable amount of ORV [off road vehicle] use and subsequent erosion because of extensive non-planned trail development."

Other activities, such as cross country skiing, snowmobiling, and horseback riding, have developed in an unplanned manner. Such unplanned and uncontrolled use increases the possibility of injury by users and diminishes their overall recreational enjoyment.

The existing Cheboygan–Black Mountain Snowmobile Trail, 30 percent of which lay within the proposed recreation area, received moderately heavy use on weekends, the existing ORV trail light to moderate use in the summer. But "heavy ORV use occurs on the slopes of the old downhill ski area."[248]

What else lay behind the DNR decision is uncertain. In July 1988, the president of the CTLA, James McPherson, described the proposal as one for for "an ATV [all terrain vehicle], ORV recreational area" and linked it "to pressures applied from recreational groups due in part to the closing of the Pigeon River area and legislative demand for the DNR to 'break even' economically by filling vacant camp sites." (The Black Lake and Twin Lakes campgrounds were parts of the Black Mountain "planning area.") The Nature Conservancy noted that in its state recreation plan, the DNR had a recommendation that trails be created or set aside for ORV use and that the DNR, to accomplish this and to regulate ORV use, had been looking for sites. It proposed one for Island Lake Recreation Area near Brighton; at the time of the conservancy's letter, that proposal was in court. (Island Lake has no provision for ATVs, and snowmobiling is limited.) A second area was proposed near Benton Harbor, but the conservancy believed it "unlikely that that area will materialize either."[249]

Responding in November 1988 to a letter sent by McPherson to Gov. James Blanchard, Henry Webster, the State Forester, focused entirely on the regulation of ORVs. Revised rules already existed; they would go into effect ninety days after the Natural Resources Commission certified that 1,500 miles of ORV trails had been designated (500 more were needed).[250]

> Since additional regulation is so important, we ask for and need support from concerned citizens as [sic] yourself in the accomplishment. Whether or not such trails must play a part in the plan for the Black Mountain area is yet being examined by our planners and their local citizens advisory group.

Webster appears not to have known that McPherson was the representative of one of those local citizens groups. Nor evidently did he know that, by the date of his letter, the DNR had already drafted development and maintenance guidelines that prescribed ATV and motorcycle trails on Black Mountain.

Ironically, the first proposal for recreational development of the area appears to have been an action measure proposal from the Huron Pines Resource Conservation and Development Area Council in February 1987 for an extensive cross-country ski trail network.[251] The cover of the Black Mountain Recreation Area Development Plan (April 1989) centered on the figure of a cross-country skier much larger than the snowmobile in the upper left of the cover and the ATV in the lower right.

In March 1988, the Forest Management Division of the DNR had notified the CTLA and other "use interest" groups of its intention to form a recreational plan for the Black Mountain area and invited it to join a committee formed as part of the planning process. Workshops were held in June, July, and September. While the DNR referred to the parties invited to join as a "representative group," the list of invitees was heavily weighted toward organizations with an interest in economic development, such as the Cheboygan County and Presque Isle County Economic Development Corporations, the Cheboygan and Onaway Chambers of Commerce, and the Presque Isle Tourism Council. (In the draft development plan of April 1989, the economic rationale for development is quite explicit, in contrast to the draft development and management guidelines of September 1988.)

Representatives from ATV, motorcycle, and snowmobile groups were present. Three skiers and one horseback rider appeared on the list. The only representation of nearby residents was the CTLA and the Black Lake Association. In his letter to the Nature Conservancy, James McPherson had commented, "You can see by the enclosed 'guest' list that we are somewhat overwhelmed."[252] In a press interview, he asked, "Where was the Audubon Society? Where was the Nature Conservancy[?]"[253]

At the second workshop, the group representatives were asked to respond to four questions; their answers were to be used to develop guidelines. The questions were as follows:

What forest-based uses would you like to see for the Black Mountain Management Unit?

What are potential conflicts among the listed possible uses or between the uses and other sources?

How can the potential use conflicts or problems you identified earlier be prevented, eliminated, or minimized?

What should the DNR do in terms of design or use guidelines for your activity?[254]

In rank order, the answer to the first was hunting and cross-country skiing, hiking, snowmobiling, parking and staging area, ATVs, and educational nature trails. Fourteen other possibilities ranked lower, including forest management and wildlife education, camping, motorized and nonmotorized biking, erosion control, fitness trails, handicapped use, and downhill skiing.[255]

Again, in rank order, the answer to the second was security and police protection, timber harvesting, trespass on private property, motorized vehicles in areas of residence, noise control, overuse and a deteriorating environment, and lack of awareness and consistent laws or rules for motorized vehicles. Ranking near the bottom was a cluster of concerns regarding motorized vehicles—motorcycles, ATVs, snowmobiles, and four-wheel drive vehicles. At the very bottom were dust control and the coexistence of hikers and hunters.

Proposed resolutions of conflicts were not ranked but listed in conjunction with the conflict(s) they were to address. For example, the suggestion to deal with dust control, the effect of motorized vehicles on residents, noise control, and possible disharmony between hikers and ATV riders was the use of large vehicle-registration numbers. Similarly, dust control, safety and emergency services, and noise from motorized vehicles were to be dealt with by a safety inspection of vehicles at registration. There were no less than six suggestions to deal with lack of awareness and consistent laws or rules for motorized vehicles: permanent assignment of personnel to inform and enforce, provision of a place to register users, local regulations of ORV use to be included at every information point, provision of maps and rules at information points, informing local public safety forces about the uses and location of uses, and news releases from county road commissions.

Apparently, no answers were given directly to the last question. Instead, they seemed to have been bundled into or to be implicit in the responses to question three.

Based on this process, the draft document laid out development and maintenance guidelines for Black Mountain. There were no specific development guidelines for hunting; maintenance guidelines were to provide adequate signage indicating hunting seasons and possibly to close trails during gun deer season.

For cross-country skiing, there were eleven development guidelines, including parallel and skating trails, a trail width of eight feet, short and easy trails near the parking lots, and providing vistas, overlooks, and variety in scenery on the trails. The maintenance guidelines were small timber cuts—"remember the aesthetics"—along with leaving trees with confidence markers along the trails when cutting and erecting signs and barriers to prevent motorized use. (Intrusions by ORVs appear to have been rare.) The guidelines for hiking development duplicated five of those for skiing and added a possible fitness and handicapped trail. The trails have remained in good condition, and some have been used for cross-country running as well as skiing and hiking. The winter trails are groomed by a local ski club (in partnership with the DNR and the Top of Michigan Trails Council), and for more than a decade, Black Mountain has hosted the Nordic Ski Classic at the end of February or beginning of March.

It was decided that the existing snowmobile trails were enough; what had to be done was to develop the parking lots and staging areas and to introduce no facilities near the Twin Lakes area. (In fact, there is a parking lot and vault toilet and access to several trails between the southernmost bay of Twin Lakes and the isolated lake.) Maintenance required only signage and barriers to keep snowmobilers on the snowmobile trails.

ATV and motorcycle use was to be combined, trails were to be curvy and winding and fifty inches wide, the bowl (the old ski site) in sec. 12 would be designated a scramble area, and there were to be no facilities near the Twin Lakes area. Maintenance guidelines involved only confidence markers, signage, and barriers.

One of the CTLA's objections to the DNR proposal, presented by Jim McPherson, was that it did not provide for adequate supervision of the new trails. Bob Slater, district forest manager, recognized the validity

of McPherson's concerns and acknowledged the difficulty of monitoring miles of crisscrossing trails. "We're going to rely on peer enforcement."[256]

The nature trail was to be less than one mile and not cross or be close to a motorized trail. Timber cutting was to be minimal; "where cutting occurs, use as an education tool." (In one degree or another, these practices were to apply to all cutting on Black Mountain.)

Development guidelines for other activities (swimming, picnicking, camping) included possible expansion but also specified that the Twin Lakes area was for quiet use only and the upper Black Lake campground was for motorized use. The DNR did not explain how the rasp, whine, and bark of ATV, motorcycle, and snowmobile engines on and around Black Mountain would not make the Twin Lakes area inescapably *un*quiet. The natural state of the area is silence, and therefore, sound carries rather than being submerged into background noise.[257] The situation was exacerbated by the fact that riders on the major ORV trail coming down

off Black Mountain at the south end of Twin Lakes could use Krouse Road as a shortcut to pick up the trail near the north end.

The single development guideline for timber management was "Key value is recreation. Forest aesthetics will be of primary concern." As for maintenance, cuts would be small and screened from the trails, and both the noise factor and the time of years would be carefully considered for timbering operations.

In April 1989, the DNR produced a draft Black Mountain Forest Recreation Area development plan that was clearly the offspring of the previous year's process. But it added a three-phase schedule of implementation expected to take ten years, cost projections of just over $186,000 for implementation, and projected annual maintenance costs of just over $80,000 in the first year and just over $45,000 in subsequent years. Annual review of the project, including public meetings, would occur. Once finished, triennial public meetings would be held. (None of these have occurred.)

ATVs were the primary concern for residents of Twin Lakes. The files of the CTLA contain newspaper clippings, including one entitled, "ATV Terror," reporting that 12 percent of wildfires in Michigan were the result of off-road vehicles lacking the mandatory spark arrestor in the muffler; that "all-terrain vehicle operators are already tormenting wildlife, land, water and people in the north country this spring"; that a Sault man was hospitalized in Traverse City when he lost control of his ATV on a curve (road use was illegal, the driver's license was expired, and alcohol and high speed were involved) and ran straight into a car whose driver had stopped when he saw the ATV out of control; and that the Michigan Motorcycle Dealers' Association had successfully prompted some television stations to remove a public service announcement sponsored by the Michigan State Medical Society regarding the dangers of ATVs.[258]

> An estimated 300,000 ATV-related injuries have been treated in emergency rooms nationwide since 1982. Injuries include paralysis of the legs, paralysis of the arms and legs, brain damage, and broken bones. More than 1,000 people have died as a result of ATV accidents since 1982—over 50 of them in Michigan. Almost half of the dead in Michigan were children under 16 years old.

Four months before the draft development plan was produced, a Cheboygan High School junior was critically injured in an ATV accident, suffering amputation of his left foot, removal of his spleen and a kidney, and surgery to repair internal injuries, all at Northern Michigan Hospital in Petoskey, followed by transfer to the intensive care unit of the University of Michigan in Ann Arbor. Another clipping noted that the gas tax legislation to fund expansion of trails required "that some of it be used to repair erosion and other damage caused by indiscriminate ORV activity."[259]

In time, however, the CTLA was won over. As quoted in the fall 1990 issue of the *Natural Resources Register*, a DNR publication, Chuck Williams, president of the CTLA, said,

> We had some concerns in the beginning.[260] But Bob Slater and Mike Mang (DNR forest resource planner) have worked hard for a long time on this development plan. Little by little, our association has come around. We wanted to bring a group out to show we all think the DNR is doing a great job.

The "group" that came out was a part of 150 people who volunteered for an all-day work bee in cooperation with the DNR to clean up the proposed recreation area (in the case of Elnora Godfrey and the Seconskys, it was the abandoned ski area), erase "outlaw" ORV trails, and take steps to control erosion.[261]

The abandoned ski area became the core of the sixty-five-acre ORV scramble area. It is now an environmental nightmare of pulverized sand, exposed tree roots, and eroding gullies. Black Mountain has the misfortune of containing one of two scramble areas in state forests and one of five in the state (the other three are in a national forest, a county park, and a state park in the dune country of Lake Michigan). Inevitably, unauthorized scramble areas have also appeared on Black Mountain.

---

[213] Gannon and Paddock. Markley W. Paddock was assistant to the director and administrative manager of the UMBS and an individual with a deep and varied background in agriculture, ecology, geography, and wildlife management. Paddock later became a member of the board of directors of Tip of the Mitt Watershed Council. For John Gannon, see note 3.

[214] pp. 84–85. But there is a lyric quality to Gannon's opening description of Twin Lakes in his "Report on the Water Quality Status of Twin Lakes (Grant Twp., Cheboygan Co., Mich.) with Special Reference to the Impact of Campgrounds" (June 1974).

[215] Letter, Dr. John E. Gannon to Mr. and Mrs. Brooks Godfrey, November 1, 1974, enclosing a copy of the report. John E. Gannon was a limnologist and fisheries research biologist at the International Joint Commission's Great Lakes Regional Office in the capacity of senior scientist. He received a BS in biology at Wayne State University, an MS in fisheries at the University of Michigan, and a PhD in zoology (limnology) at the University of Wisconsin. Following graduate school, he was resident scientist for six years at the UMBS before serving in various capacities with the IJC and the Great Lakes Science Center of the U.S. Geological Survey.

The campground involved exactly the kind of decision making regarding land use that was central to the Gannon-Paddock investigation. See Gannon-Paddock, pp. 243–244.

[216] *Report.*

[217] Letter, Gannon to Godfrey; *Report*, pp. 2, 5–6. The report identified the basins of Twin Lakes by letters of the alphabet, beginning with the southernmost. Erosion is evident at the Smith Road campground, even though it has been closed in several years since 1974.

[218] Gannon and Paddock, p. 85. See also James Bricker and John E. Gannon, "Limnological investigation of Hoop Lake — A Northern Michigan Bog." *Michigan Academecian*, 9:1 (Summer 1976), pp. 25–42.

[219] *Cheboygan News*, May 3, 1974. In his letter of transmittal, John Gannon commented that on reflection, "tackling this problem through a lawyer and the courts" was a mistake. "I strongly feel that if the proper environmental authorities at all governmental levels would have been contacted in the first place, the new campground would not have been built." That "mistake" was not made again.

[220] CTLA Newsletter, June 4, 1988. Formation of the association in 1978 may seem late in the game, certainly relative to the Black Lake Association, created in 1920 out of a concern with diminishing populations of lake sturgeon and walleye. On the other hand, the Mullett Lake Area Preservation Society was not organized until 1985. And arguably, the CTLA has a longer and denser record of coordination with TOMWC than either of the other two.

[221] Articles of Incorporation, December 4, 1978, in Twin Lakes Files (electronic), "Incorporation."

[222] Constitution and By-Laws 1979-1980 of Cheboygan Twin Lakes Assn., Twin Lakes Files (electronic), "By-Laws."

[223] Letter, Elnora Godfrey to Thomas J. Anderson, Chairman of the Joint Committee on Administrative Rules, Michigan Legislature, September 6, 1979. For discussion of these activities, see chapters 8, 9, and 10.

[224] Letter, CTLA to Remus, June 30, 1979; Department of the Army, Detroit District, Corps of Engineers, NCECO-LP Process No. 7908758/79-5-38, PROPOSED BOAT RAMP IN TWIN LAKE NEAR MANNING, MICHIGAN, undated.

[225] Department of the Army, Detroit District, Corps of Engineers, NCECO-LP Process No. 7908758/79-5-38, PROPOSED BOAT RAMP IN TWIN LAKE NEAR MANNING, MICHIGAN, undated.

[226] Letter, CTLA to Remus, June 30, 1979.

[227] The identification of the site as "located approximately 1.5 miles easterly from the intersection of Twin Lakes and Chamberlain Roads" also reflected map reading rather than local knowledge. The map included with the public notice was a general highway map of Cheboygan County from the State Highway Commission.
The 2013 fish survey of Twin Lakes by the DNR noted "the steep drop-offs to deep water" close to shore.

[228] Some years later, in 1997, a property owner exercised for himself the same right on a lesser scale, and like an avenging angel, the DEQ penalized him.

[229] Letter, Davy to Seconsky, July 11, 1979; letter, Smith to Hart, July 10, 1979.

[230] Bratschi to Davy, August 16, 1979.

[231] Department of the Army, Detroit District, Corps of Engineers, PERMITS ISSUED/DENIED DURING AUGUST 1979, September 21, 1979.

[232] *CDT*, 7.23.1984.

[233] Letter, Ann Stranaly, Secretary, and Elnora Godfrey, Corresponding Secretary, to Ronald O. Skoog et al., February 15, 1985.

[234] Letter, Henry H. Webster, State Forester, to Ann Stranaly, March 14, 1985.

[235] *CDT*, April 8, 1985.

[236] Letter, Robert Van Stee, Area Forest Manager, to Elnora Godfrey, nd.

[237] The *CDT* clipping in the CTLA files has the date 6/96 handwritten on it.

[238] Newsletter, June 2014.

[239] *Detroit News*, September 7, 1986. In another article in the *News*, the guard's case was summarized as "its existing bombing range at Camp Grayling . . . is inadequate, and the new facility will be safe, with only a small portion in the center actually used for bombing."

[240] *CDT*, September 5, 1986.

[241] *Detroit News,* September 23, 1986.

[242] Governor's Office, Press Release, September 24, 1986; Letter, Robert W. Davis to Godfrey, October 17, 1986; *CDT*, date unknown, September 23, 1986, September 30, 1986; *Detroit News*, September 7, 1986.

243 Letter, CTLA to various, September 8, 1986. One of the less carefully considered arguments for the creation of the bombing range that appeared in the Department of Military Affairs project outline was that it would "significantly reduce noise problems generated by present operations" at Grayling by providing "a large block of contiguous land which is not subject to civilian encroachment."

244 Letter, Davis to Godfrey, March 13, 1987; letter, Pridnia to Vivian Thompson, March 18, 1987; letter, John McGregor to Godfrey, March 31, 1987; letter, Levin to Godfrey, June 4, 1987.

245 *CDT*, March 13, 1987, April 23. 1987, June 26, 1987.

246 Newsletter, February 17, 1988.

247 Newsletter, June 4, 1988.

248 DNR, "Black Mountain Plan Development and Management Guidelines," September 1988, pp. 1–3. "ORV" has a short definition but a broad range: a motor vehicle used in off-road recreational travel, including four-wheel drive vehicles, dune buggies, three- and four-wheel all-terrain vehicles (ATVs), trail motorcycles, and amphibious and air-cushioned vehicles. The "Black Mountain Plan Development Plan" (pp. 1–2, 6–10) of April 1989 filled in a few more details of the unplanned use. A designated motorcycle trail, five miles of which lay within the proposed recreational area, received light to moderate use in the summer. ATVs were making their own trails, opening up old fire lanes, and using existing roads. ATVs, motorcycles, and snowmobiles all "scrambled" at the old ski slope.

249 Letter, McPherson to Michigan Chapter, The Nature Conservancy, July 21, 1988; letter, Thomas M. Woiwode to McPherson, August 15, 1988.

250 Letter, Webster to McPherson, November 14, 1988.

251 DNR, "Black Mountain Forest Recreation Area Development Plan," April 1989, p. 3. Hereafter identified as "BMFRADP."

252 "BMFRADP," Appendix A; letter, McPherson to Michigan Chapter, The Nature Conservancy, July 21, 1988.

253 *CDT*, August 4, 1988.

254 Agenda, Second Public Workshop. July 16, 1988, in "BMFRADP," Appendix C, p. 30.

255 For this and the following paragraphs, see "BMFRADP," Appendices D and E, pp. 32–42.

256 *CDT*, August 4, 1988.

257 Allegedly, the quietest place in the continental United States is located at N 47°51′959″/W 123°52′221″, in the Hoh Rain Forest of Olympic National Park in the State of Washington (at the same elevation as Twin Lakes). For proponents of active recreation, no matter how extreme, quiet areas designated by rule are NFZs, "no-fun zones."

258 Vehicles like ATVs and snowmobiles have inescapable drawbacks: they burn hydrocarbon, and they are noisy. But in areas like Northern Michigan, they have legitimate usefulness, and there are acceptable modes of operation. But motorized recreation is much more problematic, especially when the vehicle is in the hands of a short-term visitor. Money from urban weekenders is an important part of local economies. But the psychology of the owner/driver and the nature of short-term escapes from work and the city may encourage behaviors that damage or destroy the nature of the area, disturb residents, and injure or kill the driver or others. The industry and the State of Michigan have exacerbated the problem by encouraging the participation of children. The industry's advertising is of no help: it stresses aggression, power, and speed. And counties, in competition for recreational dollars, have opened county roads to ATV use. It may be said that there exist unfair stereotypes of the recreational driver, but those stereotypes have their roots in the experiences of farmers, medical personnel, and police.
And little has changed over time. Forty years ago, in its introduction, the Gannon-Paddock report commented, "The recreation industry provides products and places for play and the instigation to use them. However, snowmobiles, trail bikes, and other off-the-road recreational vehicles are used irresponsibly; tearing up vital dune grass, disturbing wildlife habitat, and shattering the serenity of the woods in all seasons."

259 *CDT*, January 13, 1989; *North Woods Call*, January 1989.

260 Natural Resources Register, Fall 1990, p. 15.

261 Newsletter, April 17, 1990.

Chapter 8 Lake Management and Preservation

The files of the CTLA contain a spiral-bound copy of a lake management manual published by the Northeast Michigan Council of Governments (NEMCOG) in 1978. Handwritten on a cover is the notation "Property of Elnora Godfrey," followed by her address on Smith Road. Lake management and preservation, the purpose of the manual, was also the initial and primary aim of the CTLA.

High-Speed Boating

The first step of the association was to secure a high-speed boating ordinance. While there is no record in the association files of who took the initiative or how it was brought about, the administrative rules proposed by the DNR, Law Enforcement Division, for approval by the Joint Committee on Administrative Rules of the Michigan Legislature in October 1979 included the following:

High-speed boating ordinance:

TWIN LAKES - R281.716.7 — High-speed boating and water skiing prohibited

7. On the waters of Twin lakes [sic], sections 2, 3, 34, and 35, T36N, RIE, Grant township, Cheboygan county, it is unlawful for the operator of a vessel to:

   (a) Operate a vessel at high speed.
   (b) Have in tow or otherwise assist in the propulsion of a person on water skis, a water sled, kite, surfboard, or other similar contrivance.

(The rule had been drafted as early as March 19, 1979.) In a letter of response to notification of the hearing to be held in Lansing on October 2, Elnora Godfrey implied that high-speed boating and water skiing were common enough on Twin Lakes to damage and erode the shoreline and to wash out "our blue gill and bass beds . . . each year." In time, it became apparent that high-speed boating was also a danger to waterfowl, especially to the loons that arrived when the ice broke and remained on the lake, raising their young, until the onset of fall. The rule was certified as approved on October 2, 1979. Subsequently incorporated in the county code, it was to take effect February 13, 1980.[262]

Two areas of misunderstanding of this ordinance have appeared from time to time. One is the belief that Twin Lakes was designated a no-wake lake. That was the stated understanding of the Secluded Land Company of De Soto, Wisconsin, when it bought 660 feet of shoreline on the north side of the Big Bay in 2000. In 2007, minutes of the trustees May meeting noted, "More NO WAKE signs are needed on the lake by the boat launch and the State Park." And the minutes of the association's first annual meeting later that month reported, "There are no old No Wake Lake signs available." In fact, it seems no such signs were ever posted on the lake; the use of the phrase reflects misunderstanding. A year later, members attending the first annual meeting were reminded to be aware of high-speed boaters: "[T]he concern is swimmers and wildlife and the fact that it is a no wake lake."[263] Not even the lone survivor among the oldest signs, its paint badly faded and flaking, mentioned "no wake," only "no high speed."

The stimulus to discussion of the ordinance in 2000 was the personal watercraft or jet ski. The land company was selling seclusion rather than high-speed activity and had found jet skiers rarely launched on no-wake lakes, a factor in its purchase of the land on Twin Lakes. (One jet skier did appear in 2006, for as long as it took the sheriff's office to be flooded with phone calls.) The meaning of "no wake" was checked with the DNR, and its severe restriction of speed was specifically rejected by the membership of the association. (Among other things, establishing a "slow–no wake" restriction would also have involved a cumbersome rule-making process.) Nevertheless, Twin Lakes is occasionally referred to as a no-wake lake.[264]

The conclusion drawn by one member who had checked with the DNR was that residents could do nothing to keep jet skis off the lake. In a literal sense, that conclusion may have been true. In a practical sense, it was not. As the sheriff and a deputy pointed out in a meeting with the trustees in July, 2003, Michigan law makes it all but impossible to legally operate jet skis on Twin Lakes.[265]

The other area of misunderstanding (or uncertainty) is what constitutes "high-speed boating." At least as early as 1992 and probably earlier, a resident "inquired as to whether the speed limit could be defined as to what exactly determined high speed." The question arose again in 2000 and 2006. At the time of the ordinance's passage and thereafter, the legal definition of "high-speed boating" was clear: "a speed at which or above which a motor boat reaches a planing condition." By contrast, a "slow–no wake speed" is "the slowest speed at which headway can be made and it is still possible to maintain steering control" or "the use of a vessel at a very slow speed so that the resulting wake or wash is minimal."[266] The source of the uncertainty appears to be the discrepancy between the generous speed provided for in the definition of "high speed" and what most reasonable people consider a safe boating speed on a small lake with swimmers, waterfowl, logs and stumps, an irregular bottom, and a vulnerable shoreline. That speed is less than planing or near-planing speed and greater than the near motionlessness of a no-wake zone. There is no administrative category that fits a common-sense notion of safe speed on a lake like Twin Lakes.[267]

From February 13, 1980, onward, the CTLA faced two problems in connection with the ordinance: making known the rule and enforcing the rule.

The vehicle for making known the ordinance was signage. The first mention of "high speed" signage in the surviving records is in the minutes of the trustees meeting of May 13, 1998. But that discussion was about repair and repainting of existing signs. Leon Byron, John King, and Robert Schultz volunteered to take down the signs, and Doris Rodriguez to repaint them. The discussion also concerned the possibility of placing a sign at the Page Road boat launch and perhaps including a notice to be aware of loon habitat. Little more than a year later, it was suggested that more signs be placed around the lake; Leon Byron would paint them, and John King and Kenneth Hebert would place them.[268]

In November 2000, the association decided to end the need to repaint wood (or strand-board) signs by purchasing metal signs. During the winter of 2000–2001, metal signs were placed, including two welcome signs at the Page Road boat launch and the campground dock. Six years later, it was believed that "More NO WAKE signs are needed on the lake by the boat launch and the State Park"; more signs, reworded, were to be ordered.[269]

The lake is host to largemouth bass, northern pike, rock bass, bluegill and sunfish. The green frog, spring peeper, mink frog, leopard frog and other amphibians live in the aquatic vegetation. Trees – among them white and red pine, maple, white cedar, white birch, beech, hemlock, aspen and eastern larch - dominate the plants of the ecosystem. Ferns, trillium, bluebead and trout lilies, marsh marigolds, wild blueberries and other plants abound. Aquatic and shoreline vegetation includes rushes, sedges, grass of Parnassus (bog-stars), sun dew, red osier dogwood, yellow water lilies and, later in summer, fragrant white water lilies.

Cheboygan Twin Lakes Association
P.O. Box 5164, Cheboygan MI 49721

Welcome to Twin Lakes

Sustaining an Environment for Generations to Come

Twin Lakes is an ideal place for recreation and residence. We urge you to respect this special place by:

- Observing the prohibition of high-speed boating
- Not disturbing the water fowl
- Being alert to swimmers
- Keeping noise levels low
- Insuring your boat, trailer, and equipment are clean
- Respecting the property of others

In 2008, a committee of Richard Duke, Stuart Gage, and Thomas Knox undertook to produce a consistent message in different media and settings: a trifold brochure for CTLA members and lake residents, a set of suggestions with explanation for visitors at the Page Road launch and the Smith Road campground, and new signs on the lake. The signs, placed over the winter of 2008–2009, warned against high speed, alerted boaters to the presence of swimmers, and urged that waterfowl not be disturbed. The text for the Page Road launch was in place by the spring of 2009, though its protective case was subsequently shattered by an unknown visitor and had to be rebuilt. (The Smith Road campground was closed at this time.) The brochures were mailed with the April 2010 newsletter and otherwise distributed.[270]

A Special Place

Twin Lakes is an ecosystem, a place where animals, plants, microbes and the physical environment interact. Its centerpiece is the complex of bays and channels that make up the lake itself.

For many reasons, some purely natural, some the result of human actions, the water is exceptionally clear and pure. Lack of direct exposure to agricultural and industrial activity protects the lake from problems ranging from excessive nutrients to siltation to mercury pollution. Twin Lakes is fed by springs; thus, it does not receive silt or pollution from other places. Small size, shore vegetation, aquatic plants, minimal currents, protection from wind and wave action, and low-speed boating all help to insure that the organic material on the bottom remains stable, reducing turbidity. Much of the shoreline is a dense and diverse belt of aquatic grasses, trees and other vegetation that helps to hold soil, filter contaminants, provide habitat, and shade shoreline areas.

A Place to Live

Based on long-term monitoring, the Tip of the Mitt Watershed Council identified Twin Lakes as a "gem" lake in 2008. But, as the Council's report noted, "this great land comes with … great responsibility."

The Twin Lakes system provides habitat for a variety of species, including humans, and many make this complex environment their home.

The Twin Lakes community is deservedly proud of this special place. And it is determined to protect and preserve this gem for current and future generations of all the species for whom this diverse ecology is home.

Animals and Plants

Birds and water fowl in the ecosystem, many of them threatened species, include bald eagles, osprey, common terns, belted kingfishers, blue herons, trumpeter swans, common loons, mergansers, pheasant, grouse, wild turkey and many smaller woodland birds.

Field, forest, and wetland dwellers range from black bear, white-tailed deer, coyotes, fox, beaver, river otter, martens, and raccoons to the usual smaller fauna such as rabbits, squirrels and chipmunks.

The community of Twin Lakes welcomes visitors to share responsibly with them the enjoyment of this special place. We ask that you please:

Observe the ordinance prohibiting high-speed boating

Low-speed operation protects all species on the lake, including water fowl and human swimmers. It also reduces wake damage to the natural shoreline that offers refuge to the juvenile fish population. The lake's fish population depends on natural reproduction, not stocking. Additionally, low-speed operation will protect the boater who is not familiar with the irregular bottom and submerged objects in Twin Lakes.

Do not disturb the water fowl

The water fowl that nest on Twin Lakes need quiet water and a lack of human intrusion. Adult birds are at their most stressed and anxious as they nest. Once hatched, the young race through the remaining weeks of summer to gain the strength and survival skills they will need for fall migration and a return to Twin Lakes in future years. This growth can be observed from watercraft on the lake, but boats should keep their distance (150 feet minimum).

Be alert to the presence of swimmers

Many of the bays of Twin Lakes have clearly visible moored swim platforms, but there are also areas where swimmers enter the water from docks and their presence is less obvious. Swimming is not a summertime activity only; there are hardy (wet-suited) souls who swim at almost any time when the lake is ice-free.

Help prevent noise pollution

One of the joys of fishing or camping is the quiet. Quiet is also important to virtually all animals and it is one reason lake residents have chosen to settle here.

Be sure your boat, trailer, and equipment are clean

The deadly fish virus VHS (viral hemorrhagic septicemia), non-native aquatic life, and invasive plant species can devastate the fragile ecology of a small lake system like Twin Lakes. Be sure to follow DNR procedures regarding unused bait, live wells and bilges, and cleaning and drying of all equipment.

Cheboygan Twin Lakes Association, PO Box 5164, Cheboygan MI 49721

The association could not carry out enforcement. At most, it could urge safe low-speed operation on its members and other boaters. Who was responsible to enforce was uncertain. The provision existed in the administrative rules of the DNR and thus in state law; it also existed in the marine section of the county code. But the DNR habitually complains (often with justification) of too few officers to carry out its responsibilities, and the Cheboygan County Marine Division, as noted on the website of the sheriff's department, is responsible to patrol "44 inland lakes, 420 miles of streams, 34.5 miles of Lake Huron, and 182.3 miles of inland lake shoreline."[271]

In 1993, then president Earl Boyea suggested that members might want to report high-speed boating "to the DNR or appropriate authority." A motion was passed "that the DNR be contacted to find out who has the responsibility for the Twin Lakes area and . . . let them know of our concerns."[272] In 1999, a newsletter reported that trustees had shared stories about high-speed boating and the harassment of loons. "DNR has said they will issue tickets for these offenses, but it's difficult to get officers here in time to catch offenders in the act."[273] No solution was suggested other than urging members to obey the laws and to ask violators gently to do the same. (More recently, the advice has been not to engage at all with violators.)

In 2003, a newsletter advised calling the sheriff's department with the registration number of the boat. But the problem of getting an officer to the lake to observe the violation was the same as with the DNR, and getting the registration number off a boat moving at high speed is a difficult task, even on a small lake. The same advice was given in a 2006 newsletter.[274]

Lake Level and the Dam

The second immediate concern of the association was control of the lake level. This was important not only for boating, especially passage through the channels connecting the bays, but also for the survival and reproduction of fish and fowl and the preservation of shoreline. And the question of lake level very soon became tied to concern over the condition of the Truscott Drive (or Owens Creek outlet or Twin Lakes outlet) dam itself.[275] (In his 1974 report, John Gannon had referred to the outlet as "controlled by a flimsy board structure at the outflow.")

In 1985, several residents appear to have written to divisions within the DNR expressing concern over water level and control of water level. Thomas Lowell, responding to Elnora Godfrey, suggested two alternative routes to take regarding water level: work with the private owner who had control over the dam and gain an easement to access and operate the dam or to petition the county commissioners to have a legal lake level established, maintenance of which would then become legally enforceable.[276]

The letter from Steve and Julia Seconsky, to which Lawrence Witte responded, appears to have focused on the condition of the dam and the possibility of state funds for repair. Having dismissed that possibility, Witte suggested establishing a legal lake level as a means to spread future repair and maintenance costs over all the property owners who benefitted. (The Inland Lake Level Act is the controlling legislation in this matter.) Witte's letter enclosed a list of the advantages and disadvantages of establishing legal lake levels. Aside from spreading the costs, the advantages listed include stabilized water levels; maximized recreational benefits; provision for winter drawdown, resulting in benefits to lake properties and lake ecology; maximized "fisheries, wildlife, and aesthetic values"; and placing responsibility for maintaining the level in local government, specifically the county commissioners and the drain commissioner. The disadvantages were the costs (and the reluctance of property owners to approve special assessment zones, even when they would benefit), the length of time required to get a legal level established, and possible damage to pike spawning.[277]

The outlet, June 1984 (Photographs courtesy of Jerry Beehler and John Ressler)

(While Lowell stated flatly that there was no legal lake level for Twin Lakes and Witte very clearly implied that there was none, a DNR official in Cheboygan was quoted in a contemporary newspaper article as saying there were court-established high- and low-water levels for the lake. The same official said that the association had put in the dam "several years ago and has maintained it since." The article also quoted Elnora Godfrey as saying she believed the Waterways Division should be responsible for the upkeep of the dam but that the association, with permission to "trespass," had maintained it for several years.[278])

Planks over outlet

Spillway entrance and controls

The disadvantages of petitioning to establish a legal lake level apparently prevailed. In fact, the association had secured an easement from one property owner on Truscott Drive on August 27, 1980, "to make necessary repairs to the Owens Creek Dam to maintain a reasonable water level in [the] lake." Steve Seconsky signed for the association, and Clayton Cannis witnessed the document. (The same property owner allowed the association to marshal supplies on his land for the 2009 erosion prevention project.) On August 4, 1985, the association secured from two of its members another easement on Truscott Road that again gave it the necessary access to control water levels and maintain the dam.

> We the undersigned & owners of Truscott Lane, Twin Lakes, Cheboygan County, on which the Owens Creek Spillway is located, have as of this date 8/4/85 given the Twin Lakes Assn., perpetual, or as long as they (the Assn.) exist, an easement to access & repair and operate that structure.

The statement was drafted by Elnora Godfrey, witnessed by Clarence Archambo, notarized by Clayton Cannis, and signed by Gerald and Doris Truscott.[279]

The history of the dam (or dams) involves some speculation. Oral testimony indicates that the first dam, probably a small earthen dam and spill gate, was built by Alva Page in the 1930s. There is some reason (though not much) to believe that a new dam was built in the 1950s; the evidence is more friable second- or thirdhand memory than anything else, and exactly what constitutes building a new dam as opposed to doing a repair is arguable. As indicated above, at least one DNR official thought the association had put in the dam "several years ago [around 1980?] and has maintained it since." "Putting in" seems most unlikely, whereas the assumption of responsibility for maintenance seems quite certain as of 1980. But assumption of maintenance would be of a structure that already existed. Clearly though, the dam, an earthwork with the simplest of controls and an earthen spillway running beneath a dirt and plank road, was deteriorating over time.

(In connection with the nature and condition of the outlet dam, it is worth considering these observations from the *Manual on Small Earth Dams*. An earthen embankment "is easily damaged or destroyed by water flowing on, over, or against it." To deal with this, a spillway is essential but also the most technically difficult part of dam building. The embankment must be adequately compacted during construction. Otherwise, it will lack structural integrity and offer channels for seepage. Earthen dams "require continual maintenance to prevent erosion, tree growth, subsidence, animal and insect damage, and seepage."[280])

By 1985, repair of the dam was seen as a crisis. (Clearly, if inferentially, the condition of the dam was a subject of acute concern in 1984, and in all likelihood, it had been a matter of apprehension for many years before.) A report by the UMBS suggested that if the dam were to wash out, the lake level would drop at least twelve inches, Twin Lakes would be reduced to three separate lakes, and several residences would be isolated. According to the *CDT* article, "The dam appears to be a flimsy, wooden structure which has borne more weight than it should and does not look as if its durability will last much longer." In addition to its location on private property, a dirt-and-plank road with no weight limit passed over the dam, giving access to cottages on the northern edge of the lake.[281]

Repair of the dam represented a financial crisis for the CTLA. The association voted to spend, $2,700–$3,000 on repair. This sum represented all its cash assets and then some. The association's cash on hand at the time was $2,048; exhausting all of it would probably have brought about dissolution. A June 17, 1985, letter asked members and lake neighbors to provide financial support. By earlier July, support on the order of $1,260 had come in, and more was hoped for.[282]

The result was that the first major renovation of the dam was undertaken and completed; its prime mover was Claude Ressler.[283] (Previously, the DNR may have paid infrequent and inadequate attention to the dam. But that is uncertain, indeed unlikely. Two nearby residents (Bruns and Dubois) had graveled around the dam as appeared necessary, but this was the barest maintenance and did not address the basic issues. What exactly the CTLA may have done by way of maintenance is unknown.) What emerged from what proved to be the first stage of a two-stage process was a dam with a strongly secured embankment, a heavy conduit, and a spillway with rocks placed on the spongy soil at its end.

Aside from the bombing range, the March 1987 newsletter included this comment from Elnora Godfrey.

> Once again, the spillway will be brought up [at the annual meeting in May] and this time in detail. Last fall, all the boards were removed early, too early, and not replaced. We have one disabled man that could not get into his boat due to low water, and if he would further injure himself, we would have no one but ourselves to blame, and I certainly would not want something like that to accept as even a part of my fault.

(In current and long-standing practice, the lake level is adjusted to the extent of the few inches represented by one or two boards. Only very heavy rains will necessitate greater adjustment. The CTLA is not free to act as it might wish with respect to the dam; it is obligated to maintain a flow in the outlet creek sufficient to sustain wildlife in and around the creek and to avoid infringing on the riparian rights of property owners along the creek.)

In contrast, in her 1988 summary of the accomplishments of the association in its first ten years, Elnora Godfrey commented,

> We have, through the cooperation and generosity of our members and a few nonmembers, managed with donations, built the best cotton-picking spillway, and related gauges in the whole

state of Michigan![284] We raised $3,000. This amount pretty well covered the cost. Very little was taked [sic] from our funds. We were so proud of you! It does prove pulling together works. You don't just wave a magic wand and nice things happen.

The process [Claude Ressler is maneuvering the metal plate]
(Photographs courtesy of John Ressler)

Still, a year later, a group of residents worked on the spillway outlet of the dam, as reported in a handwritten "[résumé] of work done on the outlet of spillway tube" provided by Claude Ressler. (The spillway had been scheduled to be a topic of discussion at the annual meeting in May 1987 and may have been brought up at earlier meetings.[285] "Deterioration of the banks" was a topic at the trustees meeting on June 14, 1989.[286])

On July 27th, our crew started the job. Had to pick out a lot of stones from the creek before we could start. These stones for some reason kept finding their way off the bank and the end of the tube & into the creek & the lake on the other side.

This was the reason for cementing the outlet in.

The result: spillway face

The process

The result: spillway end

We used seven bales of straw, wired & wired down to hold the cement from running out into the creek.

On the 28th [of July] 1989, our crew of men from the association poured grout cement all around the stones to hold them in place.

We mixed our own cement on the job. The mix was a soupy mixture of fine stones & sand. Pour it in with buckets. Did a good job.

On Tuesday August 1st 1989, we had a cement truck from Onaway to pour the top over the stones & finish the job.

Our crew of men from the association were on hand to take care of the work.

John & myself wish to thank all the fellows for their support & muscle.

Thanks

Claude Ressler

John King

Redy [sic] Mix 3yds	$229.84
10 Bags Cement 1 yd Sand	71.77
7 Bale's [sic] Straw	<u>7.00</u>
Total of Repairs	$308.61

Three years later, in hopes of discouraging unilateral lake-level management by humans and by beavers, a grill was installed to cover the dam opening. The work was finished in the fall of 1992. The grill was custom-built and custom-fit and served the dual purpose of keeping large debris out of the spillway and preventing tampering with the lake level. In place, the grill denied access to the boards that control lake level and was secured by locks. Recently, this arrangement has been modified to permit free movement of floating vegetation into the outlet creek while still satisfying the two original purposes.

Once again, however, the cost drastically reduced association assets. Welding of the grill work exceeded estimates. Not having had a chance to raise monies to cover the unexpected expenses, the association made a partial payment ($500, or roughly 70 percent of the total cost), the remainder to be paid the following spring.

As a direct result of its reduced finances, "we will need to think of some new ideas for raising needed cash for the Association. One idea already received is a plan for a combined garage and bake sale, with a portion of the proceeds going to the Association." The first such sale was held June 26, 1993, and was a success. In the August meeting of the trustees, "a general discussion was . . . held as to whether the Association would continue with an annual fund raiser, such as the Bake Sale/Garage Sale that was held this past June."[287]

> Due to the excellent results, it was generally agreed that the project would continue, and it was suggested that next years [sic] project could be expanded upon to include a mens [sic] project.

Over the years, quite apart from major repair, the dam and lake level have required constant surveillance, maintenance, and adjustment. The most common problems stemmed from beavers, in the case of the dam, and rainfall, in the case of lake levels. Entries in the minutes of the 2006 and 2010 trustees meetings may stand for all such efforts: "The fall cleanup of the dam was done and readied for winter"; "Beavers are back. Water level had been high but going down slowly due to constant diligence of cleaning the dam."[288] Such maintenance has been paid for out of the association's general fund. One of the most common topics in trustees meetings over the decades has been lake level. This work has been performed by a relatively small number of men; in a facsimile of chronological order since the earlier 1980s—Steve Seconsky, Robert Schultz, Charles Williams, Dagfin ("Swede") Nilsen, Earl Boyea, Karl Kalis, Gerald Griessel, and Leonard Page.

The first intimation of a need to carry out another major repair on the dam appeared in late 2006, with contact of the DNR regarding the surface of the road over the dam and a suggestion that the DNR and property owners be asked if the association could put rocks on the side of the road. In 2008, two members checked to see "if gravel needs to be added behind sheeting on shoreline."

By the end of August, it was known that a significant erosion stabilization project on the shoreline was needed. Verbal permission to proceed had been received from the DEQ, and a grant was being sought to cover at least a quarter of the cost (estimated at $2,500–$3,500 to remediate twenty-five feet on each side of the dam).

By early October, William Thompson, the association's lead on the project, had contacted TOMWC, specifically Jennifer Gelb, TOMWC's restoration ecologist. Repairs were put on hold for the winter. In May, Thompson reported that Gelb would visit the site during the summer and that while grants were available from the Cheboygan River Watershed Committee, the committee would designate the contractor and control what was done.

By early July, Gelb had looked at the dam site and indicated that the job could be done and would qualify for grant funds if the CTLA participated in the actual work. In August, she explained to a trustees meeting what could be done to control erosion around the dam and on lakeside properties. While a grant might be available, funds for dam erosion work were limited. She could draw up plans under a grant, or the CTLA could pay for it and then do the work. In early September, a grant was still a possibility, but if everything was approved, the work needed to be done by people on the lake by the end of October. (Ultimately, a grant was received from the U.S. Fish and Wildlife Service.) A motion to spend $2,000 from a certificate of deposit held for just such projects was passed by a large margin.[289]

In two days in the second week of October, large rocks were placed at the base of the shoreline and small rocks added. With one exception, the heavy equipment used in the project was provided by CTLA members. Gravel was added to the road to repair damage from the heavy equipment. Coir (coconut fiber) "logs" were on order and expected to be placed in November. This first stage had been covered by a grant, and Gelb was reportedly impressed by the extent of volunteerism. As of the second week in November, the remaining supplies were in place.

In the third week of November (an unusually warm November, to the annoyance of deer hunters), the work was completed with placement of the coir logs, secured by earth anchors, and graveling of the road. The hope was that indigenous natural vegetation would establish itself on the bank; if not, planting would be resorted to. In the end, the CTLA did not have to cover the major costs of remediation. (The following spring, the CTLA made a larger-than-usual donation to TOMWC and encouraged CTLA members to join; a number were already members of TOMWC.)[290]

The Boat Ramp

There is a single point of entry for boats on Twin Lakes, at the end of Page Road. The road itself did not run to the lake until the 1960s, when the County Road Commission extended the dirt road to the lake and placed two concrete slabs recovered from work on I-75 at the edge of the water. Before then, the road ran only as far as the Page farm, and those on the farm went through field and forest to get to the lake's shore.

The county neglected to place any signs at or near the end of the road. In October 2004, the CTLA trustees discussed an incident in Grand Traverse County in which a car made a wrong turn and drove off a boat launch, killing four persons. They wondered if it could happen at the end of Page Road. A nearby resident reported that it already had, though without injury. (In November 1999, a motorist drove a new Ford Explorer down the boat ramp and "into the lake about 100 feet.")[291] The trustees decided to ask the county to install appropriate signs.

In June 1997, a trustees meeting discussed, at length, possible improvements to the boat ramp. Boats had proved difficult to launch, and at least one person had fallen more than once on the cement slab. Members of the association inspecting the site believed the area could be improved and mishaps prevented if "debris" could be pulled out and a walkway built along the cement ramp. A motion to this effect was made and unanimously approved, with the proviso that the County Road Commission give its approval. The project was approved, and within weeks, stumps and logs were removed from the area and a short wooden walkway constructed on its eastern side to help in boat launching. The cost to the association was $154.28 for lumber and $13.00 for hardware.[292]

The launch did not reappear as a topic again until October 2004, at which point discussion was tabled until spring. (The primary reason the trustees decided not to vote on repairs to the launch was dismay at the number and behaviors of nonresidents using the launch.) Once more, it disappeared for a time, showing up only in May 2010, when John Hirschler reported that he had inquired about what was needed to repair the hole at the end of the boat ramp, and Leon Byron moved that the CTLA proceed to get the permit needed to make repairs.

A land and water management specialist at the Department of Natural Resources and the Environment (DNRE) had said only a simple permit, perhaps $75, was required and suggested laying down a sheeting material (GeoTech) and covering it with rocks. (The basic problem was a drop-off or hole on the southwest end of the ramp, which could cause the rear end of vehicles to become submerged and which could catch trailer wheels.) By mid-July, Dick Duke, Stuart Gage, and Tom Knox had been named a ramp committee to resolve issues at the boat ramp, especially the drop-off. The committee reported a month later. The possible solutions were fairly simple and quite expensive (a large metal ramp extension that could be put in in the spring and removed in the fall) or very simple and quite inexpensive (dump a load of *clean* gravel).[293]

As of the annual fall meeting in early September, two members had further researched the problem of the drop-off at the boat launch and were planning to attend the township meeting in a few days to ask for financial assistance for repairs on the ground that the launch was a public facility. At this point, things became complicated. It appeared that the association would have to pay $500 for a permit from the DNRE, which had oversight of Twin Lakes, because the launch was on "municipal" property, not residential property, where the fee would have been $50–$75. The DNRE wanted approval from the county since the launch was off a county road, and the county wanted the township to become involved.[294]

Preceded by a letter to the township explaining the request for assistance with the fee and emphasizing that the CTLA was not asking for money for the costs of actual repair, members of the association attended the October meeting of the township board. One response to the request was that the board did not want to set a precedent by giving funds to the CTLA for Twin Lakes. It was pointed out that precedent had long since been set with grants to the Black Lake Association to address zebra mussels, Eurasian milfoil, and swimmer's itch and for other projects. The township supervisor had contacted the Cheboygan County Road Commission (CCRC) regarding "road ends." He was told the CCRC was responsible for road ends only to the water's edge and would not help repair the boat launch.

The supervisor then spoke of conducting a survey and doing a cleanup of the launch area, including a clean-out of the shoreline vegetation. The CTLA representatives responded that the association did not want repair of the road end and that the shore vegetation "is *not* a mess": "the mess is the garbage left by those using the site, such as [C]oke bottles full of urine, empty bags, and liquor bottles at [the] boat launch." One of the trustees reasoned, "If you are going to spend the money on the survey etc. and they are not asking for us to repair the launch area, why not just give them the money for the permit?" The decision was to table the request.[295]

A good deal of frustration was expressed in the next CTLA trustees meeting. In part, it was directed at government entities that could make decisions without regard to the residents and could impose obligations and costs but would not accept responsibility. And in part, it focused on the nature of the launch. It was a public launch, not built, owned, or controlled by the lake residents, open to everyone without payment of any fee. But to the residents (in the form of the CTLA and nearby property owners) fell responsibility for maintaining the ramp and the launch area, "including cleaning up after public users." (While the CCRC had access to thirty-three feet of land on each side of the road, measured from the road's midpoint, the CCRC had made no provision for parking or sanitation. Both wound up on adjoining private property.)[296]

The November meeting of the trustees included the reading of a letter from DNRE explaining the application fee, cost estimates of two methods of repair, a report of the insistence of the township supervisor that creosoted telephone poles were needed, and a report as well of the apparent willingness of the township to split costs fifty-fifty. In its November meeting, the township board seems to have agreed to provide the cost of the permit fee and perhaps fund half of the project.[297] This agreement is not mentioned in the official minutes of the meeting. The decision was to reassess repair in the spring.[298]

Subsequently, a decision was made by the CTLA to proceed with repair using clean gravel. Arrangements were made to have the gravel delivered, and volunteers shoveled, raked, and compacted the material into an effective remedy. The site continues to be monitored.

The Island

An island—a low-lying combination of wetlands and thick forest, slightly over ninety acres in all, with a ridge forming its spine—separates the three largest of the bays. The southern half is the property of the federal government, the northern half the property of the State of Michigan, though neither has shown much interest in its share. The island is unoccupied and undeveloped. It is a favored resort for all forms of animal life in the area, aquatic, avian, and terrestrial. It is also a fruitful location for bio-acoustic research and a site of geocaching. Only in recent years has it appeared in discussions and documents as a source of concern. The concern stems from use and abuse by visitors. Specifically, the concern is with fire, cutting, and trash. There is no firepit on the island, a state requirement for an open fire. Nevertheless, open fires have been common, some of them frighteningly large. Fire could easily leap the narrow distance to the mainland. Similarly, there is to be no unlicensed cutting of standing trees on state land. That has been completely ignored in many instances on the island. Visitors often do not practice "carry in, carry out." Trash removal then falls to residents. More broadly, camping on state land requires permission of the DNR and is not permitted when there is a state camping facility within a mile of the site, as is the case on Twin Lakes. Similarly, camping on federal land requires an approved request and is not permitted when there is a camping facility within a mile of the site. As of later 2015, the CTLA, with the assistance of the DNR and contact with the U.S. Forest Service, may have succeeded in addressing these issues. (To the surprise of the forest's superintendent, the federal half of the island is a part of the ninety-year-old Hiawatha National Forest. The Forest Service describes the forest as located in the Upper Peninsula.)

Lake Monitoring

"Lake monitoring" on Twin Lakes, as distinct from the "lake level monitoring" already referred to, is concerned with the quality of the water and is a prime example of citizen science. (While reports on lake level are common in the surviving minutes of trustees meetings, there is no mention of the quality of the water until 2003.) Tip of the Mitt began its volunteer lake monitoring program (VLM), a program of annual testing of the water in lakes in Northern Michigan, in 1984. (DNR monitoring, specifically laboratory testing of samples, ended in 1983.) In 1987, it initiated its comprehensive water quality monitoring program (CM), a triennial collection of more sophisticated information. Typically, it involves gathering data for multiple parameters at the surface, middle, and bottom in each water column.[299]

The association joined TOMWC in 1987. It planned to have members trained to test lake water and to undertake systematic testing in 1988. Monitoring seems to have begun in that year (a report from TOMWC would suggest so), but the first mention in the newsletter is of James McPherson, immediate past president of the CTLA, testing the lake's clarity in 1989. Among the "gem" lakes monitored by volunteers, Twin Lakes in Cheboygan County and Thumb Lake in Charlevoix County have, by far, the longest runs of data, although in the case of Twin Lakes, there are interruptions.[300]

In the VLM program, volunteers on Twin Lakes measured Secchi disc depths in the five basins (TOMWC's count) of the lake. (The Secchi disc is a disc eight inches in diameter painted black and white alternately in its four quarters.) Quality calculations were based on the Carlson Trophic State Index (TSI) to determine if a lake was oligotrophic, mesotrophic, or eutrophic. There is not an absolute relationship between a lake's status and its water quality, but in general, oligotrophic will equate to high water quality, mesotrophic to moderate water quality, and eutrophic to poor water quality. Low-nutrient oligotrophic lakes have a high degree of clarity because of the relative absence of suspended algae. High-nutrient eutrophic lakes have low clarity because of the algae suspended in the water. Nutrient load may be increased by any number of human activities. The eutrophic lake may also have periods in which there is no oxygen at its deepest levels; in contrast, the oligotrophic lake will have little or no deepwater oxygen depletion.[301]

The easiest though not necessarily the most accurate method, Secchi disc depth is a widely used means of estimating water quality. (The most accurate combines Secchi readings, chlorophyll-a concentration, and phosphorus concentration. The VLM did add chlorophyll-a sampling in 1991. Measuring the amount of chlorophyll-a, present in all green plants, in the water provides a measure of the amount of phytoplankton, which is directly related to the nutrient level.) The TSI scale ranges from 0 to 100, with the best water quality occurring at the low end of the scale. On this scale, 0–39 designates an oligotrophic body of water, 39–49 a mesotrophic, and 50–100 a eutrophic.

In 1988, the Secchi disc depth (the point at which the disc could no longer be seen) for the basins of Twin Lakes ranged from 13.8 to 16.7 feet, an average of 15.4, producing TSI numbers tightly bunched between 37 and 39, an average of 37.6. In 1997, the average Secchi number was just above 15, and the overall TSI for Twin Lakes was 32, ranking it seventh in water quality of the bodies of water tested. As the chart below shows, the average Secchi depth of Twin Lakes since that date has ranged from roughly 12 to almost 20 feet, hovering for the most part around 15 feet. In 2015, the seasonal average Secchi depth was 14 feet and the TSI score 40, the next year 15 feet and 38.[302]

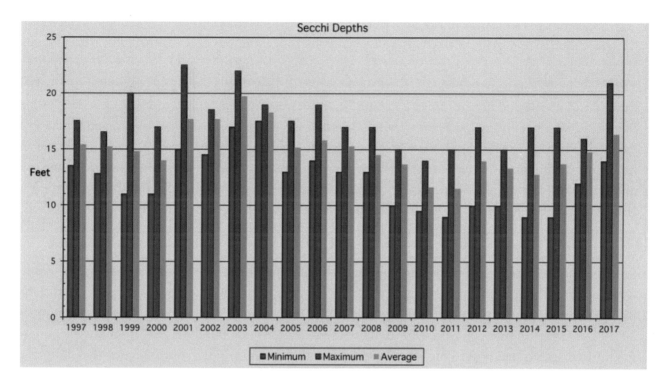

The CM gathers information on temperature, dissolved oxygen, pH, conductivity, total phosphorus, total nitrogen, chloride, and water clarity. Twin Lakes has been monitored every third year since the program's inception in 1987.

Temperature is taken in early spring to ensure that a lake is not stratified (the density of water varies with temperature, and deep lakes may well be stratified) and to determine the percent saturation of oxygen (cold water can hold more oxygen than warm water, and generally, the closer the dissolved oxygen to the saturation point, which varies with temperature, the better the quality of the water). Of lakes surveyed in 2013, the temperature range was 36°F (Torch Lake) to slightly over 58°F (Wildwood Lake). Twin Lakes was just under 54°F, in a narrow range of temperature shared with many other lakes.[303]

Oxygen is required by all organisms and dissolves into water from the atmosphere and from plant and algal photosynthesis. State law requires a minimum 5–7 parts per million (PPM). Surface readings on Twin Lakes in 1995, 1998, 2001, 2004, 2007, and 2010 produced an average of 11.07 PPM, plus or minus 2 PPM. The range of the lakes monitored in 2013 was 9.7 PPM (Paradise Lake) to 14.97 PPM (Bass Lake). Twin Lakes was 11.25. (However, in 2004, Twin Lakes accounted for the lowest level recorded until then in this group of lakes, 0.94, a measurement taken at the deepest point in the lake (over 70 feet), where oxygen depletion is typical for many lakes.) The range in 2016 was 9.99 PPM (Lancaster Lake) to 13.61 PPM (Mullett Lake); Twin Lakes was 12.09 PPM.

pH is a measure of the acidity or alkalinity of the water. Neutral is 7; numbers below 7 are acid, numbers above alkaline. If the number falls outside the range 5.5–8.5, most aquatic organisms become stressed, and some species may diminish or disappear. State water quality standards require that all waters be in the range 6.0–9.0. In 2013, the pH range of the bodies of water monitored was from 7.90 (Larks Lake) to 8.54 (Marion Lake). Twin Lakes was 8.33. (In 2010, the range was far less narrow, from 7.72 (Lancaster Lake) to 11.32 (Ben-Way Lake). Twin Lakes was 8.32.) In 2016, the range was 6.04 (Deer Lake) to 8.70 (Wildwood Lake). Twin Lakes was 7.06, the lowest pH number in the lake's recorded history; the reading in 1995 was 7.46, but samples over the next fifteen years averaged 8.25 with virtually no fluctuation.

Conductivity is a measure of the ability of water to carry an electrical current. That ability depends on the concentration of ions in the water. Steadily increasing concentrations generally occur in areas of human activity and may indicate pollution is occurring. The conductivity measures in bodies of water monitored by TOMWC in 2013 ranged from 174.1 microSiemens (µS) at Lancaster Lake to 816.1 µS at Spring Lake in Emmet County. Twin Lakes recorded 275.8 µS. In 2010, the numbers ranged from 190.1 µS at Nowland Lake to 529.9 µS at Spring Lake, with Twin Lakes at 259.6 µS. Spring Lake had been an outlier and was joined by Mud Lake (618.73 µS), the two lakes adjacent in an area of major roads and of commercial and residential development in the Petoskey–Harbor Springs area. They might also be the most extreme cases of an incipient trend of slowly increasing conductivity in the bodies of water surveyed.[304] In 2016, Mud Lake remained the outlier (504.63 µS), while Thayer Lake recorded an extraordinary 44.17 µS. Twin Lakes remained constant (250.40 µS). The Twin Lakes readings are slightly lower but otherwise consistent with readings between 1995 and 2010.

Phosphorus is the most important nutrient for plant productivity in surface waters. A body of water is considered phosphorus limited if the ratio of nitrogen to phosphorus (much less common than nitrogen and carbon) exceeds 15:1. The United States Environmental Protection Agency recommends 10 PPB or less of total phosphorus for lakes (Michigan does not have water quality standards for nutrients). Surface water considered to be of high quality usually approximates that numerical standard. Readings in 2010 ranged from 0.7 PPB on Torch Lake to 13.3 PPB on Munro Lake. Twin Lakes registered 9.7 PPB. In 2013, the low end of the range was <1 PPB on Charlevoix, Elk, Round, and Torch Lakes (the last registered 0.0), the upper end 17.0 PPB on Crooked Lake. Twin Lakes showed 4.7 PPB. The range in 2016 was 0.7 PPB (Wildwood Lake) to 61.8 (Skegemog Lake). Twin Lakes recorded 7.0 PPB. Significant decreases in total phosphorus may result from a substantial presence of zebra and quagga mussels. In 1995, Twin Lakes registered 24.0 PPB, an outlier that has to be disregarded; the next four samplings averaged 7.67 PPB within a range of 0.7 PPB.

Nitrogen is another essential nutrient and an abundant one. This nutrient occurs naturally. Nitrogen pollution, however, is generally the result of a human presence (e.g., the use of fertilizer, failing septic systems, storm water runoff). In general, the highest levels of nitrogen are found in small shallow inland lakes and the lowest in large deep inland lakes and the Upper Great Lakes. Results in 2010 ranged from 247 PPB on Silver Lake at Wolverine to 1,475 PPB on Spring Lake. Twin Lakes had a concentration of 393 PPB. In 2013, Wilson Lake in Antrim County registered 215 PPB, Spring Lake and Mud Lake 1,192 PPB and 1,288 PPB, respectively. Twin Lakes recorded 291 PPB. Three years later, Thumb Lake showed the lowest concentration (60 PPB) and Spring Lake the highest (2,476 PPB). Twin Lakes remained at the lower end of the range (294 PPB). These numbers are consistent with those recorded on the lake in 1998–2007, on average 330 PPB.

Chloride, a component of salt, is naturally present in low levels in Northern Michigan because of the marine origins of its bedrock. Chloride is also present in many substances associated with human activity, such as road salt, road brine, water-softener salts, automotive fluids, bleach, and leachings from septic systems. At levels below 1,000 PPM, most aquatic organisms are not affected by chloride.

But increasing chloride levels suggest that pollutants are reaching streams, rivers, and lakes. Readings in 2010 ranged from 2.2 PPM at Twin Lakes to 90.0 PPM on Spring Lake. Readings in 2013 fell between 2.3 PPM at Twin Lakes and 137.9 PPB on Spring Lake (Mud Lake showed 77.3 PPB, the second-highest reading). In 2016, the Twin Lakes reading had risen to 3.38 PPM, still the lowest in a range that topped out at 94.49 PPM (Spring Lake). While the presence of chloride in Twin Lakes is very low, the apparent trend is troubling: the average of samples 1998–2007 was 1.725 PPB with virtually no variation until 2007.

Chlorophyll-a is a pigment used by plants to photosynthesize. Measuring chlorophyll concentrations provides a notion of the density of phytoplankton (or microalgae). The higher the chlorophyll concentrations, the greater the density of the phytoplankton and the biological productivity of the lake. Measuring chlorophyll concentration is also a means to determine whether changes of water clarity are the result of phytoplankton densities or some other cause or causes. TOMWC began monitoring chlorophyll in 1991, but the early monitoring was not uniform, and the data is consequently somewhat broken up. In the case of Twin Lakes, data is available from 2008 onward. From 2008 through 2011, the readings are relatively consistent—2.25, 2.26, 2.03, and 2.30 PPB. From 2012 through 2016, the readings show decline—1.63, 1.62, 1.18, 1.15, and 1.15 PPB. The decline corresponds to what is now known to be the arrival of phytoplankton-consuming zebra mussels and follows a pattern that has been seen on a number of lakes, including nearby Black and Mullett Lakes.

In 2002, TOMWC conducted a shoreline survey of Douglas, Long, Munro, and Twin Lakes as a part of the Cheboygan River/Lower Black River Watershed Initiative headed by the NEMCOG. The focus of the survey was Cladophora (a green algae sometimes called "mermaid's hair"). Cladophora occurs naturally in small quantities in Northern Michigan lakes, and the conditions of its growth are well known. If large dense growths or mats of Cladophora appear, it is because nutrients are concentrating at levels incompatible with high water quality. Those nutrients may originate naturally, but they may also be the product of lawn fertilizing, septic system leaching, agricultural practices, soil erosion, and/or wetland destruction. Thus, Cladophora growth becomes a useful proxy for nutrient pollution.

Of the property parcels identified on Douglas and Munro, about half showed habitat suitable for Cladophora. On Long Lake, nearly 90 percent of properties had such habitat, on Twin Lakes less than 10 percent. Of these properties, roughly a third on Douglas, Long, and Munro showed noticeable growths of Cladophora or other filiform green algae, mostly in association with developed properties. (The percentage of developed properties was nearly the same on each of the lakes.) No Twin Lakes property has a similar showing. Despite conditions that naturally generate some of the characteristics of "accelerated shoreline erosion" ("leaning or downed trees or trees with exposed roots" and 'undercut banks") on certain parts of the lake, only 15 percent of Twin Lakes properties displayed shoreline erosion. The comparable figures for Douglas, Long, and Munro were 31, 38, and 24 percent, respectively. A shoreline greenbelt (or "vegetated buffer strip") of diverse vegetation is considered a crucial element in maintaining shoreline integrity and water quality. Nearly two-thirds of the properties on Twin Lakes displayed "excellent" or "good" greenbelts; two-thirds of these were "excellent." By contrast, "excellent" or "good" greenbelts existed on only 12.5 percent of properties on Douglas Lake, 11.5 percent of those on Long Lake, and 11 percent of those on Munro Lake.[305]

Depending on the specific setting and circumstances, a natural or vegetated buffer strip will slow runoff, allowing sediments, nutrients, and chemicals to filter out before the water enters the lake; shade the nearshore, lowering the water temperature and thereby increasing dissolved oxygen and protecting aquatic life; prevent erosion; and enhance food sources in the nearshore area, especially the "aufwuchs," or collections of small plants and animals that appear as growths on open surfaces.

The survey's description of an excellent shoreline greenbelt is a fair description of many properties on Twin Lakes.

> Very little disturbance of the natural vegetation outside the "footprint" of the house, especially along the shoreline (including emergent rushes and other aquatic vegetation). These properties have the appearance of a cottage tucked into the woods and are often difficult to observe from the water during the growing season. This is the best category, one that property owners should strive to attain to ensure maximum water quality protection and biodiversity.

By contrast, 81 percent of Burt Lake's shoreline is "lawn to the water's edge."[306]

The conclusion of a 2009 study of 40 inland lakes in Vermont states the case succinctly. "… conversion of treed shorelines to lawn may seem harmless to humans, but the chemical, physical, and biological components of the littoral biotope [i.e., the shallow near-shore habitat] are radically changed by this activity."[307]

> The natural community of aquatic and terrestrial organisms that has evolved to grow, reproduce, and survive there will change or disappear as the biotope undergoes the physical, chemical, and biological transformation to something with substantially diminished habitat quality. Minimizing the extent of shoreline conversion from forested land to lawns within the buffer zone and maximizing the extent of naturally buffered shores will help ensure that the natural community of lacustrine species endures.

An earlier study (2002) of over three hundred lakes in the eight states of the Northeastern United States judged that lakes with visible human activity in at least half of the shoreline stations visited "had highly disturbed shoreline habitat."[308]

Steep slopes in areas of sandy soil are especially vulnerable to erosion. Some of the Twin Lakes shore is very little elevated. But a good deal of the shoreline, including all of the isolated lake, lies at the base of steep slopes that are nearly pure sand. Erosion has been avoided because in almost all cases, the natural vegetation has been left on the slope, especially trees, and structures have been well set back.

Understanding the importance of a "natural" shoreline and preserving that shoreline may seem simple matters; they are not. One reason is that biologists and ecologists perceive the shoreline differently than do lakefront property owners. A study of Long Lake and Des Moines Lake in Burnett County, Wisconsin, reveals the differences. (Des Moines Lake is nearly identical in size to Twin Lakes, and lots on both Wisconsin lakes are mostly small parcels, as are those on Twin Lakes.) Of 163 lakefront lots, biologists described eighty-two as "groomed" (mowed lawn to a sandy beach). Residents described only four of the eighty-two as groomed, while characterizing fifty-eight as "mixed" (part natural and part groomed) and twenty as natural.[309] In effect, lakeshores are subject to the Lake Wobegon effect—almost all are seen as above average by lakefront owners, more natural than, in fact, they are. These owners are the stewards of lakeshores in the United States; their perceptions—or misperceptions—matter. The most important achievement of the Twin Lakes community, and the CTLA has been to educate its members and to preserve much of the lake's natural shoreline.

In its 2012 report on the lakes of the Black River watershed, TOMWC indicated that the productivity of Twin Lakes was increasing: clarity had gradually decreased, and algae presence had gradually increased. A warming climate was perhaps contributing to this increasing productivity, though excessive nutrient input from human activity around the lake and in the watershed may also play a role. "However, the likelihood of nutrient pollution in the lake is considered to be quite low due to the fact that the Twin Lakes watershed is largely pristine and [to] the Twin Lake Association's active role in educating riparian landowners about the importance of properly managing shoreline properties to prevent nutrient pollution." (Data on phosphorus concentration in the lake suggest that it was not playing a role; the trend line for phosphorus oscillates but is slightly downward over the last twenty years.) In short, Twin Lakes might be making a transition from oligotrophic to mesotrophic, perhaps because of aging, possibly as a consequence of climate change. If so, that process appears to have been interrupted by the arrival of zebra mussels.

In 1974, John Gannon identified five elements as potentially undoing the local ecological balance: the small size of the lake, the total length of the shoreline with its high shoreline development factor, water levels because no legal lake level had been established, sandy soils, and phosphorus loading. There is nothing to be done about lake size, the length of the shoreline, and the sandy soils. There is also still no legal lake level. But shoreline development has been restrained and shoreline preservation has been, for the most part, exemplary. Water levels have been monitored and controlled by residents, in keeping with the best science. And as indicated above, phosphorus loading has not been a factor.

Lake monitoring, like supervision of the dam, has been the work of a relatively few persons over the course of twenty-five years—James McPherson, David Sherman, Randolph Mateer, Leon Byron, John Ressler, and Elwin Cole. Their work is being continued by a group of residents and part-time residents. In recent years, what these men have been doing over decades has been recognized as "citizen science" and its practitioners, with respect and appreciation, as "citizen scientists."[310] (While their activity did not result in a body of longitudinal data, those who researched and carried out loosestrife control may be considered "citizen scientists" as well, along with those who conducted fish surveys and investigated the carrying capacity of the lake. Current science has underlain almost all measures taken regarding the lake.)

Education

As TOMWC observed, a primary task of the CTLA has been to educate riparian landowners about the importance of managing shoreline properties. Often that education has utilized the personnel and printed materials of TOMWC. But while the focus of its educational activity has never strayed far from that concern, it has encompassed a wide range of closely and, in a few cases, not-so-closely related subjects.

As a part of its diverse population, Twin Lakes has had the good fortune to include environmental scientists. This has provided yet another channel for the dissemination and understanding of current scientific information. Thus, Dean Haynes, professor of entomology at Michigan State University, "shared information about the relationships between lake levels, insect control, [and] food production (nutrients). His recommendation was to try to establish controls that mimicked the natural rise and fall of a lake."[311] And Stuart Gage, also a professor of entomology at MSU, has shared his soundscape ecology research carried out at Twin Lakes and contributed information and insight on a wide range of questions. The association has also financed, at least partially, the attendance of members at meetings of organizations, such as MICorps, concerned with lake management and the preservation of water quality.

The CTLA has consistently sought out information, however difficult the effort, in response to members' questions, such as that concerning the chemical composition of the road brine used by the county to hold down dust on the roads accessing the lake. (In 2012, the brine contained the metal calcium and the volatile organic compounds benzene, ethylbenzene, toluene, and other xylenes as well as chloride, all of it being sprayed on a dirt road that, at some points, is at the top of a steep slope leading down to the lake.) It also has brought personnel from the DNR and the Cheboygan sheriff's department to speak with its members as well as taking the initiative to meet with persons from various governmental bodies and departments and provide reports to the membership.

The membership may well know more than it might wish to know about invasive species, primarily purple loosestrife, Eurasian milfoil, nonnative phragmites, carp, and zebra and quagga mussels; extractive industries, primarily hydraulic fracturing and the withdrawal of groundwater for bottling; and the functioning (or malfunctioning) of local and state government. And they most certainly have learned much about fish, water quality, shoreline health, and lake management.

---

[262] Certificate of Approval, October 2, 1979, in CTLA Files; letter, Elnora Godfrey to Thomas J. Anderson, 10.2.1979. Three public hearings were held on the rule.

"Having evolved nesting in wetlands with little wave action, the common loon and black tern build nests of mud and vegetation very close to the water surface. A common cause of nest failure for these species is anthropogenically caused wave action," i.e., waves caused by motorized boats and jet skis. Joelle Gehring, "Terrestrial game and nongame fauna," in *MGG*, p. 356.

[263] CTLA Newsletter, August 2000; Minutes, Trustees Meeting, 5.9.2007; Minutes, Twin Lakes Association First Annual Meeting, 5.27.2007, 5.25.2008.

Hereafter, the CTLA Newsletter will be cited as "Newsletter." Similarly, the minutes of trustees meetings will be cited as "Minutes"; the minutes of other meeting will be specified.

The existence of "Slow–No Wake Speed" elsewhere in the county may encourage this mistaken belief. Such provisions exist on the Black River, the Cheboygan River, the Crooked River, and the Indian River and its connected channels and canals as well as on Weber Lake. (http://www.michigan.gov/dnr/0,4570,7-153-10366_37141_37701-38722--,00.html).

The "first" annual meeting refers to the annual meeting in late May. The other annual meeting is in early September.

[264] Newsletter, April 2000, August 2000, October 2006. In the October 2006 trustees meeting, there was "[d]iscussion of 'what is high speed' and 'question of can we amend ordinance?'" (Minutes, 10.10.2006).

[265] Minutes, CTLA Spring Meeting, 5.29.2000; Minutes, Trustees Meeting, 7.12.2000; Newsletter, July 2003. The Natural Resources and Environmental Protection Act, MCL 324.80209, prohibits PWCs traveling perpendicular to a shore to operate

within two hundred feet of that shore, except at a slow–no wake speed; requires PWCs, unless operated at a slow–no wake speed, to "maintain a distance of not less than 100 feet from a dock, raft, or buoyed or occupied bathing or swimming area, a person in the water or on the water in a personal flotation device, or a vessel moored, anchored, drifting, or sitting in dead water"; and disallows operation of a PWC within two hundred feet of "a submerged diver, vessel engaged in underwater diving activities, or a flotation device displaying the international diving insignia."

[266] Michigan Compiled Laws, 281.1008, Marine Safety Act (1967); MCL, 324.80201, Natural Resources and Environmental Protection Act (1994).

[267] Minutes, 11.11.1992, 5.10.2000, 5.29.2000, 10.10.2006. The practical effect of the discrepancy appeared in the September 2005 newsletter. "Other complaints have been made about a particular pontoon that routinely speeds across the lakes. Although it may not fall under the speeding definition, it still represents a danger to those of us who like to use the lakes for slower activities." See also the July 2008 newsletter.

[268] Minutes, 5.13.1998, 5.24.1998, 7.8.1998, 5.30.1999, 9.5.1999, 10.13.1999; Newsletter, 4.1.1999.

[269] Minutes, 11.8.2000, 5.9.2001, 5.27.2007.

[270] Minutes, 7.9.2008, 8.13.2008, 8.31.2008, 10.8.2008, 11.12.2008, 4.8.2009, 5.24.2009, 8.12.2009; Newsletter, July 2008, November 2008, May 2009. The Smith Road campground reopened in 2014.

[271] http://www.cheboygancounty.net/marinesnowmobile_patrol/

[272] Minutes, 4.14.1993.

[273] Newsletter, 4.1.1999.

[274] Newsletter, April 2003, July 2003, September 2005, December 2006.

[275] Control of lake level can be crucial in many cases for many reasons. Black Lake, for example, had problems with water level after the Alverno Dam was built on the Lower Black River in 1905. Before the dam was built, Black Lake was a natural lake about four and a half to five feet lower than the level maintained by the dam; "in effect, it is an artificial body of water." (In that respect, Twin Lakes is as well.)

With the lake at the higher level, the spring breakup and spring rains produced floods and associated ice damage, shore erosion, and septic effusion. In the years 1944–1968, there were serious flooding problems five times, with especially serious flooding in 1960. In spring, it was common for the water level to rise two feet or more above the winter-maintained level, and in 1960, it rose four and a half feet. If the dam were removed or its gates left open, Black Lake would revert to its natural level, causing the shoreline to retreat into the lake from one half to three-quarter miles in most sections, destroying more than a third of the fish productive area of the lake and virtually eliminating fish spawning grounds.

The Department of Conservation, which was first made aware of the flooding problem in 1941 and studied Black Lake for years thereafter, proposed a solution in the 1960s that foundered on the issue of a special tax assessment zone by which the property owners would pay the costs. Library of Michigan, QH98 .B53 1968, *Black Lake Water Level Control Problem: Cheboygan-Presque Isle Counties* (Lansing[?]: Michigan Department of Natural Resources[?], 1968); *CDT*, 7.8.1967, 7.11.1967, 7.14.1967. The issue of the dam and water levels in Black Lake has persisted. See, for example, *CDT*, 4.5.1985, and the files held by the TOMWC. In their 1974 survey of residents in Cheboygan and Emmet Counties, Robert Marans and John Wellman asked for evaluation of the condition of the lakes and rivers they lived on. Slightly over 20 percent of respondents (N=805) cited algae and weeds, on the one hand, and fluctuating water levels, on the other, as conditions that existed, though they were not serious. Another 16 percent reported the first and considered the condition a serious problem. Fourteen percent viewed fluctuating water levels as a serious condition. Similar percentages reported increasing taxes (11 percent) and poor fishing (17 percent) as conditions that existed, though they were not serious.

But these last two achieved much higher ratings as serious problems. Over half (51 percent) identified increasing taxes as a serious problem, and nearly a quarter (23 percent) thought poor fishing a serious problem. "Fluctuating water levels were considered critical on Black Lake and, to a lesser extent, on Mullett, Crooked, and Douglas Lakes as well as on the rivers. Residents of Black, Mullett, and Crooked Lakes reported the greatest number of serious problems; those on Burt and Douglas Lakes reported the fewest." Marans and Wellman, pp. 63–64.

[276] Letter, Thomas E. Lowell to Godfrey, July 24, 1985. Lowell was in the Lands Division of the DNR.

[277] Letter, Lawrence N. Witte to Seconsky, July 30, 1985. Witte was chief of the Engineering Water Management Division of the DNR. Anyone with foreknowledge in 1985 of the office of the drain commissioner in Cheboygan County in more recent years would not have been reassured.

[278] *CDT*, July 15, 1986.

[279] See copies in CTLA files. The official name of Truscott Lane or Truscott Road is Truscott Drive.

[280] Tim Stephens, *Manual on Small Earth Dams: A Guide to Siting, Design and Construction* (Rome: Food and Agriculture Organization of the United Nations, 2010), p. 13. See also the even more densely technical Bureau of Reclamation, U.S. Department of the Interior, *Design of Small Dams* (3rd ed., 1987).

[281] *CDT*, July 15, 1985. In effect, collapse of the dam would return the lake to its condition in the 1930s or earlier.

[282] *CDT*, July 15, 1985.

[283] Claude Ressler (1920–2002), an infantryman and squad leader in WWII, was a founder of the CTLA and six times its president as well as many times its treasurer. He bought what remains the family property on the lake in 1963. After retiring from the Oakland County Road Commission in 1979, he and his wife, Merry Maxine Russell, moved to the lake. He first came to know of the lake through a fellow employee of the road commission, Herbert Westervelt. Hunting and fishing were the attractions.

[284] Newsletter, June 4, 1988.

[285] Newsletter, March 23, 1987.

[286] Minutes, 6.15.1989.

[287] This was also the period in which substantial funds were being raised for gypsy moth spraying. Newsletter, 2.3.1993; Minutes, 4.14.1993, 5.12.1993, 6.9.1993, 7.3.1993, 8.11.1993. See the March 10, 1994, newsletter for successful results. For subsequent sales, see Minutes 6.8.1994, 10.11.2000, 5.11.2005, 11.9.2005, 7.9.2006, 9.3.2006, 10.10.2006, 11.8.2006, 4.11.2007, 5.25.2008, 7.9.2009, 8.13.2008, 8.31.2008, 8.31.2008, 10.8.2008, 10.8.2008, 11.12.2008, 5.24.2009, 7.8.2009, 8.12.2009, 9.6.2009, 10.14.2009, 11.11.2009, 5.12.2010, 5.30.2010.

[288] Minutes, 11.8.2006, 5.12.2010.

[289] Minutes, 11.8.2006 4,.11.2007, 5.25.2008, 7.9.2008, 8.31.2008, 5.24.2009, 10.8.2008, 11.12.2008, 7.8.2009, 8.12.2009, 9.6.2009; Newsletter, July 2008, November 2008, July 2009, September 2009

[290] Minutes, 10.14.2009, 11.11.2009, 4.14.2010; Newsletter, November 2009.

[291] *CDT*, 11.15.1999.

[292] Newsletter, November 2004; Minutes, 6.11.1997, 8.13.1997.

[293] Minutes, 10.13.2004, 5.30.2010, 7.14.2010, 8.11.2010; Newsletter, November 2004, June 2010.

[294] Minutes, Twin Lakes Association Annual Fall Meeting, 9.5.2010; Newsletter, November 2010.

[295] Minutes, Grant Township Board Meeting, 10.12.2010.

[296] Minutes, 10.13.2010. Similar frustration appeared in connection with Michigan's Public Law 56 of 2012. The law was intended to address "inappropriate use" of public road ends designated for public water access. The law prohibits private docks, piers, boat hoists, and similar structures from being placed at public road ends and makes it a misdemeanor to use public road ends for placing boat hoists or boat anchorage systems, mooring or docking boats between midnight and sunrise, and installing a dock or wharf. The penalty is a $500 fine for each violation, each twenty-four-hour period constituting a separate violation. In the September 2012 township meeting, the board was informed that the CCRC was considering abandoning road ends in favor of townships. (Page Road is one of six road ends in Grant Township.) The board's response was to have the township clerk check with the township's insurance company to see if roads ends increased the township's liability (the answer was no) and to have the township clerk draft a letter to the CCRC expressing the township's interest in acquiring the road ends and inquiring about the procedure to do so.
The CTLA was asked who had built the walkway on the side of the launch area, a project the county had approved some years earlier. The concern was the township's falling afoul of the new law (even though the law's target is obstruction of public use, which is clearly not an issue with the walkway) and its possible liability and responsibility to remove the walkway. The association prefers to believe the structure is the work of an unknown hand. As of 2014, the township had acquired the road end. Minutes, Grant Township Meeting, July 2012, September 2012.

[297] Minutes, 11.10.2010.

[298] Minutes, 11.10.2010; Newsletter, November 2010.

[299] See the Tip of the Mitt Watershed Council website; Minutes, 7.9.2003, 8.13.2003.

[300] Newsletter, February 17, 1988, June 15, 1989; TOMWC Volunteer Lake Monitoring 1988 Water Quality — Twin Lakes; The Gem Lakes of Northern Michigan 2008 Report.

[301] TOMWC Volunteer Lake Monitoring 1988 Water Quality — Twin Lakes; The Gem Lakes of Northern Michigan 2008 Report.

[302] TOMWC Volunteer Lake Monitoring 1988 Water Quality — Twin Lakes; The Gem Lakes of Northern Michigan 2008 Report; Newsletter, April 1, 1999, November 2001, April 2003; TOMWC Current Reflections, Spring 2016, Spring 2017; CWQM Database, https://www.watershedcouncil.org/comprehensive-water-quality-monitoring.html. The ranges cited are for lakes only; rivers, streams, and creeks tend to have somewhat different characteristics.

[303] http://www.watershedcouncil.org/learn/water%20terminology/; http://issuu.com/ watershedcouncil/ docs/2012_black_river_watershed_profile?mode=a_p; TOMWC Volunteer Water Quality Monitoring Programs 2014 Report. Many of TOMWC's reports and publications contain all or much of the information that follows.

[304] Spring and Mud lakes had been identified in the Gannon-Paddock study (pp. 101–102) as "extremely productive water bodies that appear to have been influenced by past human activities," specifically a brewery near the shore of Spring Lake that "undoubtedly used the lake for dumping of high nutrient wastes."

[305] Cheboygan River/Lower Black River Watershed Initiative 2006–07 Update, ch. 6, pp. 6–13.

[306] Newsletter, July 2007.

[307] K. Merrell, E. A. Howe, and S. Warren, "Examining shorelines, littorally," *Lake Line* 29(1), 14.

[308] T. R. Whittier, S. G. Paulsen, D. P. Larsen, S. A. Peterson, A. T. Herlihy, and P. R. Kauffman, "Indicators of ecological stress and their extent in the population of Northeastern lakes: A regional scale assessment," *Bioscience* 52(3): 245.

[309] Great Lakes Echo, August 6, 2013: http:/greatlakesecho.org/author/great-lakes-echo/.

[310] One of many definitions of this term, supplanting an older meaning, can now be found in the *Oxford English Dictionary*: "citizen scientist — n. *(a)* a scientist whose work is characterized by a sense of responsibility to serve the best interests of the wider community (now *rare*); *(b)* a member of the general public who engages in scientific work, often in collaboration with or under the direction of professional scientists and scientific institutions; an amateur scientist."

[311] Minutes, 7.10.2002. Dean L. Haynes (1932–2010) was a university-distinguished professor of entomology at Michigan State University, where he taught and researched in 1966–1994. His specialization was the ecologically sensitive, highly intricate, and very practical field of integrated pest management (IPM). Gage created a multidisciplinary earth system science course for honors undergraduates, has maintained research-related relationships with colleagues at Queensland University (Australia) and the University of Alaska (Fairbanks), and remains director of the Remote Environmental Assessment Laboratory (REAL) at MSU.

Chapter 9 Fish and the DNR

Fish have been important in the history of Twin Lakes. They were a primary attraction for those who built cabins or cottages from the 1940s onward, and they remain so for visitors, especially bass fishermen in the spring. Fish (and trees) account for most of the contacts—and difficult moments—between lake residents and the DNR. Fish were the subject of the one truly divisive issue in the history of the CTLA, the one instance in which some members of the organization preferred to pursue their wishes rather than the science.

Conservation officers apparently gathered some records of fish on Twin Lakes through direct contact and creel surveys in the 1930s, 1940s, and 1950s, but there is no evidence of fish planting in Twin Lakes until 1956 and none after that until 1979. In 1953, for example, the state planted seventy-five thousand trout in Cheboygan County but none in Twin Lakes.[312] In the fall of 1956, the Department of Conservation restocked the isolated lake (what the Department of Conservation then referred to as South Twin Lake or Twin Lake 1) with bass and bluegill. This was in response to a major fish kill in the lake in early February. Deep snow cover had prevented sunlight from penetrating, thereby stopping the growth of vegetation and the release of oxygen that was a part of plant growth: the fish—bluegill, bullhead, northern pike, perch and sunfish—suffocated. The department did not find similar kills in what it then called North Twin Lake or in Munro Lake or French Farm Lake to the north and west. Nevertheless, all of Twin Lakes was to undergo stocking, though there is no evidence that it actually occurred.[313]

Muskellunge

On thirty-two occasions between 1979 and 2011, the DNR planted fish in Twin Lake 1, in all but two instances brown trout of one strain or another, in the two exceptions (2008, 2010) rainbow trout.[314] In the 1989 Black Mountain Forest Recreational Area Development Plan, East Twin Lake is described as a trout lake stocked annually with one thousand yearling brook trout, as subject to special fishing regulations and to chemical treatment on a ten-year rotation to control competing "rough fish" populations and as a proposed site for annual plants of grayling yearlings and a catch-and-release grayling fishery. In the main body of the lake (Twin Lakes 2, 3, 4, 5 to the DNR) the agency planted tiger muskellunge in 1976 and 1978 and splake fourteen times between 1982 and 1993. [315]

Over a three-week period in June and July 1979, the Fisheries Division of the DNR conducted a netting survey on Twin Lakes, using trap, gill, and fyke nets. Bluegills and largemouth bass were the fish taken most abundantly in the trap and fyke nets. Only four tiger muskellunge were taken; while their growth was acceptable, clearly, their survival level was not. Rough fish, specifically brown bullhead and bowfin, accounted for 30 percent, by weight, of the fish netted. Other fish caught were pumpkinseeds, rock bass, and northern pike. The gill nets produced cisco in abundance, along with yellow perch, largemouth bass, rock bass, and northern pike. With the exception of yellow perch and northern pike, all species of fish were growing at or above state averages. Comparison to a partial gill net survey in 1968 showed little change in the species composition of the lake but revealed increases in growth rates and numbers of most species. The survey report recommended an end to the planting of tiger muskellunge as the lake appeared unable to support esocid populations. It also recommended that special restrictions be placed on the taking of bluegill and bass to preserve the bluegill population. As well, the report suggested preliminary investigation of whether the deeper waters of the lake offered a niche for salmonids.[316]

In July 1980, the CTLA petitioned the DNR to move the opening day for bass and bluegill from late May (an error: the actual opening date was the last Saturday in April) to the middle of June or to hold a public hearing on declaring Twin Lakes a late-opening lake for those species. The rationale was that since the DNR had moved the opening date back, stocks of these fish, dependent on natural reproduction, had declined. (Twin Lakes had never been stocked with these fish.) The cold water of the spring-fed lake delayed spawning enough that fishermen were taking fish at the peak of their reproductive season. Simply moving the date, it was asserted, would bring about natural restocking of the lake. The statement specifically favoring the shift to the later date bore nearly ninety signatures.[317]

David P. Borgeson, the assistant chief of the fisheries program of the Fisheries Division of the DNR, replied. (The CTLA had also written State Senator Mitch Irwin, who reported that he had heard from Howard Tanner, Director of the DNR, understood that Borgeson had communicated with the association, and asked that it contact him again if matters were not resolved to its satisfaction.)[318]

Borgeson suggested that moving the opening date for bass to late April, even though it caused fish to be caught before spawning or while on the spawning beds, did not adversely affect the bass population. What did affect bass populations, he said, was size limitations. For that reason, in 1976, the DNR had raised the ten-inch limit to a twelve-inch limit and was still evaluating the change. Even in "special problem areas where statewide regulations don't seem to work," presumably including Twin Lakes, a later opening date would not help. Instead, state biologists were experimenting with "slot size limitations." (Slot-size limits protected certain size ranges of fish, requiring release of those within "the slot" or size range; more abundant smaller fish could be kept, while intermediate-sized fish were to be recycled through catch and release.)[319]

At its fall meeting in 1980, the CTLA, almost unanimously, rejected the idea of planting trout in the lake in the fall of 1980 or spring of 1981 and opted for the planting of bass, bluegill, and other panfish. Three reasons were offered to explain the overwhelming negative. Retired people living on fixed incomes did not want to buy the required trout stamp; to allow word to get out—much less to advertise—that trout had been planted in Twin Lakes would bring an influx of fishermen to an already overcrowded lake; and the three attempts of the DNR to plant trout in East Twin Lake had been a "dismal failure."[320]

Ten days later, Steve Swan, district fish biologist, responded, suggesting a meeting with the lake association. He also noted, with considered understatement, that "if you class the potential to consistently catch 12–15″ brook trout as a 'dismal failure,' we may have difficulty developing an acceptable fisheries management program for you."

Elnora Godfrey responded on behalf of the CTLA in mid-October. She hardly backed away from the "dismal failure" remark, noting that Twin Lakes 1 had been poisoned at least twice and closed to fishing. "We do have waterfront property owners that are left with no lake to fish, unless they carry their boats to [the] rest of the Chain of Lakes." Explaining that most of the members of the TLA were summer people but some members of its fish committee would be coming north for hunting season, she requested a meeting sometime after November 18.[321]

Three members of the CTLA (Glenn Grim, Jim Leister, and Steve Seconsky) met with three representatives of the Fisheries Division of the DNR (Swan, Warren Alward, and Mason Shouder). Swan explained the past and present management of East Twin Lake and the need for periodic chemical treatments. He asked that word be gotten out that the DNR did not need help in planting fish, as with the yellow perch planted in the lake before the chemical treatment a year earlier. The CTLA again asked that the opening day of bass season be delayed until mid-June; again, its argument was that bass spawned later in Twin Lakes because of its cooler water, and a later date would prevent bass being caught off spawning redds and reduce the fishing pressure. (The association would vote unanimously for such a step in its annual meeting in May 1981.) Brush shelters were discussed, with agreement that some of the existing shelters were working but agreement also that the depth contours of Twin Lakes limited the areas in which shelters could be placed. Shouder reviewed the netting survey of the previous year, reporting that planting of tiger muskellunge had ended and the planting of trout had been proposed and would be followed up if the lake association supported the plan. (Originally, rainbow trout were considered, but subsequently, brown trout or splake became the choices in light of the large cisco population of the lake.) The outlet dam and resulting lake level were discussed inconclusively. Alward explained the idea of slotted size limits and the effect of such restrictions on bass and panfish populations.[322]

Splake

At its annual meeting in May 1981, the association approved, unanimously, having the DNR plant either brown trout or splake. At its fall meeting a few months later, the association agreed to ask the DNR whether it would plant small game fish, specifically but not exclusively perch, along with the trout or splake and, if not, to find out if the association could buy and plant fingerlings itself. By April 1982, the DNR had responded to several questions. There would be no fish plantings in Twin Lakes given the loss of thousands of fingerlings as a result of vandalism and oxygen pump failure at the hatchery. (In fact, by late June, the DNR had planted six thousand splake in the lake.) The department recommended against stocking the lake with perch because of the overabundance of stunted perch brought up in its fish survey; this was one of the reasons they recommended planting with splake. The opening date for bass fishing had been moved as an experiment on several small lakes in the area, and the results were not yet known.[323]

In 1989, no splake were planted in Twin Lakes because of the closure of the Cherry Creek Fish Hatchery. There was some discussion of planting brown trout. The newsletter added,

> Talking to some of the people who fish the Lakes has brought out some of the following comments.[324] More bedding, Bluegill, Bass, etc. have been spotted this year than last. Pike fishing seems to be up. Splake have been seen but are hard to catch. Perch sizes are up, with some 12″ perch being caught. Some believe that stabilizing the lake level has been beneficial to the fish population and size.

A 1991 fishing survey conducted by the CTLA produced thirty returned questionnaires filled out by thirty-eight people.[325] With regard to preferences in fish to stock, multiple choices permitted, bluegill was the overwhelming choice, followed by the tightly bunched group of smallmouth bass, perch, and pike. There was only one instance in which splake was chosen. (The CTLA had use of a half-acre breeding pond, ten feet deep, on Black River Road and planned to release whatever fish were bred there into Twin Lakes.[326]) The most commonly caught species of fish in the previous five years were bluegill, bass, pike, rock bass, and sunfish. The number of bluegill caught appears to have been in the thousands, if respondents are to be believed. The number of fishermen catching pike and the probable number of pike caught seem large for a lake that was officially considered inhospitable to that order of fish. Conversely, the number of fishermen catching perch appears to be low, and the number of those catching cisco and splake was very low indeed. Asked if they had seen brook trout, lake trout, rainbow trout, or walleye caught on Twin Lakes, few responded positively, and the total of fish reportedly taken was seven. Roughly two-thirds of those responding practiced catch and release; fewer than half the respondents had fished at Twin Lakes

1. (A contemporary summary of the results shows the following: thirty-seven responses; a slightly less overwhelming preference for bluegill; fairly even numbers of bluegill, pike, and bass caught in the previous five years, followed then by rock bass, sunfish, and perch; eight trout/walleye caught; and a slightly lower percentage practicing catch and release.)

In December 1991, the fish committee met with Shouder. A fish survey by DNR that was to have been done in 1991 had not occurred because of budget cuts and an overburdened workforce. That left unanswered the question of whether planting of splake had been successful in Twin Lakes. The association's 1991 survey raised grave doubts that it had. Very few splake were reported caught in the previous five years. Only one respondent indicated that he had caught or seen caught a splake over five pounds in weight. (Between 1982 and 1993, the DNR planted nearly seventy thousand splake in Twin Lakes.) The association asked for a fish survey in 1992 (or 1993 if it could not be done earlier; the last had been done in 1981), offering whatever assistance the DNR might need. It also asked to meet with Jan Fenski, fisheries biologist at the Gaylord office of the DNR.[327]

In response, Fenski agreed that it was time to evaluate the situation. It was not immediately clear why a successful program of planting in other lakes was not translating to Twin Lakes. She said she would schedule a netting survey of Twin Lakes in late October or early November as well as water analyses, especially oxygen profiles, in August, when the lake was temperature stratified. Additionally, she asked that members of the association gather splake scales so that fisheries could determine age and growth rates and perhaps determine if fish from one year were surviving better than fish from another year and compare growth rates in Twin Lakes with growth rates on other lakes.[328]

Fenski and Shouder met with Dave Sherman and others in February 1992 at Sherman's home. Fenski spoke of doing a complete survey of Twin Lakes, and she and Shouder agreed that the spillway and gauges had helped to keep the water level even and the spawning beds in good condition. A year later, it was reported that Earl Boyea, president of the CTLA, had received a response from the DNR regarding future fish plantings in Twin Lakes. Planting of splake would be stopped because of the low survival rate. Future planting had not been ruled out, but there was debate as to what fish to use in any future planting. In the meantime, the DNR reported that there were plenty of bass and pike. In the April trustees' meeting, Boyea reported that this would be the last year in which splake would be planted and, in the May meeting, that 6,500 splake had been planted at the beginning of the month.[329]

To Plant or Not to Plant

CTLA files are largely silent about what followed in the years immediately after. But residents' concern with the fishing quality of the lake did not disappear. At a meeting of the association in July 1994, it was reported that the DNR had no plans to stock Twin Lakes in the future. A DNR officer, speaking to the trustees on another topic, had offered that answer in response to a question in April 1994, and the same report was given at the spring meeting in May 1995. At the October 1998 trustees' meeting, two members indicated that they would like to investigate stocking catchable fish. At the May 1999 meeting of the trustees, the subject of planting walleye in Twin Lakes was broached. At the July meeting, it was reported that the DNR had classified Twin Lakes as unsuitable for walleye reproduction and would not stock them. There was discussion of stocking carried out by the CTLA itself. A month later, stocking crappie was suggested. As of early September, efforts to follow up on that suggestion with the DNR had been unavailing. In October, it was reported that the DNR would "check" the lake to see how suitable it might be for crappie or walleye.[330]

In February 2000, an informal meeting centered on discussion of fish stocking and fish shelters. One attendee had contacted a supplier to find out the costs of stocking crappie. It was decided to research further what type of fish shelter would be best for the soft bottom of Twin Lakes. Some members expressed concern at allowing the state to become too involved and others recommended proceeding slowly to preserve the lake's natural balance and to ensure that improvements not draw large numbers of outside fishermen.[331]

Subsequently, four members (Ken Hebert, John King, Randy Mateer, and Jerry Rogers) met with DNR fish biologist Dave Borgeson in Gaylord to discuss what could be done to improve the population and size of fish in the lake. The essence of Borgeson's response was that any given lake can support only a certain number of fish; that, if predator fish and food fish are in balance, all species should reach maximum numbers and size; and, by implication, that any problem at Twin Lakes was a problem of overfishing, which destroyed the balance. His suggestion was to try education: convince those fishing the lake to restrict the number of fish they kept in the interests of maintaining the natural balance. He also indicated that brush piles and fish shelters would not increase the number of fish and that stocking additional species would not improve the fishing. But he did promise to schedule a fish survey within a few months.[332]

At the May meeting of the trustees, the president reviewed what had occurred over the winter with respect to fish shelters, stocking, and a fish survey and reported that individuals, not the CTLA, had taken up a collection and the lake had been stocked with black crappies. The two members of the association's stocking committee, Leon Byron and Ken Hebert, expressed concern that this action, coming while the committee was working with the DNR to resolve the question of stocking suitability and before the DNR was able to survey the lake and present the results (Twin Lakes had been moved "to the head of the list of lakes to survey"), would undercut the credibility of the association with the DNR. They added that the DNR had asked that fishermen on the lake keep a creel log of the fish caught, kept, and released during the summer.[333]

At the spring meeting of the CTLA nearly three weeks later, Leon Byron explained the DNR's desire that its fish study be accompanied by a creel survey for June and July. The primary data to be gathered were length of time fished, species caught, number caught, number released, and the basin fished. Jerry Rogers outlined the steps leading to the stocking of the four hundred nine-inch black crappies as well as blue gills and minnows at the end of April. He also discussed the shelters, as many as eight, that were to be placed, with DNR permission, in one basin. Lack of shelters had been one topic of discussion, as had gulls eating stock planted in the daytime and the lack of insect life at the bottom of the food chain. A motion was made that the association not buy fish; the vote was a tie. (The planting and shelters had been privately funded.) A subsequent motion to table the issue until the September meeting of the association passed.[334]

Six weeks later, at the July trustees meeting, there was discussion of the legality of stocking, the possibility of help from the DNR, the size of fish that would produce the highest survival rate, the effect of planted fish on the food chain, and measures to improve habitat. In August, it was reported that Borgeson had agreed to speak at a special meeting. Leon Byron summarized the analysis of the July creel surveys and commented on the lack of water clarity, the temperature and turnover temperature, the effect of low rainfall, and the changes produced in the thermocline twenty feet below the surface.[335]

The DNR did its netting study in June 2000, and the CTLA collected surveys of fishermen in June and July. Borgeson spoke to the association on August 22 regarding the results of the netting study and the fish surveys. He indicated that fishing pressure is felt much more quickly on small lakes than large, that Twin Lakes could support only so many "pounds of fish" per acre, that it is easy to "fish out" fish of legal size, and that the problem was not with residents who were relatively conservative in the fish they took but with outsiders who were not concerned with fishing Twin Lakes in the future. But his suggestion was to leave the lake alone to function naturally. Stocking other species, he said, would not change the overall population because the food supply was fixed. Stocking also carried the risk that the stocked species would prey on the eggs or young of fish already established in the lake. Brush shelters, while they provided hiding places for young fish, did not increase overall population.[336]

His comment that people living on lakes in Southern Michigan would be happy with the number of fish in Twin Lakes does not appear to have been persuasive. A note in the files and a letter written to Borgeson in 2000 indicate that the association may have been interested in sponsoring an independent survey. Ann Baughman, a water resource specialist at TOMWC, reported in September 2000 that she had spoken with Mark Luttenton, an aquatic biologist at Grand Valley State University, about assessing the lake's overall productivity, carrying capacity for fish, and fisheries habitat. By implication, she would also contact the University of Michigan Biological Station on the same subject. But her note also conveyed the following: "When Mark and I discussed the situation at Twin Lakes, he really believes many people have too high of expectations for fisheries productivity in oligotrophic lakes like Twin. These low nutrients, which result in the clear water, limit the amount of fish and other aquatic life it can support."[337] (Twin Lakes has generally been considered marginally oligotrophic, nutrient poor with low productivity. More recent changes in valuations used to formulate the trophic status index of lakes in the region suggest that it could be bumped upward into the lower range of mesotrophic or moderately productive).[338]

In the association's summer meeting in September, Leon Byron moved that $600 be spent to buy bluegills for a one-time stocking after a permit had been secured from the DNR. The money was to be a combination of privately raised funds and the relatively small sum in the association treasury earmarked for stocking. The motion carried, with dissenting votes. ($550 was to plant five-inch to seven-inch bluegills.) In the summer of 2001, five hundred bluegills were introduced into the lake, along with forty pounds of minnows to serve as a food supply. Money collected independently of the association paid most of the cost, but the organization did provide some funding from a one-time stocking fund and from the general fund.[339]

The DNR's fish growth analysis, produced in August 2001, reported that 43 percent of fish age groups were at or above the state average of length for species and age. Younger bluegill and pike and rock bass in general were shorter than the state average. Only largemouth bass and pumpkinseed were longer.[340]

Fish and fishing continued to come up in trustees' meetings with regularity. In July 2001, it was suggested that another fish survey be mailed out next spring with the newsletter, to be collected in July 2002. The September 2001 trustees' meeting included a presentation of the results of the DNR survey, followed by lengthy discussion. Questions included "Where do we go from here?" and "Has anyone caught any crappies?" It was observed that there were more fishermen, evident in part because of the greater number of cars parked at the boat launch at the end of Page Road. That, in turn, raised the question of responsibility for the launching ramp and the possibility of eliminating parking in the area. (In 2002, the DNR agreed to monitor the boat launch area after receiving reports of preseason bass fishing in 2001.) The question of stocking (specifically, "native fish") was raised again. On the one hand, it was suggested to devise a plan to improve the lake and, on the other, to remember that Borgeson had said Twin Lakes was to be envied and recommended that nothing be done to change it. And for the first time, the question was raised about the possibility of zebra mussels affecting the clarity of the water and how this might alter the balance of plankton in the lake.

In April 2002, a committee reported that it was too early to evaluate the previous summer's stocking and the quality of fishing on the lake. The president, Karl Kalis, reported a conversation with a professor at Grand Valley State University regarding the possibility of a student doing lake studies over the summer. (The subject of a student doing a lake study had been broached earlier, in the October and September 2001 trustees' meetings.) The cost appeared to be prohibitive, and it was decided to rely on the services offered by TOMWC. In both meetings in May 2002, it was reported that the DNR would monitor poaching at the dam, and in the second meeting, doing another survey of lake fishermen was discussed, with no action taken.[341]

A motion was made in the May 2004 annual meeting to use $800 to purchase fish for the lake. (Fish stocking had been discussed in the trustees' meeting a few weeks earlier, but no action had been taken. The subject had also been raised in the August 2003 meeting of the trustees.) In the ensuing discussion, the question of whether the organization had the funds to sustain stocking was raised, and it was suggested as well that a decision on this matter should be submitted to the entire membership, not just those present. The motion was defeated by nearly a 2-1 margin, with several abstentions. Another issue was revisited with a suggestion that the organization check with the DNR to see if it would support moving the opening date for bass fishing to mid-June; the reasons to do so were those stated in 1980 and 1981.[342] (The date has not been changed.)

In 2013, the DNR carried out a decennial survey of Twin Lakes. Over 1,300 fish representing fourteen species were caught—"the relatively high catch numbers and diversity are representative of other natural lakes in upper Michigan with a diversity of habitat types." Panfish—in order of their abundance, bluegill, yellow perch, rock bass, and pumpkinseed—made up 71 percent of the total catch by number and 30 percent by weight. Predators—largemouth bass, northern pike, and bowfin—made up 8 percent of the total catch by number and 64 percent by weight.[343]

The DNR's summary analysis was the following:

> [T]he current fish community and environment of Twin Lakes 2, 3, 4, 5 can be generally characterized as having: 1) a moderately productive set of lake basins with good water clarity, a strong summer thermocline, and good dissolved oxygen levels throughout much of the water column (for the major lake basins), 2) a panfish community with moderate diversity and dominated by bluegill, 3) an average to slow growing panfish community, 4) a limited predator population not dependent on stocking and dominated by largemouth bass, 5) a northern pike population that is common and slow growing, 6) a cold water niche for some lake basins that historically and currently contains cisco, and 6) a non-game fish community dominated by bullheads and a relatively diverse shiner, minnow, and darter community.

That panfish were described as showing moderate diversity and relatively low quality was largely a result of the small size and slow growth of the fish. It was judged that, in part, these conditions were natural to these fish and, in part, perhaps because of relatively low levels of nutrients in the water system. In the case of bluegill, it might also result from overfishing. Largemouth bass were identified as the "keystone species" of Twin Lakes. The bass also showed slow growth relative to their fellows across the state, but that growth rate is often encountered in natural lakes in Northern Michigan. Pike as well showed a slow growth rate.

Chemical analysis of largemouth bass showed no presence of PCB, DDT, chlordane, or toxaphene but did show mercury in a concentration as high as 0.9 PPM and a mean concentration of 0.61 PPM. Largemouth and smallmouth bass from the lake were already covered by a statewide advisory to eat no more than two meals per month of bass smaller than eighteen inches or one meal per month of bass larger than eighteen inches. The recommendation was to further restrict intake: one meal per month of Twin Lakes bass smaller than eighteen inches or no more than six meals per year of bass larger than eighteen inches. Mercury was the sole reason. And statewide, mercury is the reason behind recommended restricted consumption of black crappie, bluegill, northern pike, rock bass, sunfish, and yellow perch, the other most common fish in Twin Lakes.[344]

The other species collected are common to most natural lakes in Northern Michigan, with the exception of cisco. Collection of cisco was very limited to hold down mortality of the fish. Cisco are identified by the state as a threatened species and are not present in most natural lakes in Northern Michigan. The species requires lakes that stratify thermally in the summer and contain high amounts of dissolved oxygen in the colder water below the thermocline. Human presence and activity on lakes often reduces those oxygen levels and thus cisco. The presence of cisco then has become a marker of high water quality and limited human influence. Cisco were relatively common in Twin Lakes in earlier surveys (1979, 1992) as well as in the 2013 survey but not in 2000; whether that exception has any significance is unknown.

---

[312] Godby Jr., N. A., T. C. Wills, T. A. Cwalinski, and B. Bury, *Draft Cheboygan River Assessment* (Ann Arbor: MDNR, Fisheries Division, 2011), Appendix 4; *CDT*, 6.17.53.

[313] *CDT*, 2.17.1956, 6.16.1956.

[314] DNR Fish Stocking Database.

[315]; "Black Mountain Forest Recreation Area Development Plan," pp. 11, 22.

[316] DNR Report, Fish Netting Survey, in Twin Lakes Files (electronic), "Fish." This DNR survey apparently resulted from efforts of the new CTLA to improve fishing on the lake. See Elnora Godfrey's statement in the CTLA Newsletter, 6.4.1988: "We have had a fish survey done on the lakes and at the DNR's advice planted 6,000 splake per year to help eliminate smaller fish."

[317] Letter and petition, no addressee, 7.16.1980.

[318] Letter, Irwin to Seconsky and Godfrey, 8.20.1980.

[319] Letter, Borgeson to Seconsky, 7.31.1980.

[320] Letter, no addressee, 9.7.1980.

[321] Letter, Godfrey to Swan, 10.15.1980.

[322] Summary of November 24, 1980, meeting between the Twin Lakes Association and Department of Natural Resources, Fisheries Division, representatives, in Twin Lakes Files (electronic), "Fish."

[323] Letter, CTLA to Swan, 9.8.1981; CTLA Newsletter, 4.26.1982, 6.24.1982.

[324] CTLA Newsletter, 6.15.1989.

[325] CTLA Fish Survey; CTLA Fish Survey Results, in Twin Lakes Files (electronic), "Fish."

[326] Letter, Dave Sherman to Members and Friends, 5.2.1991; CTLA Newsletter, 4.15.1991.

[327] Draft Cheboygan River Assessment, p. 196; letter, CTLA to Fenske (sic), 12.14.1991.

[328] Letter, Jan Fenski to Elnora Godfrey, 1.24.1992.

[329] CTLA Newsletter, 8.8.1992, February 1993; CTLA Trustees Meeting Minutes, 4.14.1993, 5.12.1993.

[330] CTLA Newsletter, August 1999; CTLA Summer Meeting Minutes, 9.5.1999; CTLA Trustees Meeting Minutes, 8.11.1999, 7.14.1999, 8.11.1999, 10.13.1999, 10.14.1998, 4.13.1994; CTLA Spring Meeting Minutes, 5.30.1999, 5.28.1995; Minutes, Fourth of July Meeting, 7.2.1994.

[331] CTLA Newsletter, April 2000. Notably, the responsibility to convince those fishing the lake to restrict the number of fish they kept in the interests of maintaining the natural balance was not the responsibility of the DNR.

[332] CTLA Trustees Meeting Minutes, 2.15.2000; CTLA Newsletter, April 2000.

[333] CTLA Trustees Meeting Minutes, 5.10.2000.

[334] Minutes, CLA Spring Meeting, 5.29.2000.

[335] Minutes, CTLA Trustee Meeting, 7.12.2000, 8.9.2000.

[336] Minutes, CTLA meeting with Dave Borgeson, August 22, 2000; CTLA Newsletter, November 2000.

[337] Sheet headed in handwriting, "Communication from Ann Baughman 9/00," in Twin Lakes Files (electronic), "Fish"; letter, Jeanette Mateer to David Borgeson, no date (probably July 2000); Minutes, Trustees Meeting, 10.11.2000, 11.8.2000, 5.9.20011, 5.27.2001. Baughman had spoken at the October 1999 meeting of trustees.

[338] See Tip of the Mitt Watershed Council, "The Lakes of Northern Michigan 2008 Report." Comment by Kevin Cronk, 3.8.2012.

[339] CTLA Newsletter, August 2001; Minutes, CTLA Summer Meeting, 9.3.2000; Minutes, CTLA Trustees Meeting, 10.11.2000.

340 DNR, Fish Growth Analysis, 8.27.2001, in Twin Lakes Files (electronic), "Fish."

341 CTLA Trustees Meeting Minutes, 7.11.2001, 9.2.2001, 10.10.2001, 11.7.2001, 4.8.2002, 5.8.2002, 5.26.2002; CTLA Newsletter, April 2002, August 2002; Minutes, CTLA Spring Meeting, 5.26.2002.

342 CTLA Annual Meeting Minutes, 5.30.2004; CTLA Trustees Meeting Minutes, 5.12.2004, 8.13.2003; CTLA Newsletter, May 2004.

343 Cwalinski at https://www.michigan.gov/documents/dnr/2013-168_447221_7.pdf.

344 Michigan Department of Community Health, *2016 ESF Guide*.

Chapter 10 Other Business

From time to time, the community of Twin Lakes has had to deal with issues not tied directly to the condition and management of the lake or the well-being of its inhabitants but that affected life in and on the lake. Free-running domestic animals, barking dogs, and animal waste were, perhaps, the least and least frequent of these occasional problems; there are few complaints recorded in the trustees minutes. [345] Reports of beaver activity are a bit more common. But other issues and involvements have been more substantial and sustained.

Charity

From an early date, the association appears to have contributed to local organizations and programs, even though the constitution made no provision for such activity. [346] At least one of its social activities, the Christmas party, has intended to raise monies and/or contributions in kind for a charity or charities. On the other hand, the contributions have almost always been modest.

In the late 1980s and 1990s, recipients of contributions included the Salvation Army, the Cheboygan Humane Society, several food banks, the Hospice of the Straits, and two families that lost their homes and possessions to fire. In some cases, the contributions were in kind (in 1989, the third Christmas party produced four large boxes of food for the Salvation Army and over five hundred pounds of dog food for the Humane Society). In other cases, the contributions were cash, sums from as little as $12 to the de facto upper limit of $200.

At the fall annual meeting in 1994, the treasurer reported that from time to time, he received requests from charities, such as the Cancer Society, for donations and asked for comments and suggestions from the members. It was agreed that donations should go to a local charity.

The one specific suggestion appearing in the minutes is that the association donate $200 annually to the Hospice of the Straits since some members "have already needed their services and were well satisfied with them." (Gerald Truscott would die in the hospice four weeks later.) A motion to that effect was passed with the understanding that the trustees would consider whether it was financially possible to continue the contribution on an annual basis. In planning the Christmas party at the next meeting of the trustees, it was suggested that a raffle be added, with the proceeds going to the hospice; a raffle remains a part of the Christmas party. [347]

The Christmas party, now more than a quarter-century old, remains a fixture on the local social calendar and continues to have charity as one of its purposes. And from time to time, the association has made modest contributions from its general fund to organizations of a different stripe, such as the Michigan Loon Association, TOMWC, and the Michigan Loon Preservation Association. [348]

Gypsy Moth Spraying

In 1992, members of the association had become concerned by the damage caused by gypsy moth larvae. At that time, it appeared the county did not plan to spray. A committee of Elnora Godfrey, Claude Ressler, Charles Rodriguez, David Sherman, and Margaret Wiest was appointed, and a canvas of Twin

Lakes–area residents conducted to determine the feasibility of the CTLA contracting to do the spraying. By February 1993, over $2,700, held in a separate account, had been contributed to the gypsy moth project.

As of early February the county decided to spray areas it designated as "Hot Spots." The Twin Lakes area was one of those. Because the county indicated that more than one spraying a year would not be cost-effective and did not appear to be planning on spraying the next year, while the Association was unsure at this point that one spraying would be effective, it was decided to hold the contributions in the event that spraying the next year proved to be necessary.

At the June trustees meeting, the president, Earl Boyea, reported that the balloons had been placed and spraying would occur as soon as the weather broke. He also suggested asking Elnora Godfrey, Charles Rodriguez, and David Sherman if they would continue to serve as a gypsy moth committee since the association might want to consider spraying in the next year. The committee was to check with the county to see if another spraying would be necessary. The answer a few weeks later was no; reports from testing in the county showed little sign of egg masses. That information coincided with the association's belief, based on observations and reports, that the one spraying had been sufficient.

A motion was passed to return all contributions. In a subsequent meeting, it was decided that the cost of spraying Truscott Drive, not a part of the county's spraying plan, would be borne by the CTLA rather than split up among the more than ninety individual contributors. (The cost was $120, and the fund had earned $90 in interest.) By November 1993, all funds collected were reported to have been returned to contributors. (In May 1994, the treasurer said that all funds had been returned with a single exception, a contributor who could not be located.)[349]

Adopt-a-Forest

Eileen Schultz, secretary of the CTLA, read about the DNR's Adopt-a-Forest program in the September/October issue of *Michigan Natural Resources* magazine and presented a report on it in the November 1993 meeting of the trustees. The trustees subsequently approved a motion to set up a meeting with a representative of the department. (Members of the CTLA had participated in the Black Mountain cleanup in 1990.)

As described by the DNR, "the goal of the Adopt-A-Forest program is to enhance the enjoyment of public forest lands by eliminating illegal dumping and to increase the awareness of recycling opportunities for waste materials found" in the nearly four million acres of state forest land. (To this day, Cheboygan County has one of the higher numbers of known illegal dump sites of any county in the state.) The program is now sponsored jointly by the DNR, the DEQ, the U.S. Forest Service, the Michigan Forest Resource Alliance, and private organizations. The area of interest to the trustees was the forest bordering Twin Lakes Road and Doriva Beach Road.[350]

Not having received a reply from the DNR, Schultz wrote again in mid-February 1994 in hopes that a representative might appear at the April meeting of the trustees. Tim Paulus of the Forestry Division attended and agreed to provide a dumpster, gloves, heavy plastic bags, and some help. Clarence Archambo, then Grant Township supervisor, volunteered to provide a front-end loader.

It was left to the CTLA to tour the area in question and then arrange a date with the DNR and Archambo. But at the next meeting of the trustees, the project was put on hold for the year because no dumpster could be reserved (the DNR had agreed to cover the cost to the extent of $300–$500, but all that was available was a compactor at a cost of $450). At the annual meeting in July, the membership was briefed on the Adopt-a-Forest program; a tentative date of May 12–14, 1995, had been set, and Archambo had reserved a dumpster.[351]

Bob Slater of the Forest Management Division attended the April 1995 meeting of the trustees to express DNR's continued interest and to indicate what the DNR could contribute. Archambo had reserved a forty-yard dumpster for the proposed cleanup dates, negotiating the rate of $650 down to the $400 charged the township. Slater doubted that the DNR could bear the entire cost, and Archambo suggested that the township and the department split the cost. Claude Ressler would seek to procure a front-end loader. Plans were finalized in the next trustees meeting; in the meantime, Ressler had arranged for use of the county's front-end loader, which proved to be absolutely necessary.[352]

Fifteen CTLA members packed the forty-yard dumpster, clearing some four hundred acres but leaving some trash to be picked up the following year in conjunction with the association's annual road cleanup. That effort was scheduled for May 23–25. Archambo was able to obtain a dumpster for $550, $250 of which was covered by the DNR and the rest by the township. The April 1997 newsletter that reported the completed cleanup also "asked all members to abide by the law and not use the surrounding forest as a dumping ground" and noted that the township did provide dumpsters twice a year. (The DNR had closed the Grant Township dump on Doriva Beach Road in 1982.) To this day, one of the important pieces of information conveyed to its membership in newsletters and meetings by the CTLA is the dates dumpsters will be available.

In follow-up, the DNR placed "No Dumping" signs at trail entrances along Doriva Beach Road, agreed to check the Smith Road campground to see if more trash barrels were needed there, presented the association with a plaque in appreciation, and placed four signs in the areas of the cleanup that recognized the efforts of the CTLA.[353]

Adopt-a-Road

In September 1990, the year the Michigan Department of Transportation established its Adopt-a-Highway program, David Sherman drafted a letter on behalf of the association expressing its desire to participate. The CTLA volunteered itself to adopt the then existing public access roads to the lake (Godin, Page, Reynolds, Smith) as well as Twin Lakes Road from a point just west of Reynolds Road to Krouse Road and all of Krouse Road to the Alpena State Road, a total distance of nearly seven miles. Nothing appears to have come of this effort.[354]

In May 2000, Robert Schultz suggested that the association apply to Adopt-a-Road, a version of MDOT's program at the county level, and request parts of Twin Lakes and Doriva Beach Road. At the summer meeting of the association, the president, John King, shared information about the program and announced that the CTLA would maintain Doriva Beach Road as far as Cedar Beach Road and Twin Lakes Road for a mile to the east of the Twin Lakes Road–Doriva Beach Road intersection. The first cleanup was done by four couples on September 14, and the area finally decided on was Doriva Beach Road from Twin Lakes Road to Restmore Road and Twin Lakes Road from Chamberlain Road eastward to the curve at the DNR parking site. Dutifully, each year, members of the CTLA walk and bag along the same stretches of road.[355]

It is unclear whether the association (or perhaps just a group of its members) carried out its own road cleanup program in the 1990s. There is a single statement in the surviving records that suggests it may have; Eileen Schultz, writing in the 1996 newsletter and addressing the trash left in the previous spring's Adopt-a-Forest cleanup, said, "plans are to clean-up the remaining trash this spring along with the Association's annual spring clean-up of the area's roadways."[356] That would link together the two efforts; much of the roadside ultimately adopted by the association in 2000 lay alongside the area it had cleaned in 1995 and 1996.

Dumping

Trash, especially heavy trash, removal is a continuing problem in rural areas. (The letter heading for the Adopt-a-Forest program was "TRASH: It's Out of Hand on Wild Land." As of 2008, Cheboygan County ranked third in the state of Michigan in the number of identified illegal dump sites, closer to Roscommon County, the first ranked, than to the two other northern counties on the list, Montmorency and Mackinac.) In the case of Grant Township, the DNR closed the township dump in 1982 and again in 1996. In April 1997, it was suggested that the association might hire a shredder to deal with the brush generated by spring cleanups. In September 2001, a box spring and mattress were picked up by members of the CTLA, only to have other large items dumped at the same place within weeks. In November 2006, the trustees learned that the DNR was closing the gravel pit on Krouse Road to restore it to "pristine condition," thereby making it illegal to dump there. (The pit has not yet been restored to pristine condition, though it has been cleaned up. In fact, the CRC gave up its lease on the pit only in March 2015.)[357] Grant Township also declined to participate in a recycling program (over half the material found in illegal dump sites is recyclable).

In the association's first annual meeting in May 2008, a resident inquired whether it was legal "to throw stuff in the lake (i.e., Christmas trees)." In the next trustees meeting, a member hoped that residents would become more informed about putting Christmas trees and other items in the lake for fish habitat.[358] As the DNR has indicated, the practice is not useful in terms of fish populations on Twin Lakes, nor is it healthy for the lake. (In the 1980s, the DNR unenthusiastically agreed to the placement of fish shelters on the lake, but the number was limited and the sites carefully chosen.) But the issue reappeared in 2017 as one individual apparently tried to create his own "fishing hole" conveniently close to shore.

Invasive Species and Disease

Twin Lakes has been spared VHS (viral hemorrhagic septicemia), *phragmites Australis*, and swimmer's itch (produced by flatworm parasites in the family *Schistosomatidae*), perhaps because of the lake ecology, perhaps because of an effective DNR program of informing boaters and campers, perhaps because of luck, which may be in danger of running out.[359]

But discussion of purple loosestrife first appeared in the trustees minutes of November 2000, has continued to make frequent appearances ever since, and occasioned an annual event in the lake's calendar. Mention of zebra mussels occurred even earlier.[360]

Purple Loosestrife Phragmites Eurasian Watermilfoil Zebra Mussel

The first commitment to remove loosestrife came at the association meeting nearly a year later. The newsletter following that meeting mentioned the threat of loosestrife to native plants and waterfowl breeding area and discussed two methods of control. One was to introduce the *Galerucella* beetle (or black-margined loosestrife beetle), whose use of the loosestrife plant as a food supply can reduce its ability to produce seeds, lessen its ability to compete with other plants, and weaken or kill the loosestrife. The other was to carefully remove the flower heads during the growing season, the recommended method for small infestations of the sort at Twin Lakes at that time.[361]

In April 2002, it was planned that a group would have a work bee, when the ice was off the lake, to pull up the purple loosestrife, bag it, and burn it. In May, the timing was "when boats are in the lake." At the association's spring meeting later in May, the timing was "when boats are available and the species can be recognized," and the goal was "to dig out as much as possible, bagging it to limit the distribution of seeds." A scientist/member shared other ideas for eradication, including using an herbicide in a nonpolluting way. In a later trustees meeting, he spoke about biological controls. In September, a small group worked from shore on a fifteen-by-fifteen-foot area, digging or pulling out the plant by its roots and uncovering a growth of native bullrushes.[362]

> Removal is not easy and can only be done from shore, but it is possible since it is usually found in the soft, wet soil.

> It's evident a much larger work force will be necessary if we ever hope to make a noticeable dent in the loosestrife growth, and we'll be asking volunteers again next fall.

> It is not our intent to eradicate the plant but to keep it under control.

In April 2004, there was discussion of involving the Green Dinosaurs, a Cheboygan High School environmental group, or other school groups in helping remove loosestrife or doing lake testing. There was no further discussion until November, when Leonard Page volunteered to head a committee to research and address the problem, "which may involve hiring day laborers to assist in the manual labor." The following April, eradication was again discussed, and a resident was to be asked if an area of his property could be used to test the herbicide Roundup dropped into cut-off stems and brushed on the leaves of the plant. (The suggestion to cut the tops off the loosestrife and then use an eye dropper to drip Roundup into the hollow stem had come from Scott McEwen, water resources program director for TOMWC, speaking at the November 2003 trustees meeting.)[363]

On June 4, 2008, five residents of Twin Lakes traveled west to spend a wet and slippery Wednesday morning collecting *Galerucella* beetles in a bog near Petoskey and returned to place the beetles on purple loosestrife by the boat launch and on Krouse Road. (The collection trip was sponsored by TOMWC.) But in August, a meeting concluded that loosestrife was spreading, and it was suggested that the flowers be cut off and burned, a step requiring the permission of the property owners on whose shore the plant was found. At the fall meeting a few weeks later, residents were encouraged to cut off the flowering heads to prevent seed diffusion but to watch for the beetles and their larvae and leave them undisturbed in the patch.[364]

In early October 2008, it was decided to ask another scientist/member to involve himself in the loosestrife program. Postponed several times because of weather, the collection trip to a different site in 2009 harvested another set of beetles to place on the lake's loosestrife; evidence of the previous year's beetles was seen as the new beetles were placed by hand. In both August and September meetings, there was mention of the need for volunteers and the suggestion that the flowers be cut, bagged, and put in the trash or pulled or dug up. Soon after, four residents (Elwin and Marilyn Coll, Stuart Gage, and John Ressler) cut and removed six bags of loosestrife from a large patch along the Krouse Road shoreline. In the November trustees meeting, there was discussion of a report in the Burt Lake Preservation newsletter stating that if the tops of the plant were cut off, the loosestrife would spread. "That is not true. We are on the right track on Twin Lakes by cutting and removing the tops of the plants."[365]

Beetles and larvae were collected again in 2010 and placed on the loosestrife; plant heads were also cut. The now annual occasion of beetle collection and placement was carried out yet again in 2011. By this point, the effects of the efforts were beginning to be clearly visible: the loosestrife did not appear to be spreading, the beetles were remaining on the loosestrife, the larvae of the previous year produced "a healthy crop" of beetles, and many of the plants' leaves had been eaten.[366] But it was decided that beetle collection would be replaced by beetle purchase, whenever they were available at an affordable price. Since 2015, beetles have continued to be purchased and placed in combination with shore surveys and physical removal, when possible.

Shoreline Construction and Development

In 1997, there was "a lengthy discussion" in the trustees meeting about monitoring construction along the shoreline. The stimulus to discussion was a property that had been entirely cleared down to the lake and where sand had been brought in along the shoreline. In a meeting six years later, Scott McEwen of TOMWC was asked about "lake beaching," dumping sand into the lake to form a beach. He responded that sand is the worst possible bottom material because it will not allow growth of the food sources necessary to support fish and that wave and/or ice action will quickly cause the muck to cover the sand. The residents of Twin Lakes clearly understood this in the late 1970s, when the CTLA had prevented the Army Corps of Engineers from dumping sand and stone along the shoreline at the Smith Road campground. In a more distant past, there had been an instance of importing sand to the lake and, in a still more distant past, more than one case of filling. The decision in 1997 was to check with the DNR and the county to see if all codes and permit requirements had been complied with. In the end, the DNR required limited remediation.[367]

A similar clearing of a property off Loon Nest Lane took place in 2009; no sand was introduced, but the forest was clear-cut, and only the roots of shoreline cedars were left. Technically legal, this action reflected the inadequacies of the county zoning code. Property owners are merely "encouraged" to establish a vegetative buffer zone within forty feet of the water's edge, and the rest of the provision uses "should" and "may be." By contrast, a vegetative strip of one hundred feet "shall be" left on either bank of the Pigeon River and the Upper Black River, and clear-cutting "is generally not permitted." (The property in question was soon abandoned by those responsible for the clear-cutting.)[368]

In the interim between these episodes, a true development issue arose off Loon Nest Lane on the most northern on the basins. The first mention of proposed development was a report by Leonard Page to the trustees in their meeting of August 2005. At the fall meeting of the association in September, Melvin and Theresa O'Connor presented a plan for eleven shoreline lots with access to the lake and sixteen back lots without access to the lake. A majority supported a motion to hire Leonard Page for $1.00 to represent the association with the County Planning Commission. The dominant apprehensions expressed involved the additional pressure on the lake system from so large a development (cabins and cottages on Twin Lakes had always been built one at a time), the precedent for large-scale development that would be set, the volume of traffic on Krouse Road and Loon Nest Lane, and the likelihood that the properties without lake access would acquire lake access.

Meetings in September 2005 and June 2006 discussed the development and reviewed and approved letters to the County Planning Commission opposing it. In April 2007, the trustees approved a letter to the Zoning Board of Appeals concerning, specifically, the Phase 2 development site and heard a report on Phase 2 in their May meeting. In the first annual meeting a few weeks later, it was reported that the Zoning

Board of Appeals had rejected the appeal. Suggestions included holding a meeting to pursue other options, hiring a hydrology expert to do a water assessment as the basis for an appeal (appeal of the decision had to be made within thirty days), and waiting for Phase 3. The vote was, overwhelmingly, to wait for Phase 3 to take any further action.[369]

By late August, at the initiative of a resident on the northern bay, there had been communication between the developer and the Little Traverse Nature Conservancy over appraisal and sale of the land for a nature preserve. To satisfy the board of the conservancy, there needed to be a substantial show of interest, in the form of monetary pledges, from the residents of the lake. And the appraisal was paid for by a combination of individual contributions and $300 provided by the CTLA. By July 2008, negotiations had ended, apparently because of the developer's dissatisfaction with the value set by the appraiser; two docks had been built on the bay. The property with infrastructure remains without further building, though two shoreline parcels has been sold, along with corresponding backlots.[370]

Krouse Road

Krouse Road is the only road to the lake that goes somewhere and therefore can be used as a through route. Page, Reynolds, Smith Twin Trail, Godin, and Loon Nest Roads all dead-end at the lakeshore (or, in the case of Godin, circles along the lakeshore and returns to the entry point). All are also straight roads (in the case of Godin, the roadway to the circle is straight) and relatively broad.

In contrast, Krouse Road is a narrow twisting road that dips and rises along the eastern side of the lake from Twin Lakes Road to a three-way intersection with Orchard Beach Road and the Alpena State Highway in forest north of the lake. On the land side of the road, privately owned property at the southern end gives way to state-owned land for much of the road's length. Krouse Road had been an area of concern for the CTLA in 1984–1985 because of proposed clear-cutting and safety and damage issues arising from logging. In 1994, the DNR was again planning to cut along Krouse Road but this time reassured the CTLA that it intended to cut alternate rows of trees rather than clear-cut.[371]

The first appearance of concern with ORVs was in the trustees minutes of October 1999, when it was suggested that someone from DNR come to speak about the use of ORVs and the DNR's responsibility to monitor ORV use. ORVs, specifically all-terrain vehicles or ATVs, had been a major concern of the CTLA in connection with the creation of the Black Mountain Forest Recreation Area in 1988–1989. Two years later, following complaints from lake residents about the misuse of ORVs on county roads around the lake, the trustees received information from the sheriff's department about ORV speeds and discussed the possibility of having a residential speed limit posted on Krouse Road. (ORVs were allowed on county roads but had to travel slowly, according to the sheriff's department. The 2009 county ORV ordinance prescribed twenty-five miles per hour on the far right of maintained county roads in such a manner as not to interfere with the flow of traffic. The speed limit on Krouse Road in 1999 was fifty-five miles per hour; it is not unusual to see ORVs traveling on the right of county roads at fifty miles per hour or more, and it is not possible for ORVs to travel on Krouse Road without interfering with traffic flow.)[372]

Having heard rumors that the CCRC planned to widen Krouse Road, the CTLA, in February 2002, requested a copy of the minutes of the latest township meeting. The minutes indicated that a lake resident had objected to widening Krouse Road to the standard sixty-six-foot width because many cottages and cabins stood within this distance. (At its southern end, structures were built literally to the roadside, or the road was plowed right up to the structures; widening the road to thirty-three feet on each side of the midline would require moving or, more likely, destroying cottages and cabins on both sides of the road.) The board noted that "their [sic] was some misunderstanding of the road work." A resident of Loon Nest

Lane had asked the township to ditch and widen a four-hundred-foot section of Krouse near its intersection with Loon Nest Lane. The board then voted unanimously in favor of a clarifying motion: "Krouse Rd will be graveled and graded with no widening done, the widening may be done on the corner of Loon's Nest Lane and Krouse Rd."[373]

The CTLA also discussed reducing the speed limit on Krouse Road from fifty-five to twenty-five miles per hour. "The twp., state, and CCRC makes [sic] the decision, with two agreeing to change the speed limit." The township agreed to send the association a letter supporting a reduced speed limit on Krouse Road, and the association encouraged its members living on Krouse Road to send letters to its president stating their support to move the project along.[374] Ultimately, the authorities decided to reduce the speed limit to twenty miles per hour in the vicinity of the lake and thirty miles per hour in the deeper forest.

In November 2003, it was reported that the CCRC had decided to deal with the narrowness of Krouse Road by building a road connecting Lodge Road, which runs off Twin Lakes Road at the Krouse Road intersection, with Krouse Road near Godin Circle. (For residents of Krouse Road, the problem was not its narrowness but its use as a shortcut by ORVs and other vehicles, creating traffic load and noise and safety issues.) Construction was to be completed before the end of the year.[375]

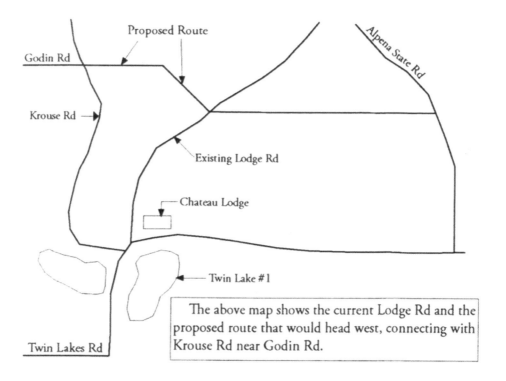

The above map shows the current Lodge Rd and the proposed route that would head west, connecting with Krouse Rd near Godin Rd.

The April newsletter corrected that account. The construction being done on Lodge Road was being done by the owners of the Chateau North, who were developing land they owned. The proposed bypass of Krouse Road was at a much earlier stage. The township had to submit an application and plans to the DNR because most of the road would cross state land. Crossing private land was an as yet unanswered question. At the December township meeting, money had been appropriated to pay for the application to the DNR. But in March, at the township's annual meeting, the cost of construction was outlined, and the only bid to be received was reported, bringing about a decision to suspend the project. It has since silently disappeared. (Ultimately, the DNR refused to allow the proposed road to pass over state land. Its grounds were the detriment to the land, resources, and public recreation, the light traffic in the area, and a lack of obligation "to allow a new road to small private land ownerships that already have at least two options to reach their property.")[376]

Disturbance and Noise

In 1998, there was mention in a trustees meeting of a trailer/camper in which someone was living on Krouse Road and causing disturbance. The county zoning department was contacted, and the camper was moved. Under law, tents and trailers can be used as temporary dwellings for no more than thirty days and then only when located on a site with an acceptable potable water source and sewage facilities. An officer of the Zoning Division was invited to speak to a meeting of the association regarding law in such situations but declined. (At another point, someone decided to pioneer on forested state land on the southwestern side of the lake; the DNR abruptly ended that adventure.)[377]

Five years later, a situation arose, similar in that it involved disturbance but amounting to much more than simple disturbance, affected a substantial part of the lake's population, and was not amenable to solution by enforcement of the zoning code. Combining a serious purpose and a sense of humor, a resident created the Twin Lakes Noise Abatement Group (NAG). He enumerated the problem, listed actions to take, and provided a complaint registry form. What was involved was a constellation of behaviors broadly described as "noise and loud boisterous behavior on private property as well as on the lake" but including specifically "loud radio, fast boating, loud vulgarity and swearing, drinking & driving, etc." The "etc." included large bonfires. Acknowledging several complaints about conduct on the lake, an April 2003 newsletter led with a relatively broad unspecific pair of statements regarding noise and high-speed boating. But the July newsletter focused sharply on the behaviors and steps to take.[378]

In the meantime, NAG had been organized (it was a network rather than anything more substantial) and had distributed information and suggestions. It noted that noise and loud boisterous behavior on private property and on the lake had increased over two years; in one case, it was particularly intense and intolerable. The problem was not occasional but chronic, in summertime almost daily. The behaviors not only were intrusive on other residents but also diminished the property values of many of those living on the lake. For lack of a county noise ordinance, the sheriff's department was of little help (though it indicated some willingness to intervene after 10:00 p.m.).[379]

The proposed response was to bring together a network of neighbors willing to cooperate; to document every incident to facilitate complaints to the police and possibly to be used by an attorney in a nuisance abatement case; to review all township and county codes and deed restrictions for provisions that might be helpful; to have a delegation meet with the police; to encourage police to patrol Krouse Road at the end of the working day to intercept drunk drivers; to trigger large numbers of simultaneous complaints to the police ("the squeaky wheel"); to work with the township and county to develop a noise and/or public nuisance ordinance; to have an attorney notify the owner of the property (the occupant was the source of the trouble) that all possible legal action would be taken if the nuisance was not abated; and to meet periodically to review what progress had been made.[380]

By mid-May or soon after, Twin Lakes residents had won a promise from township officers to look into adopting a noise ordinance. (No noise ordinance resulted.) The sheriff had informed residents that while there was no noise ordinance, there was an enforceable state blasphemy law that criminalized use of profane or vulgar language before women and children. (In fact, the 105-year-old law had been struck down by the Michigan Court of Appeals in April 2002.) The sheriff, Dale V. Clarmont, had visited and spoken with the occupant of the property in question. (At a later meeting with the trustees, the sheriff commented that "communication is 80 percent of our job"; in this case, the communication was direct and unvarnished.) For their own reasons, the Michigan State Police had also visited the property.[381]

The July newsletter prescribed calling the sheriff's department to report loud parties late at night and to report public use of foul language (and keeping a log of incidents). High-speed boating should also be reported to the sheriff's department, ideally with the registration number of the vessel. The CTLA would contact the DNR to see what could be done about bonfires. In the meantime, the sheriff indicated he would rely on talking to the individuals involved where no enforceable law existed, as in the case of bonfires.

The newsletter concluded by setting the problem in the context of development. "As more residences are built and more people come to the lake, problems such as these will become commonplace unless we take steps now to preserve the solitude of our lake. To do this, we must work together as an Association, with the support of our local law enforcement agencies." It is true that the source of the greatest problem was property that had been parceled out and sold only a few years before and was now having residences built on it. But the real source of the problem was an urban background of a sort that suggested to occupants they were in a wilderness and could do as they wished and that produced relationships and behaviors that did not translate well to a small lake community.[382]

Over time, behaviors were changed, and the situation was resolved; concern with noise shifted back to occasional concerns with barking dogs. The trustees shared noise and dog problems at their April 2004 meeting without taking action. But the November 2004 newsletter reported two further serious episodes, the last two, at a pair of locations. One involved a frequent noise offender and the other alleged drunks accosting a child on Krouse Road. The sheriff's department and the state police responded to calls. A note in the June 2008 newsletter merely reminded its readers that sound carries a long way on the lake. "Respect your neighbors and keep noise to a minimum, including barking dogs. Even from a distance, constantly barking dogs can be annoying."[383]

Nesting

In an effort that paralleled the building of brush shelters for fish (see chapter 9), the association has provided bird nesting boxes and loon nesting platforms, the first unobtrusive, the second nearly invisible. The nesting boxes were built over the winter of 2002–2003 by four residents using wood donated by one of them and placed around the lake by two other residents. The boxes were intended for wood ducks and swallows, the one for their beauty, the other for their appetite for insects. Volunteers have maintained the boxes. In 2009, the association installed a second loon float in an effort to encourage loons to nest in safer, less exposed areas. (An older float in another part of the lake had been repaired over the previous winter.)[384]

---

[345] Minutes, 11.11.1992. In this incident, a resident complained vigorously to the trustees and was told the minutes incorporating his complaints would be read at the next meeting. Disappointed, he filed a complaint with the sheriff's department, which resulted in an arrest warrant for his neighbor and a subsequent court appearance and minor fine.

[346] Article III of the by-laws defines the purpose of the association: "to advance the mutual interest of the owners of property on Twin Lakes and the surrounding area; to provide for the beautification, improvement, care, and protection of such property; and to preserve the facilities for fishing, boating, bathing, and the mutual enjoyment of the lake and surrounding areas." (by-laws, revised and restated, 2007). There is no language elsewhere in the document that applies to charitable contributions. In the wake of (relatively) large donations voted through the May 2010 meeting of the association in a manner that concerned some members, the trustees considered the subject of charitable contributions in their next two meetings. The upshot was two proposed amendments to the by-laws that limited annual contributions to local charities to $200, including "the good and welfare . . . illness and death of Association members and their families."

[347] Minutes, 9.3.1994 (Annual Fall Meeting), 10.12.1994, 11.9.1994, 4.12.1995.

[348] Minutes, 7.14.1999; Newsletter, July 2009, June 2010.

[349] Newsletter, 2.3.1993; Minutes, 4.14.1993, 5.12.1993, 6.9.1993, 7.3.1993, 9.4.1993, 10.13.1993, 10.28.1993, 11.10.1993, 5.10.1994. In 1989, David Sherman, writing in the newsletter, had warned those who had not yet come up to Twin Lakes to expect hosts of caterpillars, fat birds, and bare trees, but these were not gypsy moths (Newsletter, 6.15.1989).

[350] Letter, Schultz to VanStee, 11.18.1993; Minutes, 11.10.93; https://www.michigan.gov/dnr/0,4570,7-153-10366_10871-27529--,00.html.

[351] Letter, Schultz to VanStee, 2.28.1994; Minutes, 4.13.1994, 5.10.1994, 6.8.1994, 7.2.1994; Newsletter, 3.10.1994.

[352] Minutes, 4.12.1995, 5.10.1995, 5.28.1995, 4.19.1995, 3.15.1996, 4.5.1997.

[353] Newsletter, 3.15.1996, 4.5.1997, 4.26.1982, 6.24.1982; Minutes, 5.8.1996, 5.26.1996, 7.22.1995, 11.8.1995; *CDT*, 11.12.1995.

[354] Letter, Sherman to Unknown Addressee, 9.11.1990.

[355] Minutes, 5.10.2000, 9.3.2000, 11.8.2000.

[356] Newsletter, 3.15.1996. The Schultzes also link the two program. Eileen Schultz initiated involvement in Adopt-a-Forest, and Robert Schultz initiated involvement in Adopt-a-Road, the motion proposed by his wife and approved by the trustees.

[357] *CDT*, 3.5.2015.

[358] http://www.glfwda.org/archive/index.php/t-6953.html; Minutes, 8.14.1996, 4.9.1997, 11.7.2001, 11.8.2006, 5.25.2008 (Twin Lakes Association First Annual Meeting), 7.9.2008; Newsletter, August 2002, April 2005.

[359] As of the summer of 2013, the lake might not have been free of zebra mussels. Two were found on a submerged log at the end of the Big Bay. They probably arrived on the bottom of a boat recently used on one of the larger lakes in the region and not properly cleaned before being put into Twin Lakes. It remained to be seen if they multiplied in the environmental setting of the lake. The DNR subsequently concluded that there was no zebra mussel presence in Twin Lakes. Residents, however, are well aware there is such a presence. Phragmites on the lake are native, not invasive. (Newsletter, April 2009).
Similarly, the lake may not have been totally free of emerald ash borer, but its extent, if indeed it has been present, has been very limited.

[360] Minutes, 10.11.00. Nearby Black Lake, Long Lake, and Mullett Lake have long had zebra mussels.

[361] Minutes, 9.2.01; Newsletter, November 2001.

[362] Newsletter, April 2003; Minutes, 4.8.2002, 5.8.2002, 7.10.2002, 8.14.2002; Minutes, Twin Lakes Association Spring Meeting, 5.26.2002. The scientist/member was Dean Haynes.
Purple loosestrife is most easily recognized when in bloom. On Twin Lakes, blooming occurs in late July and early August.

[363] Minutes, 4.14.2004, 11.10.2004, 4.13.2005, 5.11.2005; Newsletter, November 2003.

[364] Minutes, Twin Lakes Association First Annual Meeting, 5.25.2008; Newsletter, July 2008; Minutes, 7.9.2008, 8.13.2008; Minutes, Twin Lakes Association Annual Fall Meeting, 8.31.2008.

[365] Minutes, 10.8.2008, 5.24.2009, 7.8.2009, 8.12.2009, 11.2009; Twin Lakes Association Annual Fall Meeting, 9.6.2009; Newsletter, July 2009, September 2009, November 2009. This scientist/member was Stuart Gage.

[366] Minutes, Twin Lakes Association First Annual Meeting, 5.30.2010; Minutes, 7.14.2010, 8.11.2010; Newsletter, June 2011, August 2011.

[367] Minutes, 8.13.1997; Newsletter, November 2003. See TOMWC Fact Sheet, "The Truth about Beach Sanding or 'Lakebed Restoration'" (July 2011).

[368] http://www.gpo.gov/fdsys/pkg/CZIC-kfm2399-c36-1982/html/CZIC-kfm2399-c36-1982.htm.

[369] Minutes, 8.10.2005, 9.4.2005, 9.11.2005, 6.4.2006, 4.11.2007, 5.9.2007, 5.27.2007 (First Annual Meeting). The only other projected development around Twin Lakes was Chateau Woods, behind the Black Mountain Lodge and well away from any shoreline. See chapter 6.

[370] Minutes, 9.2.2007, 10.8.2007, 11.7.2007, 5.25.2008, 7.9.2008; letter to Residents of the Twin Lakes Area, 8.20.2007.

[371] Minutes, 11.9.1994.

[372] Minutes, 10.13.1999, 10.10.2001; Newsletter, November 2001.

[373] Newsletter, April 2002. Godin Road was widened in the winter of 2002–2003: Newsletter, April 2003.

[374] Minutes, 4.8.2002; Newsletter, April 2002.

[375] Newsletter, November 2003.

[376] Newsletter, April 2004, April 2005.

[377] Minutes, 7.8.1998, 8.12.1998; http://www.gpo.gov/fdsys/pkg/CZIC-kfm2399-c36-1982/html/CZIC-kfm2399-c36-1982.htm.

[378] CTLA files, "The Problem"; Newsletter, April 2003. Concern may have been expressed as early as 2002 regarding high-speed boating and noise; see undated handwritten notes on what appear to be trustee meetings. Similarly, concern was expressed over bonfires as early as July 2001, but whether their source was the same is unknown; see Minutes, 7.11.2001.

[379] CTLA files, "The Problem."

[380] CTLA files, "Action to Take."

[381] Minutes, 5.14.2003, 5.25.2003; http://www.freedomforum.org/templates/document.asp?documentID=15992.

[382] Newsletter, July 2003.

[383] Minutes, 4.14.2004; Newsletter, November 2008.

[384] Newsletter, April 2003, November 2003, April 2005, April 2009, July 2009; Minutes, 5.24.2009.

Chapter 11 Community in the Woods

The process by which Twin Lakes survived in its present condition is complex, fragile, and not altogether probable. The process has interwoven natural, political, economic, and social factors. The process could have broken down at almost any point. And the odds on any desirable lake in the United States surviving in good condition are fairly low.

Some elements in the process are natural and fortuitous. Twin Lakes lies at a relatively high elevation in a watershed that is relatively "clean." It is surrounded by forest and is not in immediate proximity to agricultural or industrial operations. (Only 1 percent of the lake's watershed is actively agricultural; none is industrial.) Its water source is springs, not a river that brings its own burden of use into play. It is a small lake, its size a mixed blessing but, on balance, positive and extremely important in its history. On the one hand, its size reduces the impact of wind, especially since for most of its existence, it has been guarded by forest. The modest expanses of open water discourage the kinds of highly popular recreational activity that stimulate development. And its smallness makes it more "manageable" than larger lakes and encourages a sense of community. On the other hand, its size makes it much more sensitive to pollution and invasive species. However, even with logging and development, an unusually high percentage of its natural shoreline vegetation has survived to serve as a natural filter. Relatively little of the shoreline has been filled in, and revetting is rare and, where it exists, minimal and "natural."

Commercialization has largely bypassed Twin Lakes. Unlike Black, Burt, and Mullett, Twin Lakes was not accessible by rail. And no matter what the chamber of commerce may have said about "good roads," it would generally have been considered difficult to reach. (Ernie Hover referred to the local roads as "corduroy roads," by which he meant badly potholed and deeply rutted.) The campgrounds were much smaller, with fewer amenities than those on Black, Burt, and Mullett. The "resorts" of the 1930s and thereafter were few, small, and simple. No restaurant or lodge for the public existed until at least the later 1960s and, more likely, the 1970s. Residential growth did not come in force until the 1970s and 1980s, and even then, it was of an individualized nature. While large-scale commercialized residential development of a conventional sort became a possibility in the late 1970s and has continued to be a threat, it has not yet fully materialized.

On the other hand, an effective lake community had emerged by 1980, the product of a coincidence of timing. The Gannon-Paddock survey of Northern Michigan lakes and Project CLEAR overlapped the DNR decision to install the Smith Road campground at a time when environmental awareness had been raised by tracts such as Rachel Carson's *Silent Spring* and serious interest in "lake management" had appeared, as evidenced by the manual printed by the NEMCOG in 1978.

In both the academic and the real world, *community* is a word of many shades and many meanings. At the very least, "community" may, confusingly, refer to a geographical place, a group of people, a body of common or habitual interactions, and/or a set of shared interests, values, and relationships. Some elements that make for community may be common, if not universal; others are particular, perhaps unique.

As a geographical community, Twin Lakes is contradictory. First, there is not even the usual rural crossroads with a post office, convenience store, and possibly a family restaurant flanked by a few houses. In the conventional geographical sense of community, "there is no there there."[385] Second, Twin Lakes is relatively small. The lake is dwarfed by the better-known lakes in the northern half of the Lower Peninsula. Smallness is generally considered to be a facilitator of community.

But this small lake is divided into a series of bays, and its shoreline, long, complex, and heavily vegetated, belies its small acreage. The result is that residents can see the dwellings of only a few others from their own property or from any one point on the lake itself. Similarly, residents out on the lake can be seen only when they are in a particular bay. Thus, there is not the visual reminder of "community" that prevails on more conventionally formed and open lakes. It is also the case that, quite unlike many lakes and quite apart from any question of private property, there is no beach and virtually no shoreline that can be glanced along or walked.

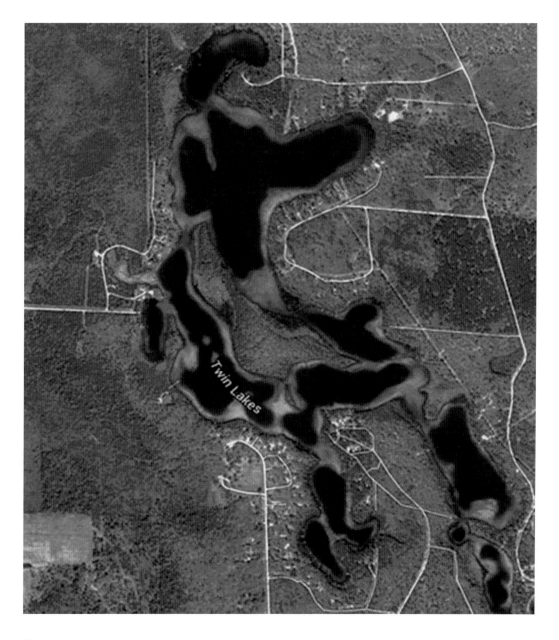

As well, there is no circumferential or shore road from which all or most of the lake can be glimpsed, if only momentarily. Instead, there are forested access roads that dive straight into the lakeshore and dead end (Smith, Twin Trail, Godin, Loon Nest, Page, Truscott, Reynolds). Crawford Road and Grim Circle are accessible only from two of these access roads. Krouse is a bit of an exception in that it runs somewhere from Twin Lakes Road to an intersection with the Alpena State Road and Orchard Beach Road. Krouse is the access road for the southeast side of the lake where cottages are built right along the road, but as it stretches north, Krouse moves farther away from the lake. Here, long access roads run off it (Godin, Loon Nest), or long and obscured two-tracks lead to residences located many forested yards off the road.

Thus, the base unit of community on Twin Lakes is the neighborhood defined by the access roads.[386] At CTLA meetings, it is common for everyone to introduce or reintroduce themselves by name and access road. And there are trustees with oversight and reporting responsibilities for each of the roads. Quite apart from more formal social intercourse, interactions on the roads are a result of walking or stopping to help a neighbor or meeting the neighbor's dog before meeting the neighbor or passing slowly in vehicles. The product of these interactions was described many years ago by the urbanist Jane Jacobs in the context of city planning and city neighborhoods.[387]

> [Most of the contact in a neighborhood] is ostensibly utterly trivial, but the sum is not trivial at all. The sum of such casual, public contact at a local level—most of it fortuitous . . . all of it metered by the person concerned and not thrust upon him by anyone—is a feeling for the public identity of people, a web of public respect and trust, and a resource in time of personal and neighborhood need.

(Contrary to a common assumption, Americans do not readily and regularly interact with neighbors. For several reasons, the level of such interaction on Twin Lakes is higher than the norm.)

These lake neighborhoods have the appearance of organic growths, mostly maturing one residence at a time rather than having been imposed on the land all at once, as in typical American development. And in most cases, the neighborhoods include households that have been on the lake for many years, in some cases two or more generations.

What else then may contribute to the sense of community that has existed? Despite the influx of newcomers over the last half century or more, marriage, family relationships, and family history have played significant roles. Pages have been present near the lake for over a hundred years. Alva, Lyle, Clyde, Alton, Edsel, and Leonard Page have owned property on or in the vicinity of the lakeshore.[388] Doris Page Rodriguez and her husband, Charles, a former president of the CTLA, have lived on the lake since the 1980s. The presence of Spiekhouts and Hovers on the lake goes back to the 1930s and 1940s. An array of Heberts appeared in Cheboygan County as early as 1880, along with Boyeas, O'Neills, O'Connors, and McKays. Two generations of Boyeas are now present on the lake. The Godins, Spiekhouts, Heberts, McPhedrans, and Weekses have all been linked by marriage and by geographical proximity on Godin Circle. Similarly, Griessel and Shultz, Field and Ressler, Williams and Kalis, Witkowski and Fox, Panyard and O'Neill, and Bordt and Page have been joined by family relationships.

The nature of the residential pattern and modern modes of communication are also factors. Twin Lakes is not the summer vacation lake held fondly in memory by many urban dwellers, especially in the east. While less than half of its population is year-round, at least some of the remainder live roughly half of the year on Twin Lakes. A few, while not year-round residents, come to the lake for varying lengths of time throughout the year. Thus, the lake population fluctuates within a somewhat limited range throughout much of the year, though it is certainly higher in June, July, and August (and lower in the heart of winter). But there is not the explosion of summer people that occurs on many other lakes, and the life of the lake is not locked into summer, the favorite frame of nostalgic writers and moviemakers.

Electronic mail, texting, and the telephone make communication inexpensive, easy, and frequent[389] so that many of the non-year-round residents never lose track of the lake community. Between Labor Day and Memorial Day, members of the CTLA will receive two or three substantial newsletters, most of them electronically. (Thirty years ago, it would be one slight newsletter delivered by the United States Post Office. The CTLA newsletter goes back almost forty years to a pre-electronic age.) Notifications will be sent of special events such as Earth Day, Tip of the Mitt programs, sightings of rarely seen animals, and meetings with the regional officials of the Forest Management Division of the DNR. Other news of particular importance finds its way among community members in one way or another, mostly electronically. While not intrusive or overwhelming, such communication preserves the ties to the place and the people.

A perhaps quite important contributor to community cohesion, interlayering with that of family relationships, is social-class integration in the lake population. Twin Lakes—and Northeastern Michigan, more generally—did not attract the wealth from Detroit, Chicago, Milwaukee, and elsewhere that can be found on the west coast of Michigan from points south of Grand Traverse Bay to points north of Harbor Springs, in Les Cheneaux islands off the southeastern coast of the Upper Peninsula, or inland on Lakes Burt and Mullett. (Already in the mid-1920s, the photographic display of "Cheboygan on the Straits of Mackinac" included a picture labeled "Along Millionaires Row, Near Sagers on Burt Lake.") This is not to say that there is no money on the lake but only that there are very few egregious displays of economic well-being, nor is there apparent social competition or a local economy of a type that serves and can exist only in the presence of great wealth. For the most part, residences are modest and practical, often older, or, if larger and contemporary, usually built in such a way as to merge unobtrusively into the lake environment. Property prices do not match prices prevailing along the Lake Michigan shore or inland lakeshores to the west.

One facet of social integration is the frequency with which individuals knew one another in a work environment beyond Twin Lakes (e.g., Herbert Westervelt and Claude Ressler in the Oakland County Road Commission or any number of individuals in the automobile industry or two members of the Michigan State University faculty) or knew of one another as residents of some place other than Twin Lakes (e.g., the Ohio residents who mostly come from a remarkably small area in West Central and Central Ohio and the cluster of Indiana residents from St. Joseph County). What either relationship means is that the process that Jane Jacobs described had already taken place or was well along before residency on the Lake. (Either or both of these work and residential associations may also have involved family connections.)[390]

A corollary of social integration was a population that possessed developed occupational skills that could be directed to the needs arising on the lake. Quite apart from other communication, residents could speak to one another through different sets of practical skills applied to those needs. The dam spillway, the literature and signs, the environmental awareness and lake monitoring, the ability to organize activities and mobilize campaigns, the dam renovation of the 1980s and the later erosion prevention project, the CTLA logotype, and the detailed consideration of issues in trustees and association meetings are all examples of this phenomenon. A brief glance at the occupations of residents past and present reveals a broad range of automotive industry workers, including executives, engineers, supervisors, testing lab personnel, line workers, repairmen, maintenance workers, and salesmen. Education has been represented by professors in science and nonscience disciplines, primary- and secondary-school teachers and counselors, specialists in information technology, and a school cook. The roster of other occupations includes army NCO, artist, auditor, beautician, bookkeeper, butcher, carpenter, chemist, coke oven operator, diesel engine mechanic, DNR employee, dry waller, farmer, Internal Revenue Service manager, law enforcement officer, lawyer, long-haul truck driver, machinist, mechanic for an auto racing team, millwright, navy NCO, painter, plaster contractor, plumbing and heating salesman, railroad worker, real estate broker, refrigeration technician, road construction supervisor, roofer, secretary, social worker, telephone lineman, tool-and-die maker, and well driller. Most of the time, the variety and availability of these skills as well as a powerful voluntarism have made it possible for lake residents to rely on themselves to do whatever has had to be done.[391]

The lake itself is central to community. To a significant degree, the balance between collective and individual elements in lake society has been imposed by the lake, its layout, and its needs. Sightings of fellow residents occur on the water. Perhaps as they fish, drifting in the early morning mist. Or in evening promenades by boat that give a sense of the lake as a whole and an awareness of current conditions and produce "ship-to-shore" communications, however fleeting. Or in unplanned meetings on the lake where news and opinions are quietly exchanged. It is virtually impossible to traverse the lake without observation or engagement. In effect, it is the Main Street of a small village or town. (The exception, at least to engagement, would be nonresident turtle hunters running silent in the darkness of night without the legally required bow, stern, and overhead lights.)

Though difficult to verify, it is tempting to suggest that just as the lake and its needs define the balance between collective and individual elements in local society, the lake and its surroundings choose those who reside on its shores. Or the lake in combination with its attractions to those who come and stay—natural beauty, solitude, fishing, and hunting. Its residents tend to be quiet-spoken, resourceful, self-sufficient yet companionable, careful but at ease on water and in forest, and concerned with the setting, appearance, and utility of their dwellings and outbuildings. If these seem contradictory in some respects, it needs to be said that fishing and hunting may often be solitary enterprises, but part of their joy is in the telling and that, for those who stay, a decision has been made to reside, not just visit.

Yet another element in the creation of a community, crucial in integrating the neighborhoods into the larger entity, is the lake association, the CTLA. It has been an inclusive and participatory organization that, in various degrees, has been advocative, charitable, educational, governing, and social (not to mention inexpensive). With its roots in the early environmental movement, the CTLA brought together lake residents, many of them relatively recent arrivals, around lake management, itself a relatively new idea (as opposed to organized protection of property values or the undertaking of physical "improvements" on a lake). The most succinct statement of the CTLA's purpose is found in its first annual report for nonprofit corporations in 1979: "To exercise all powers within the Law to protect the health, rights, welfare, and ecology of Twin Lakes & Watershed."

In the summer 1984 *Watershed Council Informer*, then the ambiguously titled newsletter of the TOMWC, the question was asked, "Why Have a Lake Association?" Its answer was

> A strong lake association has many advantages. It can bring together the energies, talents, and funds of individuals for common, planned efforts. A lake association can also: 1) act as a unified voice representing the lake's best interests before government units, 2) take advantage of governmental programs and services, 3) monitor and influence decisions on lake use and protection, and 4) identify and correct specific problems.

The CTLA has done all these.

The association has been the organized voice of the lake to township and county authorities, state agencies and politicians, the federal government, and nongovernmental organizations. It has been the vehicle to frame and articulate agreement on a number of goals: maintaining the dam and thus appropriately controlling lake levels; guarding and monitoring the quality of the water and thus whatever contributes to that quality; protecting loons and other wildlife (even tolerating beavers, so long as they do not seriously damage the lake or property); controlling or preventing the establishment of invasive species; and keeping abreast of environmental science and informing its membership. It has also shaped a community calendar in the form of events that are open to all residents, not just all members: the spring and fall meetings/picnics of the association, the trustees meetings on the second Wednesday of each month in the spring, summer, and fall, the potluck dinners in members' homes that take the place of trustees meetings in the winter months, the Fourth of July boat parade and picnic, and the Christmas party.

In *Bowling Alone*, Robert D. Putnam wrote of the waxing and waning of civic engagement and social capital in America. "Social capital" refers to "connections among individuals—social networks and the norms of reciprocity and trustworthiness that arise from them."[392] In general, the more substantial its social capital, the better a community functions. In Putnam's view, "the fabric of American community life," having strengthened in the three decades before 1960, began to unravel in the 1960s and 1970s and came apart even more rapidly in the 1980s and 1990s. Using a vast and diverse array of sociological evidence, Putnam seeks to establish the trends in community life and to explain the causes of the trends, their consequences, and the remedies for civic disengagement.

Putnam investigated whether small groups and environmental groups (the CTLA could be placed in both categories) bucked the prevailing trends of the 1980s and 1990s. Those trends were a lack of newly formed organizations and loss of membership in existing organizations. He found that growth occurred among small groups but that it was highly selective. For the most part, it consisted of the expansion of grassroots activism among evangelical conservatives and the growth in the number of self-help and support groups (e.g., AA, Al-Anon).[393]

Major environmental organizations unquestionably grew substantially and consistently from 1960 through the mid-1990s. But only a few of them had local chapters, and only a very small minority of members ever attended those local chapters that did exist. Direct mail was the primary form of communication, and "membership" consisted almost entirely of mailing in a contribution.[394]

On the other hand, some observers of the environmental movement have insisted that a fundamental change in the movement since the 1970s has been rapid growth in the number and prominence of grassroots organizations. Putnam returns a verdict of "not proved"; he can find no hard evidence that grassroots environmentalism had grown and, on the contrary, found some indications that it had declined over those decades.[395]

Interestingly, Putnam finds age, specifically generational placement rather than life cycle positioning, to be the best predictor and the most important explanation of civic engagement/disengagement. And appropriately, the movement from one generation to another is, for him, the key to understanding the course of civic involvement in the twentieth century.

What Putnam calls a "long civic generation" was born between 1910 and 1940, its core cohort being those persons born between 1925 and 1930. It experienced the Depression and World War II and, as younger adults, the postwar economic boom. For the most part, it set up homes and families in the 1950s, the Eisenhower years. Consistently, it showed a high level of civic engagement and social capital.[396]

The boomer generation, the children of the long civic generation, experienced the civil rights movement (in which some participated) and racial violence, the "big muddy" of Vietnam (but mostly not as combatants), and, as young adults, the assassinations of three national leaders, Watergate, and economic stagflation. It was also the first generation to grow up with television. Highly educated, "slow to marry and quick to divorce," less trusting than its parents' generation and less engaged, more individualistic and "libertarian" and materialistic, the boomers participated far less in all forms of community involvement, even the simplest and least time-consuming, than those who had gone before.

The Sightline Project of the Stanford (University) Center on Longevity, in its February 2016 report, repeatedly describes the fifty-five- to sixty-four-year-old cohort (one of six studied) as more isolated and less engaged than the same age cohort twenty years earlier and, in some cases, than any contemporary cohort.[397] In summary, compared to fifty-five- to sixty-four-year-olds of twenty years ago, "members of the Baby Boom generation are less likely to be married, have weaker ties to family, friends, and neighbors, and are less likely to engage in religious or community activities." In the period 1995–2012,

> social engagement levels for all age groups [did not change] substantially, with one exception: today's 55- to 64-year-olds are less likely to be socially engaged than their predecessors. This age group, part of the Baby Boom generation, are less likely to have meaningful interactions with a spouse or partner. They have weaker ties to family, friends, and neighbors and are less likely to engage in church and other community activities than those who were the same age 20 years ago.

Similarly, this was the only age cohort to experience a marked decline in married people (7 percent between 1999 and 2011).

> The 55- to 64-year-old age group is now the least likely to interact with family who do not live with them. This departure represents a substantive change from 1995, when this age group was more connected to families than other age cohorts. But again, the 55- to 64-year-old age group is quite different from its predecessors. From 1995 to 2012, the percentage of 55- to 64-year-olds saying they could count on a family member in time of need dropped from 79 percent to 69 percent.

Gen X, the grandchildren of the long civic generation, embodies a continuation, in some respects an intensification and acceleration, of the characteristics of their parents, especially with respect to individualism and materialism. Their experience is of the economic insecurities of the 1970s and 1980s, of the uncertainties of family life (Gen X were "the children" as the rate of divorce rose to half of all marriages), and of the absence of any great collective public endeavor (such as the defeat of Nazi Germany and Imperial Japan or the civil rights movement).

In the 1960s and 1970s, Twin Lakes was settled by members of the long civic generation. Of the original officers and trustees of the CTLA, only one was born outside the early years of that generation. Of fifty property owners on Twin Lakes in 1978 whose birth dates can be ascertained, 80 percent were born within Putnam's magic window. (It is important to understand that "membership within a generation" is not a causal explanation. It is a correlation that is of interest, and at best, it may describe the attitudes of a large group, not account for the actions of specific individuals or groups of individuals.)

In the case of Twin Lakes, the lake and the needs of the lake produced a response characteristic of Putnam's long civic generation but a response that runs contrary to his trend line of the 1970s and 1980s and to his skepticism about the growth of grassroots environmentalism. (Quite noticeably, the CTLA did not seek help from or membership in any of the major environmental organizations. Indeed, it even hesitated in linking up with the TOMWC.) Unalienated from civic responsibility or politics, the organized community used the political system effectively to achieve goals that were beyond the scope of direct local action.

Are there community standards? Yes. Complaints about the behaviors of outsiders are at least as often complaints that they do not accept community standards as they are genuinely legal in nature (out-of-season fishing or hunting, for example). Quite notably, these standards are, for the most part, not written down; the speed ordinance is an exception. Twin Lakes is not a condominium or neighborhood association or gated community with written rules. (Signage on the lake, of course, is written as well as ideographic, and its purpose is to acquaint visitors with five of the standards.) This is true of the treatment of the Page Road access by visitors, the fires, cutting, and trash on the island, springtime bass fishermen going back at least to the 1970s, the harassment of the loons, the unlimited taking of fish, the lone PWC rider in the lake's history, and certain policies of the DNR. But the concern is not limited to outsiders. The shoreline episodes (1997, 2009) and noise episode (2003) are also examples of deviations from community standards and of community response. So is the comment/complaint about the known "high speed" pontoon boat operator in the 2005 newsletter and the awareness of the identity of "high speed" boaters indicated by residents in the May 2008 meeting. Application of the standards is not selective as between visitor and resident.

Like institutions from marriage to the DNR, communities are not immune to disagreement, friction, and conflict. In the case of Twin Lakes, the two instances that incorporate significant division were fish in the 1980s and 1990s (primarily over how to proceed and an unwillingness to accept the conclusions reached at length by the DNR) and development in the 2000s (still not resolved). In the first case, the community has moved on, and in the second, it waits.[398]

Yet Twin Lakes is by no means a closed community. Its members are members of a broad array of other communities: for example, the city of Cheboygan, churches, kayakers, friends of the library, hometowns, political parties, garden clubs, book clubs, regional environmental organizations, and, inescapably, University of Michigan and Michigan State University alumni. Its charities are directed to various of these other communities. And this fact of multiple community involvements may well be helpful in contributing ideas for managing the lake and to appreciation of the lake.

---

[385] Gertrude Stein's statement about Oakland, California was a cultural reference, not a geographical one. The use of her phrase here is a geographical reference, not a cultural one.

[386] I want to thank Doris Page Rodriguez for her thoughtful comment on this topic. Some lakes have multiple beach associations (Mullett is one); it may be arguable whether these should be seen as neighborhoods rather than simply as restrictive legal constructs.

[387] *The Death and Life of Great American Cities* (New York: Random House, 1961), p. 56.

[388] Edsel Page was the youngest son of Alva Page. Most recently, William Page has become a property owner on the lake.

[389] Landline telephones on the lake suffer interruption only when storms damage the lines or poles, another utility digs blindly, or the occasional heavy-equipment operator breaks a ground wire. Cell phones function on certain parts of the lake and not on others. Similarly, high-speed internet access requires line of sight to a satellite or a modem that can access a wireless system. with (As of late 2018, efforts to improve internet access for residents appear to have been successful.) Cable is unavailable.

[390] Much more difficult to assess is the extent and effect of a familiar pattern in Michigan history: individuals born and/or raised in Northern Michigan (or the Upper Peninsula) who head south to make a living and then retire in Northern Michigan, having visited more or less often in the interim.

[391] While Twin Lakes is not located at the end of the earth, its distance from the small towns of Cheboygan and Onaway and the limited services they can provide encourage self-reliance among its residents. So does the modest treasury of the CTLA.

[392] Robert D. Putnam, *Bowling Alone: The Collapse and Revival of American Community* (New York: Simon & Schuster, 2000), p. 19.

[393] Putnam, pp. 149–152, 161–162, 180. Samuel P. Hayes, in *Beauty, Health, and Permanence: Environmental Politics in the United States, 1955–1985* (Cambridge: Cambridge University Press, 1987), p. 13, drew a distinction between the history of conservation and that of environmentalism, a distinction that is not equally convincing in all its parts and is not wholly consistent with Putnam: "Environmental objectives arose out of deep-seated changes in preferences and values associated with the massive social and economic transformation in the decades after 1945. Conservation had stirred technical and political leaders and then worked its way down from the top of the political order, but environmental concerns arose later from a broader base and worked their way from the middle levels of society outward, constantly to press upon a reluctant leadership."

[394] A recent acknowledgement of a renewed membership in the Sierra Club, "the only environmental organization advocating for change at every level of government," identified the member's "chapter" (state level) and "group" (local level). But the text of the message listed only the efforts "your contribution is helping" and the many benefits the member might enjoy. There is no mention of actual participation.

[395] Putnam, pp. 154–161. The two major regional environmental organizations in Northern Michigan are the TOMWC, founded in 1979, and the Little Traverse Conservancy, founded in 1991. Both qualify as "grassroots" and participatory organizations.

For this paragraph and those that follow, see Putnam's chapter 14, "From Generation to
[396] Generation," pp. 247–276. Reading the entire chapter (and indeed the whole book) may quiet concerns about Putnam's use of the concept of "generation."

[397] http://longevity3.stanford.edu/wp-content/uploads/2016/02/Sightlines-Project-Full-2_10_2016_855pm_FOR_WEBSITE.pdf. "Seeing Our Way to Living Long, Living Well in 21st Century America," pp. 5, 19, 20, 21.

[398] There is also the one instance in which some of those attending an association meeting approved a motion from the floor while feeling pressured and later regretted their vote. Those feelings and the constitutional and financial issues raised by the motion were later addressed. See the June and November 2010 Newsletters as well as the Minutes, First Annual Meeting, 5.30.2010; Trustees Minutes, 7.14.2010, 8.11.2010; and the Minutes, Fall Meeting, 9.4.2010.

III The Future

Future lake management will depend more on the efforts of private lake associations than on top-down government regulation to keep small lakes clean and to restore those that need help.[399]

Writing of kettle lakes as a group, Robert Thorson observed, perhaps too optimistically, that they "are slightly healthier than other types of lakes of comparable size. Those that remain undeveloped are almost as vibrant as they were a century ago, although they are being invisibly damaged by aerosol fallout from remote sources of air pollution."[400]

Thorson identified the main threat facing kettles in the near term as too much development, "both of their shorelines and of the highly permeable soils between them." Excess nutrients from septic tanks, feedlots, and tillage fields produce weed overgrowth, murky water, and fish kills. "Other problems include the closure of public beaches due to fecal bacteria, the ecological leveling caused by invasive species, pharmaceutical pollution, and bioaccumulated toxins in game fish." The future worries he specified were overdevelopment, the long-term effects of climate change, and demographic shifts that "are imperiling conservation and appropriate use."

A few of these plagues are not a part of the past or present of Twin Lakes and may not be a part of its future. As of now, there is no beach, public or private, on Twin Lakes and no evidence of fecal bacteria, "ecological leveling" caused by invasive species, or the presence of pharmaceuticals. Toxins in the fish population are manageable for now. There are not even known cases of "swimmer's itch."

But that is not the same as saying there is no need to deal with the potential appearance of some or all of these. Eternal vigilance is the price of an environmentally viable lake. "No matter how remote or pristine a place may be, sooner or later, dirty energy will come calling."[401] And not only dirty energy but also acidificants, carbon monoxide, dust, mercury, nitrogen oxides, PFCs, smoke, sulfur oxides, and other pollutants from other industrial processes. (As noted earlier, mercury is already present in the fish of the lake.) It needs to be remembered that for many Americans and Canadians, the Great Lakes are first and foremost an industrial basin, that all the major industries of the basin emit pollutants, that maritime activity is international and highly industrial, and that the primary sources of energy in the North Central United States are coal, natural gas, and oil.[402]

Thus, for more than sixty years, a large oil and natural gas pipeline has run along miles of Lake Michigan shoreline in the Upper Peninsula, crossed to the Lower Peninsula along the bottom of the Straits of Mackinac, and proceeded under and near the rivers, streams, and lakes of Northern Michigan, transporting crude oil and liquids from Western Canada to Sarnia, Ontario, an economically convenient but environmentally hazardous shortcut. As economically and operationally convenient—and as environmentally problematic— is the proposal of Ontario Power Generation to dispose of nuclear waste in a deep geological repository within a mile of Lake Huron.

There are too many agents and avenues for the introduction of invasive species to avoid altogether their presence. Twin Lakes cannot be hermetically sealed off from the world, nor can it deny public access. At least one invasive is present, purple loosestrife, and it is increasingly apparent and certain that another, zebra mussels, has been introduced more recently. (Zebra mussels have been present for several years in many of the lakes in Antrim, Charlevoix, Emmet, Cheboygan, and Presque Isle Counties.) What can be done and what will continue to be necessary is surveillance, early detection, and removal or control. In the case of purple loosestrife, it is fair to say that its spread has been limited and may have actually diminished slightly, but it is unlikely ever to be eradicated. What can be done is to prevent its displacing native vegetation on a large scale. (The milfoil and phragmites found on Twin Lakes are native, not invasive. But the roster and extent of invasives in Northern Michigan is not diminishing.)

In the case of zebra mussels, there had been considerable relief felt, though it was not accompanied by complete confidence, at the DNR's declaration that Twin Lakes was free of these intruders, despite the recovery of two specimens by a resident. In fact, zebra mussels have been discovered in larger and larger numbers, and the work of the near future is to observe closely their success or failure in colonizing the lake. Beyond that, the lake must wait on further research on highly selective natural toxins that kill zebra mussels and harm nothing else and on experiment with the large-scale utilization of these toxins. (As of 2016 TOMWC, the University of Michigan Research Station, the Michigan Natural Features Inventory, the United States Geologic Survey, and others were pursuing small-scale trials of a biocontrol product (Zequanox®) composed of dead bacterial cells that interfere with the digestion of zebra and quagga mussels, eventually killing them. For several reasons, even if the trials are successful, biocontrol using this product appears unlikely to be in the future of Twin Lakes.)

Alternatively, it could witness what Black Lake may be experiencing, an ongoing ecosystem adjustment that integrates the mussels into a new equilibrium. The chlorophyll-a concentrations in Black Lake fell drastically in the years between 1994 and 2009, coincident with its infestation with zebra mussels. The concentrations then rose for four years into the range recorded in 1991–1994 before falling in 2014–2015, yet remaining above the lowest levels of 2006–2009. In essence, the ecosystem, through its phytoplankton productivity, may be dictating the size of the mussel population it can tolerate. But the price of that adjustment has not been studied and the influence of lake size on such an adjustment is unknown (Black Lake is nearly fifty times the size of Twin Lakes).

The lake community will also need to be alert to quagga mussels, an invasive species that affects lake ecologies in the same way as zebra mussels and that have been found in Lake Charlevoix and Crooked Lake to the west and in nearby Mullett Lake. As with other invasives, its most likely vector is boat hulls that are not cleaned.

Monitoring of the lake must continue to identify any effects on water quality of airborne pollutants and to track a primary covert source of pollution in lakes, the leaching of septic facilities. Eventually, almost all septic systems, no matter how well looked after, will fail. And some of the septic systems on the lake are almost certainly nearing the end of their useful life. The size and the soil of Twin Lakes makes such monitoring all the more necessary. Large-scale residential development would intensify the hazard. The aging of the lake is unavoidable, but the acceleration of aging is not. Chemical analyses up to now are encouraging, and the lake's "canaries in the coal mine," fish, especially cisco, continue to thrive within the limits of the lake's inherent ability to support aquatic life.

The historically colonial character of much of Northern Michigan's economy presents its own dangers. Outsiders have come in, exploited, profited, and left without creating a sustainable segment of the economy or providing remediation. The early lumber industry was just such, and so is much of the present-day Great Lakes mining industry. The dangers to Twin Lakes of this sort of economic colonialism involve groundwater. The industries are water bottling and hydraulic fracturing. Both involve drawing down groundwater and the second risks polluting it.[403]

"Water mining" became an issue in 1999 with Nestlé Waters North America/Ice Mountain's plans to draw water from Newaygo and Mecosta Counties in West Central Michigan, its building of a bottling plant in the village of Stanwood (the Mecosta County village's population was 211), and the unwillingness of the MDEQ to effectively monitor or limit withdrawals. The legal issues were two: immediate environmental harm to bodies of water and to wetlands and habitat in the area where the spring water pumping was occurring; and the threat to the public trust doctrine by which the natural resources (including groundwater) of the state belong to the people of the state.

Michigan Citizens for Water Conservation (MCWC) won the argument of environmental damage in both the local court and in the Michigan Court of Appeals. The court of appeals, however, recognized water interests of Nestlé/Ice Mountain that had to be balanced, it said, with the water interests of the riparian landowners. A balance satisfactory to the court was achieved in 2009 in an agreement under which Nestlé ended its illegal withdrawals, reduced legal withdrawals by nearly half, and recognized the need for reduced pumping in the spring and summer. Nevertheless, the loopholes in Michigan's law and enforcement and the precedent for water diversion continue to exist, and Nestlé is now (2017–2018) seeking a large increase in permitted withdrawals.[404]

"Hydraulic fracturing" may as appropriately be called "hydrofracturing" or "hydrologic fracturing." It requires the injection under pressure of huge amounts of water mixed with mysterious proprietary brews of chemicals and, assuming anyone is watching, the responsible storage of the large but hazardous volumes of used liquid. On the one hand, "fracking" can draw down groundwater reserves in the areas in which it is practiced, and on the other hand, its disposal of fluid can infiltrate groundwater reserves. In the case of Michigan, the geologic underground and groundwater reservoir is mostly limestone, not granite. It is very much subject to fracture, dissolution, and infiltration.

But the state government and the utilities, large and small, are committed to coal-burning, oil, and natural gas. (There are now almost three thousand oil and gas wells in the Cheboygan River watershed, most of them in its southern portion. Geology limits drilling farther north.) Large corporations and the national government have an interest in making the United States an energy exporter. Fracturing therefore remains a threat to any and all areas with the relevant geological formations and a lack of political weight.[405] Similarly, areas that lie along pipeline routes or have storage facilities are at greater risk. The leakage of methane, for example, is a frequent feature of fracking and of gas delivery and storage systems. (The government of Michigan is committed to full exploitation of the state's natural resources, specifically of gas, lumber, and minerals.)

From its inception, the CTLA was able to mobilize politically and to work effectively with local and state politicians to achieve its ends (which were mostly preventive or reductive). Whether the political system is or will be as responsive and cooperative is very much open to question.

Ready access to the relevant science and a willingness to pursue and apply that science have had a central role in the continued health of the lake. The science has been delivered in a variety of modes, some one-time, others informal: the Gannon-Paddock investigation, the Gannon campground evaluation, the NEMCOG lake management manual, the presentations and/or comments of scientists resident on the lake, and articles that CTLA members have come across or sought out. But there is also an institutional basis for the continuing acquisition of the important knowledge in the form of TOMWC, the DNR, and the MDEQ. As Thorsen might comment, the problem is not and will not be knowledge of sound science: it is and will be the ability and willingness to act on it.

The relationship with the DNR is likely to remain ambivalent. The DNR is a complex political entity with many functions and divisions. It also has many constituencies, some internal and others external. Lacking political power and economic importance, a small body of residents and part-time residents on a small northeastern lake barely figures among those constituencies. At the same time, the DNR has authority over the lake and activity on the lake and the adjoining forest. When responsive, it is a source of information and direction on state policy and environmental science, and it has shown that it can be helpful in achieving certain goals. But for the most part, the DNR does not seem to want to exercise its authority, which is probably, on balance, a good thing. (That has not been true with respect to the state-owned portion of the island.) In part, that is because its myriad larger responsibilities appear to take precedence. But it is also an agency that commits itself inflexibly to certain policies, changeable over time but not variable from locality to locality at any given time, and it is an agency whose policies can be driven by politics and lobbying at the state level.

Thus, the Fisheries Division has shown up every ten years (more or less) and produced reports on lake fish populations that are useful and mostly positive. On the other hand, at points where there was concern with fish in the lake, the DNR produced "one size fits all" responses (tiger muskellunge and splake) that were inappropriate to the locality. Similarly, the Forest Resources Division takes pride in its scientific management of the state forest that surrounds Twin Lakes, of which Black Mountain is a part, and is concerned with formulating contracts with commercial loggers. Once through the introductory reassurances, however, "scientific management," is more concerned with the volume of timber recovery (certainly on the part of the contractor and state politicians) than with buffers and takes little account of the aesthetic and economic consequences of ill-advised cutting near residential lakes. (Large-scale clear-cutting has become much more common in the Twin Lakes–Black Mountain area in recent years.) The Parks and Recreation Division is concerned with maximizing campground utilization, with little concern for the effects on area residents or the behavior of campers. The conservation officers (COs) of the Law Enforcement Division are indeed "a unique class of law enforcement officer" but are rarely available to lake residents to enforce exactly the laws and regulations that are their charge; when responsive, their efforts have been widely appreciated. For the most part, residents must rely on the county sheriff's department or very cautious conversation with offenders or simply accept the violations of law, regulation, and common sense.[406]

Climate change is occurring, and Northern Michigan may have already seen some of its consequences. Warming water, for example, ended thirty years of the DNR's planting trout in the isolated lake. What its long-term implications may be are, by definition, uncertain; the long-term change has not yet occurred. But it is clearly in process. Average air temperatures in the Great Lakes region of the United States have increased 2.0°F in the last century, and ice coverage on the Great Lakes has declined over 70 percent in the last thirty-five years. Daily maximum precipitation has increased 10–20 percent in the Midwest in little more than a century. How to respond effectively to what is, as yet, not clearly known is also uncertain. For example, the effect of carbon dioxide absorption by freshwater lakes on marine life is little investigated.[407] What is certain is that the sources and consequences of climate change cannot be effectively addressed in isolation at the local level except at two extremes, the most blatant cases and the seemingly least offensive cases.

Twin Lakes is located at forty-five degrees north latitude, a line that is significant for now because the greatest measured warming to date has occurred north of that latitude. (It is an imaginary line, not a barrier against warming, which is occurring regardless of latitude.) To the north, the Arctic is warming roughly twice as fast as the rest of the planet, Greenland is melting, and from Alaska across Canada to Greenland, the traditional Inuit culture based on hunting, trapping, and fishing is endangered.

A suggestion of the effects of climate change on Twin Lakes may be found in a survey of other areas at or near forty-five degrees north latitude. In Oregon, vintners face the problem of the pinot noir grape, long the staple of a region producing the finest pinot noir wines in the United States, a grape highly vulnerable to warmer temperatures, and now "the polar bear" of the local industry. Similar problems exist in other wine-producing areas in approximately the same latitude, notably the New York Finger Lakes region, Bordeaux, and Burgundy.

To the east, the glaciers of Glacier National Park will have totally disappeared by 2030, if not sooner. At Yellowstone, there are thirty fewer days per year with snow on the ground, eighty more days per year above freezing, and a growing season thirty days longer than half a century ago. (As of late 2016, Glacier, sitting at the head of three major watersheds, had also closed all park waters to boating, both motorized and nonmotorized, because quagga mussels and larvae had been detected. The ban has now been replaced by very stringent restrictions on boating, especially on motorized boating.)

On Lake of the Woods in Minnesota, Ontario, and Manitoba, larger and larger algal (*cyanobacteria*) blooms appear each year despite decades of reduced nutrient pollution from paper mills and town sewer systems. The causes are complex, but likely contributors include two effects of climate change: higher average water temperatures that produce thirty more ice-free days a year (in effect a longer growing season for algae); and diminished winds (in a calmer lake, top and bottom waters mix less, with colder low-oxygen water settling to the bottom, where it picks up phosphorus from sediment).

In New York's Finger Lake district, vintners have already seen higher temperatures and more extreme weather events. The lakes harbor both zebra mussels and quagga mussels. But one of the lakes has also just encountered *Hydrilla verticillata,* an aggressively invasive aquatic weed that is able to survive the milder winters, can choke channels up to thirty feet deep, and that Florida and California have spent millions of dollars trying to control. Another lake is infested with Asian clams (*Corbicula fluminea*), another invasive species that reproduce profusely, alter the food chain in the lake, and contribute to algal growth. And the area must now contend with the Hemlock woolly adelgid (*Adelges tsugae*), a nonnative aphid-like insect that has been making its way north for years and can reduce hemlocks to skeletons, destroying their role in preserving the healthy creek habitats that feed the lakes.[408]

A once familiar danger may be reappearing. In 2015, more than ten million acres burned in the United States, a record; in 2017, nearly as many acres burned, and the U.S. Forest Service has reported that fire seasons are now almost eighty days longer than fifty years ago. Indeed, in some areas, fire is no longer a seasonal but a year-round concern. The increase is tied to higher annual temperatures.

Another suggestion of the effects of climate change in an environment similar in some respects to that of Twin Lakes can be found in Richard Primack's *Walden Warming: Climate Change Comes to Thoreau's Woods.* What Primack has so far detected is significantly earlier thawing of Walden Pond than in Thoreau's time, similarly earlier flowering times of local plants, as well as substantial extinction and/or greatly reduced populations of certain plants, changed flight times of butterflies, and different arrival times for some species of birds. What may appear to humans as only slight changes in the order of things locally are nevertheless devastating or progressively destructive, given the complex interplay and interdependence of plants, insects, birds, amphibians, and fish.[409] (Similarly, in Yellowstone, change in the timing and volume of spring snowmelt will affect water levels, the growth of vegetation, and the movement of wildlife from bison to trout to bees.)

On the East Coast, the Gulf of Maine and the North Atlantic off the shores of the United States have warmed so rapidly that after more than five hundred years, sustainable cod fishing has become close to impossible. Similarly, the warming of the Gulf of Maine supported a vast expansion of lobstering, beginning in the 1980s; continued warming now and in the immediate future threatens to destroy the industry. The pitch pine of New England and New York confront a new nemesis in the form of the southern pine beetle, which is extending its range northward as winter temperatures warm. It is possible that the beetles might reach the Great Lakes region, where red and jack pine would be especially vulnerable.

It is also possible that the venomous recluse spider will become resident in Michigan. Normally not to be found above thirty-nine degrees north latitude, in recent years, they have been found in a number of Michigan counties, including Emmet, to the west of Cheboygan. Like many other invasive species, they are carried into Michigan, but the milder winters have allowed them to survive and, in a few cases, establish settlements.

In Bordeaux, vintners are contemplating replacement of merlot grapes, long the staple of the region, because an earlier ripening date of a few weeks, the result of rising temperatures, leaves them overripe by the time other grapes have matured. In Burgundy, the incidence of violent, devastating summer hailstorms has increased, causing in one case loss of well over half the crop.

In Alpine Switzerland, Mount Blanc, the Matterhorn, the Eiger, and the Jungfrau, summits within straight-lines distances of fifty miles of each other, are parts of glacial systems that continue the seasonal rhythm of growth and melting. What has changed is the rate and timing of melting and retreat. On the accustomed rhythm depends skiing, tourism, service industries, and the livelihoods of millions. What changed rhythms can support is not known. (In this case, more than climate warming is involved; pollution is a factor. *The Sound of Music* stereotypes of the Alpine region, like the "Up North" images of the Great Lakes, are misleading: the Alpine region is an area of heavy commercial, industrial, residential, and transportation system development.)

But the greatest threat to Twin Lakes, as to most similar lakes, is much more obvious and familiar than climate warming: overdevelopment. In this case, acceptable or appropriate development means knowing when enough is enough, an insight only occasionally acted on where Michigan lakes or other natural resources are involved. Development is an element of environmental and climate change that *can* be addressed at the local level. It may involve septic migration into groundwater and lakes, demand for fossil-fuel–generated power, inappropriate land usage, disregard of natural hydrology, deforestation and loss of carbon storage, depletion of fish and game, and destruction of the natural protections on lakes.

Demography may also play a role in the threat. The median age of the Twin Lakes community is considerably higher than those of Cheboygan County, the state of Michigan, or the United States. In some respects, it is a retirement community. Therefore, the questions of inheritance and the disposition of property by heirs who may have made their lives and careers at a distance and do not value the lake property as their parents or grandparents did always lurk in the background. This is especially the case in those few instances in which a dispersed family owns large acreage that could be divided into small lots. It is also the case, for different reasons, with the Smith Road campground.[410]

Similarly, the CTLA will have to make a demographic transition. To remain an effective institution, it will have to inculcate environmental values and voluntarism in a generation for which neither appears to be a prominent component of living, and it will have to successfully recruit both leadership and membership. Demographics is a greater challenge than finances.

Planning and zoning regulations and their application by local agencies and boards are also crucial elements in the extent and outcome of development. Typically, these bodies do not include members from the affected lake communities. Moreover, they tend, understandably, to be more concerned with economic growth and tax bases than with the environment.

On both the smaller and the larger stage, the degree to which the environmentalism of the 1970s and 1980s has been internalized by American society may be decisive. The Canadian environmentalist David Suzuki, an "elder" in such matters, has argued that the environmentalists of that era, a disappeared or disappearing generation, failed to change the way in which humans understand the world and their place in it. They won a good many battles over clear-cutting forests, offshore oil drilling, dams, and supertankers. But they saw the battle as the issue and the victory as the accomplishment—*fini*! And therefore, they "fundamentally failed" to "shift the perceptual lenses through which we see our place on the planet," to restore what humans until recently have always known, "that we're part of nature and utterly dependent on the natural world for our wellbeing and survival." That failure helps explain why the same battles are being fought so many years later.[411]

Robert Thorson makes related points in two observations about kettle lakes. The first is that scientists and engineers know what to do, but they do not have "the background data needed to make a diagnosis, the money to fill a prescription, and the legal power to implement rehabilitation." The second is his comment, both a commonplace and an essential insight, that "modern lake management is mostly people management." Hence his conclusion, quoted at the start of this chapter: future lake management will depend more on the efforts of private lake associations than on government regulation if small lakes are to be preserved or restored. To be successful, that requires a strong sense and structure of community. On Twin Lakes, the community has compiled "the background data," found the money or volunteer labor to accomplish what was needed, and acquired the necessary legal status to rehabilitate and preserve.

---

[399] Thorson, p. 10. It was tempting to open this chapter with one or both of two quotations, each from a "philosopher" (or perhaps philosophers) in his own right.

Most men, it seems to me, do not care for Nature and would sell their share in all her beauty, as long as they may live, for a stated sum—many for a glass of rum. Thank God men cannot as yet fly and lay waste the sky as well as the earth!

— Henry David Thoreau, *Journal*, 3 January 1861

Prediction is very difficult, especially if it's about the future.

— Niels Bohr, Yogi Berra, and/or others

[400] Thorson, pp. 9–10.

[401] Bobby McEnaney, Deputy Director, NRDC Western Renewable Energy Project, Land & Wildlife Program, quoted in *On Earth*, Spring 2014, 43.

[402] See Biodiversity Research Institute in partnership with the Great Lakes Commission and the University of Wisconsin-La Crosse, *Great Lakes Mercury Connections: The Extent and Effects of Mercury Pollution in the Great Lakes Region* (Gorham, Maine: 2011).

[403] In 1906, before the State Board of (Tax) Equalization, two representatives of Cheboygan County argued the colonial case: outside logging companies were taking lumber out of the county and refusing to sell the land they owned to farmers, thus diminishing the (taxable) wealth of the county (Archives of Michigan, RG 65-5, Minutes, State Board of Equalization, pp. 90–93).

Samuel J. Smith opened for the county. "Of [the personal tax base,] there is over one-third of that that is forest products, lumber, logs, and poles, something that is transient and will be out of our reach in less than a year. We will never see it again. It is something of little value to the county . . . The lumber is taking the wealth out of our county faster than the natural improvements will bring it in . . . the lumber business is retarding the progress of our county. They cut those lands, there are a great deal of those lands, or a lot of them, rather, that is all right for agricultural purposes. All the hardwood lands, they are cutting, and that is principally all we have left . . . and the lumbermen are not selling those lands, they are holding on to them, they are afraid of selling them because they are afraid of farmers coming in there and clearing up this land and setting fires and destroying the timber. This is all right on their part, but it is not right so far as helping out our county is concerned." J. I. Barrett followed up and had to answer repeated questions from a member of the board.

Mr. Bradley: Who is cutting the timber?

Mr. Barrett: The timber is largely cut by Bay City parties.

Mr. Bradley: It is all going out of the county?

Mr. Barrett: It is all going out of the county, that is nearly all, there is the Emory [sic]. Martin Lumber Company there and the Olds, they are quite large concerns, but most of the timber is cut by the Frank Buhl Lumber Company and Johnson & Wylie, all of Bay City or the lower part of the state.

Mr. Bradley: How many acres of hardwood timber have you in Cheboygan now?

Mr. Barrett: I could not tell you.

Mr. Bradley: Who is that owned by?

Mr. Barrett: By those people I spoke of, largely.

Mr. Bradley: All that standing timber is owned by outside parties?

Mr. Barrett: Nearly all by outside parties, with the exception of the Olds people and the Martin Lumber Company, they own quite a lot, but as I say, there are four or five large firms lumbering and take the lumber out, the other people of course make it there and leave the benefit there. The land is all right, that is the hardwood lands.

Mr. Bradley: Are they making farms of it?

Mr. Barrett: Well, where they can get it, in that connection, the outside lumber firms are not putting their lands on the market for the simple reason they don't want any one to go in there and commence clearing until they get through lumbering; there is always more or less danger of fire where a man goes in and clears up a farm, when there is standing timber around it.

[404] See http://www.savemiwater.org/mcwcvsnestle/ and http://wearemichigan.com/WorldWaterWars/UnitedStates/Michigan/index.htm. For a broader perspective on "water wars" in the Great Lakes region, see Peter Annin, *The Great Lakes Water Wars* (Washington, DC: Island Press, 2006). Ironically, Nestlé often appears in magazine articles as a leader in global water issues and "water stewardship." For example, see "What is Water Worth?" in *Fortune* (May 19, 2014).

Before the 2009 settlement had been reached, Nestlé had expanded extraction operations to neighboring Osceola County and in 2017 applied to withdraw 400 gallons per minute from a well near the small town of Evart, a rate determined to be "harmful" in the case of Mecosta. Nestlé currently pays the state of Michigan $200 a year to withdraw 130 million gallons of water. See Caroline Winter, "The Nestlé Bottled Water Cycle," *Business Week*, September 25, 2017.

Since 2015, Nestlé has been embroiled in lawsuits with conservation groups, been the sole subject of a report by the California State Water Resource Control Board, and has had to enter mediation sessions with the U.S. Forest Service—all of these involving the company's withdrawals of water from the San Bernadino National Forest. As of June 2018, the Forest Service had given Nestlé sixty days to accept a three-year permit hedged with environmental protections. The effectiveness of the restrictions depends on their specifics and enforcement.

The question of the company's water rights remains open (more accurately, murky). Nestlé reportedly withdrew as much as 162 million gallons of water a year, for which it paid annually $500–$600. The control board has estimated that Nestlé had a right to less than 15 percent even of the much smaller figure (62.6 million gallons) that the company reports as the average of its withdrawals from 1947 to 2015.

[405] In an earlier version of the enthusiasm for hidden energy sources in Michigan, several property owners on Twin Lakes granted exploratory oil and gas leases in the 1960s and '70s, and the DNR granted such leases wholesale. Little or nothing came of them. In recent years, the phenomenon has been reproduced as residents have been beset with agents seeking rights to frack. As many in Pennsylvania and New York have found, it is a poor bargain.

[406] For one of the grimmest pictures possible of DNR politics, drawn by a resident of the Upper Peninsula, see Joseph Heywood's mystery novels comprising the Woods Cop series.

[407] Something is known of carbon dioxide levels in seawater, resultant acidification, and effects on marine life. That is not true of freshwater lakes and rivers, which, in some respects, are more difficult to investigate and more varied. The primary research has been done in Germany and shows that carbon dioxide not only produces acidification but also acts directly on marine organisms such as water fleas, minnows, and mussels. Over thirty-five years, the carbon dioxide levels in the water of these German reservoirs have tripled, and the pH levels have declined at a much faster rate than is true of seawater. The levels of acidity found in this study are expected to be those of the Great Lakes by 2100. A related study of eleven lakes in Wisconsin over twenty-five years showed no significant change in carbon dioxide levels; the difference in results may

reflect the difficulties in measuring carbon dioxide in freshwater and the variability to be expected in different bodies of freshwater. See https://www.nytimes.com/2018/01/11/science/climate-change-lakes-streams.html; http://onlinelibrary.wiley.com/doi/10.1002/2017JG003794/ abstract; and https://www.pbs.org/newshour/science/fossil-fuels-are-making-freshwater-lakes-more-acidic-at-triple-the rate-of-oceans.

[408] Michigan has had some experience with *Adelges tsugae* as a result of imports of hemlock from eastern areas of the country in which it has become endemic. Therefore, importation of hemlock into Michigan is restricted, and importation from areas of known infection is banned. In recent years, multiple infestations have been detected and treated in Southwestern Michigan, two in the Detroit area, and one in Emmet County, to the west of Cheboygan. An abundance of old hemlocks is one of the distinctive features of forest in the upper half of Lower Michigan and the Upper Peninsula.

[409] Richard B. Primack, *Walden Warming: Climate Change Comes to Thoreau's Woods* (Chicago: University of Chicago Press, 2014). For a recent survey of the same sort of change in the Colorado Rockies, see www.npr.org/2018/07/23/630181622/spring-is-springing-sooner-throwing-natures-rhythms-out-of-whack.

Located in Eastern Massachusetts at forty-two degrees north latitude, Walden Pond is a kettle hole with glacial origins set in an area of bogs and river meadows. Its depth is roughly the same as that of Twin Lakes, and it also has a thermocline, as Thoreau discovered in 1860. However, it is significantly smaller, less than a third of the acreage of Twin Lakes, and it exists in a much more urban area than Eastern Cheboygan County.

Contrary to many assumptions, Walden Pond, when Henry David Thoreau spent his two years living there in the mid-nineteenth century, was hardly pristine; the land had been logged and farmed, as had that around Twin Lakes. Similarly, Walden Pond was part of a community, and Thoreau was a social being. He did not seek eremitic isolation. Instead, he sought a life of simplicity, solitude when he wished it, and intercourse at other times. After all, it was Concord he walked about for hours each day for years before and after his sojourn on the pond, recording the detailed observations that are a basis of Primack's botanical study. And it was an admiring neighbor who continued those observations into the twentieth century.

The technical name for the study of cyclic and seasonal natural phenomena of the sort Primack has carried out at Walden is phenology.

[410] This problem is not limited to lakes and lakeshores. Across the United States, the age of forest landowners has been increasing, and the size of privately owned forest parcels has been shrinking. These private owners hold more than half the forest lands in the country; the owners' average age is over sixty.

Owners of smaller parcels are less likely to invest in a forestry management plans [sic], and managing for wildlife is more difficult than on larger plots . . . And once the land gets cut up, it's more likely it will be developed, and once developed, there's no chance it will ever again be a working forest . . . Though many forest landowners are deeply attached to their property, that affinity can be harder to pass on than a legal deed. "Many of the offspring, grandchildren are more urbanized and don't have the interest or the roots in the land."

See the Associated Press article written by Wilson Ring, Vermont correspondent of the AP, available in many electronic and paper sources, including http://bigstory.ap.org/article/53ebaf50e7414812a4eea02043482be8/private-forest-owners-aging-parcels-shrinking.

[411] Moyers & Company, May 9, 2014, http://billmoyers.com/episode/full-show-time-to-get-real-on-climate-change/.

Appendix I

***Soil Survey of Cheboygan County, Michigan* (1991):**

8 — Tawas peat. This deep, nearly level, very poorly drained soil is in drainageways and depressions on plains. It is subject to ponding. Individual areas are irregularly shaped and are 3 to more than 900 acres in size.

Typically, the surface layer is dark brown peat about 2 inches thick. The lower organic layers extend to a depth of about 44 inches. In sequence downward, they are black and very dark brown muck; very dark grayish brown mucky peat; and dark brown muck. The substratum to a depth of about 60 inches is gray sand. In some place [sic], the muck is more than 51 inches thick. In other places, the organic material is acid. In some areas, the substratum is loamy . . .

This soil is poorly suited to woodland. Windthrow is a hazard, and the equipment limitation, seedling mortality, and plant competition are management concerns . . .

This soil is unsuited to recreational development because of the seasonal high water table and instability of the organic material.

This soil generally is unsuited to building site development and septic tank absorption fields because of the hazard of ponding, the high water table, low soil strength, and a high potential for frost action . . . (p. 18)

77 — Bruce fine sandy loam. This deep, nearly level, poorly drained soil is in low areas. It is subject to ponding. Individual areas are irregularly shaped and range from 5 to more than 300 acres in size . . . limitation, seedling mortality, and plant competition are management concerns . . .

This soil is unsuited to recreational development because of the seasonal high water table, the moderately slow permeability, and the ponding.

This soil is unsuited to building site development and septic tank absorption fields. The instability of cutbanks and the ponding are limitations on building sites. The moderately slow permeability and the ponding are limitations on sites for septic tank absorption fields. (p. 80)

24B — Ocqueoc fine sand, 0–6 percent slopes. This deep, nearly level and undulating, well drained soil is on low knolls and ridges in the uplands and on broad plains. Individuals areas are irregularly shaped and range from 3 to more than 100 acres in size.

Typically, the surface layer is dark brown fine sand about 8 inches thick. The subsoil is about 18 inches thick. It is dark reddish brown, very friable fine sand in the upper part; strong brown and yellowish brown, very friable sand in the next part; and light yellowish brown, very friable very fine sand in the lower part. The substratum to a depth of about 60 inches is stratified. It is pink very fine sand and silt in the upper part and light brown very fine sand, silt, very fine sandy loam, and loamy very fine sand in the lower part. In places, depth to the substratum is less than 20 inches . . .

This soil is fairly well suited to such crops as small grains and grasses and legumes. Maintaining the organic matter content and controlling soil blowing are management concerns . . .

Most areas are used as woodland. The equipment limitation, seedling mortality, and plant competition are management concerns . . .

This soil is suited to recreational development. The sandy surface layer is a limitation . . .

This soil is moderately well suited to building site development but is poorly suited to septic tank absorption fields. The moderate shrink-swell potential and the instability of cutbanks are limitations on building sites . . . The moderately slow permeability is a limitation on sites for septic tank absorption fields. (pp. 38–39)

20B — Mancelona sand, 0–6 percent slopes. This deep, nearly level, and undulating, somewhat excessively drained soil is on knolls, ridges, and broad plains in the uplands. Individual areas are irregularly shaped and range from 3 to more than 200 acres in size. [The "deep, gently rolling, somewhat excessively drained" Mancelona sand, 6 to 12 percent slopes, "is on knolls, ridges, and side slopes in the uplands. Individual areas are irregularly shaped and range from 3 to more than 100 acres in size."]

Typically, about 1 inch of black, well decomposed forest litter is at the surface. The subsurface layer is dark brown sand about 7 inches thick. The subsoil is about 24 inches thick. It is dark brown, very friable and friable loamy sand in the upper part and dark brown, friable sandy loam in the lower part. The substratum to a depth of about 60 inches is light yellowish brown, calcareous, very gravelly coarse sand. In places, the subsoil is redder . . .

Such crops as corn, oats, alfalfa, and mixed grasses can be grown on this soil. Conserving moisture during dry periods, controlling soil blowing, and maintaining or increasing the organic matter content are management concerns . . . [Mancelona sand, 6 to 12 percent slope, is "fairly suited" to crops such as small grain, grasses and legumes. Water erosion and blowing soil are hazards.]

Most areas are used as woodland. The equipment limitation, seedling mortality, and plant competition are management concerns . . .

This soil is unsuited to most recreational development. The sandy surface layer is a limitation . . .

This soil is well suited to building site development but is poorly suited to septic tank absorption fields. The instability of cutbanks is a limitation on building sites . . . A poor filtering capacity is a limitations on sites for septic tank absorption fields. The soil readily absorbs but does not adequately filter the effluent. The poor filtering capacity can result in the pollution of groundwater. [Mancelona sand, 6 to 12 percent slope, is "moderately well suited" to building site development but poorly suited to septic tank absorption fields. The slope is an added limitation to those of Mancelona sand, 0 to 6 percent slope.] (pp. 32–34)

13D — Rubicon sand, 18–30 percent slopes. This deep, hilly and steep, excessively drained soil is on ridges, hills, and high knolls in the uplands. Individuals areas are from 3 to more than 300 acres in size.

Typically, the surface layer is mixed black and light brownish gray sand about [1] inch thick. The subsurface layer is light brownish gray sand about 5 inches thick. The subsoil is very friable sand about thirty inches thick. The upper part is dark brown, the next part is dark yellowish brown, and the lower part is yellowish brown. The substratum to a depth of about 60 inches is light yellowish brown sand. In some places, the subsoil is darker. In other places, the substratum has thin bands of loamy sand . . .

Most areas are used as woodland. Erosion is a hazard, and the equipment limitation and seedling mortality are management concerns . . .

If this soil is used for recreational purposes, the sandy surface layer and the slope are limitations . . .

This soil is poorly suited to building site development and septic tank absorption fields. The slope and the instability of cutbanks are limitations on building sites . . . The slope and a poor filtering capacity are limitations on sites for septic tank absorption fields . . . The soil readily absorbs but does not adequately filter the effluent. The poor filtering capacity can result in the pollution of groundwater. (pp. 24–25)

[The characterization and comment above concerning Rubicon sand are repeated with respect to Kalkaska sand, 12 to 30 percent slopes. Only the description differs.] Typically, the surface layer is mixed very dark gray and light gray sand about 2 inches thick. The subsurface layer is pinkish gray sand about 10 inches thick. The subsoil is sand about 23 inches thick. The upper part is dark reddish brown and friable, the next part is strong brown and loose, and the lower part is brownish yellow and loose. The substratum to a depth of about 60 inches is light yellowish brown sand. In some places, the upper part of the subsoil is thinner. In other places, the subsoil has many thin bands of loamy sand. (pp. 20–21) [Rare outside Michigan, Kalkaska sand is the state sand.]

Appendix 2

CTLA Officers

Presidents:

Steve Seconsky

Claude Ressler

James McPherson

Charles Williams

Charles Rodriguez

Earl Boyea

Robert Schultz

John King

Karl Kalis

Dick Robinson

Susan Page

John Ressler

In most cases, presidents had previously served as vice president. The longest serving president and vice president have been Susan Page and John Ressler.

While there have been several treasurers over the years, the longest serving have been Claude Ressler and, by a wide margin, Randy Mateer.

The office (or offices) of secretary have been occupied by a number of members (often the duties have been split) but most notably, in the early years of the association, by Elnora Godfrey and, in more recent years, by Jeanette Mateer.

For many years, the newsletter (usually one or two a year for the first twenty years of the CTLA's existence but now four or five) was the responsibility of the secretary, but more recently and for many years, it has been the work of Randy Mateer.

Appendix 3

T37N R1E Section 34: Jefferson Crawford and the Department of Conservation

In 1922, the State of Michigan sought a patent for land on the northern end of the lake in T37, sec. 34. The General Land Office produced a supplemental plat of the area without fieldwork, using only the nineteenth-century surveys and survey notes. The result was ten lots (lot 10 was the northern half of the island) and a memorandum, as shown below.

In 1952, the activities of Jefferson Crawford caught the eye of a land appraiser for the Michigan Department of Conservation. His interoffice communication began,

> In working on Case No. 26983-X, Jefferson A. Crawford, RD 2, Cheboygan, it has become evident that the above described property [government lots 6, 7, 8, and 9 in T37N R1E sec. 34] on Big Twin Lake . . . was unpatented Federal lands. No record of disposition was contained in the memo, taken from a supplemental plat received from H. S. Gibbs [covering this section]. Property contains water frontage and in part corrects erroneous original survey. All of the land is within the Black Lake State Forest and is desirable for public ownership. Negotiations toward that end are hereby recommended and suggested.

The communication continued with a bit of history and an example of the problem. The original survey of 1840, rerun in 1841, was not "entirely correct." Subsequent plats in 1854 and 1904 revised the original platting and added lots to the original five.

> A complete change of Lot numberings and area covered by the individual government lots was apparently authorized in a Land Office survey in 1922, which presumably is the present authority for designation of Lots. As a case in point, present owner of Government Lot 3, Mr. Crawford, assumes his ownership to cover land now platted as Government Lot 6. His title rests in tax title procedure. Inasmuch as he infers that he owns what is now Government Lot 6 and is proceeding towards metes and bounds disposal of all of his extensive holdings on the lake, steps should be taken to safeguard lands we now own on the lake and Government Lots we could hope to acquire through exchange with the U.S. Forest Service and the Bureau of Land Management.

The communication ends with a suggestion that the Forestry Division of the department be made aware that there existed several different surveys involving Twin Lakes in Towns 36 and 37 North and a recommendation for a resurvey "to safeguard public property on the lake" (T. R. Tucker to C. E. Millar, 8.9.1952).

A month later, the Lands Division asked the Bureau of Land Management, "Has government lot 6, T37N R1E sec. 34, State of Michigan, according to the supplemental government survey of 1922, been disposed of by the United States?" The memorandum on the 1922 plat indicated only that the lots were subject to disposal.

> The present owner of Government Lot 3, according to reports submitted to this office by our field man, is subdividing the lot according to the survey approved December 30, 1854, which includes Lot 6 . . . instead of the 7.80 acres included in the parcel lying east of the fictitious meander line of the 1840 survey.

The Lands Division also wanted to know which of the other lots resulting from the 1922 survey remained unpatented. "Some of these descriptions are under a proposed exchange with this department, and there is serious doubt in our minds as to the present ownership of the new lots created by the survey of 1922" (J. L. Stephansky to Bureau of Land Management, 9.9.1952).

The answer came in a letter from the Bureau of Land Management two months later.

Lots 6, 7, 8, 9 and 10 of sec. 34, as shown by plat approved June 6, 1922, were included in an approved swamp land selection by the State and were patented on October 3, 1923. Patents issued for lots 1, 2, 3, and 4 . . . were based on [the 1841 or 1854 plats]. Title to lot 5 is based upon plat approved May 28, 1904.

Citing a 1914 case before the U.S. Supreme Court, the bureau concluded "that since patent for lot 3 is based on the 1841 plat, there is no conflict as between the patents issued for lots 3 and 6 of this section" (To Department of Conservation, Attention: Mr. J. L. Stephansky, 11.12.1952).

The Crawfords apparently learned a cautionary lesson. In later sales (1959, 1960, 1966) by the Crawfords to Francis J. Sawyer, for example, the descriptions in the deed included the phrase "where it intersects the northeast corner of Government Lot 5 in accordance with the supplemental Plat approved May 28, 1904, by the Department of the Interior, General Land Office, Washington, D.C."

Bibliography

Articles, Papers, and Pamphlets:

W. A. Burgis and D. F. Eschman. "Late-Wisconsinan History of Northeastern Lower Michigan," Midwest Friends of the Pleistocene Thirtieth Annual Field Conference, May 29–31, 1981 (sponsored by Department of Geological Sciences, the University of Michigan), Landform Units in Northeastern Michigan.

"Cheboygan Up-to-Date" (1898).

William R. Farrand. "The Glacial Lakes around Michigan" (Bulletin 4, revised. Lansing: DEQ, Geological Survey Division, 1998).

William C. Fitt. "Locomotives Without Tracks: Michigan's Phoenix Log Haulers," *Michigan History* (September/October 1982), 46–48.

Jean Gothro, "The Story of Camp Grayling," typescript, 1949.

Guy Gugliotta. "When Did Humans Come to the Americas?" *Smithsonian*, February 2013 (and http://www.smithsonianmag.com/science-nature/When-Did-Humans-Come-to-the-Americas-187951111.html?c=y&page=5).

Glenn Hodges. "Tracking the first Americans," *National Geographic*, January 2015 (and http://ngm.nationalgeographic.com/2015/01/first-americans/hodges-text).

Allan M. Johnson, Robert V. Kesling, Richard T. Lilienthal, and Harry O. Sorensen. "The Maple Block Knoll Reef in the Bush Bay Dolostone (Silurian, Engadine Group), Northern Peninsula of Michigan" (Ann Arbor: University of Michigan, Museum of Paleontology, Papers on Paleontology No. 20, 1979).

Claire V. Korn. "Yesterday through Tomorrow: Michigan State Parks" (East Lansing: Michigan State University Press, 1989).

Kenneth K. Landes, George M. Ehlers, and George M. Stanley. "Geology of the Mackinac Straits Region and Sub-surface Geology of Northern Southern Peninsula" (Lansing: Department of Conservation, Geological Survey Division: Publication 44, Geological Series 37, 1945).

Dorothy G. Pohl and Norman E. Brown. "The history of roads in Michigan" (http://www.michiganhighways.org/history4.html).

Maria Quinlan. "Lumbering in Michigan" (http://seekingmichigan.org/wp-content/ uploads/2013/09/ Lumbering-in-Michigan.pdf).

J. C. Ryan. "Minnesota logging railroads" (http://collections.mnhs.org/MNHistoryMagazine/articles/27/ v27i04p300-308.pdf).

Randall J. Schaetzl. "Late Pleistocene Ice-flow Directions and the Age of Glacial Landscapes in Northern Lower Michigan," *Physical Geography*, 22 (2001), 28–41.

Randall J. Schaetzl, Scott A. Drzyzga, Beth N. Weisenborn, Kevin A. Kincare, Xiomara C. Lepczyk, Karsten Shein, Cathryn M. Dowd, and John Linker. "Measurement, Correlation, and Mapping of Glacial Lake Algonquin Shorelines in Northern Michigan," *Annals of the Association of American Geographers*, 92:3 (2002), 399-415.

Randall J. Schaetzl, Frank J. Krist. Paul R. Rindfleisch, Johan Liebens, and Thomas E. Williams, "Postglacial Landscape Evolution of Northeastern Lower Michigan Interpreted from Soils and Sediments," *Annals of the Association of American Geographers*, 90:3 (2000), 443–466.

Tip of the Mitt Fact Sheet, "The Truth about Beach Sanding or 'Lakebed Restoration'" (July 2011).

Books:

Dennis A. Albert and Patrick J. Comer. *Atlas of Early Michigan's Forests, Grasslands, and Wetlands* (East Lansing: Michigan State University Press, 2008).

Peter Annin. *The Great Lakes Water Wars* (Washington, DC: Island Press, 2006).

Biographical History of Northern Michigan Containing Biographies of Prominent Citizens (B. F. Bowen and Company, 1905).

William B. Botti and Michael D. Moore. *Michigan's State Forests: A Century of Stewardship* (East Lansing: Michigan State University Press, 2006).

Charles E. Cleland. *Rites of Conquest: The History and Culture of Michigan's Native Americans* (Ann Arbor: University of Michigan Press, 1992).

Edmund J. Danziger. *Great Lakes Indian Accommodation and Resistance during the Early Reservation Years, 1850–1900* (Ann Arbor: University of Michigan Press, 2009).

Dave Dempsey. *Ruin and Recovery: Michigan's Rise as a Conservation Leader* (Ann Arbor: University of Michigan Press, 2001).

Donald I. Dickmann and Larry A. Leefers. *The Forests of Michigan* (Ann Arbor: University of Michigan Press, 2003).

John Adam Dorr and Donald F. Eschman. *Geology of Michigan* (Ann Arbor: University of Michigan Press, 1970).

Timothy Egan. *The Big Burn: Teddy Roosevelt and the Fire That Saved America* (Boston: Houghton Mifflin Harcourt, 2009).

Robert S. Ford and Frank M. Landers. *Local Government in Cheboygan County* (Ann Arbor: University of Michigan Press, 1940).

Samuel P. Hayes, in *Beauty, Health, and Permanence: Environmental Politics in the United States, 1955–1985* (Cambridge: Cambridge University Press, 1987).

Wilbert B. Hinsdale. *Archaeological Atlas of Michigan* (Ann Arbor: University of Michigan Press, 1931).

———. *Primitive Man in Michigan* (Ann Arbor: University of Michigan, 1925).

Historical Society of Michigan. *Michigan Pioneer and Historical Collections* (Lansing, 1888).

J. Alan Holman. *Ancient Life of the Great Lakes Basin* (Ann Arbor: University of Michigan Press, 1995).

John A. lko, comp. *An Annotated Listing of Ojibwa Chiefs 1690–1890* (Troy, NY: Whitston Publishing Co., 1995).

Jane Jacobs. *The Death and Life of Great American Cities* (New York: Random House, 1961).

Myrna M. Killey. *Illinois's Ice Age Legacy*, 2nd ed. (Champaign: Illinois State Geological Survey, 2007).

Elizabeth Kolbert. *The Sixth Extinction* (New York: Henry Holt & Co., 2014).

Raymond G. Kuhl. *On Their Own Power: A History of Michigan's Electric Cooperatives* (Okemos, MI: Michigan Electric Cooperative Association, 1998).

Michael A. McDonnell. *Masters of Empire: Great Lakes Indians and the Making of America* (New York: Hill and Wang, 2015).

Patrick Russell LeBeau. *Rethinking Michigan Indian History* (East Lansing: Michigan State University Press, 2005).

Frank Leverett et al. *Flowing Wells and Municipal Water Supplies in the Southern Portion of the Southern Peninsula of Michigan* (Washington: GPO, 1906).

Robert W. Marrans et al. *Waterfront living: A report on permanent and seasonal residents in northern Michigan* (urban environmental research program, Survey Research Center, Institute for Social Research, the University of Michigan; Ann Arbor: The Institute, 1976.)

Robert W. Marans and John D. Wellman. *The Quality of Nonmetropolitan Livings: Evaluations, Behaviors, and Expectations of Northern Michigan Residents* (Ann Arbor: Survey, Institute for Social Research, 1978).

Forrest B. Meek and Carl J. Bajema. *Railways and Tramways: A Chronicle of Michigan's Logging Railroads* (Clare, MI: White Pine Historical Society, 1989).

Perry H. Merrill. *Roosevelt's Forest Army: A History of the Civilian Conservation Corps 1933–1942* (Montpelier, VT: Perry H. Merrill, 1981).

Michigan Official Directory and Legislative Manual for the Years 1903–1904 (Lansing: R. Smith Print. Co., State Printers and Binders, 1903)

Michigan Reports: Cases Decided in the Supreme Court of Michigan.

W. R. Middleton. *Cheboygan County Atlas* (Cheboygan: W. R. Middleton, 1913).

P. A. & J. W. Myers, Surveyors and Draughtsmen, Plat Book of Cheboygan County, Michigan. Drawn from Actual Surveys and the County Records (Minneapolis: The Consolidated Publishing Co., 1902).

Knute J. Nadelhoffer, Alan J. Hogg Jr., and Brian A. Hazlett, eds. *The Changing Environment of Northern Michigan* (Ann Arbor: University of Michigan Press, 2010).

Herbert Nagel. *The Metz Fire of 1908* (Presque Isle Historical Society, 1979).

Northwestern Reporter.

David D. Oliver. *Centennial History of Alpena County, Michigan* (Alpena: Argus Printing House, 1903).

Ellis Olson. *Wood Butchers of the North, with Cheboygan Logmarks*, 2nd ed. (Cheboygan: Cheboygan Daily Tribune, printer, 1989).

Perry F. Powers. *A History of Northern Michigan and Its People* (Chicago: Lewis Publishing Co., 1912).

Richard B. Primack. *Walden Warming: Climate Change Comes to Thoreau's Woods* (Chicago: University of Chicago Press, 2014).

Robert D. Putnam. *Bowling Alone: The Collapse and Revival of American Community* (New York: Simon & Schuster, 2000).

Walter Romig. *Michigan Place Names: The History of the Founding and the Naming of More Than Five Thousand Past and Present Michigan Communities* (Contributor Larry B. Massie; Detroit: Wayne State University Press, 1986).

Randall Schaetzl, editor in chief. *Michigan Geography and Geology* (New York: Pearson Custom Publishing, 2009).

Henry R. Schoolcraft. *Narrative Journal of Travels Through the Northwestern Regions of the United States Extending from Detroit through the Great Chain of American Lakes to the Sources of the Mississippi River in the Year 1820* (East Lansing: The Michigan State College Press, 1953).

Betty Sodders. *Michigan on Fire* (Thunder Bay Press, 1997).

Lawrence M. Sommers, ed. *The Atlas of Michigan* (East Lansing: Michigan State University Press, 1977).

Tim Stephens. *Manual on Small Earth Dams: A Guide to Siting, Design, and Construction* (Rome: Food and Agriculture Organization of the United Nations, 2010).

Helen Hornbeck Tanner, ed. *Atlas of Great Lakes Indian History* (Norman: published for the Newberry Library by the University of Oklahoma Press, 1987).

Henry David Thoreau. *The Writings of Henry David Thoreau, Journal.* VIII November 1, 1855-August 15, 1856. F.B. Sanborn and Bradford Torrey, eds. (Boston and New York: Houghton Mifflin and Company, 1906).

Robert M. Thorson. *Beyond Walden: The Hidden History of America's Kettle Lakes and Ponds* (New York: Walker & Co., 2009).

The Traverse Region, Historical and Descriptive, with Illustrations of Scenery and Portraits and Biographical Sketches of Some of Its Prominent Men and Pioneers (Chicago: HR Page & Co., 1884),

Alan S. Trenhaile. *Geomorphology: A Canadian Perspective* (Toronto: Oxford University Press, 1998).

Gordon Turner. *Pioneering North* (Cheboygan Daily Tribune, 1987).

Virgil J. Vogel. *Indian Names in Michigan* (Ann Arbor: The University of Michigan Press, 1986).

Michael Williams. *Americans and Their Forests: A Historical Geography* (Cambridge: Cambridge University Press, 1989).

CTLA Files:

CTLA files include the minutes of association meetings and of the meetings of the trustees, the CTLA newsletters, correspondence between the CTLA and various individuals and organizations, and a miscellany of membership lists, picnic planning notes, newspaper clippings, and such.

Electronic:

S. G. Berquist. "The Glacial History and Development of Michigan" (no date) (http://www.michigan.gov/documents/deq/Glacial_History_Bergquist_306034_7.pdf).

Dun & Bradstreet Rating Book 1907 (http://cheboygancountymi.org/dir/1907db.html).

"Geology in Michigan — DEQ" (http://www.michigan.gov/documents/deq/ogs-gimdl-GTLH_geo_307674_7.pdf).

"Glacial Lakes" (http://www.geo.msu.edu/geogmich/glacial.html).

http://www.ang.af.mil/history/heritage.asp

http://bigstory.ap.org/article/53ebaf50e7414812a4eea02043482be8/private-forest-owners-aging-parcels-shrinking

http://www.cheboygancounty.net/marinesnowmobile_patrol/

http://cheboygantoday.com/wp-content/uploads/2012/07/CT-2010.pdf

http://www.census.gov/hhes/www/income/data/historical/state/state1.html

http://www.everingham.com/family/data2/article011.html

http://www.glfwda.org/archive/index.php/t-6953.html

http://umbs.lsa.umich.edu/research/research_sites

http://umbs.lsa.umich.edu/research/researchsite/twin-lakes.
htm?order=field_project_years_active_value2&sort=asc

http://www.savemiwater.org/mcwcvsnestle/

http://wearemichigan.com/WorldWaterWars/UnitedStates/Michigan/index.htm

R. W. Kelley, comp. *Geology Notes for Upper Peninsula Traveling Workshop* (Lansing: Geological Survey Division, Michigan Department of Conservation, 1957) (http://www.michigan.gov/documents/deq/ GIMDL-GGGNUP_302335_7.pdf).

Moyers & Company, May 9, 2014 (http://billmoyers.com/episode/full-show-time-to-get-real-on-climate-change/).

Polk's Cheboygan City Directory 1910 (http://www.migenweb.org/cheboygan/dir/1910busdir2.html).

Polk's Cheboygan City Directory 1916 (http://cheboygancountymi.org/dir/1916cc2.html).

Polk's County Directory 1916 (http://cheboygancountymi.org/dir/1916cc7.html).

Randall J. Schaetzl. "Karst Country of the NE Lower Peninsula" (http://web2.geo.msu.edu/geogmich/ NE-MIkarst.html).

Government:

W. B. Allen. Flowing Wells in Michigan 1974 (Water Information Series Report 2. Prepared by the United States Geological Survey in cooperation with the Michigan Department of Natural Resources. Lansing: State of Michigan, Dept. of Natural Resources, Geological Survey Division, 1977).

Archives of Michigan. MS 2011-34, Map of Rivers and Lakes, Cheboygan and Presque Isle Counties.

Archives of Michigan. RG 58-017, Public Domain Commission, State Forests — Cheboygan.

Archives of Michigan. RG 65-5, Minutes, State Board of Equalization.

Archives of Michigan. RG 94-380, Rural Property Inventory, Cheboygan County, 1936–1939.

Cheboygan County Planning Commission. Cheboygan County Comprehensive Plan (2002).

G. P. Cooper. A fisheries survey of Twin lakes, near Indian River, Cheboygan County (Fisheries research report 1044, 1946).

Department of Conservation. Biennial Reports.

Department of Labor. Annual Report of the Department of Labor of the State of Michigan.

Z. C. Foster et al. Soil Survey of Cheboygan County (Washington, DC: U.S. GPO, 1939).

Frank Leverett et al. Flowing Wells and Municipal Water Supplies in the Southern Portion of the Southern Peninsula of Michigan (Washington, DC: GPO, 1906).

Michigan Compiled Laws.

Michigan County Atlas of General Highway Maps for 1940.

NEMCOG. Cheboygan River/Lower Black River Watershed Initiative 2006–07 Update.

United States Department of Agriculture, Soil Conservation Service, in cooperation with Michigan Department of Agriculture, Michigan Agricultural Experiment Station, and Michigan Technological University. Soil Survey of Cheboygan County, Michigan, 1991.

United States Archives. Michigan Land Patents Database.

United States Bureau of the Census. Twelfth Census,1900. Michigan.

United States Bureau of the Census. Thirteenth Census, 1910. Michigan.

United States Bureau of the Census. Fourteenth Census, 1920. Michigan.

United States Bureau of the Census. Fifteenth Census, 1930. Michigan.

United States Bureau of the Census. Sixteenth Census, 1940. Michigan

United States Department of Agriculture, Soil Conservation Service, in cooperation with the Michigan Agricultural Experiment Station, and the Michigan Department of Conservation. Soil Survey of Cheboygan County, Michigan, 1939.

US-23 Sunrise Side Heritage Route Management Plan Supporting Documentation.

Newspapers and Periodicals:
Cheboygan Democrat

Cheboygan Daily Tribune

Cheboygan News

Detroit News

Fortune

New York Times

On Earth

"Our Story," Celebrating 150 Years of Cheboygan Business History, Special Supplement to the *Cheboygan Daily Tribune*, August 2010.

Presque Isle County Advance

Oral History:
Randolph Mateer, comp. *Twin Lakes Oral History* (unpublished, 1990).

Public Domain Commission/Department of Conservation/Department of Natural Resources:

Archives of Michigan. RG 91-37, State Forest Plantation Record, 1910–1941, 1949–1959.

Black Lake Water Level Control Problem: Cheboygan-Presque Isle Counties (Lansing[?]: Michigan Department of Natural Resources[?], 1968).

Tim A. Cwalinski, Senior Fisheries Biologist, Gaylord. *Michigan Dept. of Natural Resources Status of the Fishery Resource Report*: Twin Lakes 2-5 (2014).

DNR. Black Mountain Plan: Development and Management Guidelines, Draft, September 1988.

DNR. Black Mountain Forest Recreation Area Development Plan, April 1989.

Godby Jr., N. A., T. C. Wills, T. A. Cwalinski, and B. Bury. 2011. Draft Cheboygan River Assessment (Ann Arbor: MDNR, Fisheries Division, 2011).

Michigan Department of Conservation. Forest Fire Report Calendar Year 1938.

Official map showing state parks, fish hatcheries, game reserves, fire towers, and national forests purchases units in Michigan (Lansing: Department of Conservation, 1929).

J. A. Mitchell and D. Robson. *Forest Fires and Fire Control in Michigan* (Lansing: Michigan Dept. of Conservation in cooperation with U.S. Dept. of Agriculture, Forest Service, 1950).

Proceedings of the Public Domain Commission (Lansing: Wynkoop Hallenbeck Crawford, 1916), vol. 7.

A Review of Bear Management in Michigan (Lansing: DNR, 2008).

Reports:

Biodiversity Research Institute in partnership with the Great Lakes Commission and the University of Wisconsin-La Crosse. *Great Lakes Mercury Connections: The Extent and Effects of Mercury Pollution in the Great Lakes Region* (Gorham, ME: 2011).

John E. Gannon. *Report on the Water Quality Status of Twin Lakes (Grant Twp., Cheboygan Co., Mich.) with Special Reference to the Impact of Campgrounds* (June 1974).

John E. Gannon and Mark W. Paddock in cooperation with project staff of the Northern Michigan Environmental Research Program. *Investigations into Ecological and Sociological Determinants of Land-use Decisions — A Study of Inland Lake Watersheds in Northern Michigan* (Pellston, MI: University of Michigan Biological Station, 1974).

Proceedings of the Forestry Convention Held in Grand Rapids, Mich., January 26 and 27, 1888, under the auspices of the Independent Forestry Commission. Bulletin 32, Department of Botany and Forestry, Agricultural College, Michigan (Lansing: Thorp & Godfrey, 1888).

Report of the Commission of Inquiry, Tax Lands and Forestry, to the Governor and Legislature of the State (Lansing: Wynkoop, Hallenbeck, Crawford, 1908).

Daniel J. Stynes, JiaJia Zheng, and Susan I. Stewart. *Seasonal Homes and Natural Resources: Patterns of Use and Impact in Michigan.* General Technical Report NC-194 (St. Paul, MN: U.S. Dept. of Agriculture, Forest Service, North Central Forest Experiment Station, 1997).

Theses and Dissertations:

Lloyd M. Atwood. "Cheboygan as a Nineteenth Century Lumber Area" (Wayne State University MA Thesis, 1947).

James B. Smith. "Lumbertowns in the Cutover: A Comparative Study of the Stage Hypothesis of Urban Growth" (Dissertation, University of Wisconsin, 1973).

Printed in the United States
By Bookmasters